The Court of Justice of the European Union as an Institutional Actor

The EU Treaties bind the Court of Justice of the European Union as an institution of the Union. But what does that mean for judicial lawmaking within the EU legal order? And how might any limits set out in the EU Treaties be effectively applied to the Court of Justice as lawmaker? This book interrogates these fundamental and underexplored questions at a critical juncture in European integration. It argues that the EU Treaties should be considered to function as the principal touchstones for assessing the internal constitutionality, and hence legitimacy, of all Union institutional activity – including the work of the Court. It then examines how far the Court of Justice complies with the EU Treaty framework in the exercise of its interpretative functions. The results of that analysis are striking and offer scholars powerful new insights into the nature and limits of the Court's role within the EU legal order.

Thomas Horsley is Senior Lecturer at Liverpool Law School, University of Liverpool. He has published widely in leading international journals and edited collections on EU law and European integration. His most recent work analyses the impact of the UK's exit from the European Union on UK courts. He completed his PhD at the University of Edinburgh (2009–2011), funded by the UK Arts and Humanities Research Council.

Cambridge Studies in European Law and Policy

This series aims to produce original works that contain a critical analysis of the state of the law in particular areas of European law and set out different perspectives and suggestions for its future development. It also aims to encourage a range of work on law, legal institutions and legal phenomena in Europe, including 'law in context' approaches. The titles in the series will be of interest to academics; policy makers; policy formers who are interested in European legal, commercial and political affairs; practising lawyers, including the judiciary; and advanced law students and researchers.

Books in the Series

The Court of Justice of the European Union as an Institutional Actor: Judicial Lawmaking and its Limits
Thomas Horsley

Redefining European Economic Integration
Dariusz Adamski

Human Rights in the Council of Europe and the European Union
Steven Greer, Janneke Gerards and Rosie Slowe

Core Socio-Economic Rights and the European Court of Human Rights
Ingrid Leijten

New Labour Laws in Old Member States
Rebecca Zahn

The Governance of EU Fundamental Rights
Mark Dawson

The International Responsibility of the European Union: From Competence to Normative Control
Andrés Delgado Casteleiro

Frontex and Non-Refoulement: The International Responsibility of the EU
Roberta Mungianu

Gendering European Working Time Regimes: The Working Time Directive and the Case of Poland
Ania Zbyszewska

EU Renewable Electricity Law and Policy: From National Targets to a Common Market
Tim Maxian Rusche

European Constitutionalism
Kaarlo Tuori

Brokering Europe: Euro-Lawyers and the Making of a Transnational Polity
Antoine Vauchez

Services Liberalization in the EU and the WTO: Concepts, Standards and Regulatory Approaches
Marcus Klamert

Referendums and the European Union: A Comparative Enquiry
Fernando Mendez, Mario Mendez and Vasiliki Triga

The Allocation of Regulatory Competence in the EU Emissions Trading Scheme
Jospehine Van Zeben

The Eurozone Crisis
Kaarlo Tuori and Klaus Tuori

International Trade Disputes and EU Liability
Anne Thies

The Limits of Legal Reasoning and the European Court of Justice
Gerard Conway

New Governance and the Transformation of European Law: Coordinating EU Social Law and Policy
Mark Dawson

The Lisbon Treaty: A Legal and Political Analysis
Jean-Claude Piris

The European Union's Fight against Corruption: The Evolving Policy towards Member States and Candidate Countries
Patrycja Szarek-Mason

The Ethos of Europe: Values, Law and Justice in the EU
Andrew Williams

State and Market in European Union Law: The Public and Private Spheres of the Internal Market before the EU Courts
Wolf Sauter and Harm Schepel

The European Civil Code: The Way Forward
Hugh Collins

Ethical Dimensions of the Foreign Policy of the European Union: A Legal Appraisal
Urfan Khaliq

Implementing EU Pollution Control: Law and Integration
Bettina Lange

European Broadcasting Law and Policy
Jackie Harrison and Lorna Woods

The Transformation of Citizenship in the European Union: Electoral Rights and the Restructuring of Political Space
Jo Shaw

The Constitution for Europe: A Legal Analysis
Jean-Claude Piris

The European Convention on Human Rights: Achievements, Problems and Prospects
Steven Greer

Social Rights and Market Freedom in the European Constitution: A Labour Law Perspective
Stefano Giubboni

EU Enlargement and the Constitutions of Central and Eastern Europe
Anneli Albi

Free Trade, Fair Trade, and Green Trade in and with the EU: Process-Based Measures within the EU Legal Order
Laurens Ankersmit

The Court of Justice of the European Union as an Institutional Actor

Judicial Lawmaking and its Limits

Thomas Horsley
University of Liverpool

CAMBRIDGE
UNIVERSITY PRESS

CAMBRIDGE
UNIVERSITY PRESS

University Printing House, Cambridge CB2 8BS, United Kingdom

One Liberty Plaza, 20th Floor, New York, NY 10006, USA

477 Williamstown Road, Port Melbourne, VIC 3207, Australia

314-321, 3rd Floor, Plot 3, Splendor Forum, Jasola District Centre, New Delhi - 110025, India

79 Anson Road, #06-04/06, Singapore 079906

Cambridge University Press is part of the University of Cambridge.

It furthers the University's mission by disseminating knowledge in the pursuit of education, learning and research at the highest international levels of excellence.

www.cambridge.org
Information on this title: www.cambridge.org/9781107124035
DOI: 10.1017/9781316403792

First published 2018

A catalogue record for this publication is available from the British Library

Library of Congress Cataloging-in-Publication Data
Names: Horsley, Thomas, 1984–, author.
Title: The Court of Justice of the European Union as an institutional actor : judicial lawmaking and its limits / Thomas Horsley, University of Liverpool.
Description: New York, NY : Cambridge University Press, 2018. | Includes bibliographical references and index.
Identifiers: LCCN 2017057910 | ISBN 9781107124035 (hardback : alk. paper)
Subjects: LCSH: Court of Justice of the European Union.
Classification: LCC KJE5461 .H67 2018 | DDC 347.24/01–dc23
LC record available at https://lccn.loc.gov/2017057910

ISBN 978-1-107-12403-5 Hardback
ISBN 978-1-107-56113-7 Paperback

The [Union] is based on the rule of law, inasmuch as neither its Member States nor its institutions can avoid review of the conformity of their acts with the basic constitutional charter, the [Treaties].[1]

[1] Joined Cases C-402/05 P and C-415/05, *P Kadi and Al Barakaat International Foundation* v. *Council and Commission* EU:C:2008:461 at para. 281. See also, Case 294/83, *Parti écologiste 'Les Verts'* v. *European Parliament* EU:C:1986:166 at para. 23 and Opinion 2/13 *Draft Agreement on Accession of the EU to the European Convention on Human Rights* EU:C:2014:2454 at para. 163.

Contents

Series Editors' Preface

The role of the Court of Justice of the European Union as an institutional actor is often overlooked; this book by Thomas Horsley should ensure the rectification of that oversight. Horsley applies the Treaty framework to the Court as a means to problematise that institution's role within the EU legal order. Having done so, he asks how the Court and its interlocutors can (and should) respond to the existence of three contemporary problems for EU judicial activity: judicial challenges to constituent authority; judicial challenges to Treaty limits on EU policymaking; and judicial challenges to EU legislative frameworks. On the way, Horsley examines the formal status of Union law and the conditions under which it applies within Member States; the locus of EU political authority within the EU legal order; and the objectives, values and limits governing European integration. He sees the Court's institutional positions on each of these three key issues for EU constitutionalism as offering paradigmatic examples of acts of constitutional contestation. He illustrates well how the Court uses Treaty norms as tools to challenge substantive policy choices made by the Union legislature.

There has in fact been a long history of such challenges – sometimes at the behest of individuals faced with obstacles to the exercise of their freedoms aggravated by inactivity of the legislature, and famous cases like *Reyners* spring to mind. The Court's duty when faced with failures to act by the Council was well set out in a celebrated article by the great judge Pierre Pescatore, '*La carence du législateur communautaire et le devoir du juge*' in Lüke et al. (eds.), *Rechtsvergleichung, Europarecht und Staatenintegration (Gedächtnisschrift für Léontin-Jean Constantinesco*, Heymans, Cologne, 1983) 559–580. The Union legislature may want to take a more nuanced view than one might expect from the Treaties, but it does not mean that it can deprive Union citizens of their rights under the Treaties, or restrict them without clear Treaty-based authority, something that the Court rightly points out as appropriate.

Horsley does not merely identify problems, he makes four specific reform proposals to strengthen the legitimacy of the Court's institutional role within the Treaty framework as a Union institution. His proposals are both theoretically stimulating and practical in their conception.

For all these reasons we very much welcome this perceptive work as a welcome and indeed timely addition to our series *Cambridge Studies in European Law and Policy*.

Laurence Gormley
Jo Shaw

Preface

The new millennium has not been easy on the European Union (EU). It has gifted the EU and its Member States a series of constitutional, economic and humanitarian crises in rapid succession. Each new crisis has placed enormous strain on the EU's institutional framework and posed renewed challenges to the legitimacy of European integration. The United Kingdom's notification to the European Council in March 2017 of its intention to exit the European Union has added yet another layer of complexity.

Under such challenging circumstances, it is tempting for EU legal scholars to rally instinctively to the defence of the European Union and its institutions. And let us be clear, there are good reasons to do so. More than ever, Europe's citizens deserve to be much better informed about what the European Union does (and does *not* do); how it achieves its objectives; and, most importantly, where they (the citizens) fit within its institutional architecture. The need to strengthen the connection between the EU and the citizens it serves through credible (and accessible) scholarship is more pressing than ever. Recent years have witnessed a proliferation of political movements within many Member States that consciously set out to *mis*inform citizens about the relative costs and benefits of European integration.

Nevertheless, even at times of heightened political crisis, it remains the responsibility of EU legal scholars to offer critical perspectives on European integration based on robust, objective analysis. This book is written firmly in that spirit. The critical perspective it adopts with specific reference to EU judicial lawmaking challenges head-on many of the things that EU legal scholars defend (or at least have come to accept) as incontrovertible 'truths' in European integration. This is done not to undermine the Court or, more broadly, to support further denigration of the European Union and its institutions. The aim is to enhance the legitimacy of EU judicial lawmaking by reinforcing the normative foundations of the Court's institutional role within the EU legal order. This book's intellectual point of departure, core argument and concluding reform proposals all serve that basic aspiration.

Acknowledgements

Writing this book would not have been possible without the encouragement and support of so many people. I am particularly indebted to my colleagues at Liverpool Law School, especially Michael Dougan, Steph Reynolds, Mike Gordon, Andrew Woodhouse, Katy Sowery, Craig Purshouse, Greg Messenger and Eleanor Drywood. It is a privilege to work among such a wonderful group of extremely sharp minds. An additional note of thanks is due to Michael Dougan, who, in true scholarly tradition, has generously offered so much of his time to help me succeed with the writing of this book. Michael's support and encouragement is matched only by his superb intellect and good humour. I also owe an enormous expression of gratitude to Niamh Nic Shuibhne for her rigorous training as my PhD supervisor and for her comments on the draft manuscript.

Individual chapters of this book have benefitted from conversations with numerous colleagues working throughout Europe, notably Marie-Pierre Granger and Paul Beaumont. I am also grateful to many others, not least those who have taken time to provide me with feedback on my article, 'Reflections on the Role of the Court of Justice as the "Motor" of European Integration: Legal Limits to Judicial Lawmaking' (2013) 50 *Common Market Law Review*, 931. This monograph is an attempt to develop the arguments advanced in that exploratory article. It would also not have been completed without the hard work and patience of my editor, Kim Hughes, and her team at Cambridge University Press.

Finally, I wish to thank Matt for his love and support and my parents for always encouraging me to learn, achieve more and go further in life.

Table of Cases

Court of Justice

Joined Cases C-92/92 and C-326/92, *Phil Collins* v. *Imtrat Handelsgesellschaft mbH* EU:C:1993:847
Case C-57/93, *Vroege* EU:C:1994:352
Joined Cases C-46/93 and C-48/93, *Brasserie du Pêcheur SA* v. *Bundesrepublik Deutschland and The Queen* v. *Secretary of State for Transport, ex parte: Factortame Ltd and others* EU:C:1996:79
Case C-415/93, *Union royale belge des sociétés de football association ASBL* v. *Bosman* EU:C:1995:463
Case C-450/93, *Kalanke* v. *Freie Hansestadt Bremen* EU:C:1995:322
Opinion 2/94, *Accession by the Community to the European Convention for the Protection of Human Rights and Fundamental Freedoms* EU:C:1996:140
Case C-61/94, *Commission* v. *Germany (International Dairy Agreement)* EU:C:1996:313
Joined Cases C-163/94, C-165/94 and C-250/94, *Criminal proceedings against Sanz de Lera and Others* EU:C:1995:451
Case C-265/95, *Commission* v. *France (Strawberries)* EU:C:1997:595
Case C-388/95, *Belgium* v. *Spain (Designations of Origin)* EU:C:2000:244
Case C-85/96, *Martínez Sala* v. *Freistaat Bayern* EU:C:1998:217
Case C-149/96, *Portugal* v. *Council (Textiles)* EU:C:1999:574
Case C-274/96, *Bickel and Franz* EU:C:1998:563
Case C-281/98, *Angonese v. Cassa di Risparmio di Bolzano* SpA EU:C:2000:296
Case C-367/98, *Commission* v. *Portugal (Golden Shares)* EU:C:2002:326
Case C-376/98, *Germany* v. *Parliament and Council (Tobacco Advertising)* EU:C:2000:544
Case C-9/99, *Echirolles Distribution SA* v. *Association du Dauphiné and Others* EU:C:2000:532
Case C-157/99, *Geraets-Smits* v. *Stichting Ziekenfonds VGZ and Peerbooms* v. *Stichting CZ Groep Zorgverzekeringen* EU:C:2001:404
Case C-184/99, *Grzelczyk* v. *Centre public d'aide sociale d'Ottignies-Louvain-la-Neuve* EU:C:2001:458
Case C-385/99, *Müller-Fauré and van Riet* EU:C:2003:270
Case C-493/99, *Baumbast and R* v. *Secretary of State for the Home Department* EU:C:2002:493
Opinion 1/00, *Proposed Agreement between the European Community and non-Member States on the establishment of a European Common Aviation Area* EU:C:2002:231
Case C-50/00 P, *Unión de Pequeños Agricultores* v. *Council* EU:C:2002:462.
Case C-112/00, *Schmidberger, Internationale Transporte und Planzüge* v. *Republik Österreich* EU:C:2003:333
Case C-253/00, *Muñoz y Cia SA* v. *Frumar Ltd* EU:C:2002:497
Case C-280/00, *Altmark Trans GmbH and Regierungspräsidium Magdeburg* v. *Nahverkehrsgesellschaft Altmark GmbH* EU:C:2003:415
Case C-224/01, *Köbler* v. *Republik Österreich* EU:C:2003:513
Case C-36/02, *Omega Spielhallen- und Automatenaufstellungs-GmbH* EU:C:2004:614
Case C-49/02, *Heidelberger Bauchemie GmbH* EU:C:2004:384
Case C-110/02, *Commission* v. *Council (State Aid)* EU:C:2004:395

Case C-138/02, *Collins* v. *Secretary of State for Work and Pensions* EU:C:2004:172
Case C-148/02, *Garcia Avello* v. *Belgian State* EU:C:2003:539
Case C-200/02, *Zhu and Chen* v. *Secretary of State for the Home Department* EU:C:2004:639
Case C-224/02, *Pusa* v. *Osuuspankkien Keskinäinen Vakuutusyhtiö* EU:C:2004:273
Case C-105/03, *Pupino* EU:C:2005:386
Case C-173/03, *Traghetti del Mediterraneo SpA* v. *Italy* EU:C:2006:391
Case C-176/03, *Commission* v. *Council (Environmental Sanctions)* EU:C:2005:542
Case C-209/03, *Bidar* v. *London Borough of Ealing and Secretary of State for Education and Skills* EU:C:2005:169
Case C-380/03, *Germany* v. *European Parliament and Council (Tobacco Advertising II)* EU:C:2006:772
Case C-403/03, *Schempp* v. *Finanzamt München V* EU:C:2005:446
Case C-446/03, *Marks & Spencer plc* v. *David Halsey (Her Majesty's Inspector of Taxes)* EU:C:2005:763
Case C-503/03, *Commission* v. *Spain (Schengen Information System)* EU:C:2006:74
Case C-144/04, *Mangold* v. *Helm* EU:C:2005:709
Case C-145/04, *Spain* v. *United Kingdom (Electoral Rights)* EU:C:2006:543
Case C-258/04, *Office national de l'emploi* v. *Ioannis Ioannidis* EU:C:2005:559
Case C-311/04, *Algemene Scheeps Agentuur Dordrecht* EU:C:2006:23
Case C-345/04 P, *Gestoras Pro Amnistia and Others* v. *Council* EU:C:2007:11
Case C-372/04, *Watts* v. *Bedford Primary Care Trust and Secretary of State for Health* EU:C:2006:325
Case C-490/04, *Commission* v. *Germany (Posted Workers)* EU:C:2007:430
Case C-76/05, *Schwarz and Gootjes-Schwarz* v. *Finanzamt Bergisch Gladbach* EU:C:2007:492
Case C-101/05, *Skatteverket* v. *A* EU:C:2007:804
Case C-192/05, *Tas-Hagen and Tas* v. *Raadskamer WUBO van de Pensioen- en Uitkeringsraad* EU:C:2006:676
Case C-284/05, *Commission* v. *Finland (Military Equipment)* EU:C:2009:778
Case C-341/05, *Laval un Partneri Ltd* v. *Svenska Byggnadsarbetareförbundet* EU:C:2007:809
Joined Cases C-402/05 P and C-415/05, *P Kadi and Al Barakaat International Foundation* v. *Council and Commission* EU:C:2008:461
Case C-438/05, *International Transport Workers' Federation and Finnish Seamen's Union* v. *Viking Line ABP* EU:C:2007:772
Case C-268/06, *Impact* v. *Minister for Agriculture and Food and Others* EU:C:2008:223
C-411/06, *Commission* v. *Parliament and Council (Waste Shipments)* EU:C:2009:189
Case C-141/07, *Commission* v. *Germany (Pharmacies)* EU:C:2008:492

Case C-351/07, *Fachverband der Buch- und Medienwirtschaft* v. *LIBRO Handelsgesellschaft mbH* EU:C:2009:276

Joined Cases C-402/07 and Case C-432/07, *Sturgeon* v. *Condor Flugdienst GmbH and Böck and Lepuschitz* v. *Air France SA* EU:C:2009:716

Case C-555/07, *Kücükdeveci* v. *Swedex GmbH & Co. KG* EU:C:2010:21

Joined Cases C-22/08 and C-23/08, *Vatsouras and Koupatantze* EU:C:2009:344

Case C-73/08, *Bressol and Others* v. *Gouvernement de la Communauté française* EU:C:2010:181

Case C-127/08, *Metock and Others* v. *Minister for Justice, Equality and Law Reform* EU:C:2008:449

Case C-135/08, *Rottman* v. *Freistaat Bayern* EU:C:2010:104

Case C-382/08, *Neukirchinger* v. *Bezirkshauptmannschaft Grieskirchen* EU:C:2011:27

Case C-484/08, *Caja de Ahorros y Monte de Piedad de Madrid* EU:C:2010:309

Opinion 1/09, *Draft Agreement on the Creation of a Unified Patent Litigation System* EU:C:2011:123

Case C-34/09, *Ruiz Zambrano* v. *Office national de l'emploi* EU:C:2011:124

Case C-236/09, *Test-Achats ASBL and Others* v. *Conseil des ministres* EU:C:2011:100

Case C-439/09, *Pierre Fabre Dermo-Cosmétique SAS* v. *Président de l'Autorité de la concurrence* EU:C:2011:649

Case C-117/10, *Commission* v. *Council (State Aid)* EU:C:2013:786

Case C-364/10, *Hungary* v. *Slovakia* EU:C:2012:630

Joined Cases C-581/10 and Case C-629/20, *Nelson and Others* v. *Deutsche Lufthansa AG and TUI Travel plc and Others* v. *Civil Aviation Authority* EU:C:2012:657

Case C-617/10, *Åklagaren* v. *Åkerberg Fransson* EU:C:2013:105

Case 300/11, *ZZ* v. *Secretary of State for the Home Department* EU:C:2013:363

Case C-399/11, *Melloni* EU:C:2013:107

Case C-256/11, *Dereci and Others* v. *Bundesministerium für Inneres* EU:C:2011:734

Case C-583/11 P, *Inuit Tapiriit Kanatami and Others* v. *Parliament and Council* EU:C:2013:625

Case C-628/11, *Criminal proceedings against International Jet Management GmbH* EU:C:2014:171

Case C-131/12, *Google Spain SL and Google Inc.* v. *Agencia Española de Protección de Datos (AEPD) and Costeja González* EU:C:2014:317

Case C-270/12, *United Kingdom* v. *Parliament and Council (Short Selling)* EU:C:2014:18

Joined Cases C-293/12 and C-594/12, *Digital Rights Ireland and Seitlinger and others* EU:C:2014:238

Case C-370/12, *Pringle* v. *Government of Ireland and Others* EU:C:2012:756

Case C-507/12, *Jessy Saint Prix* v. *Secretary of State for Work and Pensions* EU:C:2014:2007

Opinion 2/13, *Draft Agreement on Accession of the EU to the European Convention on Human Rights* EU:C:2014:2454

Case C-333/13, *Dano and Dano* v. *Jobcenter Leipzig* EU:C:2014:2358
Case C-409/13, *Council* v. *Commission (Macro Financial Assistance)* EU:C:2015:217
Case C-424/13, *Zuchtvieh-Export GmbH* v. *Stadt Kempten* EU:C:2015:259
Case C-425/13, *Commission* v. *Council (Emissions Trading)* EU:C:2015:483
Case C-508/13, *Estonia* v. *Parliament and Council* EU:C:2015:403
Case C-650/13, *Delvigne* v. *Commune de Lesparre Médoc and Préfet de la Gironde* EU:C:2015:648
Case C-62/14, *Gauweiler and Others* v. *Deutscher Bundestag* EU:C:2015:400
Case C-67/14, *Jobcenter Berlin Neukölln* v. *Alimanovic and Others* EU:C:2015:597
Case C-299/14, *Garcia-Nieto and Others* EU:C:2016:114
Case C-308/14, *Commission* v. *United Kingdom (Social Security)* EU:C:2016:436
Case C-362/14, *Schrems* v. *Data Protection Commissioner* EU:C 2015:650
Case C-441/14, *Dansk Industri (DI), acting on behalf of Ajos A/S* v. *Estate of Karsten Eigil Rasmussen* EU:C:2016:278
Case C-648/15, *Austria* v. *Germany (Double Taxation)* EU:C:2017:664
Case C-490/16, *A.S.* v. *Slovenia* EU:C:2017:585
Case C-646/16, *Jafari and Jafari* v. *Bundesamt für Fremdenwesen und Asyl* EU:C:2017:586

General Court

Case T-115/94, *Opel Austria GmbH* v. *Council* EU:T:1997:3
Case T-450/12, *Anagnostakis* v. *Commission* EU:T:2015:739
Case T-479/14, *Kendrion* v. *European Union* EU:T:2017:48
Case T-577/14, *Gascogne Sack Deutschland GmbH* EU:T:2017:1
Case T-673/15, *Guardian Europe* v. *European Union* EU:T:2017:377

European Court of Human Rights

Hirst v. *the United Kingdom (No. 2)* [2005] ECHR 681

Permanent Court of International Justice

Advisory Opinion of 3 March 1928, *Jurisdiction of the Courts of Danzig*, PCIJ, Series B, No. 15

Member State Courts

Belgium

Cour de cassion (B), decision of 27 May 1971, *SA Fromagerie franco-Suisse Le Ski*, JT, 1971 460
Arbitragehof/Cour d'Arbitrage, decision n. 26/92 of 16 October 1991, *Commune de Lanaken*

Czech Republic

Ústanví soud, judgment of November 26, 2008, *Treaty of Lisbon I*, PI. ÚS 19/08
Ústanví soud, judgment of November 3, 2009, *Treaty of Lisbon II*, PI. ÚS 29/09
Ústanví soud, judgment of January 31, 2012, *Slovak Pensions*, Pl. ÚS 5/12

Denmark

Danish Supreme Court, judgment of 6 April 1998, *Carlsen* v. *Rasmussen*, Case I 361/1997
Danish Supreme Court, judgment of 6 December 2016, Dansk Industri (DI) acting for *Ajos A/S* v. *The estate left by A*, Case I 15/2014

France

Conseil d'Etat, Decision of 20 October 1989, *Nicolo*, RTDeur., 136
Conseil Constitutionnel, Décision No 2006–540 DC, 27 July 2006
Conseil Constitutionnel, Décision No 2006–543 DC, 30 November 2006

Germany

Bundesverfassungsgericht, Decision of 29 May 1974, *Solange I*, BVerfGE 37, 271
Bundesverfassungsgericht, Decision of 12 October 1993, *Treaty of Maastricht*, BVerfGE 89, 155
Bundesverfassungsgericht, Decision of June 30, 2009, *Lisbon Decision*, 2 BvE 2/08
Bundesverfassungsgericht, Decision of 6 July 2010, *Honeywell*, 2 BvR 2661/06

Italy

Corte costituzionale, Decision n. 183/73 of December 27 1973, *Frontini*, 18 Guir. Cost. I 2401

Latvia

Satversmes tiesa, judgment of 7 April 2009, *Lisbon*, Case No. 2008–35–01

Lithuania

Konstitucinis Teismas, Ruling of December 4, 2008

Luxembourg

Cour de Cassation, Decision of 14 July 1954, Pas.lux, Vol. 16, 150

Poland

Trybunal Konstytucyjny, Decision of 11 May 2004, *Accession Treaty*, K 18/04
Trybunal Konstytucyjny, Decision of 24 November 2010, *Lisbon Treaty*, K 32/09

Portugal

Supremo Tribunal Administrativo, October 27, 1999, Case 45389-A

Spain

Tribunal Constitucional, Declaration 1/2004 of 13 December 2004

United Kingdom

R. v. *Secretary of State for Transport, Ex p. Factortame and Others* (No. 2) [1991] 1 A.C. 603
Hirst v. *the United Kingdom* (No. 2) [2005] ECHR 681
R. (on the application of Chester) v. *Secretary of State for Justice* [2013] UKSC 63
R. (on the application of GI (Sudan)) v. *Secretary of State for the Home Department* [2012] EWCA Civ 867
R. (HS2 Action Alliance Ltd) v. *Secretary of State for Transport* [2014] UKSC 3
Pham v. *Secretary of State for the Home Department* [2015] UKSC 19

Introduction

This book examines the role of the Court of Justice of the European Union as an institutional actor in EU integration. Its principal aim is to assess how far the Court complies with the EU Treaty framework in the exercise of its attributed functions. The book argues that the EU Treaties remain the principal touchstones for assessing the internal constitutionality, and hence legitimacy, of all Union institutional activity – including the work of the Court. The use of the EU Treaty framework to scrutinise the Court's interpretative choices is an innovative approach to the study of EU judicial lawmaking and its limits. Legal scholars (and the Court itself) presently overlook the application *to the Court* of the EU Treaty framework as a tool to determine the internal constitutionality of its institutional activities. The core claim of this book is that such an entrenched perspective fundamentally obscures the Court's position within the EU legal order *as an institution of the Union*. The implications of that claim are potentially transformative when coupled with the Court's historically dynamic approach to the exercise of its interpretative functions.

The remainder of this introduction outlines the component parts of the core argument developed in this book. Section I frames the background to the discussion. It outlines the Court's functions under the Treaty framework and the significance of its institutional contribution to the process of European integration. Thereafter, it points to a critical gap in the scrutiny of EU institutional activity for compliance with the Treaty framework. Specifically, the Court is identified as the only Union institution whose activities are presently not routinely scrutinised (by itself or by others) for compliance with the EU Treaties.

Section II introduces the intellectual framework developed in this book to scrutinise EU judicial activity for compliance with the Treaty framework. It offers an overview of the book's original claims concerning the status, function and limits of the EU Treaties as the principal touchstones for assessing the internal constitutionality of all Union institutional activity – including the work of the Court.

Section III precises the findings of the review of EU judicial activity for compliance with the Treaty framework as constitutional touchstone. More precisely, it foregrounds the argument that the Treaty framework and the Court of Justice have adopted and maintained fundamentally distinct statements on what this book defines as the three key issues for EU constitutionalism: *the formal status of Union law and the conditions under which it applies within Member States* (Constitutional Issue No. 1); *the locus of political authority within the EU legal order* (Constitutional Issue No. 2); and *the objectives, values and limits governing European integration* (Constitutional Issue No. 3). The Court's adoption, and subsequent robust defence, of its own distinct institutional statements on each of these three issues gives rise to paradigmatic examples of what this monograph conceptualises as acts of *constitutional contestation*.

Section IV summarises the book's conclusions. First, it details how this monograph uses the responses of the Court's interlocutors (Member States, national courts and EU scholars) to transform the identified acts of constitutional contestation into three contemporary problems for EU judicial lawmaking. Secondly, it links the existence of these problems with contemporary debates about EU integration, its limits and the democratic credentials of Union policymaking. Finally, it sets out four specific reform proposals in outline form as part of a constructive attempt to align the exercise of EU judicial functions more closely with the demands of the Treaty framework as constitutional touchstone. This process of alignment is absolutely critical. It serves directly to reinforce the legitimacy of the Court's contribution to European integration as an institution of the Union.

I The Court of Justice and European Integration

I.1 The Court's Functions under the EU Treaty Framework

The EU Treaties confer specific functions on the Court. These include competence to adjudicate on the validity of secondary EU law and competence to interpret both primary (Treaty) and secondary EU law.[1]

[1] See, in particular, Art. 263 TFEU and Art. 267 TFEU.

Additionally, the Court is empowered to hear infringement actions raised by (usually) the Commission against Member States for alleged breaches of Union law.[2] Furthermore, the Court may also be engaged to rule on the compatibility of draft agreements concluded between the European Union and third countries and/or other international organisations.[3] It is also enjoys jurisdiction in a range of other specific instances, including in any dispute relating to the subject matter of the Treaties submitted to it under a special agreement concluded between Member States.[4]

In the exercise of its attributed functions, the Court of Justice is guided by an overarching mandate to ensure that, in the interpretation and application of the Treaties, the law is observed (Article 19 TEU). The Court's role in EU integration under the Treaty framework remains strikingly unchanged despite successive Treaty amendments.

I.2 The Court of Justice as the 'Motor' of European Integration

The Court of Justice's contribution to the EU integration process through the exercise of its conferred judicial functions is widely acknowledged, remarkable and enduring.[5] Exercising its interpretative functions, the Court of Justice has radically recast the nature of the EU legal order and, in particular, the relationship between EU and Member State law. Furthermore, employing these same competences, the Court has continued to make significant contributions to the development of substantive Union law, including in the areas of intra-EU movement;[6]

[2] See Art. 258 TFEU. See also, by analogy, Art. 259 TFEU.

[3] See Art. 218(11) TFEU.

[4] See Art. 273 TFEU, interpreted in Case C-648/15, *Austria* v. *Germany (Double Taxation)* EU:C:2017:664. See also Arts. 272, 274 and 275 TFEU.

[5] E. Stein, 'Lawyers, Judges, and the Making of a Transnational Constitution' (1981) 75 *American Journal of International Law*, 1; F. Mancini, 'The Making of a Constitution for Europe' (1989) 26 *Common Market Law Review*, 595; J. H. H. Weiler, 'The Transformation of Europe' (1991) 100 *Yale Law Journal*, 2403; J. Shaw and G. Moore (eds.), *The New Legal Dynamics of European Union* (Oxford: Oxford University Press, 1996); K. Alter, *Establishing the Supremacy of European Law* (Oxford: Oxford University Press, 2001); A. Stone Sweet, *The Judicial Construction of Europe* (Oxford: Oxford University Press, 2004) and H. de Waele, 'The Role of the Court of Justice in the Integration Process: A Contemporary and Normative Assessment' (2010) 6(1) *Hanse Law Review*, 3. See also, A. Rosas, E. Levits and Y. Bot (eds.), *The Court of Justice and the Construction of Europe: Analyses and Perspectives on Sixty Years of Case-Law* (The Hague: T.M.C. Asser Press, 2013).

[6] For discussion, see e.g., N. Nic Shuibhne (ed.) *Regulating the Internal Market* (Cheltenham: Elgar, 2006) and C. Barnard, *The Substantive Law of the EU: The Four Freedoms* (5th edn) (Oxford: Oxford University Press, 2016).

competition law;[7] data protection;[8] external relations;[9] and EU citizenship.[10] The Court has also played a critical role in determining the internal constitutionality of acts of the EU institutions. This has included the development of an autonomous system of EU fundamental rights protection.[11] More recently, the Court has been called upon to rule on the constitutionality of the Union's responses to the Eurozone financial crisis and its efforts to accede to the European Convention on Human Rights.[12] In relation to the ongoing migrant crisis, the Court has also been requested to determine the impact of the arrival of an exceptionally large number of third-country nationals wishing to obtain international protection on the application of Regulation 604/2013 EU (the Dublin III Regulation).[13]

[7] For discussion, see e.g., D. Gerber, 'The Transformation of European Community Competition Law?' (2004) 35 *Harvard International Law Journal*, 127; J. Goyder and A. Albors-Llorens, *Goyder's EC Competition Law* (5th edn) (Oxford: Oxford University Press, 2009) and N. Petit, 'The Future of the Court of Justice in EU Competition Law: New Role and Responsibilities' in Rosas, Levits and Bot, *The Court of Justice and the Construction of Europe*, n. 5.

[8] See esp., Case C-131/12, *Google Spain SL and Google Inc.* v. *Agencia Española de Protección de Datos (AEPD) and González* EU:C:2014:317 and Case C-362/14, *Schrems* v. *Data Protection Commissioner* EU:C:2015:650. For discussion, see e.g., L. Azoulai M. van der Sluis, 'Institutionalizing Personal Data Protection in Times of Global Institutional Distrust: *Schrems*' (2016) 53(5) *Common Market Law Review*, 1343 and T. Horsley, '"The Court Hereby Rules . . ." – Legal Developments in EU Fundamental Rights Protection' (2015) 53(5) *Journal of Common Market Studies*, 108.

[9] For discussion, see e.g., M. Cremona (ed.), *The European Court of Justice and External Relations Law* (Oxford: Hart Publishing, 2014).

[10] For discussion, see e.g., E. Spaventa, 'Seeing the Wood Despite the Trees? On the Scope of Union Citizenship and its Constitutional Effects' (2008) 45(1) *Common Market Law Review*, 13; M. Dougan, N. Nic Shuibhne and E. Spaventa (eds.), *Empowerment and Disempowerment of the European Citizen* (Oxford: Hart Publishing, 2012) and D. Thym (ed.), *Questioning EU Citizenship: Judges and the Limits of Free Movement and Solidarity in the EU* (Oxford: Hart Publishing, 2017).

[11] See esp., Case 11/70, *Internationale Handelsgesellschaft mbH* v. *Einfuhr- und Vorratsstelle für Getreide und Futtermittel* EU:C:1970:114; Case 4/73, *Nold, Kohlen- und Baustoffgroßhandlung* v. *Commission* EU:C:1974:51 and Opinion 2/94, *Accession by the Community to the European Convention for the Protection of Human Rights and Fundamental Freedoms* EU:C:1996:140.

[12] Case C-370/12, *Pringle* v. *Government of Ireland and Others* EU:C:2012:756; Case C-62/14, *Gauweiler and Others* v. *Deutscher Bundestag* EU:C:2015:400 and Opinion 2/13, *Draft Agreement on Accession of the EU to the European Convention on Human Rights* EU:C:2014:2454.

[13] See Case C-490/16, *A.S.* v. *Slovenia* EU:C:2017:585 and Case C-646/16, *Jafari and Jafari* v. *Bundesamt für Fremdenwesen und Asyl* EU:C:2017:586. Regulation (EU) No. 604/2013 of the European Parliament and of the Council establishing the criteria and mechanisms for determining the Member State responsible for examining an application for international protection lodged in one of the Member States by a third-country national or a stateless person [2013] OJ L 180/31.

I.3 A Blind Spot Overlooked

Among the EU institutions, the Court remains uniquely distinguished as an actor in the integration process. It is the only Union institution whose activities are not routinely scrutinised (by itself or by others) for compliance with the EU Treaties. The Treaty framework is employed without question to measure the constitutionality of acts of the EU legislative and administrative institutions (as well as the activities of the Member States).[14] The exercise of political authority by the European Council, Council, Parliament and Commission is scrutinised against a range of normative limits set out in the Treaty framework.[15] The applicable limits have steadily increased over time as a consequence of repeated amendments to the founding Treaty framework and include, *inter alia*, the principles of conferral (Article 5(2) TEU), subsidiarity (Article 5(3) TEU) and proportionality (Article 5(4) TEU) as well as the protection of national identity (Article 4(2) TEU).

By contrast, the constitutionality of EU judicial activity is rarely discussed with direct reference to the Treaty framework.[16] The judgments in *Gascogne Sack Deutschland GmbH* and *Guardian Europe* v. *European Union* in the sphere of competition policy remain the exception. In both decisions, the Court ruled, with reference to the EU Charter, that the Union was liable to compensate undertakings for losses incurred as a result of the General Court's undue delay in hearing competition proceedings.[17] Beyond that set of cases, however, the potential impact of the Treaty framework in connection with assessments of EU judicial activity and its legitimacy is rarely examined.[18] Discussion of the Court and the Treaty

[14] From a long list of illustrations, see e.g., Case C-376/98, *Germany* v. *Parliament and Council (Tobacco Advertising)* EU:C:2000:544; Case C-370/12, *Pringle*, n. 12; Opinion 2/13, *Draft Agreement on Accession of the EU to the European Convention on Human Rights*, n. 12; Case C-409/13, *Council* v. *Commission (Macro Financial Assistance)* EU:C:2015:217 and Case C-62/14, *Gauweiler and Others*, n. 12.

[15] See Art. 263 TFEU. See also Art. 218(11) TFEU.

[16] None of the leading textbooks on EU law or works on the Court of Justice addresses the application of the EU Treaty framework *to the Court* as a source of normative restraint on the exercise of its attributed functions.

[17] Case T-577/14, *Gascogne Sack Deutschland GmbH* EU:T:2017:1 and Case T-673/15, *Guardian Europe* v. *European Union* EU:T:2017:377. See also, Case T-479/14, *Kendrion* v. *European Union* EU:T:2017:48.

[18] See, G. A. Bermann, 'Taking Subsidiarity Seriously: Federalism in the European Community and the United States' (1994) 94 *Columbia Law Review*, 331; T. Schilling, 'Subsidiarity as a Rule and a Principle' (1994) 14 *Yearbook of European Law* 203; G. de Búrca, 'The Principle of Subsidiarity and the Court of Justice as an Institutional Actor' (1998) 36(2) *Journal of Common Market Studies*, 217; P. Craig,

framework is typically focused on analysing the strength of the Court's role in the enforcement of Treaty norms against other Union institutions and/or the Member States.[19] Elsewhere, EU scholars reflect in great detail on the enduring impact of the Court's interpretative choices on both the vertical and horizontal balance of competences within the EU legal order.[20] With respect to the exercise of its own attributed functions, however, there is no sustained discussion of the potential impact of the Treaty framework on the scope of the Court's authority.[21] Analyses of EU judicial power – and its limits – look to other sources of normative restraint.

For most EU legal scholars, the legitimacy of the Court's activities continues to be assessed primarily with reference to generally accepted (Western) standards of good constitutional adjudication.[22] As Adams et al. summarise, the dominant approach in the literature remains focused on assessing: 'Whether the [Court's] judgments display sufficient consistency, whether the outcomes are well-founded, whether the results were reasonably predictable and whether the ECJ defers to the EU legislature and the Member States whenever appropriate.'[23] Crucially, this

'The ECJ and the Ultra Vires Action: A Conceptual Analysis' (2011) 48 *Common Market Law Review*, 395; T. Horsley, 'Reflections on the Role of the Court of Justice as the "Motor" of European Integration: Legal Limits to Judicial Policymaking' (2013) 50 *Common Market Law Review*, 931 and E. Cloots, *National Identity in EU Law* (Oxford: Oxford University Press, 2015).

19 See e.g., A. von Bogdandy and J. Bast, 'The European Union's Vertical Order of Competences: The Current Law and Proposals for Its Reform' (2002) 39 *Common Market Law Review*, 227; S. Weatherill, 'Competence Creep and Competence Control' (2004) 23(1) *Yearbook of European Law*, 1; S. Weatherill, 'The Limits of Legislative Harmonization Ten Years after *Tobacco Advertising*: How the Court's Case Law Has become a "Drafting Guide"' (2011) 12 *German Law Journal*, 827 and S. Adam and F. J. M. Parras, 'The European Stability Mechanism through the Legal Meanderings of the Union's Constitutionalism: Comment on *Pringle*' (2013) 38(6) *European Law Review*, 848.

20 See recently, e.g., H. W. Micklitz and B. de. Witte (eds.), *The European Court of Justice and the Autonomy of the Member States* (Antwerp: Insentia, 2012); M. Adams, H. de Waele, J. Meeusen and G. Straetmans (eds.), *Judging Europe's Judges: The Legitimacy of the Case Law of the European Court of Justice* (Oxford: Hart Publishing, 2013) and M. Dawson, B. de Witte and E. Muir (eds.), *Judicial Activism at the European Court of Justice* (Cheltenham: Elgar, 2013).

21 For the principal exceptions, see n. 18 and the literature cited therein.

22 See e.g., Adams et al., *Judging Europe's Judges*, n. 20 and Dawson et al., *Judicial Activism at the European Court of Justice*, n. 20 and N. Nic Shuibhne, *The Coherence of EU Free Movement Law: Constitutional Responsibility and the Court of Justice* (Oxford: Oxford University Press, 2013).

23 M. Adams et al., 'Introduction: Judging Europe's Judges' in Adams et al., *Judging Europe's Judges*, n. 20, at p. 8.

highly developed body of work overlooks the Treaties' function as principal touchstones on the internal constitutionality of EU judicial activity.[24] It takes its cue instead from the Court's own jurisprudence, specifically its institutional positions on the three key issues for EU constitutionalism (see further Section III).

I.4 A Fundamental Omission in Existing Legal Analyses of the Court

The absence of a comprehensive and rigorous Treaty-based critique of EU judicial activity in the scholarship is striking for two reasons. First, the Treaty framework provides no basis whatsoever to justify differentiating between the Court and the Union's administrative and political institutions with regard to compliance with its demands. The Court is formally designated an institution of the Union under Article 13 TEU. As such, along with the Union's political institutions, it is irrefutably subject to compliance with the EU Treaties.[25] Indeed, as the Court of Justice has repeatedly stated, 'the [Union] is based on the rule of law, inasmuch as neither its Member States nor its institutions can avoid review of the conformity of their acts with the basic constitutional charter, the [Treaties].'[26] Secondly, and more strikingly still, existing criticism of the Court and its role in EU integration raises concerns that the EU Treaty framework directly addresses. In particular, the principal interlocutors (Member States, national courts and EU scholars) voice concerns that the Court of Justice often plays fast and loose with the

[24] The same is true of other strands of the scholarship on the Court – examined in Chapter 6. See e.g., H. Rasmussen, *On Law and Policy in the European Court of Justice* (Dordrecht: Martinus Nijhoff Publishing, 1986); J. Bengoetxea, *The Legal Reasoning of the European Court of Justice: Towards a European Jurisprudence* (Oxford: Oxford University Press, 1993); P. Neill, *The European Court of Justice: A Case Study in Judicial Activism* (London: European Policy Forum, 1995); T. Hartley, 'The European Court, Judicial Objectivity and the Constitution of the European Union' (1996) 112 *Law Quarterly Review*, 95; G. Beck, *The Legal Reasoning of the Court of Justice of the EU* (Oxford: Hart Publishing, 2013) and S. Sankari, *European Court of Justice Legal Reasoning in Context* (Groningen: Europa Law Publishing, 2013). See also, though to a lesser extent, G. Conway, *The Limits of Legal Reasoning and the European Court of Justice* (Cambridge: Cambridge University Press, 2012).

[25] See esp., Art. 13(2) TEU.

[26] Joined Cases C-402/05 P and C-415/05, *P Kadi and Al Barakaat International Foundation* v. *Council and Commission* EU:C:2008:461 at para. 281; Case 294/83, *Parti écologiste "Les Verts"* v. *European Parliament* EU:C:1986:166 at para. 23 and Opinion 2/13, *Draft Agreement on Accession of the EU to the European Convention on Human Rights*, n. 12 at para. 163.

basic character of the EU legal order as a system of limited, attributed competences (see Article 5(2) TEU).[27] As Sharpf summarises: 'Whilst the Court's contribution to European integration is widely considered beneficial in politically correct discourses, its impact on the constitutional balance of the multilevel European polity does raise serious problems.'[28] Similarly, the Court is also routinely criticised for undermining democratic processes at both Union and national level through its approach to the judicial review of EU and Member State measures.[29] Grimm, for example, directly links the Court's case law, and its role in driving the process of 'constitutionalising' the EU legal order, with the European Union's chronic democracy deficit.[30] On his analysis, '[the Court's] confusion of elements of constitutional law with elements of ordinary law in the treaties favours the unelected and non-accountable institutions of the EU over the democratically legitimised and accountable organs'.[31]

This book addresses the persisting failure to scrutinise EU judicial activity for compliance with the demands of the Treaty framework as constitutional touchstone. In so doing, its primary contribution is to correct the asymmetry that presently arises between, on the one hand, analysis of the internal constitutionality of EU administrative/legislative activity and Member State measures and, on the other hand, assessments of the Court's institutional choices.

[27] See e.g., Rasmussen, *On Law and Policy in the European Court of Justice*, n. 24; Neill, *The European Court of Justice: A Case Study in Judicial Activism*, n. 24; Hartley, 'The European Court, Judicial Objectivity and the Constitution of the European Union', n. 24; Conway, *The Limits of Legal Reasoning and the European Court of Justice*, n. 24 and Beck, *The Legal Reasoning of the Court of Justice of the EU*, n. 24. See also in the popular press, R. Herzog and L. Gerken, 'Stop the European Court of Justice', *EU Observer*, 10 September 2008.

[28] F. Scharpf, 'Perpetual Momentum: Directed and Unconstrained?' (2012) 19(1) *Journal of European Public Policy*, 127, at p. 134.

[29] See e.g., D. Grimm, 'The Democratic Costs of Constitutionalisation: The European Case' (2015) 21(4) *European Law Journal*, 460; Scharpf, 'Perpetual Momentum: Directed and Unconstrained?', n. 28 and D. Ritleng, 'Does the European Court of Justice take Democracy Seriously? Some Thoughts about the Macro-Financial Assistance Case' (2016) 53(1) *Common Market Law Review*, 11. Similarly, the Court is also criticised for its lack of deference to Member States on sensitive matters of cultural, moral, ethical and redistributive policy. See e.g., C. Newdick, 'Citizenship, Free Movement and Health Care: Cementing Individual Rights by Corroding Social Solidarity' (2006) 43(6) *Common Market Law Review*, 1645; S. Gerards, 'Pluralism, Deference and the Margin of Appreciation Doctrine' (2011) 17(1) *European Law Review*, 80 and F. de Witte, 'Sex, Drugs & EU law: The Recognition of Moral and Ethical Diversity in EU Law' (2013) 50(6) *Common Market Law Review*, 1545.

[30] Grimm, 'The Democratic Costs of Constitutionalisation', n. 29.

[31] *Ibid.*, at p. 471.

II The Treaty Framework as Constitutional Touchstone

II.1 The EU Treaties as Constitutional Touchstones

A central claim of this book is that the EU Treaties should be viewed as the principal statements on the internal constitutionality of all EU institutional activity. This includes, as a matter of principle, the activities of the Court of Justice – an EU institution the activities of which are presently not routinely scrutinised for compliance with the Treaties. The argument that the EU Treaties apply *to the Court* as a source of normative restraint on the exercise of its institutional functions is easily constructed. It follows expressly from the EU Treaties and also finds explicit confirmation in the Court's case law (Section I.4).

Internal constitutionality is not, of course, the only possible baseline against which the legitimacy of EU judicial activity may be measured. The legitimacy of the Court of Justice's role in the EU legal order, and European integration more broadly, may be (and is) assessed from a range of complementary and/or competing perspectives.[32] The alignment of internal constitutionality (i.e., legality) with discussion of the legitimacy of EU judicial activity in this book addresses an important gap in existing legal research on the Court of Justice. More crucially, however, it also finds deeper foundations. Above all else, it acknowledges the fundamental value that Member States, through the EU Treaties, have always attached – and continue to attach – to the nature of the EU legal order as a system of limited, attributed competences.[33]

II.2 The Treaty Framework and the Three Key Issues for EU Constitutionalism

As constitutional touchstone, the EU Treaty framework performs an important normative function. It provides clarity on what this book defines as the three basic issues for EU constitutionalism. These three

[32] Legitimacy may be assessed, for example, not only in terms of legality, but also from a range of political, sociological and moral perspectives. For an overview of the main legitimacy models applied to the study of EU judicial activity, see e.g., R. Bobek, 'Of Feasibility and Silent Elephants: The Legitimacy of the Court of Justice through the Eyes of National Courts' in Adams et al., *Judging Europe's Judges*, n. 20 at pp. 198–202.

[33] See Art. 5(2) TEU and Art. 13(2) TEU.

issues are representative of questions that a public lawyer may ask, in adapted form, of any legal system based on the rule of law. They address the *how*, *who* and *what* of European integration. The first issue references *the formal status of Union law and the conditions under which it applies within Member States* (Constitutional Issue No. 1); the second addresses *the locus of political authority within the EU legal order* (Constitutional Issue No. 2); and the third is focused on identifying *the objectives, values and limits governing European integration* (Constitutional Issue No. 3).

The EU Treaty framework's statements on each of these three constitutional issues have remained strikingly consistent over time.[34] To a considerable extent, Member States, as Treaty signatories, have repeatedly (re)ratified remarkably clear positions on the fundamentals of EU integration that trace their origins back to the founding EEC Treaty. The principal changes to the EU Treaty framework over time have primarily concerned the objectives, values and limits of EU integration (Constitutional Issue No. 3). These have undergone a process of broadening and deepening. In addition, successive waves of Treaty amendment have also radically adjusted the disposition of policymaking competence between the three key political institutions (Constitutional Issue No. 2) – to enhance, first and foremost, the position of the European Parliament.

II.3 Limits to the EU Treaty Framework as Constitutional Touchstone

The EU Treaties form the centrepiece of the broader constitutional context that structures EU integration. However, they do not capture that context exhaustively. The wider context is conditioned by what this book defines as acts of *constitutional supplementation* and *constitutional contestation*.

The first of these concepts, constitutional supplementation, references acts of the EU institutions (and also Member States) that elaborate – but do *not* fundamentally contest – the EU Treaties' basic statements on the three key issues for EU constitutionalism (Section II.2). Examples include

[34] See also, G. de Búrca, 'The Institutional Development of the EU: A Constitutional Analysis' in P. Craig and G. de Búrca (eds.), *The Evolution of EU Law* (Oxford: Oxford University Press, 1999) at p. 57.

inter-institutional agreements concluded between the EU's political organs to manage the exercise of their legislative competences[35] and, in the judicial sphere, the Court's recognition of fundamental rights as 'general principles of Union law'.[36] By contrast, the concept of constitutional contestation refers to acts of the EU institutions (and Member States) that expressly *contest* the Treaties' clear position on the three basic issues for EU constitutionalism. Examples include, in the political context, Member State agreement on the 'Luxembourg Compromise'[37] and, more recently, the use of intergovernmental treaties to reform core aspects of the Treaty framework on Economic and Monetary Union in response to the Eurozone crisis.[38]

The introduction of the concepts of constitutional supplementation and constitutional contestation serves two specific objectives. First, it reveals the existence of limits to the functioning of the bare bones of the EU Treaties as touchstones on the internal constitutionality of EU institutional activity. Secondly, it establishes the framework employed in this book to structure the critique of EU judicial activity for compliance with the Treaties.

III The Court of Justice *Versus* the EU Treaty Framework

This book uses the concepts of constitutional supplementation and constitutional contestation to assess how far the Court's institutional position on the three key issues for EU constitutionalism conform to the Treaty framework's statements on each as constitutional touchstone. This leads to the identification of multiple acts of *judicial* constitutional contestation across all three basic issues for EU constitutionalism.

35 See e.g., Interinstitutional Agreement of 20 December 1994 – Accelerated working method for official codification of legislative texts [1996] OJ C102/2 and Interinstitutional Agreement between the European Parliament, the Council of the European Union and the European Commission on Better Law-Making [2016] OJ C123/1.

36 See e.g., Case 11/70, *Internationale Handelsgesellschaft*, n. 11.

37 Bulletin of the European Communities, March 1966, 3–66 at pp. 5–11.

38 Treaty establishing the European Stability Mechanism and Treaty on Stability, Coordination, and Governance in the Economic and Monetary Union. See also, similarly, Decision of the Heads of State or Government, meeting within the European Council, concerning a New Settlement for the United Kingdom within the European Union [2016] EUCO 1/16.

III.1 The Court of Justice and the Formal Status of Union Law and the Conditions under Which it Applies within Member States

First, with regard to the formal status of Union law and the conditions under which it applies within Member States (Constitutional Issue No. 1), the Court and the Treaty framework have offered and maintained fundamentally different responses.[39] The Treaties, as an expression of the political preferences of the Member States, ground EU integration in the normative framework of public international law. For example, pursuant to Article 4(3) TEU, Member States retain full control over the internal effect of Union law – in accordance with the principles and practice of international law.[40] By contrast, the Court of Justice robustly defends a vision of the EU as a 'new legal order' that is defined in opposition to international law and, further, considers the domestic effect of EU norms an exclusive matter for Union, not Member State law.[41] The source of this judicial vision is external to the Treaty framework. It represents the Court's projection onto the Treaty framework of a model of political federalism. To a great extent, that vision was also 'co-produced' with an influential body of legal scholars advocating a shared political vision for EU integration.[42]

[39] See further, Chapter 3.

[40] On Member State control over the domestic effect of EU norms, see also Art. 260 TFEU, Art. 280 TFEU and Art. 291(1) TFEU.

[41] Case 26/62, *NV Algemene Transport- en Expeditie Onderneming van Gend & Loos* v. *Netherlands Inland Revenue Administration* EU:C:1963:1 at p. 12. See also Case 6/64, *Costa* v. *E.N.E.L* EU:C:1964:66 at p. 593; Opinion 1/09, *Draft Agreement on the Creation of a Unified Patent Litigation System* EU:C:2011:123 at para. 65 and Opinion 2/13, *Draft Agreement on Accession of the EU to the European Convention on Human Rights*, n. 12 at para. 157. See also, with respect to the Court's position on the autonomy of the EU legal order in the field of external relations, Opinion 1/91, *Draft agreement between the Community, on the one hand, and the countries of the European Free Trade Association, on the other, relating to the creation of the European Economic Area* EU:C:1991:490 at para. 2 and Opinion 1/00, *Proposed agreement between the European Community and non-Member States on the establishment of a European Common Aviation Area* EU:C:2002:231.

[42] On the role of EU scholars in promoting the Court's work, see e.g., Alter, *Establishing the Supremacy of European Law*, n. 5 at p. 58 and Conway, *The Limits of Legal Reasoning and the European Court of Justice*, n. 24 at pp. 52–59. On co-production theory, see S. Janasoff (ed.), *States of Knowledge: The Co-Production of Science and the Social Order* (London: Routledge, 2004).

III.2 The Court of Justice and the Locus of Political Authority within the EU Legal Order

Secondly, the Court of Justice has also mounted a series of challenges to the EU Treaties' clear statements on the locus of political authority within the Union legal order (Constitutional Issue No. 2).[43] With respect to *constituent* authority, the Court of Justice is shown to have repeatedly challenged the position of Member States – acting collectively – under the Treaty framework as the ultimate source of constituent political authority within the EU legal order. For example, in *Parliament* v. *Council (Chernobyl)*, the Court revised the Treaty rules on standing rights in annulment actions, notwithstanding the (then) Treaty's reservation of competence to do so to Member States.[44] Similarly, in cases such as *Rottmann*, the Court has found no difficulty at all in disregarding specific acts of constitutional supplementation that Member States have collectively adopted to manage discrete issues, including, in that decision, the rules governing the acquisition and loss of Member State nationality.[45]

In addition, the Court of Justice has also subverted the formal framework structuring *EU policymaking* authority under the EU Treaties by arrogating to itself primary responsibility for Union policymaking in key areas of Union activity.[46] This has been achieved by attributing direct effect to a range of EU norms and, moreover, asserting their primacy over conflicting provisions of Member State law. In short, invoking its case law on the formal status of Union law and the conditions under which it applies within Member States (Constitutional Issue No. 1), the Court of Justice has effectively interposed itself alongside the EU legislature as direct policymaker.[47] Its policymaking functions are typically

43 See further, Chapter 4.

44 Case C-70/88, *Parliament and Council (Chernobyl)* EU:C:1990:217. See also, the Court's establishment of the right to reparation in Joined Cases C-6/90 and C-9/90, *Francovich and Others* v. *Italy* EU:C:1991:428.

45 Case C-135/08, *Rottman* v. *Freistaat Bayern* EU:C:2010:104. See also, e.g., the Court's interpretation of Protocol No. 8 relating to Article 6(2) of the Treaty on European Union on the accession of the Union to the European Convention on the Protection of Human Rights and Fundamental Freedoms [2012] OJ C 326/273 in Opinion 2/13, *Draft Agreement on Accession of the EU to the European Convention on Human Rights*, n. 12.

46 See T. Horsley, 'Institutional Dynamics Reloaded: The Court of Justice and the Development of EU Internal Market' in P. Koutrakos and J. Snell (eds.), *Research Handbook on the Law of the EU's Internal Market* (Cheltenham: Elgar, 2016). See also, R. Dehousse, *The European Court of Justice* (Basingstoke: MacMillan Press, 1998).

47 See Horsley, 'Institutional Dynamics Reloaded: The Court of Justice and the Development of EU Internal Market', n. 46 at pp. 414–422.

activated using the preliminary reference procedure, which empowers and/or compels Member State courts to make references to the Court to rule on, *inter alia*, the interpretation of provisions of Union law.

The Court's assertion of direct policymaking functions has had a transformative impact on the development of substantive EU law, so much so that in specific instances the Union legislature has subsequently done little more than transpose the Court's interpretative choices into secondary legislation.[48] However, its substantive impact notwithstanding, the Court's move to interpose itself alongside the EU legislature as direct policymaker exists in clear tension with the Treaty framework as constitutional touchstone. The EU Treaties continue as under the founding EEC Treaty to entrust primary responsibility for policymaking to the Union's political institutions: principally, the Commission, European Parliament and Council of the European Union.[49]

III.3 The Court of Justice and the Objectives, Values and Limits of EU Integration

Thirdly, the Court's approach to the Treaty framework's statements on the objectives, values and limits of EU integration (Constitutional Issue No. 3) gives rise to further acts of constitutional contestation in EU judicial activity.[50] The EU Treaties now set out a range of restraining norms that exist to manage EU institutional activity. The provisions in question include, for instance, the principles of conferral;[51] subsidiarity;[52] proportionality;[53] national identity;[54] and interinstitutional balance.[55] The Court has been routinely criticised by commentators at various points for its apparent failure to enforce these provisions effectively against other EU institutions.[56] More strikingly, however, there is

[48] See e.g., Directive 2011/24 EU on the application of patients' rights in cross-border healthcare [2011] OJ 88/45.

[49] For analysis, see e.g., See H. Wallace, M. Pollack and A. Young (eds.), *Policy-Making in the European Union* (2nd edn) (Oxford: Oxford University Press, 2014); S. Hix and B. Høyland, *The Political System of the European Union* (3rd edn) (Basingstoke: Palgrave MacMillan, 2011) and N. Nugent, *The Government and Politics of the European Union* (7th edn) (Basingstoke: Palgrave MacMillan, 2010).

[50] See further Chapter 5.

[51] Art. 5(2) TEU.

[52] Art. 5(3) TEU.

[53] Art. 5(4) TEU.

[54] Art. 4(2) TEU.

[55] Art. 13(2) TEU.

[56] See e.g., n. 19 and the literature cited therein.

evidence of its systematic disregard for the same values and limits of EU integration in connection with the exercise of its own institutional functions. This applies, first and foremost, to its interpretive choices as direct policymaker (Section III.1.2).

The Court's use of directly effective EU norms to override, sidestep or simply interrogate the Union legislature's preferences in decisions such as *Sturgeon and Others* (air passenger rights) is a paradigmatic example of constitutional contestation with regard to the Treaties' statements on the values of EU integration (falling within Constitutional Issue No. 3).[57] More precisely, the Court's disregard for the integrity of EU legislative choices undermines the increased normative weight that the EU Treaty framework now attaches to the value of representative democracy as the foundation of EU decision-making. That value is now firmly embedded within the Treaty framework as constitutional touchstone, most visibly in Article 10 TEU.

Similarly, as direct policymaker, the Court of Justice has also detached EU policymaking from the framework of limits that the Treaties now impose on EU *legislative* policymaking. This defies functional expectations. As a consequence of its move to interpose itself alongside the Union legislature as direct policymaker, the Court of Justice is legitimately to be expected to exercise its new role in accordance with the framework of limits structuring EU legislative policymaking. However, as its jurisprudence on issues such as cross-border healthcare and the right to strike demonstrate, the Court has adopted a very different approach. Specifically, it does not construe express Treaty exclusions on Union legislative competence as limits on its own functions as direct policymaker.[58] At best, such provisions are operationalised as potential

[57] Joined Cases C-402/07 and Case C-432/07, *Sturgeon* v. *Condor Flugdienst GmbH and Böck and Lepuschitz* v. *Air France SA* EU:C:2009:716. See also, e.g., Case C-138/02, *Collins* v. *Secretary of State for Work and Pensions* EU:C:2004:172; Case C-144/04, *Mangold* v. *Helm* EU:C:2005:709; Case C-236/09, *Test-Achats ASBL and Others* v. *Conseil des ministres* EU:C:2011:100; Case C-382/08, *Neukirchinger* v. *Bezirkshauptmannschaft Grieskirchen* EU:C:2011:27; Case C-34/09, *Ruiz Zambrano* v. *Office national de l'emploi* EU:C:2011:124; Joined Cases C-581/10 and Case C-629/20, *Nelson and Others* v. *Deutsche Lufthansa AG and TUI Travel plc and Others* v. *Civil Aviation Authority* EU:C:2012:657 and Case C-441/14, *Dansk Industri (DI), acting on behalf of Ajos A/S* v. *Estate of Karsten Eigil Rasmussen* EU:C:2016:278.

[58] See e.g., Case C-157/99, *Geraets-Smits* v. *Stichting Ziekenfonds VGZ and Peerbooms* v. *Stichting CZ Groep Zorgverzekeringen* EU:C:2001:404; Case C-385/99, *Müller-Fauré and van Riet* EU:C:2003:270; Case C-372/04, *Watts* v. *Bedford Primary Care Trust* EU:C:2006:325; Case C-341/05, *Laval un Partneri Ltd* v. *Svenska Byggnadsarbetareförbundet* EU:C:2007:809 and Case C-438/05, *International Transport Workers' Federation and Finnish Seamen's Union* v. *Viking Line ABP* EU:C:2007:772.

derogations to specific EU norms that the Court has ruled directly effective – and subject to a strict proportionality assessment.[59]

IV Three Contemporary Problems for EU Judicial Lawmaking, Four Reform Proposals

The individual acts of judicial constitutional contestation unmasked in this book do not exist in a legal and political vacuum. On the contrary, the Court's statements on the three issues for EU constitutionalism are bounded together closely with the activities of its principal interlocutors: namely, Member States, national courts and tribunals, and also EU scholars. These three sets of actors are empowered, to differing degrees, to respond to the Court's decisions to formulate its own independent responses on, respectively, the formal status of Union law and the conditions under which it applies within Member States (Constitutional Issue No. 1); the locus of political authority within the EU legal order (Constitutional Issue No. 2); and the objectives, values and limits governing European integration (Constitutional Issue No. 3).

The concluding chapter of this book reconsiders the three acts of judicial constitutional contestation in light of the responses of the Court's interlocutors. The result is the isolation of three contemporary problems for EU judicial activity. The first problem concerns the Court's use of its own statements on the three key issues for EU constitutionalism as tools to *challenge clear statements of constituent authority* (Problem No. 1). The second and third problems address the Court's contribution to EU integration as *direct policymaker*. On the vertical axis, the problem centres on the Court's *disregard for the range of limits that the EU Treaties impose on Union policymaking* (Problem No. 2). On the horizontal axis, it concerns the Court's *use of directly effective norms as tools to override, adjust, or step beyond the EU legislature's policy choices* (Problem No. 3).

The existence of these three contemporary problems places the Court of Justice at the very centre of critical debates about EU integration, its limits and the democratic credentials of Union policymaking. Successive Treaty amendments have sought to place clearer limits on the existence and exercise of EU competences, as well as to introduce new safeguards to

[59] See esp., Case C-341/05, *Laval un Partneri Ltd*, n. 58 at paras. 103–11. See also, by analogy and with reference to Art. 4(2) TEU and Art. 346 TFEU on national security, Case 300/11, *ZZ* v. *Secretary of State for the Home Department* EU:C:2013:363 and Case C-284/05, *Commission* v. *Finland (Military Equipment)* EU:C:2009:778.

protect Member States' autonomy in sensitive policy areas.[60] In parallel, far-reaching reforms have also been introduced into the Treaty framework in an effort to bolster the democratic qualities of Union policy-making.[61] These (and other related) reform initiatives amount to very little if the Court of Justice – one of the most powerful and influential institutions of the Union – considers that it remains free to act independently of the Treaty framework as constitutional touchstone.

The application of the Treaty framework *to the Court* as a means to problematise that institution's role within the EU legal order is this monograph's primary contribution to the scholarship on European integration. By way of conclusion, however, the book also asks how the Court and its interlocutors can (and should) respond to the existence of the three contemporary problems for EU judicial activity. Specifically, it offers four reform proposals to strengthen the legitimacy of the Court's institutional role within the Treaty framework as a Union institution.

First, and most crucially, the Court of Justice is required to demonstrate closer engagement with the EU Treaty framework when exercising its interpretative functions (Reform Proposal No. 1).[62] Secondly, legal scholars are challenged to reframe the intellectual paradigm that presently structures both explanatory and normative analysis of the Court and its case law (Reform Proposal No. 2). Thirdly, it is incumbent on Member States to improve the quality of the EU Treaty framework (Reform Proposal No. 3). Finally, and most ambitiously, Member States are also encouraged to consider the merits of establishing a stronger

60 See the introduction, at Maastricht, of e.g., Art. 3b EEC (now Art. 5 TEU) (on conferral, subsidiarity and proportionality); at Amsterdam, of e.g., Art. F(3) TEU (on national identity), Art. K(5) TEU (on national security), Art. 129(5) EEC (now Art. 168(7) TFEU) (on protection of national healthcare systems); and, at Lisbon, of e.g., Art. 4 TEU and Arts. 2–6 TFEU (on categories of competence), Art. 6 TEU (on the legal status of the EU Charter of Fundamental Rights), Art. 50 TEU (on Member State withdrawal) and Art. 65(4) TFEU (on Member State control over the liberalisation of external capital movements).

61 See the introduction, in the Single European Act, of e.g., Art. 6 (establishing the co-operative legislative procedure); at Maastricht, of e.g., Art. 8d EEC (now Art. 24 TFEU) (establishing EU citizens' right to petition the European Parliament and engage the EU Ombudsman); at Amsterdam, of e.g., Art. 189b (see now Arts. 289 and 294 TFEU) (extending the co-decision procedure) and, at Lisbon, of e.g., Art. 10 TEU (on the dual democratic basis of the Union), Art. 11(4) TEU and Regulation (EU) No. 211/2011 of the European Parliament and of the Council on the citizens' initiative [2011] OJ L65/1 (establishing the European Citizens' Initiative) and Art. 12 TEU (on the role of national parliaments).

62 That requirement is, in turn, broken down further into three specific normative prescriptions. See further Chapter 7.

institutional framework to facilitate more effective scrutiny of EU judicial activity for compliance with the EU Treaties (Reform Proposal No. 4).

The first and second proposals are the most significant. They do not require Treaty amendment and can be actioned immediately. The third and fourth proposals are presented as supplementary. They outline options for further reform to enhance the legitimacy of EU judicial activity by aligning this more closely with the Treaty framework as constitutional touchstone. The fourth is the most innovative in that respect. It prompts the Member States (and legal scholars) to consider the added value of establishing new mechanisms to monitor the Court's adherence to the EU Treaties. This goes beyond existing discussions of the advantages and disadvantages of creating a new 'EU Supreme Court' to include consideration of fresh alternatives, such as establishing a role for certain national courts and/or political institutions to support the Court of Justice as a Union institution.[63]

Outline

Chapters 1 and 2 establish the intellectual framework of enquiry. Chapter 1 defends the status of the EU Treaty framework as the principal source of normative restraint on EU institutional activity – including the work of the Court. It also explores the consequences of positioning the EU Treaties as touchstones on the internal constitutionality of EU institutional activity. Specifically, it assesses the EU Treaty framework's position on the three key issues for EU constitutionalism. Chapter 2 then reflects on the limits of the EU Treaty framework as a source of normative restraint on EU institutional activity. Most importantly, it introduces the twin concepts of constitutional contestation and constitutional supplementation that structure critique of EU judicial activity for compliance with the Treaty framework in subsequent chapters. It also highlights examples of both phenomena in non-judicial contexts. This includes an appraisal of political actors' responses to the ongoing Eurozone crisis.

[63] On proposals to establish an EU Supreme Court, see e.g., J. H. H. Weiler, 'Epilogue: The Judicial Après Nice' in G. de Búrca and J. H. H. Weiler (eds.), *The European Court of Justice* (Oxford: Oxford University Press, 2001). See also, Lindseth's proposal for a 'Conflicts Tribunal' in P. L. Lindseth, *Power and Legitimacy: Reconciling Europe and the Nation-State* (Oxford: Oxford University Press, 2010) at pp. 266–277.

Chapters 3, 4 and 5 examine the detail of the Court of Justice's position on the three fundamental issues for EU constitutionalism with a view to identifying specific sites of judicial constitutional contestation. Chapter 3 begins by critiquing against the Treaty framework (as amended), the Court's approach to defining the formal status of Union law and the conditions under which it applies within Member States (Constitutional Issue No. 1). Chapter 4 then turns to consider the Court's position on the locus of political authority within the EU legal order (Constitutional Issue No. 2), considering questions of both constituent power and policy-making competence. Thereafter, Chapter 5 concludes by assessing the Court's engagement with the objectives, values and, most crucially, limits that the EU Treaties impose on EU integration (Constitutional Issue No. 3). It focuses in particular on the existence of sites of constitutional contestation with respect to the Court's exercise of its direct policymaking functions in key areas of Union policymaking, including the free movement of services, EU citizenship and air transportation. It interrogates the Court's institutional choices as direct policymaker in these fields for compliance with specific limits and values that the EU Treaties place on Union policymaking along both the vertical (Union-Member State) and horizontal (Union-Union) axes.

Chapter 6 considers the reactions of the Court's principal interlocutors to its statements on the three key issues for EU constitutionalism. It assesses how Member States and national (constitutional) courts have responded to the Court's institutional position on the functioning of the EU Treaty framework as a normative restraint on the scope and exercise of its attributed functions. It also considers the responses of EU legal scholars. With respect to Member States and national courts, the Court's challenges to the Treaty framework are shown, to a significant extent, to be tolerated but not accepted on their own terms. By contrast, most EU legal scholars fully embrace the judicial paradigm and, moreover, have sought vigorously to defend the integrity of the Court of Justice's divergent positions on all three issues for EU constitutionalism where challenged. This is most visible in efforts to manage the gap between the EU Treaties and the Court's position on the formal status of Union law and the conditions under which it applies within Member States (Constitutional Issue No. 1) through a shift towards constitutionalism pluralism.

Chapter 7 uses the responses of the Court's interlocutors – Member States, national courts and EU scholars – to identity three problems with EU judicial activity in its present form. Put another way, the responses of the Court's interlocutors are employed as a filter to transform the identified acts of judicial constitutional contestation into three contemporary problems for EU judicial lawmaking. To manage these problems, Chapter 7 offers four reform proposals in outline form. These proposals should not be viewed in isolation, but as component parts of an overall reform strategy that is designed to enhance the legitimacy of the Court's contribution to EU integration as an institution of the Union.

1 The EU Treaty Framework as Constitutional Touchstone

> The [Union] is based on the rule of law, inasmuch as neither its Member States nor its institutions can avoid review of the conformity of their acts with the basic constitutional charter, the [Treaties].
>
> Joined Cases C-402/05 P and C-415/05, P *Kadi and Al Barakaat International Foundation* v. *Council and Commission* EU:C:2008:461 at para. 281

Introduction

This chapter examines the status and function of the EU Treaty framework as the principal touchstone for assessments of the internal constitutionality of all EU institutional activity. Its aim is twofold. First, it defends the core claim at the centre of this book that, as an institution of the Union, the Court is bound to comply with the demands of the EU Treaties. Secondly, this chapter considers the conclusions that attach to that claim. In short, it asks what is the relevance of the finding that the Treaty framework functions as the principal source of normative restraint on Union institutional activity – including the work of the Court?

Section 1 defends the EU Treaties' function as a primary source of normative restraint within the EU legal order. In summary, it argues that the EU Treaties should be viewed as the principal touchstones with regard to the internal constitutionality of all EU institutional activity. This includes, as a matter of principle, the activities of the Court of Justice – an EU institution the activities of which are presently not routinely scrutinised for compliance with the Treaties. Furthermore, it is argued that, as the Union's founding constitutional charter, the EU Treaty framework enjoys an uncharacteristically high degree of normative authority. In particular, it is submitted that the frequency, nature and scope of the various amendments serve as a direct and powerful source of 'constitutional refreshment', injecting renewed normative authority into the Treaties' statements on the formal status of EU law, the locus of EU political authority and the objectives, values and limits of EU integration.[1]

Section 2 explores the *consequences* of positioning the EU Treaties as touchstones on the internal constitutionality of EU institutional activity. In summary, this chapter contends that, as constitutional touchstone, the EU Treaty framework provides important clarity on what this book defines as the three basic issues for EU constitutionalism. These three issues are representative of questions that a public lawyer may ask, in adapted form, of any legal system based on the rule of law. They interrogate the *how*, *who* and *what* of EU integration. The first issue addresses the formal status of Union law and the conditions under which it applies within Member States (Constitutional Issue No. 1); the second concerns the locus of political authority within the EU legal order (Constitutional Issue No. 2) and the third is focused on identifying the objectives, values and limits governing European integration (Constitutional Issue No. 3).

On each of the three issues, the EU Treaty framework is shown to have remained strikingly consistent over time.[2] To a considerable extent, Member States, as Treaty signatories, have repeatedly (re)ratified remarkably clear positions on the fundamentals of EU integration that trace their origins back to the founding EEC Treaty. First, on *the formal status of Union law and the conditions under which it applies within Member States* (Constitutional Issue No. 1), the EU Treaties continue to anchor EU integration to established principles of international law. Secondly, with respect to the locus of political authority within the EU legal order (Constitutional Issue No. 2), the Treaty framework reserves constituent authority to the Member States acting collectively. At the same time, the Union's political institutions – the Commission, European Parliament and Council of the European Union – are entrusted, in varying institutional combinations, with primary responsibility for EU policymaking.[3] Lastly, the EU Treaties now outline a diverse range of objectives and values, but also prescribe an

[1] See B. de Witte, 'The Closest Thing to a Constitutional Conversation in Europe: The Semi-Permanent Treaty Revision Process' in P. Beaumont, C. Lyons and N. Walker (eds.), *Convergence and Divergence in European Public Law* (Oxford: Hart Publishing, 2002).

[2] See also G. de Búrca, 'The Institutional Development of the EU: A Constitutional Analysis' in P. Craig and G. de Búrca (eds.), *The Evolution of EU Law* (Oxford: Oxford University Press, 1999) at p. 57.

[3] See also the role of the European Council in specific policy fields such as the Common Foreign and Security Policy (Title V, Chapter 2 TEU).

ever-increasing set of limits on the existence and exercise of EU competences by Union institutions.

The principal changes to the EU Treaty framework over time have primarily concerned the objectives, values and limits of EU integration (Constitutional Issue No. 3). These have undergone a process of broadening and deepening. In addition, successive waves of Treaty amendment have also radically adjusted the disposition of policymaking competence between the three key political institutions (Constitutional Issue No. 2) – to enhance, first and foremost, the position of the European Parliament.

1 The Treaty Framework and Internal Constitutionality

This section argues that the EU Treaties are conceived, and should be viewed as, the principal instruments determining the internal constitutionality of all EU institutional activity. That argument is easily constructed: it follows expressly from the EU Treaties and also finds explicit confirmation in the Court's case law.

Thus far, discussion of the Treaty framework's function as a check on EU institutional behaviour has focused almost exclusively on the activities of the Union's legislative and administrative organs; primarily the Commission, European Parliament and Council.[4] That focus is the product of structural features, but also the result of the prevalence of a particular 'way of seeing' that has underplayed the potential role of the Treaty framework as a source of normative restraint on the activities of other EU actors – first and foremost, the Court of Justice (see further Chapter 6).[5] This chapter argues that the scope of application of that framework is not so limited and extends, without differentiation, to

[4] None of the key texts on EU law examine the function of the EU Treaty framework as a source of constitutional restraint on EU judicial activity. See P. Craig and G. de Búrca, *EU Law: Text, Cases and Materials* (6th edn) (Oxford: Oxford University Press, 2015); D. Chalmers, G. Davies and M. Monti, *European Union Law* (3rd edn) (Cambridge: Cambridge University Press, 2014); A. Dashwood et al., *Wyatt and Dashwood's European Union Law* (6th edn) (Oxford: Hart Publishing, 2011); R. Schütze, *European Constitutional Law* (Cambridge: Cambridge University Press, 2015) and P. Craig and G de Búrca, *The Evolution of EU Law* (2nd edn) (Oxford: Oxford University Press, 2011). See also, e.g., A. Dashwood, 'The Limits of European Community Powers' (1996) 21 *European Law Review*, 113; A. Estella, *The Principle of Subsidiarity and Its Critique* (Oxford: Oxford University Press, 2002) and T. Tridimas, *General Principles of EU Law* (2nd edn) (Oxford: Oxford University Press, 2007).

[5] This phrase is borrowed from J. Berger, *Ways of Seeing* (London: Penguin Classics, 2008).

encompass and mandate the scrutiny of EU judicial activities for compliance with its demands.[6]

As a constitutional touchstone, the Treaty framework benefits from an uncharacteristically high degree of normative authority. In contrast to many other constitutional charters, the EU Treaties have been comprehensively amended by the Member States at regular intervals. That process functions as an important source of 'constitutional refreshment'. Crucially, with each instance of refreshment, the Member States may also be seen to have repeatedly reconfirmed the validity of the Treaty framework's basic statements on the three key issues for EU constitutionalism regarding, first, the formal status of Union law and the conditions under which it applies within Member States (Constitutional Issue No. 1); the locus of political authority within the EU legal order (Constitutional Issue No. 2); and the objectives, values and limits governing European integration (Constitutional Issue No. 3).

1.1 The Foundations of the Treaty Framework as Constitutional Touchstone

The Treaty framework establishes the European Union and forms its basic constitutional charter. In its current form, that framework comprises two Treaties – the Treaty on European Union and the Treaty on the Functioning of the European Union, respectively, together with the EU Charter on Fundamental Rights, and a body of Protocols annexed to the Treaties. These instruments all enjoy equivalent legal status.[7]

As the Union's basic constitutional charter, the EU Treaty framework provides specific prescription on the three key issues for EU constitutionalism. Decisions, for instance, on the disposition of EU political power outlined in the EU Treaties (Constitutional Issue No. 2) determine which of the Union institutions is competent to act under specific circumstances. Likewise, the Treaties' statements on the objectives, values and limits of EU integration (Constitutional Issue No. 3) circumscribe the

[6] See earlier, T. Horsley, 'Reflections on the Role of the Court of Justice as the "Motor" of European Integration: Legal Limits to Judicial Lawmaking' (2013) 50 *Common Market Law Review*, 931. See also, G. de Búrca, 'The Principle of Subsidiarity and the Court of Justice as an Institutional Actor' (1998) 36(2) *Journal of Common Market Studies*, 214.

[7] Treaty on European Union [2016] OJ C-202/13; Treaty on the Functioning of the European Union [2016] OJ C-201/47 and Charter of Fundamental Rights of the European Union [2016] OJ C-201/389. There are presently 37 Protocols annexed to the EU Treaties. On the legal status of Protocols, see Art. 51 TEU.

substantive legal and political space within which the Union institutions may exercise their functions. Ultimately, a failure by the Union institutions to comply with the EU Treaties as the founding instruments of European integration leads necessarily to the conclusion that the activity in question is invalid as a matter of EU constitutional law.[8]

Section 2 considers the detail of the Treaty framework's substantive responses on the three issues for EU constitutionalism and their evolution over time. This section is concerned first with the *source* of the basic obligation. In short, what requires EU institutions to adhere to the constitutional charter established by the Treaty framework in the exercise of their respective functions? That source is easily located.

Article 13(2) TEU sets out the basic statement on internal constitutionality with respect to EU institutional activity. That provision mandates in clear terms that the legitimacy of all EU activity is to be assessed for compliance with the Treaty framework: 'Each institution [of the EU] shall act within the limits of the powers conferred on it in the Treaties, and in conformity with the procedures, conditions and objectives set out in them.' The Treaties offer several additional restatements of this basic requirement *lex specialis*. For example, Article 51 of the EU Charter of Fundamental Rights states that the EU institutions must respect the rights, observe the principles and promote the application of EU Charter rights when exercising their respective functions under the Treaties.[9] Similarly, Article 263 TFEU demands compliance with the Treaties and of any rule of law relating to their application as a condition of the validity of EU legal acts.

Significantly, the Court of Justice has expressly acknowledged the central function of the Treaty framework in assessments of the validity of EU institutional activities in line with the demands of Article 13(2) TEU. Most clearly, it has repeatedly observed that: 'The [Union] is based on the rule of law, inasmuch as neither its Member States nor its institutions can avoid review of the conformity of their acts with the basic constitutional charter, the [Treaties].'[10] The obligation imposed on EU institutions under Article 13(2) TFEU to act within the limits of the powers expressly attributed to them by the Treaties gives effect to the principle of conferral in Article 5(2) TEU. That provision frames in

[8] Art. 264 TFEU.

[9] Charter of Fundamental Rights, n. 7.

[10] Joined Cases C-402/05 P and C-415/05, *P Kadi and Al Barakaat International Foundation* v. *Council and Commission* EU:C:2008:461 at para. 281 and Case 294/83, *Parti écologiste "Les Verts"* v. *European Parliament* EU:C:1986:166 at para. 23.

unambiguous terms the nature of the EU legal order as a system of limited, attributed powers. According to the principle of conferral: '[T]he Union shall only act within the limits of the competences conferred upon it by the Member States in the Treaties to attain the objectives set out therein. Competences not conferred upon the Union in the Treaties remain with the Member States.'

1.2 The EU Treaty Framework's Scope of Application as Constitutional Touchstone

The use of the Treaty framework to measure the internal constitutionality of EU action is an everyday phenomenon in EU integration. The EU Treaties and, increasingly, the EU Charter on Fundamental Rights are routinely invoked to scrutinise the validity of important aspects of EU institutional activity.[11]

Engagement with, and respect for, the Treaty framework as the EU's basic constitutional charter is, first and foremost, a matter for institutions themselves. It is incumbent on each institution to ensure that it exercises its attributed functions in compliance with the Treaties. This obligation finds specific expression within parts of the EU Treaty framework. For instance, Article 1 of Protocol No. 2 requires Union institutions to ensure constant respect for two of the main limits on the exercise of Union competences under the Treaties: the principles of subsidiarity and proportionality.[12] Moreover, Article 5 mandates that the Commission justify draft legislative acts with reference to both Treaty principles.[13] That institution must provide a detailed statement outlining the basis upon which the proposed legislative measure is deemed compliant with the subsidiarity and proportionality principles, using quantitative and qualitative data to support its findings.[14]

In instances of dispute, the Treaties place the determination of questions of internal constitutionality ultimately in the hands of the Court of

[11] From an extensive list of possible examples, see e.g., Joined Cases C-293/12 and C-594/12, *Digital Rights Ireland and Seitlinger and others* EU:C:2014:238; Case C-131/12, *Google Spain SL and Google Inc.* v. *Agencia Española de Protección de Datos (AEPD) and González* EU:C:2014:317; Case C-508/13, *Estonia* v. *Parliament and Council* EU:C:2015:403 and Case C-62/14, *Gauweiler and Others* v. *Deutscher Bundestag* EU:C:2015:400.

[12] Protocol (No. 2). On the Application of the Principles of Subsidiarity and Proportionality [2016] OJ-201/206, Art. 1.

[13] *Ibid.*

[14] *Ibid.*, Art. 5. See also, Interinstitutional Agreement between the European Parliament, the Council of the European Union and the European Commission on Better Law-Making [2–16] OJ L123/1 (Title III).

Justice. Pursuant to Article 263 TFEU, Member States, EU institutions, and, under certain conditions, individual litigants may seek judicial review of EU legal acts for compliance with the Treaties. Likewise, the Court of Justice may be called upon to scrutinise the compatibility with the Treaty framework of proposed agreements concluded between the Union and international organisations.[15]

The entry into force of the Lisbon Treaty in 2009 introduced, for the first time, a new set of institutional actors into the system established to monitor EU institutional activity for compliance with the EU Treaties. Specifically, Member State parliaments now exercise a prior review function with respect to the application of the principle of subsidiarity in Article 5(3) TEU.[16] The existence of that role – which, under certain conditions, may prompt the withdrawal of EU legislative proposals on subsidiarity grounds – leaves the Court's powers intact.[17] However, to a large extent, the introduction of a new checking role for national parliaments reduces demand for judicial review *ex post*. Disputes over the quality of the Union legislature's engagement with the subsidiarity principle in the exercise of its legislative competences in areas of shared responsibility are now to be resolved primarily through political dialogue with Member State parliaments. The Court of Justice retains its judicial review powers, but, as a matter of practical institutional dynamics, is no longer the main gatekeeper in subsidiarity disputes.[18]

Intervening changes notwithstanding, an intellectual gap remains in connection with discussion of the functioning of the Treaty framework as a touchstone for scrutinising the internal constitutionality of EU institutional activity. In short, and most remarkably in light of its approach to the exercise of its institutional functions, the activities of the Court of Justice are not routinely checked – by itself or by its key

[15] Art. 218(11) TFEU. See e.g., Opinion 2/94, *Accession by the Community to the European Convention for the Protection of Human Rights and Fundamental Freedoms* EU:C:1996:140 and Opinion 2/13, *Draft Agreement on Accession of the EU to the European Convention on Human Rights* EU:C:2014:2454.

[16] A. Cygan, *Accountability, Parliamentarism and Transparency in the EU: The Role of National Parliaments* (Cheltenham: Elgar, 2013); A. J. Cornell and M. Goldoni (eds.), *National and Regional Parliaments in the EU-Legislative Procedure Post-Lisbon: The Impact of the Early Warning Mechanism* (Oxford: Hart Publishing, 2017) and K. Grant, *The Principle of Subsidiarity and Its Enforcement in the EU Legal Order: The Role of National Parliaments in the Early Warning System* (Oxford: Hart Publishing, 2018).

[17] Art. 8, Protocol (No. 2). On the Application of the Principles of Subsidiarity and Proportionality, n. 12.

[18] T. Horsley, 'Institutional Dynamics Reloaded: The Court of Justice and the Development of the EU Internal Market' in P. Koutrakos and J. Snell (eds.), *Research Handbook on the Law of the EU's Internal Market* (Cheltenham: Elgar, 2017).

interlocutors (Member States, national courts, and EU scholars) – for compliance with the demands of the EU Treaties. Discussion of the Treaty framework as the constitutional touchstone of EU integration has focused instead almost exclusively on scrutinising the institutional activities of the Union's *political* organs.[19]

The existence of such an important intellectual gap is, in part, arguably the result of structural factors. In particular, it may be seen as the logical consequence of the fact that the EU Treaties only provide mechanisms to review and/or contest the activities of the Union's political organs (e.g., Articles 263 TFEU and Article 218(11) TFEU above). By contrast, there is no mechanism within the Treaties themselves that may be routinely invoked to review the internal constitutionality of EU judicial activity. The Treaty framework positions the Court of Justice as the ultimate guardian of the EU constitutional order *vis-à-vis* its EU institutional relations. It does not, however, provide an express basis to monitor the internal constitutionality of its own interpretative choices. That omission follows directly as a result of the Treaties' clear statements on the locus of political authority within the EU legal order (see further Section 2).

Specific provisions of the Treaties do, of course, provide for the political reversal of EU Court judgments.[20] Article 65(4) TFEU, for example, empowers the Council, acting unanimously and on a proposal from a Member State, to deem restrictive tax measures concerning capital movements between the Union and third countries compatible with the Treaty. That provision, which was inserted by the Treaty of Lisbon, effectively 'claws back' from the Court of Justice the right to determine the conditions under which tax restrictions may be imposed on extra-EU capital movements.[21] Article 108(2) TFEU provides for a

[19] For exceptions, see, G. A. Bermann, 'Taking Subsidiarity Seriously: Federalism in the European Community and the United States' (1994) 94 *Columbia Law Review*, 331; T. Schilling, 'Subsidiarity as a Rule and a Principle' (1994) 14 *Yearbook of European Law*, 203; de Búrca, 'The Principle of Subsidiarity and the Court of Justice as an Institutional Actor', n. 6, at 217; P. Craig, 'The ECJ and the *Ultra Vires* Action: A Conceptual Analysis' (2011) 48 *Common Market Law Review*, 395; T. Horsley, 'Reflections on the Role of the Court of Justice as the "Motor" of European Integration: Legal Limits to Judicial Policymaking' (2013) 50 *Common Market Law Review*, 931 and E. Cloots, *National Identity in EU Law* (Oxford: Oxford University Press, 2015).

[20] A. Arnull, 'Me and My Shadow: The European Court of Justice and the Disintegration of European Union Law' (2007) 31 *Fordham International Law Journal*, 1174.

[21] For discussion see e.g., R. Murphy, 'The Dynamic Relationship of the Legislature and the Judiciary in the Pursuit of Capital Liberalisation' in P. Syrpis (ed.), *The Judiciary, the*

parallel arrangement in connection with the review of State Aid in exceptional circumstances. Judgments of the Court in other areas are also open to adjustment or reversal by Treaty amendment. For example, at Maastricht, Member States enacted a new protocol in response to the Court's decision on the application of the principle of equal treatment to occupational pension schemes.[22]

However, both sets of specific and general provisions are not conceived as mechanisms to review the constitutionality of EU judicial activity for compliance with the Treaty framework. Articles 65(4) TFEU and 108(2) TFEU make no express reference to judicial transgression at variance with the Treaty framework as the basis for judicial review. The same is also true of Article 48 TEU, outlining the ordinary and simplified Treaty revision procedures. In any case, it ultimately falls to the Court itself to adjudicate on the impact of Member State efforts to reverse or modify its own jurisprudence. Through further exercise of its interpretative competences, the Court is in a position to manage the effects of unfavourable Member State responses to its activities *qua* EU institution (see further Chapter 6).

However, the absence of any institution-specific scrutiny mechanisms does not in any sense excuse the Court of Justice from the obligation to respect the Treaty framework in the exercise of its own functions. On the contrary, as both the EU Treaties and jurisprudence confirm, the Treaty framework applies to, and thus binds, all of the Union's institutions as defined in Article 13 TEU. These are the European Parliament, the European Council, the Council, the European Commission the Court of Justice of the European Union, the European Central Bank and the Court of Auditors. As a matter of principle, therefore, the EU Treaty framework must be considered to determine the internal constitutionality of the activities of each of these institutions in equal measure. Addressing the significant and enduring gap that presently exists with respect to the assessment of judicial functions for compliance with the EU Treaties is a core objective of this book.

Legislature and the EU Internal Market (Cambridge: Cambridge University Press, 2012) and T. Horsley, 'Death, Taxes and (Targeted) Judicial Dynamism: The Free Movement of Capital in EU Law' in A. Arnull and D. Chalmers (eds.), *The Oxford Handbook of European Union Law* (Oxford: Oxford University Press, 2015).

22 See now Protocol (No. 33) Concerning Article 157 of the Treaty on the Functioning of the European Union [2016] C-202/318 in response to Case C-262/88, *Barber* v. *Guardian Royal Exchange Assurance Group* EU:C:1990:209. See also, e.g., the revision of Art. 119 EC (now Art. 157 TFEU) at Amsterdam in response to the Court's ruling in Case C-450/93, *Kalanke* v. *Freie Hansestadt Bremen* EU:C:1995:322.

1.3 The Normative Power of the EU Treaty Framework as Constitutional Touchstone

As a constitutional touchstone, the EU Treaty framework enjoys an uncharacteristic degree of normative power on the basis of the frequency, nature and scope of its repeated amendments. The Member States, as Treaty principals, have revised the Treaties (including through accession treaties) no fewer than twenty-one times in the Union's sixty-year history.[23]

In quantitative terms, this is unremarkable when compared with other national and international instruments. The German Basic Law, for example, has been amended sixty times since its entry into force in 1949.[24] Similarly, the list of amendments to the US Constitution enacted in 1789 presently runs to twenty-seven in total.[25] What is more striking, however, is the qualitative nature and scope of Member State amendments to the EU Treaty structure in its relatively short history. Whereas other constitutional charters (and the US Constitution in particular) have been subject to repeated discrete revisions, the EU Treaties, by contrast, have been comprehensively revised and (re)ratified in their entirety following in-depth, critical and often public reflection on the three fundamental issues for EU constitutionalism.

With few exceptions, the process of amending the EU Treaties has not focused on discrete (though important) issues, such as, in other constitutional contexts, extensions of the franchise;[26] the terms of the office of president;[27] the approval of privatisation processes;[28] or the introduction

23 The following Treaties amended the founding EEC Treaty: Merger Treaty (1965); Single European Act (1986); the Treaty on European Union (1992); The Treaty of Amsterdam (1997); the Treaty of Nice (2000); the Treaty of Lisbon (2007). The Accession Treaties concluded in 1973, 1981, 1986, 1995, 2004, 2007 and 2013 introduced additional amendments. Art. 49 TEU provides that accession treaties may make 'adjustments' to the Treaties – as they typically do.

24 As of 23 December 2014. See A. Tschentscher, *The Basic Law (Grundgesetz) 2016: The Constitution of the Federal Republic of Germany (May 23rd, 1949) – Introduction and Translation* (4th edn) (Würzburg: Jurisprudentia, 2016). For analysis see e.g., D. Grimm, 'The Basic Law at 60 – Identity and Change' (2010) 11(1) *German Law Journal*, 33.

25 For discussion, see e.g., G. Epps, *American Epic: Reading the U.S. Constitution* (Oxford: Oxford University Press, 2013).

26 See e.g., 15th, 19th and 26th Amendments to the US Constitution.

27 See e.g., 22nd and 25th Amendments to the US Constitution.

28 See e.g., Arts. 6a, 87e and 143a, inserted by Federal Law of 20 December 1993 (*Federal Law Gazette* I, p. 2089) and Art. 87f and Art. 143b, inserted by Federal Law of 30 August 1994 (*Federal Law Gazette* I, p. 2245).

of national conscription.[29] Rather, at each juncture, the Member States have discussed and subsequently reached political consensus on often far-reaching reforms to core aspects of the EU constitutional order.

The fundamentals of EU integration formed the centrepiece of the political reform agenda in the negotiations leading up to the adoption of the Treaty of Lisbon in 2007.[30] The substance of the negotiations addressed important aspects of the Union's institutional architecture; its decision-making instruments and procedures; its scope of competences; its system for the protection of human rights and fundamental freedoms; and the procedures for accession, withdrawal and subsequent treaty amendment – to list only the key themes.[31] This followed an earlier period of intense political deliberation prior to the adoption of the now defunct Constitutional Treaty.

The resulting changes introduced to the Treaty framework at Lisbon extend to 231 pages in the *Official Journal* and encompass far-reaching revisions across the aforementioned areas. Among other things, Member States reached agreement on the establishment of new institutional offices, including the President of the European Council and the High Representative for Foreign Affairs.[32] In addition, they agreed at Lisbon to enhance further the powers of the European Parliament in EU lawmaking processes – in the continuation of an established trend (see Section 2). Likewise, further important changes were made to the framework of limits imposed on EU institutional activity through agreement on the attribution of legal effect to the EU Charter of Fundamental Rights.[33]

The comprehensive nature of reflections on, and agreed revisions to, the fundamentals of EU constitutionalism in EU Treaty reform processes functions as a powerful source of 'constitutional refreshment'. More so than is typically the case in other political systems, the process of revising the Treaty framework may be seen, on each occasion, to revisit and

[29] See Art. 12a Basic Law, inserted by Federal Law of 24 June 1968 (*Federal Law Gazette* I, p. 709).

[30] J-C Piris, *The Lisbon Treaty: A Legal and Political Analysis* (Cambridge: CUP, 2010) and P. Craig, *The Lisbon Treaty: Law, Politics, and Treaty Reform* (Oxford: Oxford University Press, 2013). See also, D. Phinnemore, *The Treaty of Lisbon: Origins and Negotiation* (Basingstoke: Palgrave MacMillan, 2013).

[31] See M. Dougan, 'The Treaty of Lisbon 2007: Winning Mind, Not Hearts' (2008) 45 *Common Market Law Review*, 617.

[32] See Art. 15 TEU and Art. 18 TEU.

[33] See Art. 6(1) TEU and Charter of Fundamental Rights of the European Union, n. 7.

modify (or simply reaffirm) the normative foundations of the EU Treaties as the Union's basic constitutional charter. As de Witte notes:

> one can say that the revision of the European Treaties has ceased to be an incidental occurrence devoted to technical adjustments and has, instead become an ongoing concern of the member states and the EU institutions, which involves important policy choices about the institutional architecture of Europe . . . One can consider this semi-permanent revision process as one continuous conversation about the future of Europe.[34]

As an exercise in constitutional refreshment, the democratic quality of EU Treaty reform is further enhanced by the requirement that Member State governments reach unanimous political agreement on the substance of any changes to the Union's architecture. It is not simply enough, even with respect to revisions under the simplified procedure, to amend the Treaty by qualified or weighted majority as is typical within many national legal systems.[35] Furthermore, in order to take effect, all twenty-eight Member States must subsequently ratify the agreed reforms in accordance with their respective domestic requirements.[36] At the very least, this requires the approval of national legislatures. In some Member States, it can demand the direct approval of Member State citizens by referendum. Securing consensus in the European Council is only the first step. National governments must then return to their respective domestic constituents and fight to secure their approval of the proposed Treaty reforms.

2 The EU Treaties and the Three Issues for EU Constitutionalism

Section 1 defended the EU Treaties' function as a primary source of normative restraint within the EU legal order. In summary, it argued that the EU Treaties should be viewed as the principal touchstones with regard to the internal constitutionality of all EU institutional activity.

[34] De Witte, 'The Closest Thing to a Constitutional Conversation in Europe: The Semi-Permanent Treaty Revision Process', n. 1 at p. 43.

[35] National referenda on proposed revisions to the EU Treaty framework have been held in Denmark, Ireland, Italy, France, Spain, the Netherlands and Luxembourg. See further, F. Mendez, M Mendez, and V. Triga, *Referendums and the European Union: A Comparative Inquiry* (Cambridge: Cambridge University Press, 2014).

[36] See Art. 48(4) TEU (ordinary revision procedure) and Art. 48(6) TEU (simplified revision procedure).

This includes, as a matter of principle, the activities of the Court of Justice – an EU institution the activities of which are presently not routinely scrutinised for compliance with the Treaties. Furthermore, as the Union's founding constitutional charter, the EU Treaty framework was shown to enjoy an uncharacteristically high degree of normative authority. The frequency, nature and scope of the various amendments, it is argued, serves as a direct and powerful source of 'constitutional refreshment', injecting renewed normative authority into its function as constitutional touchstone.[37]

This section considers the consequences of positioning the EU Treaties as touchstones on the internal constitutionality of EU institutional activity. In summary, it asserts that the EU Treaty framework provides important clarity on what this book defines as the three key issues for EU constitutionalism.

First, on the formal status of EU law and the conditions under which it applies within Member States (Constitutional Issue No. 1), the EU Treaties continue to provide clear statements that link the EU legal order to the standard framework of international law.[38] Secondly, with respect to the locus of EU political authority within the Union legal order (Constitutional Issue No. 2), the Treaty framework is shown to reserve constituent authority to the Member States acting collectively. At the same time, it entrusts primary responsibility for EU policymaking to the Union's political institutions – the Commission, European Parliament and Council of the European Union – in varying combinations. Lastly, this Section illuminates not only the range of objectives and values, but also the ever-increasing limits that the Treaty framework establishes to structure EU institutional activity (Constitutional Issue No. 3).

Overall, the principal changes to the EU Treaty framework have primarily addressed the objectives, values and limits of EU integration. These have undergone a process of broadening and deepening. In addition, successive waves of Treaty amendment have also radically adjusted the disposition of policymaking competence between the three key

[37] De Witte, 'The Closest Thing to a Constitutional Conversation in Europe: The Semi-Permanent Treaty Revision Process', n. 1.

[38] D. G. Valentine, *The Court of Justice of the European Communities* (London: Stevens, 1965); C. Mann, *The Function of Judicial Decision in European Economic Integration* (The Hague: Springer, 1971); T. Hartley, 'The Constitutional Foundations of the European Union' (2001) 117 *Law Quarterly Review*, 225 and B. de Witte, 'Using International Law for the European Union's Domestic Affairs' in E. P. Cannizzaro, P. Wessel and A. Ramses (eds.), *International Law as Law of the European Union* (Leiden: Brill, 2011).

political institutions – to enhance, first and foremost, the position of the European Parliament.

2.1 Constitutional Issue No. 1: What Is the Formal Status of Union Law under the Treaties and under What Conditions Does It Apply within Member States?

Writing in 1971, Mann observed that: 'The legal orders of the Community rest squarely on international Treaties. They were ratified by Member State legislatures as ordinary treaties and not, as is characteristic of national constitutions, by specifically convened constitutive assemblies. Their binding force . . . must be sought in the relationship of international to national law.'[39] That assessment continues accurately to describe the formal status of EU law under the present Treaty framework.[40] It also correctly outlines the relationship between Union law and Member State law; in other words, the conditions under which EU norms shall take effect within national legal systems. In summary, the EU Treaty framework established, and has subsequently maintained, a strikingly clear and coherent response to the first key issue for EU constitutionalism: EU law is international law.

2.1.1 The Formal Status of Union Law

The formal status of EU law as international law under the Treaties is apparent, initially, from the legal framework governing their adoption and entry into force.[41] The Treaty on European Union and Treaty on the Functioning of the European Union are both international treaties, concluded and ratified by Member States in accordance with orthodox principles of public international law – and the law of treaties in particular.[42]

In more precise terms, the Member States (represented by their designated plenipotentiaries) adopted the text of the (now) EU Treaties on the

[39] Mann, *The Function of Judicial Decision in European Economic Integration*, n. 38 at p. 26.

[40] See also, T. Hartley, 'The Constitutional Foundations of the European Union,' n. 38 and de Witte, 'Using International Law for the European Union's Domestic Affairs', n. 38 at p. 134.

[41] See also, B. de Witte, 'Rules of Change in International Law: How Special Is the European Community?' (1994) *Netherlands Yearbook of International Law*, 299.

[42] On the legal framework governing international treaties, see A. Aust, *Modern Treaty Law and Practice* (3rd edn) (Cambridge: Cambridge University Press, 2013).

basis of common consent or unanimity.[43] In accordance with principles of international law, the entry into force of the EU Treaties was conditional on signatory states subsequently expressing their consent to be bound thereto in a recognised form.[44] The detail of that form of consent is a matter for the Member States as Treaty signatories.[45] The available options include, *inter alia*, the expression of consent by signature, exchange of documents, or ratification.[46] The agreed position is presently set out in Article 54 TEU and Article 357 TFEU. Both provisions outline that the respective EU Treaties shall only enter into force following: (1) ratification by each Member States in accordance with its respective national constitutional requirements and (2) the deposit of all the instruments of national ratification with the Italian Government.

The character of the EU Treaties as international Treaties has remained fundamentally unchanged over time. Most notably perhaps, the development of EU integration has not witnessed significant changes to the basic principles governing the adoption and entry into force of the EU Treaties. The entry into force of any changes to the EU Treaties is still absolutely conditional upon the agreement of, and subsequent ratification by, all Member States.[47] Post-Lisbon, two procedures now govern that process: the ordinary and simplified revision procedures. According to Article 48(2)–(5) TEU, detailing the ordinary revision procedure, reforms to the Treaties must be approved 'by common accord' of the Member States, acting through the European Council.[48] Agreed amendments then enter into force after being ratified by all Member States in accordance with their individual domestic constitutional requirements.

The procedures in Article 48(6)–(7) TEU now provide the basis to amend particular Parts of the Treaties without the need to convene a formal convention composed of representatives of national parliaments, Heads of State or Government of the Member States, the European Parliament and of the Commission. Article 48(7) TEU, for instance,

43 See Art. 9 of the Vienna Convention of the Law of Treaties and (now) the Preambles to the TEU and TFEU respectively. The Vienna Convention, of course, post-dates the adoption and entry into force of the founding EEC Treaty. It should also be noted that not all Member States are party to the Convention.

44 See Art. 11 VCLT.

45 *Ibid.*

46 Arts. 11–17 VCLT.

47 Note, however and historically, the proposal of Spinelli Group to transition to majority voting with respect to amendments to the Treaty framework. See e.g., A. Hinajeros, *The Euro Area Crisis in Constitutional Perspective* (Oxford: Oxford University Press, 2015) at p. 115.

48 See Art. 48(4) TEU.

empowers the Member States, again acting unanimously and through the European Council, to adopt a decision authorising the Council to enact legislative measures by qualified majority in particular substantive areas where unanimity is required. Crucially, however, decisions taken pursuant to the simplified decision procedure in Article 48(6)–(7) TEU still require subsequent ratification by all Member States in order to take effect. Additionally, under Article 48(7) TEU, decisions to make adjustments to either voting requirements and/or legislative procedures applicable in specific areas of EU activity are also subject to an additional hurdle: potential veto by national parliaments.

Important adjustments have been made to the legal framework structuring Treaty amendment since the entry into force of the founding EEC Treaty. However, these have not disturbed the basic paradigm of (collective) Member State control. For example, Article 48(2) TEU now provides that Member States shall act collectively through a common institution – the European Council – and by *majority* decision when determining whether and, if so, how to commence negotiations for Treaty reform under the ordinary revision procedure. More notably still, the Lisbon Treaty adjusted the requirements for the ratification of Treaty revisions agreed using the aforementioned procedure. According to Article 48(5) TEU: 'If, two years after the signature of a treaty amending the Treaties, *four fifths of the Member States* have ratified it and one or more Member State have encountered difficulties in proceeding with ratification, *the matter shall be referred to the European Council*.'[49]

The introduction of the four-fifths ratification threshold in Article 48(5) TEU was first proposed in the (now-defunct) Treaty establishing a Constitution for Europe.[50] At first sight, the reference to a four-fifths majority in connection with the ratification of Treaty amendments appears to mark a radical change. It announces a transition to a form of majority ratification that alludes to prevailing approaches often found in other international instruments. For instance, Article 48 of the Treaty establishing the European Stability Mechanism, which exists outside the framework of EU law, provides that: 'This Treaty shall enter into force on the date when instruments of ratification, approval or acceptance have been deposited by signatories *whose initial subscriptions represent no less than 90% of the total subscriptions set forth in Annex II*.'[51] On closer inspection,

[49] Emphasis added.
[50] Art. IV-443(4) CT.
[51] Treaty establishing the European Stability Mechanism [2012] D 12/3 (emphasis added). For comparison, see also Art. V of the US Constitution, which outlines that amendments

however, the legal effects of the Article 48(5) TEU are far more limited. That provision does nothing to break with the basic requirement for Member State unanimity with respect to the ratification of amendments to the EU Treaties. Article 48(5) TEU merely opens up a new, formal space for Heads of States or Government to reach a decision on how to proceed where the ratification process stalls within (at least) one Member State after a two-year period. Nothing in Article 48(5) TEU indicates that such a decision – if triggered and whatever its substance – is to be taken on any basis other than unanimity.

2.1.2 *The Domestic Application of EU Law*

Far more significantly, a review of the EU Treaty framework provides conceptual clarity on the second issue: the relationship between Union and national law. Again, in common with the rules on the adoption and ratification of the Treaties (and revisions thereof), that relationship has also been – and remains – firmly rooted in the principles and practice of international law. The EU Treaties do not make, and have never made, any special provision for the application of Union law *within* Member State legal orders.[52] On the contrary, the provisions addressing the general application of EU law, the legal effects of judgments of the Court of Justice, and the enforcement of EU legal norms, all reinforce the conclusion that the relationship between the Union and Member State legal orders remains ultimately grounded in the framework of international law.

Article 4(3) TEU sets out the principal statement on the internal application of Union law under the current Treaty framework.[53] That provision makes clear that, under the Treaties, the responsibility for the application of EU law within national legal systems rests with individual Member States as Treaties signatories: 'Member States shall take any appropriate measure, general or particular to ensure fulfilment of the obligations arising out of the Treaties or resulting from the acts of the institutions of the Union.' The Treaties' clearest statement on the application of EU norms thus requires Member States simply to *give effect* to

to the US Constitution may enter into force, throughout the United States, on the ratification of three fourths of State legislatures or by Conventions in three-fourths thereof.

52 Art. 101(2) TFEU states that anti-competitive agreements and decisions concluded between undertakings contrary to Art. 101(1) TFEU shall be 'automatically void'. However, considered in its broader context, Art. 101(2) TFEU does not, by its own authority, detach the EU Treaties from the normative framework of international law that governs the domestic effect of EU norms. See further, Chapter 3.

53 See previously Art. 5 EEC.

EU law internally as they would do ordinarily with respect to other binding international treaty commitments.[54] The Treaty framework mandates no more. The internal effect of EU legal norms is accordingly, under the EU Treaties, a matter for individual Member States alone.

The formal status of EU law as international law under the Treaties is also evidenced through a review of the provisions on the legal effects of Court of Justice judgments and the conditions governing their enforcement against defaulting Member States. With respect, first, to legal effects, the EU Treaties continue to mandate that judgments of the Court of Justice are intended only to bind Member States as contracting parties with no independent normative force within national legal systems. For example, with reference to the legal effects of judgments delivered pursuant to the infringement procedures (Articles 258 and 259 TFEU), Article 260 TFEU provides that: 'If the Court of Justice of the European Union finds that a Member State has failed to fulfil an obligation under the Treaties, *the State shall be required* to take the necessary measures to comply with the judgment of the Court.'[55] The requirement in Article 260 TFEU that Member States bring national law into line with the EU Court judgments leaves decisions regarding the internal effect of Union law entirely within the hands of the States themselves. Member States may opt to give effect to the substance of the Court's ruling against them as they best see fit. Equally, they may simply ignore it and risk further procedural action for non-compliance with their binding obligations under the EU Treaties.[56]

Strikingly, in its formative jurisprudence, the Court of Justice reached the same conclusion regarding the legal effects of decisions against Member States for non-compliance with their Treaty obligations delivered by way of preliminary reference. In relation to the legal effects of its judgments under Article 177 EEC (now Article 267 TFEU), the Court concluded in *Humblet* that the EEC Treaty: 'merely attach[es] *declaratory effect* to the decision of the Court in cases of failure to comply with the [Treaty], albeit obliging the Member States to take the necessary measures to comply with the [Court's] judgment'.[57] By contrast, under the Treaty framework, the Court of Justice is competent to declare acts of the EU institutions *void*. Article 263 TFEU provides that:

[54] See also, Art. 291(1) TFEU: 'Member States shall adopt all measures of national law necessary to implement legally binding Union acts.'

[55] Emphasis added.

[56] Pursuant to Art. 258 TFEU.

[57] Case 6/60, *Humblet* v. *Belgian State* EU:C:1960:48 at p. 569 (emphasis added).

> The Court of Justice of the European Union shall review the legality of legislative acts, of acts of the Council, of the Commission and of the European Central Bank, other than recommendations and opinions, and of acts of the European Parliament and of the European Council intended to produce legal effects *vis-à-vis* third parties. It shall also review the legality of acts of bodies, offices or agencies of the Union intended to produce legal effects *vis-à-vis* third parties.

Pursuant to Article 264 TFEU, where an action is well founded, the Court of Justice shall declare the relevant EU act void *ab initio*.[58]

The retention by Member States of full control over the internal application of EU law is reinforced by further provisions of the EU Treaties governing the enforcement of Court decisions within national legal systems. Specifically, Article 280 TFEU provides that judgments of the Court 'shall be enforceable under the conditions laid down in Article 299 TFEU'. The latter provision outlines the procedure for the enforcement of Commission and Council decisions within the Member States – in particular those imposing pecuniary obligations on natural and legal persons. According to Article 299 TFEU, the execution of such a decision is expressly designated a matter for national law. Specifically, in order to seek redress, the aggrieved party is directed to bring an enforcement action before the designated competent authority in the relevant Member State.

Overall, the EU Treaties' statements on the legal effects of Court of Justice decisions and the rules governing their domestic enforcement closely mirror those found in other international treaties. Article 19.1 of the WTO Dispute Settlement Understanding, for example, mandates, albeit in less forceful language, that: 'Where a panel or Appellate Body concludes that a [State] measure is inconsistent with a covered agreement, it shall recommend that *the Member concerned bring the measure into conformity with that agreement*.'[59] Article 46 of the European Convention for the Protection of Human Rights and Fundamental Freedoms (ECHR) outlines a similar commitment.[60] Pursuant to that provision,

[58] On the severability of EU legal acts in Art. 263 TFEU proceedings, see e.g., Case 17/74, *Transocean Marine Paint* EU:C:1974:106 and Case C-376/98, *Germany* v. *Parliament and Council (Tobacco Advertising)* EU:C:2000:544.

[59] Understanding on Rules and Procedures Governing the Settlement of Disputes (DSU), WTO Agreement 1994, Annex 2 (emphasis added).

[60] Convention for the Protection of Human Rights and Fundamental Freedoms (European Convention on Human Rights, as amended) (ECHR).

contracting states undertake to 'abide by the final judgment of the Court in any case to which they are parties'. How (and, of course, whether) they choose to do so is a matter for the state concerned.

Finally, with respect to the relationship between Union and Member State law, it is significant to note that the EU Treaties still contain no legally binding statement on the primacy of EU law *vis-à-vis* Member State law.[61] Such provisions are, of course, common features within other constitutional charters, notably: the German Basic Law (Article 31 GG) and Article VI of the United States Constitution. The latter, for example, provides that:

> This Constitution, and the Laws of the United States which shall be made in Pursuance thereof; and all Treaties made, or which shall be made, under the Authority of the United States, shall be the supreme Law of the Land; and the Judges in every State shall be bound thereby, any Thing in the Constitution or Laws of any State to the Contrary notwithstanding.

The EU Treaty framework has never incorporated a legally binding statement on the ranking of EU norms within domestic legal systems (see further Chapter 6). The principles of primacy (and direct effect) are to be found in the Court's case law (see Chapter 3).[62] Taken together with the Treaties' statements on the legal effects of Union law and, moreover, the rules governing the enforcement of Court of Justice decisions within Member States, that omission is unremarkable. The EU Treaty framework has little to say on the internal effect of Union law other than that it remains, in accordance with the principles and practice of international law, an exclusive matter for Member States in accordance with their respective constitutional traditions.

As an historical aside, it is worth noting that the EU Constitutional Treaty, had it been ratified by all Member States and entered into force, would have enshrined the primacy of Union law over national law into the Treaty framework. Articles 1–6 stated that: 'The Constitution and law adopted by the institutions of the Union in exercising competences

[61] The primacy of EU law over national law is referenced only in Declaration (No. 17) concerning Primacy [2016] C-202/344. Declarations annexed to the EU Treaties are non-binding. See A. G. Toth, 'The Legal Status of Declarations Annexed to the Single European Act' (1986) 23 *Common Market Law Review*, 803.

[62] See Case 26/62, *NV Algemene Transport- en Expeditie Onderneming van Gend & Loos* v. *Netherlands Inland Revenue Administration* EU:C:1963:1 at p. 12. See also, Case 6/64, *Costa* v. *E.N.E.L* EU:C:1964:66 at p. 593.

conferred on it shall have primacy over the law of the Member States.' It is doubtful, however, that the introduction of that provision would have effected meaningful constitutional change.[63] The entry into force of the (now defunct) Constitutional Treaty would have left the remaining features of the pre-existing (and now current) Treaty framework discussed earlier intact. Despite its title, the Constitutional Treaty remained an international Treaty. Most crucially, it would have had little obvious impact on the continued formal status of Union law as international law. In more precise terms, Article I-5(2) of the Constitutional Treaty would have simply reproduced the Treaties' principal statement on the internal application of Union law under (now) Article 4(3) TEU. As before, it outlined in clear terms the general obligation on Member States as contracting parties to: 'take any appropriate measure, general or particular, to ensure fulfilment of the obligations arising out of the Constitution or resulting from the acts of the institutions of the Union'. Notably, the Constitutional Treaty also foresaw no changes to the Treaty rules outlining the domestic effect of Court of Justice decisions and, likewise, the conditions governing their enforcement within Member States.[64] Both would have remained tied to the pre-existing legal framework first established under the EEC Treaty.

2.2 Constitutional Issue No. 2: The Locus of EU Political Authority within the EU Legal Order

The Treaty framework also provides clear statements on the second key issue for EU constitutionalism: the locus of political authority. On the one hand, it vests constituent authority, that is competence to revise and rescind the Treaties as well as determine political membership of the Union, with Member States – acting both collectively through the EU institutional framework and individually as sovereign states. On the other hand, the EU Treaties entrust responsibility for Union policymaking principally to the European Parliament, the Council and the Commission.[65] The Treaties mandate that these three institutions work

[63] See also, by analogy, Declaration (No. 17) Concerning Primacy, n. 61 – examined in Chapter 6.

[64] See Art. III-362, Art. III-380 and Art. III-401.

[65] See also the role of the European Council in specific policy fields such as the Common Foreign and Security Policy (Title V, Chapter 2 TEU).

together in differing combinations to exercise EU policymaking functions (as well as administrative and budgetary powers).[66] Furthermore, in addition to being entrusted with primary responsibility for EU policymaking, the Union's political institutions also remain principally responsible for enforcing EU legal norms against Member States.

2.2.1 Constituent Authority

With respect, first, to constituent authority, the Treaties continue as before under the founding EEC Treaty to vest final responsibility with Member States. Article 48 TEU, outlining the ordinary and simplified Treaty revision procedures, mandates that Member States, acting collectively through the European Council must ultimately reach consensus on any revisions to the Treaty framework.[67] Thereafter, that provision further requires the subsequent ratifications of agreed changes by Member States, acting individually as sovereign states, in accordance with their respective domestic constitutional requirements.[68]

Member State control over the scope of EU integration is further enhanced through other Treaty provisions, most notably Article 352 TFEU. That provision, the so-called 'flexibility clause', empowers Member States, acting collectively through the Council and again by unanimity, to adopt specific measures in certain policy areas in instances where the present Treaty structure does not provide the necessary powers to do so. Likewise, the Treaties now include a set of general and specific passerelle clauses.[69] These clauses empower Member States, acting collectively through the European Council or Council, and subject to additional varying preconditions, to substitute the requirement for unanimous voting in Council in EU decision-making processes with voting by qualified majority. In each case, the decision to adjust the

[66] See H. Wallace, M. Pollack and A. Young (eds.), *Policy-Making in the European Union* (2nd edn) (Oxford: Oxford University Press, 2014); S. Hix and B. Høyland, *The Political System of the European Union* (3rd edn) (Basingstoke: Palgrave MacMillan, 2011) and N. Nugent, *The Government and Politics of the European Union* (7th edn) (Basingstoke: Palgrave MacMillan, 2010).

[67] Art. 48(4) TEU and Art. 48(6) TEU.

[68] *Ibid.*

[69] Art. 48(7) TEU (general clause); Art. 31(3) TEU (common foreign and security policy); Art. 81(3) TFEU (judicial cooperation concerning family law); Art. 153 TFEU (social affairs); Art. 192 TFEU (environment); Art. 312(2) TFEU (multiannual financial framework) and Art. 333 TFEU (enhanced cooperation).

applicable voting procedure requires, *inter alia*, the unanimous agreement of Member States.

In addition, Article 49 TEU affords Member States, acting through the Council, control over the accession of new Member States to the European Union. As a logical corollary to that provision, the Treaty of Lisbon also introduced, for the first time, a legal basis in the Treaties for Member State withdrawal from the EU. Article 50 TEU provides that a Member State may notify the European Council of its intention to withdraw, triggering, in the first instance, a process towards the (possible) negotiation of a bilateral exit agreement. Article 50 TEU is unique amongst the Treaty provisions governing the exercise of EU constituent authority in that it provides for collective Member State action on the basis of *majority* voting in the Council.[70] However, the requirement for unanimity is retained in instances where the departing Member State wishes to extend the prescribed two-year period for the negotiation of a withdrawal agreement with the EU.[71]

2.2.2 Political Authority for Union Policymaking

On the second issue, EU policymaking authority, the Treaty framework places responsibility firmly in the hands of three of Union's key political institutions: the European Parliament, Council, and Commission. Specific provisions of the Treaty expressly empower these institutions, acting together in varying institutional combinations, to exercise defined EU policymaking functions.

For example, in the internal market, Article 46 TFEU empowers the European Parliament and Council, acting on a proposal from the Commission, to enact legal measures in order to secure the free movement of workers within the Union. The scope of that freedom is defined in Article 45 TFEU, which provides that:

1 Freedom of movement for workers shall be secured within the Union.
2 Such freedom of movement shall entail the abolition of any discrimination based on nationality between workers of the Member States as regards employment, remuneration and other conditions of work and employment.

[70] Pursuant to Art. 50(2) TEU, the Council is authorised to conclude bilateral exit agreements with departing Member States by qualified majority.
[71] Art. 50(3) TEU.

3 It shall entail the right, subject to limitations justified on grounds of public policy, public security or public health:
   (a) to accept offers of employment actually made;
   (b) to move freely within the territory of Member States for this purpose;
   (c) to stay in a Member State for the purpose of employment in accordance with the provisions governing the employment of nationals of that State laid down by law, regulation or administrative action;
   (d) to remain in the territory of a Member State after having been employed in that State, subject to conditions which shall be embodied in regulations to be drawn up by the Commission.

4 The provisions of this Article shall not apply to employment in the public service.

Under Article 46 TFEU, the European Parliament and Council are expressly directed to give effect to Article 45 TFEU by enacting EU directives and regulations to achieve the following primary objectives:

(a) ... ensuring close cooperation between national employment services;
(b) ... abolishing those administrative procedures and practices and those qualifying periods in respect of eligibility for available employment, whether resulting from national legislation or from agreements previously concluded between Member States, the maintenance of which would form an obstacle to liberalisation of the movement of workers;
(c) ... abolishing all such qualifying periods and other restrictions provided for either under national legislation or under agreements previously concluded between Member States as imposed on workers of other Member States conditions regarding the free choice of employment other than those imposed on workers of the State concerned;
(d) ... setting up appropriate machinery to bring offers of employment into touch with applications for employment and to facilitate the achievement of a balance between supply and demand in the employment market in such a way as to avoid serious threats to the standard of living and level of employment in the various regions and industries.

This basic structure outlined in Articles 45 and 46 TFEU is replicated across all areas of policymaking under the Treaties – from internal market law to social policy and competition law. It also remains fundamentally unchanged since the entry into force of the founding Treaty of Rome. What has changed through subsequent Treaty amendment is: (1) the nature and scope of EU policymaking competences under the

Treaties and (2) the disposition of political power *between Union institutions* with respect to the exercise of EU policymaking functions.[72]

The growth of Union policymaking competences started with the Single European Act and has continued thereafter.[73] To a considerable extent, the progressive expansion of Union power may be viewed as the natural consequence of the functionalist account of EU integration.[74] On that view, progress towards the establishment of a common market would inevitably give rise to the need for EU intervention in new areas as the liberalising impact of the EEC Treaty 'spilled over' into related, non-economic spheres of Member State activity. Supporting that prediction, Member States have, over time, entrusted the Union institutions with additional competence to contribute to policymaking in a range of new areas, including research and technological development;[75] the environment;[76] public health;[77] consumer protection;[78] and education and vocational training.[79]

At the same time, the increase in EU policymaking powers also attests to the Member States' clear ambitions to develop a broader basis for European integration beyond the achievement of a common market. As early as 1986 (the Single European Act), for example, the Member States

[72] See Wallace et al., *Policy-Making in the European Union*, n. 66; Hix and Høyland, *The Political System of the European Union*, n. 66 and Nugent, *The Government and Politics of the European Union*, n. 66.

[73] On the development of European Integration, see A. Arnull, 'The Single European Act' (1986) 11(5) *European Law Review*, 358; D. Curtin, 'The Constitutional Structure of the Union: A Europe of Bits and Pieces' (1993) 30 *Common Market Law Review*, 17; D. O'Keeffe (ed.), *Legal Issues of the Maastricht Treaty* (London: Wiley, 1994); P. Twomey and D. O'Keeffe (eds.), *Legal Issues of the Amsterdam Treaty* (Oxford: Hart Publishing, 1999); M. Andenas and J. Usher (eds.), *The Treaty of Nice and Beyond: Enlargement and Constitutional Reform* (Oxford: Hart Publishing, 2003) and M. Dougan, 'The Treaty of Lisbon 2007: Winning Mind, Not Hearts', n. 31. For broader discussion, see D. Dinan (ed.), *Origins and Evolution of the European Union* (2nd edn) (Oxford: Oxford University Press, 2014) and L. van Middelaar, *The Passage to Europe: How a Continent Became a Union* (London: Yale University Press, 2013).

[74] See E. Haas, *The Uniting of Europe: Political, Social, and Economic Forces 1950–1957* (Stanford: Stanford University Press, 1968); W. Sandholtz and A. Stone Sweet, 'Neo-Functionalism and Supranational Governance' in E. Jones, A. Menon and S. Weatherill (eds.), *The Oxford Handbook of the European Union* (Oxford: Oxford University Press, 2012); A. Wiener and T. Diaz, *European Integration Theory* (2nd edn) (Oxford: Oxford University Press, 2009), chapter 2 and B. Rosamond, *Theories of European Integration* (Palgrave Macmillan, 2000), chapter 3.

[75] Art. 130f EEC (see Arts. 179–190 TFEU).

[76] Art.130r EEC (see Arts. 191–193 TFEU).

[77] Art. 129 EEC (see Art. 168 TFEU).

[78] Art. 129a EEC (see Art. 169 TFEU).

[79] Art. 126 EEC (see Arts. 165–166 TFEU).

were already laying the foundations for closer integration in key areas such as foreign policy and economic and monetary Union.[80] These foundations have since been transformed into cornerstones of the European integration project – together with several other key areas. Under the Lisbon Treaty, European integration now encompasses an extensive range of regulatory activities from the internal market and economic and monetary policy, to EU citizenship, asylum policy and fundamental rights protection.[81]

In a further development, the intervening period has also seen important changes to the distribution of political authority between the (now) Union institutions. Most significantly, the powers of the European Parliament have been significantly boosted through Treaty amendments.[82] Under the EEC Treaty, the Assembly (as it was then known) was a non-elected institution comprised of representatives nominated by Member State parliaments. It had only limited advisory and supervisory powers. However, over time, its status and powers have grown considerably. The first direct elections to the renamed European Parliament took place in 1979. That institution now acts jointly with the Council in the process of adopting Union legislation under the default ordinary legislative procedure.[83] It also enjoys competence to request that the Commission bring forward proposals for action it considers necessary for the purposes of implementing the Treaties.[84] In addition to its increased legislative role, the European Parliament is now entrusted with important functions in the appointment and supervision of the other Union institutions.[85]

More recently, the drive to enhance the Union's democratic credentials has looked beyond the European Parliament to other actors and sources of democratic input. For example, successive waves of amendment have further embedded Member State parliaments into the Treaty structure as a means to enhance the Union's democratic legitimacy.

[80] See Art. 30 the Single European Act [1987] OJ L 169/1, formalising intergovernmental co-operation in foreign policy and Art. 20 introducing a new chapter on Co-operation in Economic and Monetary Policy (as Art. 102a EEC).

[81] Piris, *The Lisbon Treaty: A Legal and Political Analysis*, n. 30 and Craig, *The Lisbon Treaty: Law, Politics, and Treaty Reform*, n. 30.

[82] See B. Rittberger, *Building Europe's Parliament: Democratic Representation Beyond the Nation State* (Oxford: Oxford University Press, 2005) and R. Corbett, F. Jacobs and M. Shackleton, *The European Parliament* (8th edn) (London: Harper, 2011).

[83] Art. 289 TFEU.

[84] Art. 225 TFEU.

[85] See e.g., Arts. 234 TFEU (motion of censure against the Commission and the High Representative for Foreign Affairs) and Art. 17(7) TEU (election of the President of the European Commission).

Article 12 TEU now states that Member State parliaments 'contribute actively to the good functioning of the Union'. Most importantly, as previously illustrated, they enjoy competence to scrutinise EU legislative proposals in areas of shared competence for compliance with the principle of subsidiarity.[86] In addition, national parliaments also have competence to veto proposed amendments to the Treaties under the simplified revision procedure in Article 48(7) TEU.

Finally, in addition to being entrusted with primary responsibility for EU policymaking, the Union's political institutions also remain principally responsible for enforcing EU legal norms against Member States. Article 258 TFEU empowers the Commission to deliver 'reasoned opinions' to Member States in instances of alleged non-compliance with Treaty obligations. Where the matter is not satisfactorily resolved within a specific timeframe, the Commission, acting as gatekeeper, may elect to bring the matter before the Court of Justice. Article 259 TFEU outlines a parallel (and rarely invoked) procedure for allegations of non-compliance by Member States instigated by other Member States.[87] Under that provision, the Commission also acts as gatekeeper to the judicial process, enjoying a prior right to issue its opinion on the merits of the dispute. However, under Article 259 TFEU, Member States are not prevented from activating the Court where the Commission fails to deliver its reasoned opinion within a period of three months.

The Court's judgments on non-compliance with Treaty obligations under both Articles 258 and 258 TFEU address the defaulting Member State *qua* State. The implementation (or otherwise) of EU court judgments remains a matter for domestic law. Article 260 TFEU illuminates this point, which was noted in connection with analysis of the legal effects of EU judicial decisions within national legal systems (Section 2.1): 'If the Court of Justice of the European Union finds that a Member State has failed to fulfil an obligation under the Treaties, *the State shall be required to take the necessary measures to comply with the judgment of the*

[86] See Art. 12 TEU and Protocol (No. 2) On the Application of the Principles of Subsidiarity and Proportionality, n. 12, establishing the subsidiarity early warning procedure. For analysis, see e.g., P. Kiiver, *The Early Warning System for the Principle of Subsidiarity* (London: Routledge, 2012) and A. Cygan, 'The Parliamentarisation of EU Decision-Making: The Impact of the Treaty of Lisbon on National Parliaments' (2011) 36 *European Law Review*, 480.

[87] For rare exceptions see e.g., Case 141/78, *France* v. *United Kingdom (Marine Conservation)* EU:C:1979:225; Case C-388/95, *Belgium* v. *Spain (Designations of Origin)* EU:C:2000:244 and Case C-364/10, *Hungary* v. *Slovakia* EU:C:2012:630.

Court.'[88] The same applies with respect to demands for the payment of financial penalties, which may be attached to judgments against Member States by way of supplementary procedure. Article 260(3) TFEU refers in that connection simply to the Court's judgment giving rise to a 'payment obligation' on the part of the Member State in breach.

The Maastricht Treaty further enhanced the role of the Union's political institutions in the enforcement of Treaty norms against Member States – this time with a specific focus on ensuring compliance with the core values of EU integration.[89] These values, outlined in Article 2 TEU, include, *inter alia*, respect for human dignity, freedom, democracy, equality, and human rights (see further Section 2.3). In summary, the European Council, acting unanimously on a proposal from one-third of the Member States or the Commission after obtaining the consent of the European Parliament, is empowered to determine the existence of 'a serious and persistent breach' of any of the values outlined in Article 2 TEU. Should that breach not be satisfactorily addressed, the Treaty permits the Council to introduce specific sanctions against the Member State concerned, including the limitation of its voting rights in the Council.[90]

2.3 Constitutional Issue No. 3: The Objectives, Values and Limits of EU Integration

This final section completes analysis of the Treaty framework's position on the three baseline issues for EU constitutionalism by reviewing its key statements on the objectives, values, and limits of EU integration.[91] First, it asks, with reference to the Treaty framework, what is the process of European integration conceived to achieve? Secondly, it considers the Treaties' core statements on the range of *values* that Member States have embedded in the Treaty framework as a means to shape the activities of

88 Emphasis added.

89 C. Hillion, 'Overseeing the Rule of Law in the EU: Legal Mandate and Means' in C. Closa and D. Kochenov (eds.), *Reinforcing Rule of Law Oversight in the European Union* (Cambridge: Cambridge University Press, 2016).

90 Art. 7(3) TEU.

91 See S. Weatherill, *Law and Values in the European Union* (Oxford: Oxford University Press, 2016); J. Larik, 'On the Changing Role of the Objectives of the European Union' (2014) 63 *International Comparative Law Quarterly*, 935 and K. Lenaerts and P. Van Nuffel, *European Union Law* (3rd edn) (London: Sweet and Maxwell, 2011) at pp. 106–111. See also, A. Von Bogdandy, 'Founding Principles of EU Law: A Doctrinal Sketch' (2010) 16(2) *European Law Journal*, 95.

the EU institutions in pursuit of the Treaties' primary objectives. Finally, it highlights the increasing range of *limits* that the EU Treaties now impose on the competence of the Union institutions in connection with the realisation of the objectives and values of European integration.

Alongside adjustments to the locus of EU policymaking authority (Constitutional Issue No. 2), this is an area of considerable intervening change. Member States have repeatedly expanded the range of highly functional objectives, complementary values and general and specific limits imposed on EU institutional activity through successive Treaty amendments.

2.3.1 *The Objectives of European Integration*

With respect, first, to objectives, the central aim of European integration under the founding Treaty of Rome was 'to promote through the Community a harmonious development of economic activities, a continuous and balanced expansion, an increase in stability, an accelerated raising of the standard of living and closer relations between the [Member] States'.[92] That objective was to be achieved through a process of progressive economic integration – the establishment of a common market.[93]

The promotion of balanced economic growth and stability, inter-state relations and social progress through economic integration remains a core objective of European integration under the amended Treaty framework. According to Article 3(3) TEU, 'the Union shall establish an internal market. It shall work for the sustainable development of Europe based on balanced economic growth and price stability, a highly competitive social market economy, aiming at full employment and social progress.' The internal market concept represents a refinement of the original common market concept established under the EEC Treaty.[94] It is defined in Article 26(2) TFEU as an 'area without internal frontiers in which the free movement of goods, persons, services, and capital is ensured in accordance with the provisions of the Treaties'. Under Article 3(4) TEU, the EU's economic objectives now extend to include 'the establishment of an economic and monetary Union whose currency is the euro'.

92 Art. 2 EEC.
93 *Ibid.*
94 K. Mortelmans, 'The Common Market, the Internal Market and the Single Market, What's in a Market?' (1998) 35 *Common Market Law Review*, 101 and S. Weatherill, *The Internal Market as a Legal Concept* (Oxford: Oxford University Press, 2017).

In addition, the Treaties also now outline other key objectives alongside the aforementioned aims that have their foundations in the EEC Treaty. Overall, the revised list of objectives reflects a progressive broadening beyond the realisation of economic objectives. As de Búrca notes, EU integration began as 'a kind of pilot project of limited economic integration with a view to securing greater peace and prosperity for Member States … [but] has evolved into something much larger, more complex and more ambitious.'[95] Pursuant to Article 3 TEU, the Union's principal objective is to 'promote peace, its values and the well-being of its peoples'. It also aims to offer citizens 'an area of freedom, security, and justice' between the Member States, covering external border controls, asylum, immigration and the prevention and combatting of crime'.[96] Further objectives now include tackling social exclusion and discrimination, and the promotion of social justice protection, equality between women and men, solidarity between generations and the protection of the rights of the child (Article 3(3) TEU). Equally, under Article 3(5) TEU, the Union is also now given express aims with respect to its external relations with the wider world. Specifically, the Union is tasked with contributing 'to peace, security, the sustainable development of the Earth, solidarity and mutual respect among peoples, free and fair trade, eradication of poverty and the protection of human rights'.[97] Article 21 TEU expands further on the Union's objectives in connection with its external activities.[98]

As before under the EEC Treaty, these core objectives seek to give effect to a broader set of political aspirations outlined by the Member States in the preambles to the Treaties and Article 1 TEU. These aspirations include, first and foremost, a continued commitment by the Member States to create 'an ever-closer Union among the peoples of Europe'.[99] Importantly, the list of the Union's overarching objectives under Article 3 TEU is not a source of legal competence.[100] The realisation of the Union's core objectives under that provision is expressly

[95] G. de Búrca, 'Europe's raison d'etre' in D. Kochenov and F. Amterbrink (eds.), *The European Union's Shaping of the International Legal Order* (Cambridge: Cambridge University Press, 2013) at p. 21.

[96] Art. 3(2) TEU.

[97] Art. 3(5) TEU.

[98] See J. Larik, *Foreign Policy Objectives in European Constitutional Law* (Oxford: Oxford University Press, 2016) at p. 141.

[99] Art. 1 TEU.

[100] See Case C-339/89, *Alsthom Atlantique* EU:C:1991:28 at para. 9; Case C-9/99, *Echirolles Distribution SA* v. *Association du Dauphiné and Others* EU:C:2000:532 at para. 25 and Case C-484/08, *Caja de Ahorros y Monte de Piedad de Madrid* EU:C:2010:309 at paras. 46–47.

linked to the existence, elsewhere in the Treaty framework, of competence to act in accordance with the principle of conferral in Article 5(2) TEU. As Article 3(6) TEU details, 'The Union shall pursue its objectives by appropriate means commensurate with the competences which are conferred upon it in the Treaties.'[101]

2.3.2 *The Values of European Integration*

Turning now to values, the founding EEC Treaty had very little to say – at least expressly. It included no references to any 'values' *per se*.[102] Yet, that omission did not mean that EU integration was not, from the outset, concerned with the promotion of a specific set of political and economic values. On the contrary, through the EEC Treaty, the Member States can be seen to have a clear aspirational commitment to the fundamentals of an open market economy based on the principles of non-discrimination and undistorted competition.[103] That commitment was not absolute, of course, but qualified in key respects through the existence in the EEC Treaty of a range of exclusions and derogating provisions.[104] It was also further conditioned by the inclusion of limited social and redistributive policies, notably Title III on social policy.[105] More notably still, the EEC Treaty extended the scope of the non-discrimination principle to promote equal pay for men and women – at least to the extent that it affected the establishment of the common market.[106]

Furthermore, the founding Treaty framework implicitly, but firmly, linked European integration to the rule of law as a normative value. As the work of EU legal historians illuminates, the Court of Justice was established principally to offer Member States and economic operators judicial protection against acts of the new Community institutions.[107]

[101] See e.g., Case C-149/96, *Portugal* v. *Council (Textiles)* EU:C:1999:574 at paras. 86–87 (on the objective of economic and social cohesion in Art. 3(3) TEU).
[102] Weatherill, *Law and Values in the European Union*, n. 91 at p. 393.
[103] See esp., Art. 64 EEC, Art. 110 EEC.
[104] See Art. 36 EEC; Art. 48(3) EEC; Art. 48(4) EEC; Art. 55 EEC; Art. 56 EEC; Art. 73(2) EEC; Art. 82 EEC; Art. 84 EEC; Art. 85(3) EEC; Art. 90 EEC; Art. 93(2) EEC Art. 109 EEC; Art. 222 EEC and Art. 223 EEC.
[105] Arts. 117–130 EEC.
[106] Art. 119 EEC.
[107] A. Boerger-De Smedt, 'Negotiating the Foundations of European Law, 1950–57: The Legal History of the Treaties of Paris and Rome' (2012) 21(3) *Contemporary European History*, 339 at p. 346. See also the remarks of the Court's first President, Massimo Pilotti, at the opening of the new Court: 'The task imposed upon this Court is ... to guarantee to the parties concerned, whether they be States, enterprises, or humble

Moreover, under Article 164 EEC, the Court of Justice was entrusted with a guiding mandate to ensure that, in the interpretation and application of the EEC Treaty, the 'law is observed'. At a push, it is also possible to read into the founding Treaty an embryonic commitment to broader values such as representative democracy. From the outset, the EEC Treaty included, of course, an Assembly composed of national parliamentarians in its founding institutional structure – the body that would subsequently be transformed into a directly elected European Parliament.

The present Treaty framework continues to bind the Union and the Member States to the basic values of the founding EEC Treaty. Both sets of actors remain committed, in particular, to the principles of a 'highly competitive social market economy', based on the cornerstone principles of non-discrimination and undistorted competition.[108] Likewise, the Court's basic mandate to ensure that, in the interpretation and application of the EEC Treaty, the 'law is observed' remains unchanged.[109] At the same time, however, the range of values guiding EU integration has expanded considerably in the intervening period in line with the progressive growth in Union competence. Moreover, with the entry into force of the Lisbon Treaty, the Union's guiding set of values is now expressly defined as such in the Treaty framework.[110] These values are also now frontloaded in the Treaty framework, listed ahead of the objectives of EU integration.

According to Article 2 TEU, 'the Union is founded on the values of respect for human dignity, freedom, democracy, equality, the rule of law and respect for human rights'. This central statement of Union values reinforces existing values embedded, implicitly, in the original Treaty framework, notably respect for the rule of law and the principle of non-discrimination. In its current formulation, that latter principle is, however, no longer just concerned with nationality or gender discrimination in the context of market integration. It now extends to cover discrimination on grounds of race or ethnic origin, religion or belief, disability, age and sexual orientation across all areas of Union activity.[111]

individuals, protection against encroachment beyond those limits within which the organs of the Community must act', cited in Valentine, *The Court of Justice of the European Communities*, n. 38 at p. 4.

[108] See Art. 3(3) TEU. Post-Lisbon, undistorted competition within the internal market is referenced in Protocol No. 27 on the Internal Market and Competition [2016] OJ C 202/308.

[109] See Art. 19 TEU.

[110] See Art. 48 TEU.

[111] Art. 10 TEU. See also, Art. 21 of the Charter of Fundamental Rights, n. 7.

The commitment to respect human dignity, freedom, human rights and democracy, represent entirely new additions to the Treaty framework. The Treaty of Rome made at best only rather weak implicit references to this set of values. Their introduction into the Treaty framework can, however, be traced back relatively far in the history of EU integration. With respect to human rights, for instance, the Court of Justice took the initial step to introduce this set of new values into the EU policymaking framework. In its *Handelsgesellschaft* decision, the Court ruled that, despite no express mention in the EEC Treaty, fundamental rights formed an integral part of the Community legal order.[112] Subsequently, the Member States have repeatedly amended the Treaty framework to include ever-increasing commitments to the protection of fundamental rights. The political integration of fundamental rights into the Treaty framework culminated in the attribution of legal status to the EU Charter of Fundamental Rights at Lisbon.

The revised Article 2 TEU does not, however, set out an exhaustive list of the values of EU integration. Commitments to promote other core values in EU policymaking can now be found throughout the amended Treaties. Articles 11, 12 and 13 TFEU, for instance, define high levels of environmental protection, consumer protection and animal welfare, respectively, as key benchmarks for EU policymaking. These provisions have general application and function to ensure the promotion of specific normative aspirations in connection with the definition and implementation of all EU institutional activities.[113]

2.3.3 *The Limits on European Integration*

Lastly, the EU Treaty framework has always placed important limits on the Union institutions and the Member States. Under the EEC Treaty, the limits on (then) Community activity were principally to be found in Article 177 EEC (now Article 263 TFEU). That provision outlined four principal grounds for the judicial review of Community activity: lack of competence; infringement of an essential procedural requirement;

[112] Case 11/70, *Internationale Handelsgesellschaft mbH* v. *Einfuhr- und Vorratsstelle für Getreide und Futtermittel* EU:C:1970:114.

[113] On mainstreaming provisions, see e.g., J. Shaw, 'Mainstreaming Equality and Diversity in European Union Law and Policy' (2005) 58(1) *Current Legal Problems* 255 and R. Geyer and S. Lightfoot, 'The Strengths and Limits of New Forms of EU Governance: The Cases of Mainstreaming and Impact Assessment in EU Public Health and Sustainable Development Policy' (2010) 32 *Journal of European Integration*, 339.

infringement of the Treaty of any rule relating to its application; and the misuse of powers. Specific Treaty provisions placed further limits on Community institutional activity – actionable through Article 177 EEC. For example, Article 84 EEC precluded the Community's adoption of legal acts under Title IV on transport that apply to transport by rail, road and inland waterway. Similarly, Article 48(4) EEC excluded public service employment from the scope of the Treaty provisions on the free movement of workers. More broadly, and following patterns in international treaty making, Article 223 EEC required Community institutions to respect the essential security interests of individual Member States.

Under the EEC Treaty, Member States were limited, first and foremost, by the range of specific obligations set out within the Treaty framework.[114] These included, for example, commitments to refrain from introducing between themselves new restrictions on the importation and export of goods, services and, to a lesser extent, capital.[115] In addition, Member States were also bound under the EEC Treaty to comply with the principles of non-discrimination, equal pay and, most broadly, the duty of loyal cooperation when acting within the scope of the Treaty.[116]

Since 1957, there has been a significant increase in the range of limits that bind the Union institutions in the exercise of their Treaty competences. At the same time, Member States are also now subject to an expanded range of normative restraints to the extent that they act within the scope of the Treaties.

With respect to *Union institutions* specifically (the focus of this book), repeated amendments to the Treaty framework have broadened the basis of judicial review on grounds of 'lack of competence' under Article 263 TFEU. Alongside the principle of conferral, formalised as a general principle at Maastricht, the Treaties now prescribe two further key restrictions on Union competences: subsidiarity and proportionality. The subsidiarity principle (Article 5(3) TEU) applies to areas of shared Union and Member State competence. In essence, it requires the Union institutions to justify their motivation to act with reference to the existence of a transnational regulatory issue that is best (or better)

[114] See e.g., Art. 48 EEC (now Art. 45 TFEU) on the elimination of restrictions on the free movement of workers cited earlier.

[115] See e.g., Arts. 12, 31 and 71 EEC.

[116] See e.g., Art. 7 EEC (now Art. 18 TFEU), Art. 119 EEC (now Art. 157 TFEU) and Art. 5 EEC (now Art. 4(3) TEU).

addressed at Union level.[117] The proportionality principle in Article 5(4) TEU applies, by contrast, to all Union activity. Its function is to restrict the scope of EU activity to that which is strictly necessary to achieve the objectives of the Treaties.[118]

Subsidiarity and proportionality entered into the Treaty framework as limits on the exercise of Union competences at Maastricht. The founding Treaty did not mention subsidiarity. That Treaty had also only referenced proportionality loosely and in connection with *Member State* obligations and not Community functions.[119] The decision by Member States at Maastricht to formalise subsidiarity and proportionality as general limits on Union competences was a direct response to concerns on the part of certain states over the apparent ever-increasing expansion of Community lawmaking. In particular, the reintroduction of majority voting in the Council *de jure* and *de facto* in the internal market had significantly boosted the Community's policymaking influence at the expense of individual Member States.[120] With majority voting restored in the Council as the EEC Treaty had intended, Member States could no longer wield national vetoes. This had the immediate effect of refocusing Member State attention on the existence and enforcement of limits on Community policymaking in an effort to protect national regulatory autonomy.

Member States have also introduced a range of additional limits on EU institutional activity alongside the principles of conferral, subsidiarity and proportionality in Article 5 TEU. These limits are to be found in both the EU Treaties and accompanying protocols and differ in their levels of specificity and scope of application (see further Chapter 6). The Treaty of Lisbon, for instance, enhanced the protection of Member State competence with respect to national security pursuant to Article 223 EEC (see now, in revised form, Article 346 TFEU). It also complemented that existing concern with the introduction of express reference to respect

[117] Estella, *The Principle of Subsidiarity and Its Critique*, n. 4. See also, Bermann, 'Taking Subsidiarity Seriously: Federalism in the European Community and the United States', n. 19 and G. Davies, 'Subsidiarity: The Wrong Idea, in the Wrong Place, at the Wrong Time' (2006) 43 *Common Market Law Review*, 63.

[118] Tridimas, *General Principles of EU Law*, n. 4, chapters 3–5 and J. H. Jans, 'Proportionality Revisited' (2000) *Legal Issues of European Integration*, 239.

[119] See e.g., Art. 67 EEC, which committed Member States to the liberalisation of intra-Community capital movements 'to the extent necessary to ensure the proper functioning of the Common Market'.

[120] See e.g., J. H. H. Weiler, 'The Transformation of Europe' (1991) 100 *Yale Law Journal*, 2403 at pp. 2456–2466.

for, among other things, the national identities of the Member States. Article 4(2) TEU now provides that:

> The Union shall respect the equality of Member States before the Treaties as well as their national identities, inherent in the fundamental structures, political and constitutional, inclusive of regional and local self-government. It shall also respect their essential State functions, including ensuring the territorial integrity of the State, maintaining law and order and safeguarding national security.

Finally, EU institutional activity is also subject to compliance with the expanded range of *values* now in the Treaty framework (see Section 2.3.2). Alongside the principles of conferral, subsidiarity and proportionality – and the other specific Treaty limits – these values function as important normative restraints on the Union institutions. The transformation from *value* to *limit* follows directly from Article 263 TFEU, which provides for judicial review of Union acts on the grounds of 'infringement of the Treaties'. As a matter of principle, Union activity is therefore also subject to potential scrutiny by the Court of Justice for non-compliance with the values contained in, *inter alia*, Articles 2 TEU, as well as those outlined in Title II of the TFEU (Articles 7–17 TFEU). The functioning of the EU Charter of Fundamental Rights as an additional source of legal restraint on EU institutional activity follows expressly from Article 51(1) EUCFR. That provision mandates that the Union institutions respect EU Charter rights in the exercise of their respective functions under the Treaties.

The impact of Treaty limits on the scope for, and nature of, EU policy-making is highly provision specific. The wording of certain provisions imposes only minimum limits on EU activity. Article 12 TFEU on consumer protection, for example, simply requires that the Union institutions 'take account of' particular values when defining and implementing other EU policies.[121] A similar approach is taken with respect to the values of, among other things, environmental protection, animal welfare and the protection of human health.[122] By contrast, other Treaty provisions purport to set stronger limits on EU institutional activity. Article 4(2) TEU, for example, mandates that national security remains the sole responsibility of individual Member States. Between these two extremes, the majority of provisions in the Treaty framework demand that the

[121] On the integration of environmental protection into EU policymaking, see e.g., M. Wasmeier, 'The Integration of Environmental Protection as a General Rule for Interpreting Community Law' (2001) *Common Market Law Review*, 159.

[122] Arts. 11, 13 and 9 TFEU respectively. See e.g., Case C-424/13, *Zuchtvieh-Export GmbH v. Stadt Kempten* EU:C:2015:259.

Union institutions fully respect particular limits on Union competence and/or value commitments.

In line with the locus of EU political authority under the Treaty framework (Constitutional Issue No. 2), adherence to the limits imposed remains, in the first instance, a matter for the Union institutions themselves. The Court of Justice is, however, entrusted with competence to issue final judgment on the interpretation and application of Treaty limits in connection with EU institutional activity. Its approach to the scrutiny of EU institutional activity for compliance with the Treaty framework as constitutional touchstone has generally afforded EU institutions a broad sphere of discretion.[123]

Concluding Remarks

The legitimacy of the Court of Justice's role in the EU legal order, and European integration more broadly, may be (and is) assessed from a range of complementary and/or competing perspectives.[124] This book aligns discussion of the legitimacy of EU judicial activity with analysis of the Court's compliance with the EU Treaty framework in the exercise of its functions as an institution of the Union. This chapter has examined the status and function of the EU Treaty framework as the principal touchstone for assessments of the internal constitutionality of all EU institutional activity – including the work of the Court. In so doing, it establishes the intellectual framework that this book develops in order to scrutinise EU judicial activity in subsequent chapters (Chapters 3–5).

Section 1 defended the function of the EU Treaties as a primary source of normative restraint on the activities of the Court of Justice. In summary, it argued that the EU Treaties should be viewed as the

[123] See e.g., Case C-376/98, *Germany* v. *Parliament and Council (Tobacco Advertising)*, n. 58; Case C-370/12, *Pringle* v. *Government of Ireland and Others* ECLI:EU:C:2012:756 and Case C-62/14, *Gauweiler and Others*, n. 11. Note, however, the Court's at times stricter approach to the application of Treaty limits. See e.g., its case law on EU Charter rights, including Joined Cases C 293/12 and C 594/12, *Digital Rights Ireland*, n. 11 and Case C-362/14, *Schrems* v. *Data Protection Commissioner* EU:C:2015:650.

[124] Legitimacy may be assessed, for example, not only in terms of legality, but also from a range of political, sociological and moral perspectives. For an overview of the main legitimacy models applied to the study of EU judicial activity, see e.g., R. Bobek, 'Of Feasibility and Silent Elephants: The Legitimacy of the Court of Justice through the Eyes of National Courts' in M. Adams, H. de Waele, J. Meeusen and G. Straetmans (eds.), *Judging Europe's Judges: The Legitimacy of the Case Law of the European Court of Justice* (Oxford: Hart Publishing, 2013) at pp. 198–202.

principal touchstones with regard to the internal constitutionality of all EU institutional activity. This includes, as a matter of principle, the activities of the Court of Justice – an EU institution whose activities are presently not scrutinised routinely for compliance with the Treaties. Furthermore, as the Union's founding constitutional charter, the EU Treaty framework was shown to enjoy an uncharacteristically high degree of normative authority. The frequency, nature and scope of the various amendments, it was argued, serves as a direct and powerful source of 'constitutional refreshment', injecting renewed normative authority into the Treaties' function as constitutional touchstones.[125]

Section 2 then explored the consequences of positioning the EU Treaties as the principal touchstones for assessments of the internal constitutionality of EU institutional activity. In short, this chapter asserted that the EU Treaty framework provides important clarity on what this book identifies as the three key issues for EU constitutionalism.

First, on the formal status of Union law and the conditions under which it applies within Member States (Constitutional Issue No. 1), the EU Treaties continue to display the standard features of ordinary international treaties. Secondly, with respect to the locus of EU political authority (Constitutional Issue No. 2), the Treaty framework was shown to reserve constituent authority to the Member States acting collectively. At the same time, the Union's political institutions – the Commission, European Parliament and Council of the European Union – are entrusted, in varying institutional combinations, with primary responsibility for EU policymaking. Lastly, with reference to Constitutional Issue No. 3, the EU Treaties now outline a diverse range of objectives and values, but also prescribe an ever-increasing set of limits on the existence and exercise of EU competences that bind the Union institutions.

The principal changes to the EU Treaty framework over time have primarily concerned the objectives, values and limits of EU integration (Constitutional Issue No. 3). These have undergone a process of broadening and deepening. In addition, successive waves of Treaty amendment have also radically adjusted the disposition of policymaking competence between the three key political institutions (Constitutional Issue No. 2) – to enhance, in particular, the position of the European Parliament.

[125] See de Witte, 'The Closest Thing to a Constitutional Conversation in Europe: The Semi-Permanent Treaty Revision Process', n. 1.

Next, Chapter 2 turns to consider the limits of the EU Treaties' function as benchmarks to assess the legitimacy of EU institutional activity. It argues that, as a constitutional touchstone, the Treaty framework is neither hermetically sealed nor politically settled in its entirety. The constitutional context structuring EU integration is much richer and more dynamic. In particular, it is argued that the EU Treaty framework as constitutional touchstone is conditioned by two broader phenomena in EU integration. These are labelled, respectively: sites of *constitutional supplementation* and *constitutional contestation*.

2 The EU Treaty Framework and the Constitutional Context of European Integration

Introduction

This chapter places analysis of the EU Treaty framework's status and function as constitutional touchstone (Chapter 1) within the broader legal and political context that structures EU integration. In summary, it argues that, as constitutional touchstones, the Treaties' function is conditioned by what this chapter defines as acts of *constitutional supplementation* and *constitutional contestation*. The first of these concepts, *constitutional supplementation*, references acts of the EU institutions (and also Member States) that elaborate – but do not fundamentally contest – the EU Treaties' basic statements on the three key issues for EU constitutionalism (Chapter 1). By contrast, the concept of *constitutional contestation* refers to acts of the EU institutions (and Member States) that expressly contest the Treaties' clear position on the three basic issues for EU constitutionalism.

The introduction of the concepts of constitutional supplementation and constitutional contestation in this chapter serves two specific objectives. First, it reveals the existence of inherent limits to the functioning of the bare bones of the EU Treaties as touchstones on the internal constitutionality of EU institutional activity. Secondly, and looking ahead to the chapters that follow, it establishes the framework to structure the critique of EU judicial activity for compliance with the Treaties in the remainder of this book (Chapters 3–5).

Section 1 examines the gap that exists between the text of the Treaty framework and the 'real world' of EU integration It also introduces the twin concepts of constitutional supplementation and constitutional contestation as a new approach to theorising that important division. Sections 2 and 3 then highlight prominent examples of acts of constitutional supplementation (Section 2) and constitutional contestation (Section 3) in EU integration. Section 4 explores the relationship between acts of constitutional supplementation and constitutional contestation and the dynamics of EU Treaty reform. Finally, the chapter concludes with an assessment of the Union institutions' and Member States' responses to the Eurozone crisis as a case study in constitutional contestation (Section 5).

Throughout this chapter, constitutional supplementation is explored with reference to both EU political and judicial institutional activity. By contrast, discussion of acts of constitutional contestation (Sections 3 and 5) is restricted to analysis of *political* developments. The search for sites of constitutional contestation with reference to EU *judicial* activity – the focus of this book – begins in the next chapter.

1 The Space between: The EU Treaties and the Constitutional Context of EU Integration

In isolation, the Treaty framework does not fully capture the constitutional context that shapes the process of EU integration.[1] That context is much richer and more dynamic than that outlined by the text of the EU Treaties. As de Búrca observes:

> [A] description of the legal rules and Treaty provisions which define and purport to regulate the formal institutions of European government, without considering how those institutions actually function or the extent to which the rules in fact operate to constrain or shape institutional conduct, provides a limited constitutional account . . . a satisfactory constitutional account requires both an appreciation of how the institutions of government are supposed to function and what the safeguards are to ensure this, as a well as an appreciation of how they operate in practice.[2]

Similarly, with a specific reference to executive authority, Curtin argues that legal and structural changes to the EU Treaty framework *stricto sensu* form only one component part of a 'living constitution' that reflects the dynamic empirical reality of EU institutional activities at any single

[1] See G. de Búrca, 'The Institutional Development of the EU: A Constitutional Analysis' in P. Craig and G. de Búrca (eds.), *The Evolution of EU Law* (Oxford: Oxford University Press, 1999).

[2] *Ibid.*, at p. 63.

moment in time.[3] In an assessment that rings true of any political system, she notes that:

> Formal institutions may take flesh and shape in ways that are not originally envisaged in the formal legal rules. They may spawn new actors who, through various informal processes and legal and institutional practices, acquire and exercise tasks. Institutions become "living" and acquire a life of their own by virtue of empirical practice.[4]

EU scholars have probed the gap that exists between the formal constitutional framework structuring EU institutional activity and empirical reality.[5] Studies of the EU decision-making processes, for example, have revealed the emergence of more complex and nuanced sets of institutional arrangements in practice, which should be read alongside the formal constitutional account outlined in the Treaty framework.[6] In the legal sphere, Curtin's work has challenged the assumption that executive power rests exclusively with the Commission – an assumption formalised in the EU Treaties. Through detailed study of 'real world' practices, she reveals that executive power has, as a matter of practical experience, developed across different institutions over time to form a 'veritable patchwork'.[7] Political scientists have attempted to map similar empirical trends in the exercise of EU institutional power and, moreover, sought to locate these trends in institutional and political theory.[8]

In the broader literature on European integration, Van Middelaar juxtaposes the Treaty framework with the activities of Member States as both sovereign states and, collectively, as Member States of the Union.[9] The Treaty framework, he argues, forms the 'inner sphere' of

3 D. Curtin, *Executive Power of the European Union: Law, Practices, and the Living Constitution* (Oxford: Oxford University Press, 2009).

4 *Ibid.*, at p. 5.

5 De Búrca, 'The Institutional Development of the EU: A Constitutional Analysis', n. 1.

6 See e.g., M. Van Schendelen, 'The Council Decides: Does the Council Decide?' (1996) 34 *Journal of Common Market Studies*, 531; D. Kietz and A Maurer, 'The European Parliament in Treaty Reform: Predefining IGC's through Interinstitutional Agreements' (2007) 13(1) *European Law Journal*, 20 and H. Farrell and A. Héritier, 'Formal and Informal Institutions under Co-Decision: Continuous Constitution-Building in Europe' (2007) 30(2) *West European Politics*, 285

7 Curtin, *Executive Power of the European Union*, n. 3 at p. 20.

8 See e.g., D. S. Martinsen, *An Ever More Powerful Court? The Political Constraints of Legal Integration in the European Union* (Oxford: Oxford University Press, 2015); R. Thomson and M. Hosli, 'Who Has Power in the EU? The Commission, Council and Parliament in Legislative Decision-Making' (2006) 44(2) *Journal of Common Market Studies*, 396 and A. Héritier, *Explaining Institutional Change in Europe* (Oxford: Oxford University Press, 2007).

9 L. Van Middelaar, *The Passage to Europe* (London: Yale University Press, 2014).

European integration.[10] It exists alongside, and in tension with, both the historical understanding of States as sovereign actors in international law (the 'outer sphere' of EU integration) and a powerful, new 'intermediate sphere' of *collective* Member State activity outside (at least historically) the formal structure of the EU Treaty framework.[11] The intermediate sphere of integration, Van Middelaar argues, quickly emerged as a powerful force in EU integration. Its emergence can be seen, for example, in the establishment and growth of the European Council as a forum for intergovernmental policymaking between the Heads of State or Government of the Member States.[12]

This chapter introduces the concepts of *supplementation* and *contestation* to complement existing analyses of the space that exists between the Treaty framework and the broader context that structures EU integration. Importantly, the twin concepts do not seek to further existing studies of empirical reality – what Curtin dubs the 'dark matter' of EU integration.[13] That task is left to political scientists. The methodological approach adopted in this chapter remains firmly rooted in doctrinal analysis. The existence and visibility of important sites of supplementation and contestation at the level of doctrinal analysis provides sufficiently compelling evidence to support the underlying argument advanced in this chapter; namely that, an understanding of the constitutional context that structures EU integration cannot be gleaned from the text of the EU Treaties alone.

2 Constitutional Supplementation

Constitutional supplementation refers to acts of the EU institutions and/or Member States that serve to elaborate, but not fundamentally contest, the Treaties' core statements on the three key issues for EU constitutionalism (Chapter 1). This section highlights a number of examples from across both political and judicial activities. The chosen illustrations supplement the Treaty framework's basic statements on the second and third issues for EU constitutionalism, concerning, respectively, the locus of political authority within the Union legal order (Constitutional

10 *Ibid.*, at pp. 13–24.

11 *Ibid.*

12 In short, as Van Middelaar puts it, the history of European integration demonstrates that, whenever the EU28 speak collectively as Member States of the Union, the inner sphere (the EU institutions) 'obeys' and the outer sphere (the sovereign Member States) 'listens'.

13 Curtin, *Executive Power of the European Union*, n. 3 at p. 11.

Issue No. 2) and the objectives, values and limits of EU integration (Constitutional Issue No. 3).

Section 2.1 points to the proliferation of inter-institutional agreements concluded between the EU's political organs as paradigm examples of acts of constitutional supplementation. Section 2.2 considers the emergence of the comitology regime as another instance of constitutional supplementation with regard to the Treaty's position on the locus of political authority within the Union legal order (Constitutional Issue No. 2). Finally, Section 2.3 identifies the Court's case law on the 'general principles' of Union law as an important act of constitutional supplementation in furtherance of the Treaty framework's statements on the third issue for EU constitutionalism concerning the objectives, values and limits of EU integration (Constitutional Issue No. 3).

2.1 Inter-Institutional Agreements

Inter-institutional agreements (as well as joint declarations, and other similar instruments) adopted by the EU's political institutions are paradigmatic acts of constitutional supplementation. These instruments, adopted by the EU's political institutions to manage their relationships *inter se*, play a crucial role in supplementing the Treaties' basic statements on the locus of EU political authority (Constitutional Issue No.2).[14] As Monar argues, inter-institutional agreements are,

> so closely related to the institutional and legal framework of the Treaties that they can be regarded as a direct emanation of [that] framework. They are concluded by institutions which are set up by the Treaties; they are directed at the conduct of these institutions in the framework of the powers conferred upon them by the Treaties; they are explicitly or implicitly based on and often even clearly refer to the decision-making procedures laid down by the Treaties; and they find their limits in the provisions of the Treaties, *whose scope and context they cannot alter*.[15]

Similarly, Costa, Dehousse, and Traklová assert that inter-institutional agreements, 'stipulate the procedures provided for by the treaties and,

[14] See B. Driessen, 'Interinstitutional Conventions and Institutional Balance' (2008) 33(4) *European Law Review*, 550; B. Driessen, *Interinstitutional Conventions in EU Law* (London: Cameron, 2007) and J. Monar, 'Interinstitutional Agreements: The Phenomenon and Its New Dynamics After Maastricht' (1994) 31 *Common Market Law Review*, 693.

[15] Monar, 'Interinstitutional Agreements: The Phenomenon and Its New Dynamics After Maastricht', n. 14 at p. 700 (emphasis added). See also, Declaration (No. 3) annexed to the Treaty of Nice.

without opposing them, may include alternative arrangements which limit inter-institutional disputes and expedite the decision-making process'.[16]

The EU institutions have adopted over a hundred such supplementary measures of varying sorts in order to lubricate their inter-institutional relations under the Treaties.[17] Early examples include the agreements concluded between the Presidents of the European Commission and European Parliament;[18] the Commission's Communication on practical measures to improve relations between the Parliament and Commission;[19] and the Joint Declaration of the Parliament, Council and Commission on the establishment between the Parliament and Council of a conciliation procedure in budgetary matters.[20] More recently, the introduction and expansion of the co-decision (now ordinary) legislative procedure, along with broader efforts to enhance the efficiency and quality of EU policymaking, have given rise to further, more detailed, acts of constitutional supplementation.[21]

The existence of these supplementary agreements is necessitated, first, by the wording of the EU Treaties. The Treaties' statements on the locus of political authority within the Union provide little by way of detail on the practical arrangements governing the EU institutions' internal procedures and inter-institutional relationships. Secondly, the need for elaboration beyond the text of the Treaties is also a consequence of Member States' chosen approach to the *dispersal* of legislative and executive power within the Union. That approach distributes policymaking

[16] O. Costa, R. Dehousse and A. Traklová, 'Codecision and "Early Agreements": An Improvement or a Subversion of the Legislative Procedure?' Studies & Research, No. 84, *Notre Europe* at p. 8 (emphasis added).

[17] Driessen, *Interinstitutional Conventions in EU Law*, n. 14 at p. 275.

[18] Cited in Commission, 'Practical Measures to Strengthen the Powers of Control of the Parliament and to Improve Relations Between the Parliament and the Commission' [1973] COM (73) 999 (Annex I).

[19] Communication on Practical Measures to Strengthen the Powers of Control of the Parliament and to Improve Relations Between the Parliament and the Commission [1973] COM (73) 999.

[20] Joint Declaration of the Parliament, Council and Commission on the establishment between the Parliament and Council of a conciliation procedure in budgetary matters [1975] OJ C89/1.

[21] See e.g., Interinstitutional Agreement of 20 December 1994 –Accelerated working method for official codification of legislative texts [1996] OJ C102/2; Interinstitutional Agreement of 22 December 1998 on common guidelines for the quality of drafting of Community legislation [2002] OJ C 77/1; Joint Declaration of 13 June 2007 on practical arrangements for the co-decision procedure [2007] OJ C145/2 and Interinstitutional Agreement between the European Parliament, the Council of the European Union and the European Commission on Better Law-Making [2016] OJ C123/1.

competence across three distinct Union institutions, each of which is established to defend the interests of a rival political constituency (see Chapter 4). In so doing, the EU Treaties therefore set up the EU institutions as political 'opponents' rather than classical partners.[22] As Monar notes, 'the triangulated relationship between Commission, Council and Parliament is a dynamic or – if one likes to put it negatively – unstable one in which the institutions frequently use political and legal means available to increase their impact on the decision-making process or to defend their prerogatives'.[23] Emphatically then, the adoption of inter-institutional agreements functions both to address practical gaps in the Treaty framework and manage the political tensions between rival institutions as a direct result of its basic statements on the locus of political authority.

The Joint Declaration of the European Parliament, Council and Commission on Practical Arrangements for the Codecision Procedure offers an example *in concreto*.[24] That Declaration was adopted to provide greater clarity (and guarantees) on the respective roles of the three institutions in the co-decision legislative procedure established in Article 251 EC (now Article 294 TFEU). It details the working procedures at all stages of the co-decision procedure and formalises the structural arrangements for inter-institutional co-operation. For example, in the Joint Declaration, the Council, Parliament and Commission commit to co-operate in good faith with a view to reconciling, as far as possible, their differing political positions on specific substantive matters in order to facilitate the adoption of legislative acts at the earliest possible procedural point. Furthermore, to facilitate that objective, the Joint Declaration formalises the pre-existing system of 'trialogues' as the basis for inter-institutional co-operation under the co-decision procedure.

Moreover, the text of the Joint Declaration also provides important details on the responsibly for, and procedures governing, the finalisation, signature and communication of legislative acts adopted pursuant to the ordinary legislative procedure. None of this practical context is outlined in the bare text of Article 294 TFEU. The Declaration outlines, for instance, that the legal-linguistic services of the European Parliament and Council are jointly responsible for the finalisation of the agreed

[22] Monar, 'Interinstitutional Agreements: The Phenomenon and Its New Dynamics After Maastricht', n. 14 at pp. 694–695.

[23] *Ibid.*, at p. 695.

[24] Joint Declaration on Practical Arrangements for the Codecision Procedure, n. 21.

legislative text; that, in so far as possible, mutually acceptable standard clauses shall be used in the adopted text; and that the institutions will endeavour to make joint arrangements for the signature and announcement of legislative acts adopted under Article 294 TFEU in the presence of the media.

2.2 Comitology

The Member States' establishment of the comitology regime provides a second example of constitutional supplementation with regard to the EU Treaty framework's statements on the locus of EU political authority. In summary, that regime governs the exercise of the Commission's implementing powers. It applies wherever the EU institutions confer implementing powers on the Commission in a legally binding EU Act and, further, specify that the exercise of those powers shall be subject to Member State control.

The founding EEC Treaty had little to say on the adoption of implementing measures.[25] Article 155 EEC simply provided that the Commission was to exercise the competences conferred on it by the Council for the 'implementation' of the rules laid down by the latter. Exercising its general competence to issue decisions to achieve the Treaty's objectives,[26] the Council moved early on to confer implementing powers on the Commission in a range of areas. However, in so doing, the Council introduced a new layer of institutional control beyond the text of the Treaties to monitor the Commission's implementing activities.

In more precise terms, the Council established a system of control by committees (comprised of representatives of the Member States) that evolved into the present comitology regime.[27] Article 202 EEC, added by the Single European Act, subsequently provided a stronger basis in the Treaty for the introduction of supplementary controls on the Commission in connection with the implementation of Union law. That provision empowered the Council to confer implementing powers on the Commission in legally binding Community acts – subject to 'certain

[25] See also, K. Bradley, 'Comitology and the Law: Through a Glass, Darkly' (1992) 29(4) *Common Market Law Review*, 693 at pp. 702–704.

[26] Art. 145 EEC.

[27] For discussion of the early comitology procedures, see C. Bertram, 'Decision-Making in the E.E.C.: The Management Committee Procedure' (1968) 5(3) *Common Market Law Review*, 246 and Bradley, 'Comitology and the Law: Through a Glass, Darkly', n. 25.

requirements'.[28] It provided the basis for the adoption of the First and Second Comitology Decisions, both of which were replaced, post-Lisbon, by Regulation 182/2011.[29]

Following changes introduced at Lisbon, the revised Comitology Regulation only governs the Commission's adoption of implementing acts.[30] The Commission's adoption of what are now categorised post-Lisbon as 'delegated acts' is subject to a separate system of control.[31] In summary, the Comitology Regulation establishes two specific committee procedures that are designed to empower Member States to monitor the adoption of implementing acts by the Commission.[32] Both procedures – labelled the advisory and examination procedures – redesign and replace earlier incarnations under previous Comitology Decisions.

In contrast to the Union institutions' adoption of inter-institutional agreements (Section 2.1), the introduction of the comitology framework did not emerge primarily to fill the gaps left by the text of the EU Treaties or, likewise, simply to manage co-operation between the EU institutions.[33] Rather, the establishment of the comitology regime was principally the Member States' attempt to supplement the Treaties' basic statements on the locus of EU political authority in a manner that sought expressly to enhance their influence in EU policymaking. More precisely, through the comitology framework, Member States sought to retain a degree of control over the Commission with regard to the exercise of the implementing powers delegated to it through the Council.

2.3 The Court's Jurisprudence on 'General Principles'

EU institutional practice has also supplemented the Treaty framework's basic statements on the objectives, values and limits of EU integration

[28] See now Art. 291(2) TFEU.

[29] Council Decision 87/373/EEC laying down the procedures for the exercise of implementing powers conferred on the Commission [1987] OJ L197/33 and Council Decision 1999/468/EC laying down the procedures for the exercise of implementing powers conferred on the Commission [1009] OJ L184/23, amended by Council Decision 2006/512/EC [2006] OJ L200/11.

[30] Regulation (EU) No. 182/2011 of the European Parliament and of the Council laying down the rules and general principles concerning mechanisms for control by Member States of the Commission's exercise of implementing powers [2011] OJ L 55/13.

[31] Pursuant to Art. 290 TFEU.

[32] See, respectively, Arts. 4 and 5 of Regulation (EU) No. 182/2011, n. 30.

[33] For analysis, see J. Blom-Hansen, *The EU Comitology System in Theory and Practice: Keeping an Eye on the Commission?* (London: Palgrave MacMillan, 2011).

(Constitutional Issue No. 3). Nowhere is this clearer to see than in the Court of Justice's development of the 'general principles' of Union law as additional limits on EU institutional activity.[34] These general principles encompass, *inter alia*, the protection of fundamental rights, proportionality and equal treatment, as well as a range of specific administrative and procedural rights.[35]

The founding EEC Treaty made no express reference to the protection of general principles within the (then) Community legal order. This was particularly true with respect to fundamental rights.[36] Nevertheless, and relatively early in its case law, the Court of Justice recognised the existence of 'general principles' as important normative limits on EU institutional activity. More specifically, in *Stauder* and, thereafter, *Internationale Handelsgesellschaft* and *Nold*, the Court expressly referenced 'fundamental human rights' as 'general principles' of Community law, the observance of which it would intervene to protect in the exercise of its adjudicative functions.[37] Likewise, the Court also confirmed that the internal constitutionality of EU institutional activity is conditional on respect for legal certainty, legitimate expectations and a range of other procedural rights.[38]

[34] See T. Tridimas, *The General Principles of EU Law* (2nd edn) (Oxford: Oxford University Press, 2007).

[35] See e.g., Case 11/70, *Internationale Handelsgesellschaft mbH* v. *Einfuhr- und Vorratsstelle für Getreide und Futtermittel* EU:C:1970:114 (on fundamental rights); Case 5/73, *Schlüter* v. *Hauptzollamt Lörrach* EU:C:1973:110 (on proportionality); Case 85/76, *Hoffmann-La Roche & Co. AG* v. *Commission* EU:C:1979:36 (on the right to be heard); Case 240/78, *Atalanta Amsterdam BV* v. *Produktschap voor Vee en Vlees* EU:C:1979:160 (on proportionality); Case 374/87, *Orkem* v. *Commission* EU:C:1989:387 (on self-incrimination) and Joined Cases C-13 to C-16/92, *Driessen and Others* EU:C:1993:828 (on legitimate expectations, legal certainty, proportionality and equal treatment).

[36] That omission was unremarkable in light of the founding Treaty's principal concern: the integration of Member State economies through the establishment of the Common Market. Moreover, the domestic effect of Community measures was also, under the Treaty (Art. 5 EEC), a matter for national, not Community law (Chapter 1). By implication, it remained therefore open to individuals to scrutinise Community acts indirectly through Member State systems of fundamental rights control – as indeed occurred. See e.g., Case 11/70, *Internationale Handelsgesellschaft mbH*, n. 35 at para. 2 and Case 4/73, *Nold, Kohlen- und Baustoffgroßhandlung* v. *Commission* EU:C:1974:51 at para. 12.

[37] Case 29/69, Stauder v. Stadt Ulm EU:C:1968:57; Case 11/70, *Internationale Handelsgesellschaft mbH*, n. 35 and Case 4/73, *Nold, Kohlen- und Baustoffgroßhandlung*, n. 36.

[38] See e.g., Case 12/71, *Henck* v. *Hauptzollamt Emmerich* EU:C:1971:86 (on legal certainty); Case 78/77, *Lührs* v. *Hauptzollamt Hamburg-Jonas* EU:C:1978:20 (on legitimate expectations) and Case 85/76, *Hoffmann-La Roche*, n. 35 (on the right to be heard).

The case law on the general principles of Union law is paradigmatic of constitutional supplementation. The Court's jurisprudence adds vital flesh to the bones of its basic mandate under the Treaty framework to ensure the observance of 'the law' within the EU legal order (see Article 19 TEU). That mandate entrusts the Court of Justice with a general responsibility to monitor EU institutional activity for compliance with demands of a legal order that is rooted in the rule of law – a normative value that the general principles directly serve.

Political developments have reinforced the Court's jurisprudence on general principles as an act of constitutional supplementation. This applies, in particular, with respect to the Court's establishment of a system of EU fundamental rights protection in furtherance of the Treaties' statements on the objectives, values and limits of EU integration. For example, in 1977 the Council, Parliament and Commission adopted a Joint Declaration on Fundamental Rights.[39] In that Declaration, the three institutions committed politically to respect fundamental rights under the terms of the Court's jurisprudence. The EU institutions have also made adjustments to specific instruments of secondary Union law in light of the case law on general principles. For example, in the field of competition policy, the revised Regulation on the implementation of Articles 81 and 82 of the Treaty (now Articles 101 and 102 TFEU) expressly references compliance with the principle of legal certainty and respect for the fundamental rights of defence.[40] The Court of Justice had previously recognised both principles in its case law – including in judgments interpreting the outgoing Regulation.[41]

Most strikingly, however, Member States have used the Treaty revision processes to integrate (aspects of) the Court's case law on general principles into the Treaty framework proper. This includes introducing, at Maastricht, Articles F TEU and 3b EC to formalise, respectively, fundamental rights and proportionality as 'general principles' within the Union legal order.[42] The dynamic relationship between the concept of constitutional supplementation (and constitutional contestation – see Section 3) and the process of EU Treaty amendment is considered further in Section 4.

[39] Joint Declaration of the European Parliament, Council and Commission [1977] OJ 103/1.
[40] Council Regulation (EC) No. 1/2003 of 16 December 2002 on the implementation of the rules on competition laid down in Arts. 81 and 82 of the Treaty [2003] OJ L1/1.
[41] See e.g., Case 85/76, *Hoffmann-La Roche*, n. 35 (on the right to be heard) and Case 374/87, *Orkem*, n. 35 (on self-incrimination).
[42] See now Art. 6(3) TEU and Art. 5(4) TEU respectively.

3 Constitutional Contestation

Alongside acts of constitutional supplementation (Section 2), the broader constitutional context shaping European integration is also characterised by important sites of constitutional contestation. To repeat: constitutional contestation refers to Member State and/or EU institutional activity that directly challenges the Treaty framework's statements on the three key issues for EU constitutionalism.

The process of EU integration is punctuated with numerous attempts by the EU institutions (and also Member States) to challenge the Treaties' basic statements on the key issues for EU constitutionalism. This section highlights three prominent illustrations of constitutional contestation. The chosen examples address challenges to the Treaty framework's position on the locus of EU political authority (Constitutional Issue No. 2). They also arise in the political sphere. As noted earlier, discussion of sites of contestation in this chapter is limited to analysis of *political* developments. The search for sites of constitutional contestation in connection with EU judicial activity – the focus of this book – begins in the next chapter (Chapter 3).

The first example of constitutional contestation is adoption of the 'Luxembourg Compromise' in the Community's formative years (Section 3.1). This provided for the effective continuation of unanimous decision-making in the Council beyond the end of the transitional period prescribed in the founding Treaty. The second example considers the Member States' establishment in the 1970s of the European Council as an intergovernmental forum outside the scope of the EU Treaty framework (Section 3.2). The final, and more recent illustration, examines the detail of the (now-defunct) package of measures concluded in February 2016 to renegotiate the terms of the UK's continued membership of the European Union. (Section 3.3). chosen examples all display the distinguishing features of acts of constitutional contestation: they directly challenge the Treaty framework's clear statements on the three key issues for EU constitutionalism (Chapter 1).

3.1 The Luxembourg Compromise (1966)

The 'Luxembourg Compromise' was adopted in response to the French Government's policy of non-participation in Council decision-making during the mid-1960s – commonly referred to as the politics of the 'empty chair.'[43] That policy had its origins in a political dispute over the Commission's ambitious plans to reform the agricultural policy, the Community budget and the powers of the European Parliament. The French Government, under the direction of President De Gaulle, was strongly opposed to these proposals, which it viewed as functioning to facilitate a 'power grab' by the Community institutions to the detriment of the Member States. When talks broke down, President De Gaulle withdrew the entire French delegation from Council meetings.

The French withdrawal from the Council in July 1965 posed the first major existential challenge to the continued existence of the new Community. To bring the French delegation back on board, the other Member States conceded an agreement to maintain voting by consensus in the Council *de facto* beyond the end of the transitional period prescribed in the Treaty for the completion of the Common Market (1 January 1966). That represented an important concession. The preservation of a permanent national veto in Community policymaking was a key issue for the French – notwithstanding their previous agreement to transition to majority voting as a signatory to the founding EEC Treaty. Specifically, the agreed deal, known as the Luxembourg Compromise, provided that:

> Where, in the case of decisions which may be taken by majority vote on a proposal of the Commission, very important interests of one or more partners are at stake, the Members of the Council will endeavour, within a reasonable time, to reach solutions which can be adopted by all the Members of the Council while respecting their mutual interests and those of the Community, in accordance with Article 2 of the Treaty.
>
> With regard to the preceding paragraph, the French delegation considers that where very important interests are at stake the discussion must be continued until unanimous agreement is reached.[44]

The Luxembourg Compromise is a striking early example of an act of constitutional contestation. It directly challenged the Treaty framework's statements on the locus of political authority within the (then) Community (Constitutional Issue No. 2). More precisely, the agreed changes fundamentally revised the Treaty rules on voting procedures in the Council. In particular, the EEC Treaty expressly mandated a shift

[43] See Van Middelaar, *The Passage to Europe*, n. 9 at pp. 54–72. See also, W. Nicoll, 'The Luxembourg Compromise' (1984) 23(1) *Journal of Common Market Studies*, 33 and A. Teasdale, 'The Life and Death of the Luxembourg Compromise' (1993) 31(4) *Journal of Common Market Studies*, 567.

[44] *Bulletin of the European Communities*, March 1966, 3–66, pp. 5–11.

from unanimous to qualified majority decision-making in the Council in key areas of Community policymaking at the end of the transitional period.[45] The agreement to maintain voting by consensus *de facto* beyond that period contradicted that unambiguous prescription.

In addition, the agreed changes to the voting procedures in the Council circumvented the prescribed procedures for Treaty revision. The Member States did not activate Article 236 EEC (now Article 48 TEU) formally to revise the pre-existing Treaty rules on Council voting – despite their obvious character as Treaty amendments. That, of course, would have required convening a convention to agree changes to the Treaty and, more onerously, the subsequent ratification of these changes in accordance with Member States' respective national constitutional requirements. The agreed compromise instead took the form of an 'accord' that Member States concluded *outside the Treaty framework* at an extraordinary meeting of the Council.

3.2 The Establishment of the European Council (1974)

The Member States' decision to step outside the Treaty framework in response to the 'empty chair' crisis set the tone for subsequent political acts of constitutional contestation.[46] Such acts included the establishment of the European Council in 1974 as an intergovernmental forum to shape the process of European integration.[47] The creation of that new forum (initially) outside the Treaty framework posed further direct challenges to the founding Treaty's statements on the locus of EU political authority. In particular, the establishment of the European Council outside the Treaty framework in the mid-1970s and its subsequent rise to prominence contested the role of the Council as the exclusive

[45] Art. 8 EEC.

[46] See Van Middelaar, n. 9, who argues that Member States were acting here collectively within a new and rival 'intermediary sphere' of EU integration.

[47] The Heads of States of the European Communities established the European Council in the Paris communiqueé (1974). For analysis of the European Council, see S. Bulmer and W. Wessels, *The European Council: Decision-Making in European Politics* (Easingstoke: MacMillan, 1987) and M. T. Johnston, *The European Council: Gatekeeper of the European Community* (Boulder: Westview Press, 1994). See also, more recently, W. Wessels, *The European Council* (Basingstoke: Palgrave MacMillan, 2014) and F. Eggermont, *The Changing Role of the European Council in the Institutional Framework of the European Union: Consequences for the European Integration Process* (Antwerp: Insentia, 2012).

representative of Member States' interests in the process of European integration.[48]

Under the EEC Treaty, the Council was expressly established to represent Member State interests at Union level. Its institutional competence within the Community legal order was broadly conceived. The Council's competence under the founding Treaty was not restricted to addressing technical decision-making in specific substantive areas of Community policymaking such as trade and agriculture. Rather, its attributed functions extended to include responsibility for the management of Treaty reform processes (Article 236 EEC); agreement on the accession of new Member States (Article 237 EEC); and the conclusion of international agreements between the Community and third countries (Article 238 EEC).

On each of these issues, and prior to its integration into the Treaty framework as a Union institution, the European Council interceded to define and promote Member State interests in the European integration process.[49] In their Solemn Declaration (1983), the Heads of State or Government went so far as to assert their competence – acting through the European Council – to *displace* the Council in Community decision-making.[50] Specifically, that Declaration boldly proclaimed that, 'When the European Council acts in matters within the scope of the European Communities, it does so in its capacity as the Council within the meaning of the Treaties.'[51]

The European Council has, however, never truly acted (or aspired to act) as direct substitute for the Council on matters of day-to-day policymaking. Nonetheless, its functions have included, first, providing a forum to broker agreement on specific matters of EU policy in instances where negotiations within the Council have reached deadlock.[52] Secondly, and more sensitively, the European Council has also intervened periodically to exert influence over the Union's legislative agenda – a responsibility the EU Treaty framework vests with the Commission (Article 17 TEU). The conclusions of European Council summit meetings have, for example,

[48] F. Haynes-Renshaw and H. Wallace, *The Council of Ministers* (2nd edn) (Basingstoke: Palgrave MacMillan, 2006).

[49] For detailed analysis, see Eggermont, *The Changing Role of the European Council*, n. 47.

[50] Solemn Declaration on European Union, Stuttgart, 19 June 1983, *Bulletin of the European Communities*, 1983, at pp. 6–83.

[51] *Ibid.*, at p. 25.

[52] For analysis, see e.g., Bulmer and Wessels, *The European Council: Decision-Making in European Politics*, n. 47 and Johnston, *The European Council: Gatekeeper of the European Community*, n. 47. See also, more recently, Wessels, *The European Council*, n. 47 and Eggermont, *The Changing Role of the European Council*, n. 47.

been used as a means to commit – or at least strongly nudge – the Commission to bring forward legislative proposals in particular areas.

In addition, and more significantly, the emergence of the European Council also challenged the founding Treaty's statements on the locus of political authority with regard to broader constitutional issues. For example, beginning with its Milan summit in June 1985, the European Council seized effective control of the process of Treaty revision.[53] That body established the intergovernmental conferences that paved the way for the adoption of amendments to the EU Treaty (Treaties) through the Single European Act and at Maastricht, Amsterdam, Nice and Lisbon.[54] Moreover, in each case, it was also the forum used to secure final agreement on the substance of Treaty amendments. Prior to the entry into force of the Lisbon Treaty, the EU Treaty framework, as a constitutional touchstone, made no mention of the European Council's role in Treaty revision procedures.[55] Article 236 EEC stated that:

> The Government of any Member State or the Commission may submit to the Council proposals for the revision of this Treaty.
>
> If the *Council*, after consulting the Assembly and, where appropriate, the Commission, expresses an opinion in favour of the calling of a conference of representatives of the Governments of the Member States, such conference shall be convened by the President of the Council for the purpose of determining in common agreement the amendments to be made to this Treaty.[56]

The Lisbon Treaty revised the text of that provision to reflect institutional practice. Article 48 TEU now includes, *inter alia*, express reference to the European Council's role in the management of ordinary treaty revisions. It reads:

> If the *European Council*, after consulting the European Parliament and the Commission, adopts by a simple majority a decision in favour of examining the proposed amendments, the President of the *European Council* shall convene a Convention composed of representatives of the national Parliaments, of the Heads of State or Government of the Member States, of the European Parliament and of the Commission.[57]

[53] See e.g., Van Middelaar, *The Passage to Europe*, n. 9 at pp. 100–111.

[54] See N. Nugent, *The Government and Politics of the European Union* (7th edn) (Basingstoke: Palgrave MacMillan, 2010) at p. 175.

[55] The Maastricht Treaty introduced the first express reference to the European Council's existence (though not as an institution of the Union) (Art. D TEU). It also outlined its role within specific policy fields, such as the common foreign and security policy (Art. J.3 TEU) and economic and monetary policy (Arts. 103 and 109b EC).

[56] Emphasis added.

[57] Emphasis added.

The same is also true with respect to EU accession. The founding Treaty attributed competence to manage the accession of third states to the Union principally to the Council (Article 237 EEC). The European Council nevertheless subsequently assumed effective control, using summit meetings to reach agreement on the most important aspects of applications to join the EU. This included the adoption of specific criteria for progress towards admission to the Union pursuant to Article 48 TEU – the Copenhagen criteria.[58]

3.3 The Decision on the New Settlement for the UK within the EU (2016)

The (now-defunct) Decision on the United Kingdom's renegotiated terms of EU membership offers a third, and more recent example of constitutional contestation in the political sphere.[59] It brings together neatly the illustrations in Sections 3.1 and 3.2, highlighting Member State efforts to contest the Treaties' basic statements on the locus of EU political authority (Constitutional Issue No. 2) through (1) the circumvention of the prescribed procedures for Treaty revision (Sections 3.1 and 3.2) and (2) the assertion of direct influence over the EU legislative agenda (Section 3.2).

The UK's attempt to renegotiate the terms of its continued membership of the European Union with its EU partners was motivated entirely by domestic politics. Acting on a national election manifesto commitment, the then UK Prime Minister, David Cameron, sought to secure agreement with the EU27 on a number of domestic concerns arising as a consequence of the United Kingdom's continued membership of the EU. These concerns addressed matters of economic governance, national sovereignty, competitiveness and the free movement of EU citizens and their associated rights to access social benefits within the UK.

The Heads of State or Government reached agreement on all four issues in February 2016 as part of a proposed 'New Settlement for the UK within the European Union'. That settlement took the form of a Decision of the twenty-eight Heads of State or Government, meeting

[58] Conclusions of the Presidency of the European Council, Copenhagen, 21–22 June 1993, SN 180/1/93 REV 1.

[59] Decision of the Heads of State or Government, meeting within the European Council, concerning a New Settlement for the United Kingdom within the European Union [2016] EUCO 1/16.

within the forum of the European Council.[60] It was further supplemented by a series of Draft Declarations. The entry into force of the entire package of measures and commitments was conditional on the UK deciding, by national referendum on 23 June 2016, to remain a member of the EU. The UK's narrow vote to leave the Union (and its consequential activation of the Article 50 TEU withdrawal procedure in March 2017) has rendered the measures obsolete. Nonetheless, for present purposes, they remain an important (if now legally defunct) example of constitutional contestation in the political sphere.

The challenge to the Treaty framework's core statement on the locus of EU political authority was essentially threefold. First, the conclusion of the agreed package of measures provided a further example of Member States stepping outside the EU Treaties' institutional framework to manage important aspects of the EU *acquis* – specifically, economic and monetary union, the internal market and free movement rights. The twenty-eight Heads of State or Government adopted the Draft Decision on the UK's new settlement outside the institutional framework of the Union. The Decision was agreed *within* the European Council, but not whilst the EU Heads of State or Government were sitting *as* the European Council. Accordingly, the Draft Decision was not an act of the EU institutions, but instead a Decision taken by the EU Heads of State or Government as signatories to the EU Treaties and was legally binding only as a matter of international law.

Secondly, the proposed new settlement with the United Kingdom also directly encroached on the Commission's monopoly over legislative initiation, guaranteed under the Treaties (Article 17 TEU). Specifically, the Draft Decision committed the Commission to bring forward a range of detailed legislative proposals. These proposals included significant reforms to existing EU instruments governing, *inter alia*, the free movement of workers and the rights of EU citizens. For example, the Decision outlined that, following its entry into force, the Commission would submit proposals to amend Regulation 883/2004 on the co-ordination of social security systems to permit Member States to index the payment of child benefit to the standard of living in the Member State where the child of an EU worker actually resides.[61] Similarly, the Decision directed the Commission to establish a new alert and safeguard mechanism to

[60] *Ibid.*

[61] Regulation (EC) No. 883/2004 of the European Parliament and of the Council on the coordination of social security systems [2004] OJ L 166/1.

authorise Member States to impose temporary restrictions on access to certain in-work benefits for 'newly arriving EU workers' under exceptional circumstances.

Thirdly, the Decision also provided for the circumvention of the Treaties' amendment procedures (Article 48 TEU). In particular, the EU Heads of State or Government reached agreement on the introduction of a new 'red card' procedure to enhance the role of Member State parliaments in the scrutiny of EU legislative proposals for compliance with the subsidiarity principle. In summary, the Decision established a new role for the Council in monitoring the Union legislature's adherence to that principle under the supervision of national parliaments. More precisely, it empowered the Council to discontinue the consideration of draft legislative instruments in instances where more than 55 per cent of the votes allocated to national parliaments under the pre-existing Treaty Protocol on subsidiarity were cast against that measure within twelve weeks of its transmission to them. The attribution of a new role to Member States – through the Council, but outside the Treaty framework – was designed to bolster the pre-existing 'early warning system' introduced into the EU legal order at Lisbon. It is an example of constitutional contestation *par excellence*.

4 Constitutional Supplementation, Constitutional Contestation and the Dynamics of EU Treaty Reform

Section 1 introduced the twin concepts of constitutional supplementation and constitutional contestation to theorise the gap that exists between the text of the Treaty framework and the 'real world' of EU integration. Sections 2 and 3 then applied these concepts to highlight prominent examples of acts of constitutional supplementation (Section 2) and constitutional contestation (Section 3) in evolution of European integration. The existence of both categories of act serves to broaden the political and legal context structuring EU integration beyond the bare text of the Treaties. That process is observable at the level of doctrinal analysis through examination of legal materials; in other words, without any need to delve into studies of empirical practice – the 'dark matter' of EU integration. It is also not unique to the Union legal order. The concepts of constitutional supplementation and constitutional contestation may be applied to any legal order that is based on a founding text, including international treaties.

This section explores the relationship between acts of constitutional supplementation and constitutional contestation and the dynamics of EU Treaty reform. Section 4.1 argues that, as constitutional touchstones, the EU Treaties establish a clear pathway to normalise sites of constitutional supplementation and constitutional contestation through Treaty amendment. The integration of the Court's case law on fundamental rights as 'general principles' of Union law (Section 2.3) into the Treaty framework provides one example with reference to constitutional supplementation. Similarly, the Single European Act resolved, to a great extent, the function of the Luxembourg Compromise as an act of constitutional contestation with regard to the Treaties' position on the locus of EU political authority (Constitutional Issue No. 2) (Section 3.1).

Relatedly, this section also highlights the Court of Justice's important intermediary role in the determination of the boundary between acts of constitutional supplementation and constitutional contestation (Section 4.2). Under the Treaty framework, the Court is entrusted with the responsibility to monitor the internal constitutionality of all EU institutional activity for compliance with the EU Treaties as constitutional touchstones (Chapter 1). Exercising that responsibility, the Court has been requested, *inter alia*, to determine whether specific measures, such as the Council's introduction of the comitology procedures (Section 3.2.), constitute acts of constitutional supplementation or constitutional contestation.

4.1 Normalisation through Treaty Amendment

Member States have made routine use of the Treaty amendment procedures as a means to normalise specific acts of constitutional supplementation and/or constitutional contestation with the Treaty framework. With regard, first, to constitutional supplementation (Section 2), Member States agreed at Maastricht to normalise the Court's jurisprudence on fundamental rights as 'general principles' of Union law. This was achieved initially through the integration of Article F(2) into the Treaty framework. That provision outlined that, 'The Union shall respect fundamental rights, as guaranteed by the European Convention for the Protection of Human Rights and Fundamental Freedoms signed in Rome on 4 November 1950 and *as they result from the constitutional traditions common to the Member States, as general principles of Community law.*'[62]

[62] Emphasis added. See now Art. 6 TEU.

In a similar manner, Member States have integrated into the Treaty framework the substance of specific inter-institutional agreements as paradigm examples of acts of constitutional supplementation (Section 2.1). For example, the Treaty of Nice adopted, in modified form, the procedure for the censure of individual commissioners that was negotiated between the European Parliament and the Commission by way of a Framework Agreement in 2000.[63] Similarly, as Driessen highlights, the right to petition the European parliament in Article 227 TFEU has its origins in an inter-institutional agreement, from where it was subsequently integrated into the EU Treaties.[64] The same is true of the European Parliament's right to ask questions of the Council or make recommendations to it.[65] As these examples clearly demonstrate, the adoption of specific inter-institutional agreements as acts of constitutional supplementation has frequently served to provide the impetus for subsequent Treaty revision.[66]

The dynamic is no different with respect to acts of constitutional contestation (Section 3). For example, as signatories to the Single European Act, Member States reached formal agreement on the (re)introduction of qualified majority voting *de jure* and *de facto* in key areas of EU policymaking.[67] Whilst leaving the Luxembourg Comprise formally in place, this served effectively to reinstate the Treaty rules on qualified majority voting in the Council – as the founding Treaty prescribed. Similarly, Member States have revised the EU Treaties progressively to normalise the European Council's role within the EU legal order. This includes, for example, defining its institutional functions and competences, voting procedures, the legal status of its decisions and its involvement in the management of Treaty amendment and accession procedures. This process of normalisation culminated at Lisbon, where

63 Framework Agreement on Relations between the European Parliament and the Commission [2001] OJ C-121/122 at para. 10 and Art. 217(4) EC respectively. Note, however, that Art. 217(4) EC was repealed at Lisbon.

64 Driessen, *Interinstitutional Conventions in EU Law*, n. 14, at pp. 270–271.

65 *Ibid*. See, also pre-Lisbon, Art. 39(3) EU.

66 See Driessen, 'Interinstitutional Conventions and Institutional Balance', n. 14 at pp. 555–559 and A. Maurer, D. Kietz and C. Völkel, 'Interinstitutional Agreement in the CFSP: Parliamentarization through the Back Door?' (2005) 10(2) *European Foreign Affairs Review*, 175.

67 See Art. 7 SEA (revising Art. 149 EEC) and Art. 18 SEA (introducing Art. 110a EEC).

the European Council achieved formal recognition within the Treaty framework as an institution of the Union.

Of course, there is nothing to guarantee a neat linear progression from act of constitutional supplementation or constitutional contestation to normalisation with the Treaty framework. Everything hinges on the Member States reaching agreement to amend the Treaties. That is no easy task. As a matter of practical politics, the barriers to normalisation have increased significantly in recent years. First, EU enlargement now demands that twenty-eight, rather than six, twelve or fifteen Member States reach unanimous agreement on amendments to the Treaty framework. Secondly, progress towards normalisation is now increasingly conditioned by *national* constitutional practices. Under Article 48 TEU, each Member State must ratify the agreed Treaty amendments in accordance with its respective national constitutional requirements. Increasingly, that requires Member States to engage with, and ultimately satisfy, a specific range of domestic constitutional limits on EU Treaty reform. These include 'referendum locks' and/or other enhanced mechanisms for legislative and judicial controls on Treaty amendment.[68]

4.2 The Court of Justice as Intermediary

The Court of Justice plays an important intermediary role in determining the relationship between the EU Treaty framework as constitutional touchstone and the broader constitutional context that structures EU integration. Pursuant to Article 263 TFEU and Article 267 TFEU, the Court is charged with the responsibility to monitor the internal constitutionality of all EU institutional activity for compliance with the Treaty framework as constitutional touchstone.[69] In addition, the Court may also be called upon (at the request of Member States or EU institutions) to rule on the compatibility with the EU Treaties of international agreements concluded between the EU and third countries and/or international organisations. Where the Court concludes that the relevant

[68] For analysis of domestic judicial challenges, see recently, P. J. Castillo Ortiz, *EU Treaties and the Judicial Politics of National Courts: A Law and Politics Approach* (London: Routledge, 2016). For an example of enhanced Member State legislative controls, see e.g., the UK's *European Union Act 2011* and M. Gordon and M. Dougan, 'The United Kingdom's European Union Act 2011: "Who Won the Bloody War Anyway?"' (2013) 37(1) *European Law Review*, 3.

[69] Art. 218(11) TFEU.

agreement is not in conformity with the EU Treaty framework, that agreement may not enter into force unless it is amended, or the Treaties are revised through Article 48 TEU.[70]

The Court of Justice is frequently engaged to rule on whether specific EU and/or Member State measures are *intra vires* as acts of constitutional supplementation or *ultra vires* as acts of constitutional contestation. At times, the Court's intermediary role in determining the boundaries between acts of constitutional supplementation and constitutional contestation has been tested to its limits under extreme economic and political pressure (see further Section 5.3).[71] This section highlights two less charged, though no less significant, examples. The first addresses challenges to the compatibility with the Treaty framework of the comitology regime (Section 2.2).[72] The second reviews the Court's case law on the related issue of delegated powers.[73]

In *Köster*, the Court was requested to assess the compatibility of the comitology regime with the EU Treaty framework. More precisely, it was asked to determine whether the Council's introduction of the committee procedures in a series of early Community Regulations in the field of the common agricultural policy distorted the EEC Treaty's basic statements on the locus of EU political authority (Constitutional Issue No. 2). As previously highlighted (see Section 2.1), Member States had established these procedures, beyond the text of the (now) Treaties, to monitor (and retain control over) the Commission's activities where the Council had agreed to confer implementing powers on that institution.

The Court's conclusions in *Köster* confirmed the status of the comitology procedures as an act of constitutional supplementation. On its assessment:

> The so-called management committee procedure forms part of the detailed rules to which the Council may legitimately subject a delegation of power to the Commission ... The function [of that committee] is to ensure permanent consultation in order to guide the Commission in the exercise of the powers conferred on it by the Council and to enable the latter to substitute its own action for that of the Commission ... Consequently, and *without distorting the Community structure*

[70] See recently, e.g., Opinion 2/13, *Draft Agreement on Accession of the EU to the European Convention on Human Rights* EU:C:2014:2454.

[71] See esp. Case C-370/12, *Pringle* v. *Government of Ireland and Others* EU:C:2012:756 and Case C-62/14, *Gauweiler and Others* v. *Deutscher Bundestag* EU:C:2015:400.

[72] See e.g., Case 25/70, *Einfuhr- und Vorratsstelle für Getreide und Futtermittel* v. *Köster and Berodt & Co* EU:C:1970:115 and Case 5/77, *Tedeschi* v. *Denkavit Commerciale s.r.l.* EU:C:1977:144.

[73] See e.g., Case 9/56, *Meroni* v. *High Authority* EU:C:1958:7; Case 98/80, *Romano* v. *Institut national d'assurance maladie-invalidité* EU:C:1981:104 and Case C-270/12, *United Kingdom* v. *Parliament and Council (Short Selling)* EU:C:2014:18.

and the institutional balance, the management committee machinery enables the Council to delegate to the Commission an implementing power of appreciable scope, subject to its power to take the decision itself if necessary.[74]

With regard to the second example, on the related matter of delegated powers, the Court reached the same conclusion in *Meroni*.[75] In that case, the applicant, a private undertaking, contested the High Authority's delegation to private agencies of its competence to administer a Community scrap equalisation scheme. In its response, the Court ruled that, provided certain conditions were met, the Commission was permitted to delegate specific functions to administrative bodies and outside agencies. In other words, on those terms, the delegation of these powers constituted an act of constitutional supplementation and was, hence, *intra vires*.

The Court's decision in *Meroni* established important guidelines with respect to the delegation of EU political authority.[76] In summary, it ruled that the (then) Treaty sanctioned only the delegation of defined executive powers, the exercise of which can, therefore, be subject to strict review in light of objective criteria determined by the delegating authority.[77] By contrast, the (then) Treaty precluded the delegation of broad discretionary powers that make it possible for the beneficiary to replace the choices of the delegator within its own.[78] This basic dividing line between *intra vires* (constitutional supplementation) and *ultra vires* (constitutional contestation) measures in the context of delegated powers remains largely unchanged.[79]

5 Eurozone Crisis Management: A Study in Constitutional Contestation in the Political Sphere

The Eurozone sovereign debt crisis provides some of the clearest illustrations of acts of constitutional contestation ever seen in European integration – at least in the sphere of EU political activity. This section considers the responses of both Member States and EU institutions to that crisis as a case study in constitutional contestation.

74 Case 25/70, *Köster*, n. 72 at para. 9 (emphasis added). See also, Case 5/77, *Denkavit*, n. 72.
75 See e.g., Case 9/56, *Meroni*, n. 73; Case 98/80, *Romano*, n. 73 and Case C-270/12, *United Kingdom* v. *Parliament and Council (Short Selling)* EU:C:2014:18.
76 See *United Kingdom* v. *Parliament and Council (Short Selling)*, n. 75 at paras. 41–42.
77 Case 9/56, *Meroni*, n. 73 at pp .152–154.
78 *Ibid.*
79 See *United Kingdom* v. *Parliament and Council (Short Selling)*, n. 75.

Section 5.1 summarises the background to the Eurozone crisis. It also outlines the key political initiatives enacted in response. The solutions adopted fall into three broad categories: (1) interventions to stabilise the Eurozone; (2) action to enhance budgetary surveillance and the coordination of national economic policies; and (3) agreement on a programme of regulatory reform.[80] Section 5.2 assesses how far these solutions comply with the Treaty framework's basic statements on the three key issues for EU constitutionalism. In summary, analysis of the political responses to the Eurozone crisis exposes the existence of key acts of constitutional contestation with respect to the Treaty framework's statements on the locus of EU political authority (Constitutional Issue No. 2) and the objectives, values and limits of European integration (Constitutional Issue No. 3).

The first site of constitutional contestation identified concerns (Eurozone) Member States' use of intergovernmental agreements *outside the framework of Union law* as a means to reform key features of EMU that remain governed *within* that framework (Section 5.2.1). The use of extra-EU intergovernmental Treaties to reform the basic architecture of EMU amounts to an effective circumvention of the prescribed procedures for Treaty reform, most notably Article 48 TEU. As such, it directly contests the Treaty framework's clear statements on the locus of EU political authority with specific regard to constituent authority (Constitutional Issue No. 2).

The second site of constitutional contestation centres on the specific stabilisation measures adopted in response to the crisis (Section 5.2.2). More precisely, it relates to the European Central Bank's adoption of non-standard measures to increase financial liquidity, notably its programmes of buying Eurozone government bonds. It also encompasses the (Eurozone) Member States' establishment of the European Stability Mechanism as a permanent financial assistance scheme to manage future sovereign debt crises within the Euro area. In short, both measures directly challenge the Treaties' explicit – and unaltered – position on the core objectives, values and limits of EU integration (Constitutional Issue No. 3) in the sphere of the Economic and Monetary Union.[81]

Member States and EU institutions are fully aware of the existence of both sites of constitutional contestation. This applies, *a fortiori*, with

[80] The typology is borrowed from A. Hinarejos, *The Eurozone Crisis in Constitutional Perspective* (Oxford: Oxford University Press, 2015).

[81] *Ibid.*, at p. 19 and 22.

regard to the use of intergovernmental agreements *outside the framework of Union law* to reform key features of EMU that remain governed *within* that framework. The decision to circumvent the Treaty amendment procedures was not a free choice, but forced upon (Eurozone) Member States at the refusal of two Member States to sanction Treaty reform. Section 5.3 points to subsequent political efforts to normalise both sites of constitutional contestation with the Treaty framework as constitutional touchstone. Finally, Section 5.4 considers the Court's important contribution as intermediary in the interim period (see Section 4.2). In summary, the Court has been repeatedly requested to determine whether specific political measures adopted in response to the Eurozone crisis are *intra vires* as acts of constitutional supplementation or *ultra vires* as acts of constitutional contestation.

5.1 The Eurozone Crisis: Background and Political Responses

The Eurozone crisis was triggered by the global financial crisis that started in 2007. In the wake of that crisis, the governments of several Eurozone countries were pushed to breaking point as financial markets expressed concerns with the health of their respective underlying economies and increased their costs of borrowing above serviceable levels. Unable to refinance public debt, the governments of (particularly) Greece, Ireland and Portugal faced a sovereign debt crisis, the scale of which threatened the very stability of the entire Eurozone area.

The response to the Eurozone sovereign debt crisis has been multidimensional and engaged a broad range of institutional actors.[82] The protagonists have included not only the EU institutions and Member States (principally Eurozone States), but also other international actors such as the International Monetary Fund. The solutions adopted fall into three broad categories.[83] First, interventions were made to stabilise the Eurozone. These took the form of non-standard measures to provide

[82] For legal analysis, F. Amtenbrink, 'The Metamorphosis of European Economic and Monetary Union' in A. Arnull and D. Chalmers (eds.), *The Oxford Handbook of European Union Law* (Oxford: Oxford University Press, 2015); K. Tuori and K. Tuori, *The Eurozone Crisis: A Constitutional Analysis* (Cambridge: Cambridge University Press, 2014) and Hinajeros, *The Eurozone Crisis in Constitutional Perspective*, n. 80. See also, the Report of the House of Lords, European Union Committee, *The Euro Area Crisis*, 25th Report of Session 2010–12, HL Paper 260.

[83] The typology is borrowed from Hinajeros, *The Eurozone Crisis in Constitutional Perspective*, n. 80, chapter 3.

immediate liquidity to the Eurozone economies in trouble, coupled with the establishment of new mechanisms to provide future financial assistance.[84] Secondly, the Member States reached agreement on a stricter framework for budgetary surveillance and the co-ordination of national economic policies within the Eurozone.[85] The absence of strict rules, coupled with Eurozone States' failure to adhere to the applicable rules in practice, had directly contributed to the Eurozone crisis. Thirdly, the Member States reached agreement on a programme of key regulatory reforms, including the creation of an EU Banking Union.[86]

The solutions adopted represent a fundamental shift in approach to the governance of the Eurozone area.[87] In its original design, EMU was strictly rule-based, involving only the transfer of competences necessary to establish a currency Union between participating Member States. Eurozone States retained full fiscal autonomy, and the possibility of financial assistance (bailouts) at EU level was expressly excluded. As Hinajeros observes:

> The original EMU was rule-based . . . the main underlying approach was not to transfer policy-making powers and discretion to the EU level, but to impose certain limits on those policy-making powers and discretion at national level.[88]
>
> At its inception, EMU had the makings of an extremely decentralized system of fiscal governance, where the units maintain full fiscal sovereignty. The possibility of a bailout from the centre was explicitly excluded in the Treaty. The units maintained their full taxing powers and they were not dependent on transfers from the centre.[89]

The tripartite approach to the Eurozone crisis (stabilisation, enhanced surveillance and regulatory reform) has transformed the basic operating system of EMU governance. The introduction of stabilisation measures

[84] These measures included the European Central Bank's indirect purchasing of government bonds through its 2010 Securities Markets Programme and the announcement of its Outright Monetary Transaction scheme. Eurozone Member States also established the European Financial Stability Mechanism and, thereafter, the European Financial Stability Facility. For discussion, see Hinajeros, *The Eurozone Crisis in Constitutional Perspective*, n. 80 at pp. 16–29.

[85] See e.g., the 'Six Pack' and, subsequently, 'Two Pack' of EU legislative measures enacted in response to the crisis, together with the Treaty on Stability, Coordination and Governance signed in 2012. For discussion, see Hinajeros, *The Eurozone Crisis in Constitutional Perspective*, n. 80 at pp. 29–40.

[86] *Ibid.*, at pp. 40–48.

[87] See Tuori and Tuori, *The Eurozone Crisis: A Constitutional Analysis*, n. 82.

[88] Hinajeros, *The Eurozone Crisis in Constitutional Perspective*, n. 80 at p. 7.

[89] *Ibid.*, at pp. 54–55.

(liquidity injections and financial assistance mechanisms) challenges one of the cornerstones of EMU: the prohibition on the provision of financial assistance to Eurozone States from the centre. Likewise reforms to bolster the framework for budgetary surveillance and the co-ordination of national (Eurozone) economies at Union level have effected significant transfers of new policymaking powers to EU institutions. In particular, the role of the European Central Bank has shifted from that of a technical, non-political actor responsible for EU monetary policy, to an institution that now enjoys a significant degree of influence over national economic policies.[90]

5.2 The Eurozone Crisis and Constitutional Contestation

The detailed changes to EMU governance, together with their broader implications, are widely explored in the literature.[91] This chapter is specifically concerned with the extent to which the agreed reforms to EMU governance provide further examples of acts of constitutional contestation in the political sphere. In other words, how far do these solutions comply with the Treaty framework's basic statements on the three key issues for EU constitutionalism?

This section identifies two specific acts of constitutional contestation in that regard. The first concerns (Eurozone) Member States' use of intergovernmental agreements outside the framework of Union law as a means to reform key features of EMU that remain governed within that framework (Section 5.2.1). The second centres on the specific stabilisation measures adopted in response to the crisis (Section 5.2.2). These two sets of acts contest, respectively, the Treaty framework's statements on the locus of EU political authority (Constitutional Issue No. 2) and the objectives, values and limits of European integration (Constitutional Issue No. 3).

5.2.1 *Challenges to the Locus of EU Political Authority*

The first example of constitutional contestation addresses (Eurozone) Member States' use of intergovernmental agreements outside the

[90] *Ibid.*, at p. 9.

[91] See e.g., J. A. Caporaso and M. Rhodes (eds.), *Political and Economic Dynamics of the Eurozone Crisis* (Oxford: Oxford University Press, 2016); J. Pisani-Ferry, *The Euro Crisis and Its Aftermath* (Oxford: Oxford University Press, 2014) and T. Beukers, 'The New ECB and its Relationship with the Eurozone Member States: Between Central Bank Independence and Central Bank Intervention' (2013) 50(6) *Common Market Law Review*, 1759.

framework of Union law as a means to reform key features of EMU that formally remain governed within that framework. In response to the crisis, these Member States reached agreement on two key international Treaties. The first of these, the Treaty establishing the European Stability Mechanism (ESM), created, by means of an ordinary international Treaty, a new permanent financial assistance mechanism to address future debt crises.[92] The second Treaty negotiated outside the EU legal framework, the Treaty on Stability, Coordination and Governance in the Economic and Monetary Union (TSCG), is less significant in practical terms.[93] That Treaty addresses the second of the three responses to the Eurozone crisis: budgetary surveillance and the co-ordination of national economic policies. Its most significant feature is arguably the inclusion of an obligation on the part of Eurozone Member States to enshrine into national law a commitment fully to respect and adhere to the rules on budgetary discipline.

The use of extra-EU intergovernmental Treaties to reform the basic architecture of EMU amounts to an effective circumvention of the prescribed procedures for Treaty reform, most notably Article 48 TEU. As Craig notes, with specific reference to the TSCG:

> The Lisbon Treaty provides clear rules on amendment in art. 48 TEU, with unanimity being required for change. There are in addition detailed Treaty provisions concerning enhanced co-operation in art.20 TEU and arts 326–334 TFEU, specifying the applicable rules if some but not all states wish to do certain things under the Lisbon Treaty. No attempt was made to use the rules on enhanced co-operation to attain the ends contained in the TSCG. The EU Summit in December 2011 attempted to change the Lisbon Treaty, but failed because of the UK veto.[94]

Tomkin criticises the political decision to step outside the EU Treaty framework in order to secure key reforms to EMU governance in even stronger terms. In his view:

92 Under the ESM Treaty, Eurozone governments unable to refinance public debt under workable market conditions are able to access financial assistance, subject to strict conditionality. To access ESM support, recipient States must sign a Memorandum of Understanding prepared by the Commission, together with the European Central Bank and, where possible, the International Monetary Fund. These instruments are used to secure (or better: impose) economic reform on the Member State concerned – typically mandating strict cutbacks to public spending and programmes of privatisation.

93 For analysis, see e.g., P. Craig, 'The Stability, Coordination, and Governance Treaty: Principle, Politics and Pragmatism' (2012) 37(3) *European Law Review*, 231.

94 *Ibid.*, at p. 238.

> The decision to establish the ESM [Treaty] outside the EU legal order was intended to permit Member States to circumvent provisions prohibiting or restricting the granting of financial assistance by Member States or by the ECB. In addition, it facilitated Member States to side-step the requirement to amend the Union Treaties using the ordinary revision procedure. Taken cumulatively, the use of international agreement to bypass or circumvent provisions of Union law may be regarded as challenging the normative coherence of the Union legal order.[95]

Stepping outside the Treaty framework directly contests the Treaty framework's clear statements on the locus of political authority (Constitutional Issue No. 2) with regard not only to constituent authority. It also challenges the EU Treaties' position on the locus of EU political authority for Union policymaking in the field of EMU.

In particular, the European Parliament has emerged from the crisis as the greatest loser in institutional terms. Under the EU Treaties, the European Parliament is an integral part of the institutional framework structuring Union policymaking in the field of EMU. At the very least, it enjoys rights to be consulted on specific matters of policy. All that changed with (Eurozone) Member States' decision to reform the fundamentals of EMU through two intergovernmental treaties. As Dawson and De Witte argue, Almost all of the reforms proposed in the wake of the [Eurozone] crisis exclude the [European Parliament] to varying degrees, either by establishing procedures where its role is merely consultative, or by channeling important decisions outside the official structure of the Union altogether, relegating the role of the [European Parliament] to that of mere observer.'[96]

In addition, recourse to international instruments to reform EMU has also restructured the balance of policymaking power between Eurozone Member States *inter se*.[97] Nowhere is this clearer to see than in changes to the weighting of individual (Eurozone) Member States' voting rights. Under the ESM Treaty, for example, voting rights are allocated on the basis of capital contributions. This greatly enhances the influence of larger, richer (and typically creditor) Eurozone States over smaller States (typically recipients of financial assistance). Thus, under the ESM Treaty,

[95] J. Tomkin, 'Contradiction, Circumvention and Conceptual Gymnastics: The Impact of the Adoption of the ESM Treaty on the State of European Democracy' (2013) 14 *German Law Journal*, 169.

[96] M. Dawson and F. de Witte, 'Constitutional Balance in the EU after the Euro-Crisis' (2013) 76(5) *Modern Law Review*, 817 at p. 833.

[97] Dawson and de Witte describe this as adjusting the 'spatial balance' of power between Member States. Dawson and de Witte, 'Constitutional Balance in the EU after the Euro-Crisis', n. 96, at p. 833.

Germany holds 27 per cent of all voting rights, compared with a share of 8.5 per cent of voting when acting through the Council (i.e., within the EU).[98]

5.2.2 *Challenges to Objectives, Values and Limits of EU Integration*

The second site of constitutional contestation identified in this section concerns the specific stabilisation measures adopted in response to the crisis. More precisely, these measures include the European Central Bank's adoption of non-standard instruments to increase financial liquidity, notably its programmes of buying Eurozone government bonds. They also encompass the Eurozone Member States' establishment of the European Stability Mechanism as a permanent financial assistance scheme to manage future sovereign debt crises within the Euro area. Both sets of reforms directly challenge the Treaties' explicit – and unaltered – position on the core objectives, values and limits of EU integration (Constitutional Issue No. 3) in the sphere of EMU.[99]

In specific terms, the Treaty framework continues, as before the crisis, to maintain a robust stance on the underlying principle of full Member State fiscal responsibility. Articles 123 and 125 TFEU are clear on that point. The former provision prohibits the European System of Central Banks (ESCB), composed of the ECB and national central banks, from providing, *inter alia*, Eurozone governments with overdrafts or 'any other type of credit facilities'. That provision also prohibits ESCB members from purchasing debt instruments from Eurozone governments directly. Article 125 TFEU details the Union's 'no-bailout clause'. It provides, in equally express terms, that neither the Union nor the Member States shall be liable to assume the financial commitments of, *inter alia*, central governments of any of the other Member States.

The suite of stabilisation measures adopted in response to the Eurozone crisis is difficult to square with the Treaty framework's statements on the limits of Union competence in EMU policymaking. Article 123 TFEU is strikingly clear on the Treaties' prohibition on the provision of financial support to Member State governments through credit facilities or debt purchasing. The 'no-bailout' clause in Article 125 TFEU serves only to reinforce further the Treaty framework's baseline position on the

[98] *Ibid.*, at p. 839.

[99] See also, e.g., Hinajeros, *The Eurozone Crisis in Constitutional Perspective*, n. 80 at pp. 19 and 22.

exclusive responsibility of individual Member States for their respective financial liabilities.

5.3 Towards Normalisation with the EU Treaty Framework

Several clear attempts have been made to bridge the gaps that exist between the EU Treaty framework as constitutional touchstone and the substance and process of EMU reform. First, in March 2015, all twenty-eight Member States reached an agreement to revise Article 136 TFEU using the simplified revision procedure in an effort to address the tension between the Treaties' 'no-bailout' clause and the Eurozone States' move to establish a new financial assistance mechanism outside the Treaty framework through the ESM Treaty.[100] A new paragraph was inserted into that provision. It now includes reference to the fact that, 'The Member States whose currency is the euro may establish a stability mechanism to be activated if indispensable to safeguard the stability of the euro area as a whole. The granting of any required financial assistance will be made subject to strict conditionality.' Secondly, the principal instruments of EMU reform established outside the EU legal order anticipate their eventual normalisation within the Treaty framework. The resolution of specific points of political contestation was, for instance, engineered into the TSCG. Article 16 of that Treaty provides that its substance shall be integrated into the EU Treaty framework within, at most, a period of five years from the date of its entry into force; in other words, by 1 January 2018. The ESM Treaty, by contrast, does not expressly anticipate its normalisation within the EU Treaty framework. Nonetheless, that eventuality is highly probable as part of the next major round of Treaty reform.

5.4 The Court's Role as Intermediary in Eurozone Crisis Management

In the interim period, it has ultimately fallen to the Court of Justice to adjudicate on the internal constitutionality of both the substance and process of EMU reform.[101] Unsurprisingly, in light of the extreme political

[100] Decision 2011/199/EU amending Article 136 of the Treaty on the Functioning of the European Union with regard to a stability mechanism for Member States whose currency is the euro [2011] OJ L 91/1.

[101] For legal analysis, see Tuori and Tuori, *The Eurozone Crisis: A Constitutional Analysis*, n. 82, chapter 5 and Hinajeros, *The Eurozone Crisis in Constitutional Perspective*, n. 80, chapter 8.

and economic realities, the Court has fought extremely hard to iron out the two key sites of constitutional contestation outlined in Sections 5.2.1 and 5.2.2 through a highly considered approach to judicial interpretation.[102]

First, in *Pringle*, the Court of Justice – sitting as the Full Court – adopted a teleological approach to square the introduction of the new European Stability Mechanism with the terms of the 'no-bailout' clause in Article 125 TFEU.[103] It concluded that the aim of Article 125 TFEU was to ensure that Member States adhere to budgetary discipline as a means to achieve a 'higher objective', namely ensuring the financial stability of the Eurozone area as a whole.[104] Accordingly, the 'no-bailout' clause prohibited the provision of financial assistance to Eurozone States only where this diminished the recipient State's incentives to conduct sound budgetary policy.[105] This, the Court ruled, was not so with respect to the European Stability Mechanism, which attached strict conditionality requirements to the provision of financial assistance as a means to ensure that recipient States adhered to (or more accurately: implemented) sound budgetary policies.[106]

The referring Court in *Pringle* also requested the Court of Justice to consider the constitutionality of the Eurozone States' decision to establish the new Stability Mechanism outside the EU Treaty framework. The applicant, a member of the Irish Parliament, argued, *inter alia*, that the ESM Treaty was incompatible with the EU Treaties on the grounds that its substance directly affected matters of monetary policy within the Eurozone – an area of exclusive Union competence under the EU Treaties.[107] Specifically, the new stability mechanism encroached on the European Central Bank's 'exclusive power to regulate money supply within the euro area'. In addition, the provision of financial assistance under the

[102] See e.g., V. Borger, 'The ESM and the European Court's Predicament in *Pringle*' (2013) 14(1) *German Law Journal*, 113 at p. 114 and Hinajeros, *The Eurozone Crisis in Constitutional Perspective*, n. 80, chapter 8.

[103] Case C-370/12, *Pringle*, n. 71 at paras. 133–147. See also, Hinajeros, *The Eurozone Crisis in Constitutional Perspective*, n. 80 at pp. 125–6 and S. Adam and F. J. M. Parras, 'The European Stability Mechanism through the Legal Meanderings of the Union's Constitutionalism: Comment on *Pringle*' (2013) 38(6) *European Law Review*, 848 at pp. 860–861.

[104] At para. 135. For strong criticism, see esp., G. Beck, 'The Legal Reasoning of the Court of Justice and the Euro Crisis – the Flexibility of the Court's Cumulative Approach and the *Pringle* Case' (2013) *Maastricht Journal of European and Comparative Law*, 645. See also, G. Beck, *The Legal Reasoning of the Court of Justice of the EU* (Oxford: Hart Publishing, 2014) at p. 449.

[105] At para. 137.

[106] At paras. 138–147.

[107] See Art. 3(1)(c) TFEU.

ESM Treaty also impacted directly on inflation (and thus price stability), the management of which was again entrusted solely to the ECB under the EU Treaties.[108]

The Court of Justice rejected the applicant's arguments. It ruled that financial assistance under the ESM Treaty constituted an act of *economic*, not monetary policy. According to the Court:

> it is not the purpose of the ESM to maintain price stability [defined as the objective of EU *monetary* policy], but rather to meet the financing requirements of ESM Members, namely Member States whose currency is the euro, who are experiencing or are threatened by severe financing problems, if indispensable to safeguard the financial stability of the euro area as a whole and of its Member States.[109]

That resolved the thorny issue of Union competence, neutralising the applicant's attempt to have the ESM Treaty ruled incompatible with the EU Treaty framework on the grounds that it encroached on an area of exclusive EU responsibility (monetary policy). Of course, the Court of Justice accepted that the provision of financial assistance under the ESM Treaty might impact on the rate of inflation within the Euro area.[110] However, any such impact was considered an *indirect* consequence of granting financial assistance as an instrument of economic policy.[111]

Finally, the Court also rejected the applicant's arguments that the European Stability Mechanism affected other specific provisions of the EU Treaty framework. This included, in particular, the EU institutions' existing, limited competence under Article 122(2) TFEU to provide *ad hoc* financial assistance to Member States when it is found that a Member State is in difficulties or is seriously threatened with severe difficulties caused by natural disasters or exceptional occurrences beyond its control.[112] It also referenced the provisions on enhanced co-operation in Article 20(1) TEU, which, as Craig noted, could arguably have provided a legal basis to achieve the objectives of the TSCG *within* the existing EU Treaty framework.[113] In summary, the Full Court was satisfied that the conclusion and ratification of the ESM Treaty outside the framework of EU law did not jeopardise in any way the objectives

108 See Arts. 127(1) and 282(1)/(2) TFEU.
109 At para. 96 (emphasis added).
110 At para. 97.
111 *Ibid.*
112 At paras. 115–122.
113 Craig, 'The Stability, Coordination, and Governance Treaty: Principle, Politics and Pragmatism', n. 93 at p. 238. At paras. 166–169.

of the EU Treaties or prevent the Union institutions from exercising their competences thereunder.[114]

More recently, in *Gauweiler*, the Court of Justice was requested to review the constitutionality of another key component of EMU reform: the ECB's programme of 'Outright Monetary Transfers' (OMT). Briefly summarised, the OMT programme provides for the ECB to purchase – in unlimited quantities – sovereign bonds on secondary markets at critical junctures as a means to prevent (Eurozone) Member State governments risking default. Under the terms of the OMT programme, which was announced by the ECB in 2012 by way of press release, the purchase of sovereign bonds on secondary markets is subject to specific conditions. These technical features relate, *inter alia*, to conditionality, coverage, creditor treatment and transparency.

In the proceedings giving rise to the reference to the Court of Justice, the applicant, a German politician, and adjoining parties asserted that the ECB's OMT programme was incompatible with the EU Treaties in two principal respects. First, it was argued that, by establishing the OMT programme, the ECB had exceeded its strict mandate under the Treaty framework to manage *monetary*, not economic policy within the Eurozone. That first ground of challenge has much in common with the applicant's argument in *Pringle* concerning the compatibility of the European Stability Mechanism with the EU Treaties' 'no-bailout' clause (Article 125 TFEU). Secondly, the applicants argued that the OMT programme infringed Article 123(1) TFEU – prohibiting the European System of Central Banks (ESCB) from providing Eurozone governments with overdrafts or 'any other type of credit facilities'.

As before in *Pringle*, the Grand Chamber worked extremely hard to square circles through considered judicial interpretation to uphold the validity of the OMT programme.[115] On the first issue – the character of ECB bond buying – the Court reached the opposite conclusion to that in *Pringle* with regard to the character of the contested measures. Specifically, it ruled that the OMT programme was an instrument of monetary, not economic policy.[116] That determination was essential to support the conclusion that the OMT programme was compatible with EU Treaties. As an instrument of monetary policy, the establishment of that programme therefore fell within the exclusive competence of the Union and of the ECB in particular. Recalling its earlier conclusions in *Pringle*,

[114] At paras. 106, 114, 122, 128, 147, 152 and 169.
[115] Case C-62/14, *Gauweiler and Others*, n. 71.
[116] At paras. 46–65.

the Court was clear that this finding was unaffected by the possible indirect effects of the OMT scheme on economic policy within the Euro area – a sphere of activity for which Member States continue to retain principal responsibility under the Treaty framework.[117]

Furthermore, the Grand Chamber upheld the conditionality requirement attached to the purchase of bonds by the ECB. Under the OMT programme the ECB's purchase of government bonds on secondary markets was conditional on the beneficiary Member State complying with an agreed macroeconomic adjustment programme. In *Pringle*, the Full Court had ruled that scheme a matter of economic, not monetary policy in an effort to resolve the tension between the 'no-bailout' clause in the Treaty framework and provisions of the European Stability Mechanism.[118] In *Gauweiler*, the opposite conclusion was necessary to uphold the validity of ECB bond buying: the OMT programme required categorisation as a tool of *monetary* policy to defend its internal constitutionality.

To that end, the Court of Justice in *Gauweiler* drew a clear distinction between the purchase of government bonds on secondary markets under the terms of the ESM Treaty and the purchase of such instruments under the terms of the OMT scheme.[119] Whereas the former was considered a matter of economic policy in *Pringle*, the Court in *Gauweiler* ruled that the latter was a central instrument of monetary policymaking. In its view, the purchase of government bonds under the OMT programme was undertaken independently of macroeconomic adjustments initiatives and strictly on the basis of objectives particular to Eurozone monetary policy.[120]

On the second argument – compliance with Article 123 TFEU – the Court's task was made slightly easier by the wording of the Treaty. As noted earlier, that provision prohibits only the *direct* purchasing of government debt instruments by the ECB and not, strictly speaking, bond buying on secondary markets – as foreseen under the OMT programme. Nevertheless, the applicants maintained that the ECB's plans to purchase Eurozone Member State bonds on secondary markets remained incompatible with that provision. In short, the OMT programme was considered nothing short of an attempt to circumvent the prohibition on direct bond buying in Article 123 TFEU. The Court of Justice was acutely sensitive to this line of argument. In particular, it recognised fully that the central aim of that provision was – like that of Article 125 TFEU – to

117 At paras. 52–60.
118 At paras. 63–65.
119 *Ibid.*
120 At para. 65.

ensure that Member States follow sound budgetary policies.[121] However, in the final analysis, the Court ruled the OMT programme compatible with the Treaty framework.

In the Court's view, the ECB's programme was not, in practice, liable to have an effect equivalent to the direct purchase of government bonds. The Grand Chamber's assessment on that point relied, in particular, on additional explanations provided to the Court by the ECB.[122] The Court was satisfied by the ECB's assurances, contained within a draft decision and draft guidelines, that the primary market for sovereign bonds would not be distorted by the OMT programme. For example, the ECB indicated that the purchase of bonds on the secondary market (including details on timing and quantity) would not be announced in advance.[123] Likewise, the ECB committed to ensuring that a minimum period would be observed between the issue of debts by Member States on the primary market and their purchase by that institution on the secondary market.[124] Thus, like the ESM Treaty before it, the OMT Programme survived the Court's review and was declared compatible with the EU Treaty framework.

It is not the purpose here to add to the existing literature critiquing the Court's reasoning in its judgments scrutinising the validity of political responses to the Eurozone crisis.[125] Rather, this section has used the judgments in *Pringle* and *Gauweiler* to reinforce the centrality of the Court's role in determining the boundaries between acts of constitutional supplementation and acts of constitutional contestation (see Section 4.2). As the preceding analysis demonstrated, in both cases, the Full Court ultimately ruled these responses *inter vires* as acts of constitutional supplementation, not *ultra vires* as acts of constitutional contestation. That required interpretative efforts of herculean proportions on its part. It was arguably also absolutely essential to ensure the Eurozone's survival.

121 At para. 100.

122 At paras. 105–106.

123 At para. 106.

124 *Ibid.*

125 For strong criticism in the broader literature, see e.g., Beck, *The Legal Reasoning of the Court of Justice of the EU*, n. 104 at p. 449 and M. Everson, 'An Exercise in Legal Honesty: Re-writing the Court of Justice and the *Bundesverfassungsgericht*' (2015) 21(4) *European Law Journal*, 474.

Concluding Remarks

This chapter has placed analysis of the EU Treaty framework's status and function as constitutional touchstone (Chapter 1) within the broader legal and political context that structures EU integration. In summary, it argued that, as constitutional touchstones, the Treaties' function is conditioned by what this chapter defines as acts of *constitutional supplementation* and *constitutional contestation*. The first of these concepts, constitutional supplementation, references acts of the EU institutions (and also Member States) that elaborate – but do not fundamentally contest – the EU Treaties' basic statements on the three key issues for EU constitutionalism (Chapter 1). By contrast, the concept of constitutional contestation refers to acts of the EU institutions (and Member States) that expressly contest the Treaties' clear position on the three basic issues for EU constitutionalism.

The introduction of the concepts of constitutional supplementation and constitutional contestation in this chapter served two specific objectives. First, it revealed the existence of inherent *limits* to the functioning of the bare bones of the EU Treaties as touchstones on the internal constitutionality of EU institutional activity. Secondly, and looking ahead to the chapters that follow, it established the framework to structure the critique of EU judicial activity for compliance with the Treaties in the remainder of this book (Chapters 3–5).

3 The Court of Justice, the Treaty Framework and Constitutional Issue No. 1

[T]he founding treaties of the European Union, unlike ordinary international treaties, established a new legal order, possessing its own institutions, for the benefit of which the States have limited their sovereign rights, in ever wider fields, and the subjects of which comprise not only Member States but also their nationals. The essential characteristics of the European Union legal order thus constituted are in particular its primacy over the laws of the Member States and the direct effect of a whole series of provisions which are applicable to their nationals and to the Member States themselves.

Opinion 1/09, *Draft Agreement on the Creation of a Unified Patent Litigation System* EU:C:2011:123 at para. 65.

Introduction

Chapter 2 explored the limits of the Treaty framework as a tool to determine the internal constitutionality of EU institutional activity. In summary, it was argued that, as constitutional touchstones, the EU Treaties form the centrepiece of the broader constitutional context that structures EU integration. That context is conditioned by acts of supplementation and contestation. The distinction between the two categories turns on whether the measure in question is developed by the EU institutions and/or Member States in conformity (constitutional supplementation) or in tension (constitutional contestation) with the Treaties' basic statements on the three fundamental issues for EU constitutionalism (Chapter 1).

The next three chapters assess how far EU judicial activity conforms with the Treaty framework and its statements on the three basic issues for EU constitutionalism: the formal status of Union law and the conditions under which it applies within Member States (Constitutional Issue No. 1); the locus of EU political authority within the EU legal order

(Constitutional Issue No. 2); and the objectives, values and limits governing European integration (Constitutional Issue No. 3). The overall argument developed across the next three chapters is that the Court's institutional positions on each of the three key issues for EU constitutionalism offer paradigmatic examples of what Chapter 2 defined as acts of constitutional contestation.

This chapter is specifically concerned with the Court's statements on the first issue for EU constitutionalism, addressing *the formal status of Union law and the conditions under which it applies within Member States*. In particular, it demonstrates that the Court of Justice has formulated and, thereafter, robustly defended its own position on that issue. In summary, its approach comprises three interrelated claims. First, the Court of Justice asserts that the European Union constitutes a 'new legal order' distinct from ordinary international law.[1] Secondly, EU law is deemed to be 'autonomous' in character.[2] Thirdly, and most crucially, the Court has ruled that the application of Union law *within* Member States is exclusively a matter for Union law and governed by the principles of direct effect and primacy.[3]

The Court's statements on the formal status of Union law and the conditions under which it applies within Member States remain external to, and in contestation with, the Treaty framework as constitutional touchstone. The EU Treaties (as amended) continue to accentuate the basic character of Union law as international law. Moreover, the EU Treaty framework also continues to make no special provision for the application of Union law within Member States. On the contrary,

[1] Case 26/62, *NV Algemene Transport- en Expeditie Onderneming van Gend & Loos* v. *Netherlands Inland Revenue Administration* EU:C:1963:1, p. 12. See also Case 6/64, *Costa* v. *E.N.E.L* EU:C:1964:66 at p. 593; Opinion 1/91, *Draft agreement between the Community, on the one hand, and the countries of the European Free Trade Association, on the other, relating to the creation of the European Economic Area* EU:C:1991:490 at para. 1; Opinion 1/09, *Draft Agreement on the Creation of a Unified Patent Litigation System* EU:C:2011:123 at para. 65 and Opinion 2/13, *Draft Agreement on Accession of the EU to the European Convention on Human Rights* EU:C:2014:2454 at para. 157. See also, with respect to the Court's position on the autonomy of the EU legal order in the field of external relations, Opinion 1/91, *Draft agreement between the Community, on the one hand, and the countries of the European Free Trade Association, on the other, relating to the creation of the European Economic Area* EU:C:1991:490 at para. 2 and Opinion 1/00, *Proposed agreement between the European Community and non-Member States on the establishment of a European Common Aviation Area* EU:C:2002:231.

[2] Case 26/62, *van Gend & Loos*, n. 1 at p. 12. See also, Case 6/64, *Costa*, n. 1 at p. 593, Opinion 1/91, n. 1 at para. 2 and Opinion 1/00, n. 1 at paras. 5–46 and Opinion 2/13, n. 1 at paras, 158, 166 and 170.

[3] Case 26/62, *van Gend & Loos*, n. 1 at p. 12 and Case 6/64, *Costa*, n. 1 at, p. 593.

the provisions governing the general application of EU law, the legal effects of judgments of the Court of Justice and the enforcement of EU legal norms all reinforce the conclusion that the relationship between the Union and Member State legal orders remains ultimately grounded in the principles and practice of international law.

The Court's approach to Constitutional Issue No. 1 traces its origins back to its landmark judgments on direct effect and primacy: *Van Gend en Loos* and *Costa* v. *ENEL*.[4] The Court's conclusions in both decisions, to which it has since robustly adhered, capture that institution's particular normative view on the *finalité* of EU integration. That vision, which appears impervious to changing (Member State) attitudes to EU integration over time, was *projected onto* the Treaty framework rather than deduced from it. It forms the cornerstone of the Court's broader judicial efforts to recast the relationship between the Union and the Member States along *domestic*, rather than international lines – with the Court assuming for itself the role of EU Supreme Court *de facto* within that recast legal order.[5] That effort continues to enjoy strong support among most EU scholars, many of whom were instrumental in its construction as an act of constitutional contestation.

Section 1 examines the EU Treaties' position on the formal status of Union law and the conditions under which it applies within Member States through the lens of public international law. Section 2 contrasts that position with the Court of Justice's institutional statements on that first issue for EU constitutionalism. Finally, Section 3 locates these statements within a broader process of judicial 'constitutionalisation'.

1 The EU Treaties and the Normative Framework of International Law

This section examines the EU Treaties' basic statements on the formal status of EU law and the rules governing its scope of application within Member States through the lens of public international law (Constitutional Issue No. 1). It begins by reviewing international law as a normative

[4] *Ibid.*

[5] See E. Stein, 'Lawyers, Judges, and the Making of a Transnational Constitution' (1981) 75 *American Journal of International Law*, 1; F. Mancini, 'The Making of a Constitution for Europe' (1989) 26 *Common Market Law Review*, 595 and J. H. H. Weiler, 'The Transformation of Europe' (1991) 100 *Yale Law Journal*, 2403. See also earlier, A. W. Green, *Political Integration by Jurisprudence* (Leiden: Sijthoff, 1969).

framework structuring inter-state co-operation (Section 1.1). Specifically, it asks: what limits does international law impose on states' contractual freedom (Section 1.1.1)? To what extent does international law *by its own authority* provide for the direct penetration of domestic legal systems (Section 1.1.2)? And what tools are available to states in both domestic (Section 1.1.3) and international law (Section 1.1.4) to manage the internal application of international treaty norms?

Thereafter, Section 1.2 reappraises the EU Treaty framework – and its key statements on Constitutional Issue No. 1 – in light of the responses to these questions. In summary, it is argued that, to a great extent, the EU Treaties are strikingly conventional – and, in parts, even rather conservative – as instruments of international law. Most crucially, no special provision is made for the allocation of competence to the Union institutions – and the Court of Justice in particular – to rule on the internal application of EU norms (i.e., within Member State legal systems).

The decision, as an EU legal scholar, to explore Constitutional Issue No. 1 through the lens of public international law risks accusations of heresy! As Plender notes with reference to the founding EEC Treaty, 'No principle of Community law is more fundamental, no more frequently reiterated by the European Court, than that the Treaty establishing the European Economic Community is "more than an agreement which merely creates obligations between contracting states" but rather constitutes a new legal order capable of conferring rights and imposing obligations directly upon individuals.'[6] In the eyes of EU scholars, and also most international lawyers, the EU severed its connections with the framework of international law years ago. Whilst EU commentators pay lip service to the fact that the European Union remains established by international treaties, they quickly distinguish its character and normative operating system. In a similar manner, international lawyers now largely exclude the EU legal order from general analyses of international treaty organisations and the law of treaties.[7] Key works on international

[6] R. Plender, 'The European Court and an International Tribunal' (1983) 42(2) *Cambridge Law Journal*, 279, p. 279. See also, K. Alter, *Establishing the Supremacy of European Law* (Oxford: Oxford University Press, 2001) at p .27.

[7] On that point see E. Denza, 'Placing the European Union in International Context: Legitimacy of the Case Law' in M. Adams et al. (eds.), *Judging Europe's Judges: The Legitimacy of the Case Law of the European Court of Justice* (Oxford: Hart Publishing, 2013) at p. 176. See also, U. Khaliq, 'Treaty Conflict and the European Union, or Conflicting Perspectives on the European Union' (2012) 37 *European Law Review*, 493.

law frequently make only passing, and largely distinguishing, references to the European Union in connection with discussions of the law of treaties and, in particular, the principles governing the domestic effect of treaty norms.[8]

The fact that the study of the European Union has become largely detached from the normative framework of international law reflects the striking success of the Court of Justice's efforts to recast the nature of the EU legal order in its own preferred image. Yet, aside from the Court's jurisprudence outlining *its position* on the formal status of EU law (Section 2), there is no compelling reason to distinguish the EU Treaties from the standard framework of international law. European integration remains established by ordinary international treaties and, on that basis alone, it is appropriate to explore the Treaty framework's position – as constitutional touchstone – on Constitutional Issue No. 1 through the normative framework of international law.[9] Of particular interest in that regard is what the international law paradigm has to say on the domestic application of treaty norms; in other words, on the status of EU law *within* Member State legal systems.

1.1 International Law as a Normative Framework Structuring Inter-State Co-operation

1.1.1 *What Limits Does International Law Impose on States' Contractual Freedom?*

International law provides a structured, albeit remarkably flexible normative framework to govern co-operation and general relations between

[8] See e.g., M. Shaw, *International Law* (7th edn) (Cambridge: Cambridge University Press, 2014) at p. 177; A. Aust, *Modern Treaty Law and Practice* (3rd edn) (Cambridge: Cambridge University Press, 2013) at pp. 359–362; A. V. Lowe, *International Law* (Oxford: Oxford University Press, 2007) at pp. 5–6 and M. Dixon, R. McCorquodale and S. Williams (eds.), *Cases & Materials on International Law* (5th edn) (Oxford: Oxford University Press, 2003) at pp. 115–119. Other key works exclude the EU legal order in its entirety. See e.g., M. D. Evans (ed.), *International Law* (4th edn) (Oxford: Oxford University Press, 2014).

[9] See also, with specific respect to analysis of the EU's internal affairs, B. de Witte, 'Using International Law for the European Union's Domestic Affairs' in C. Enzo, P. Palchetti and R. A. Wessel (eds.), *International Law as Law of the European Union* (Leiden: Martinus Nijhoff, 2011) esp. at p. 134. See also, B. de Witte, 'The Closest Thing to a Constitutional Conversation in Europe: The Semi-Permanent Treaty Revision Process' in P. Beaumont, C. Lyons and N. Walker (eds.), *Convergence and Divergence in European Public Law* (Oxford: Hart Publishing, 2002) at p. 52.

sovereign states.[10] In the international context, states remain the primary actors and subjects of rights and obligations.[11] Only states have full legal capacity on the international stage – a capacity that is based on the exercise of effective control over territory that is recognised by the international community. The relationship between states in international law is horizontal, with states enjoying (formal) equality. Under the doctrine of collective responsibility, it is also states and not individual officials or public entities within states that are liable to answer for alleged breaches of international obligations.

Alongside states, the traditional actors in international law include international organisations, insurgents and, to a lesser extent, individuals.[12] For their part, individuals traditionally feature as the beneficiaries of rights and obligations established by contracting states, rather than as the direct subjects of international law.[13] Discussion of the status of individuals as international law subjects classically centred on acts of piracy, although there is some dispute over the extent to which international law has ever actually addressed individuals engaged in piracy as direct subjects of rights and obligations.[14] However, that debate aside, it is now beyond dispute that, in limited arenas, individuals have gradually come to be regarded as actors in their own right in international law, notably in the field of international criminal law.[15] Equally, certain states have also granted individuals procedural rights to petition international organisations directly and independently of domestic law in specific treaties.[16]

[10] For discussion, see e.g., A. Cassese, *International Law* (2nd edn) (Oxford: Oxford University Press, 2005) chapter 1 and K. Parlett, *The Individual in the International Legal System: Continuity and Change in International Law* (Cambridge: Cambridge University Press, 2013), chapter 1.

[11] Cassese, *International Law*, n. 10, chapter 4. See also, R. Jennings and A. Watts, *Oppenheim's International Law* (9th edn) (Oxford: Oxford University Press, 2008) at p.4 and p. 16.

[12] Cassese, *International Law*, n. 10, chapter 7. See also, Shaw, *International Law*, n. 8, chapter 5.

[13] *Ibid.*, at p. 142. For discussion, see also, R. McCorquodale, 'The Individual and the International Legal System' in M. D. Evans (ed.), *International Law*, n. 8, chapter 10 and Parlett, *The Individual in the International Legal System*, n. 10.

[14] Cassese, *International Law*, n. 10, at pp. 142–144.

[15] *Ibid.*, at p. 144. See also, McCorquodale, 'The Individual and the International Legal System', n. 13. For broader discussion, see e.g., J. Klabbers, *International Law* (2nd edn) (Cambridge: Cambridge University Press, 2017), chapter 6.

[16] *Ibid.*, at pp. 147–9. See e.g., Art. 34 of The Convention for the Protection of Human Rights and Fundamental Freedoms (European Convention on Human Rights, as amended) (ECHR).

There are few substantive limits on what states may agree to as actors on the international stage.[17] International law has classically offered states considerable freedom (and protection) to pursue their individual and collective political interests. The Vienna Convention on the Law of Treaties provides, for signatory states, a framework governing the procedures for the adoption, amendment, extinction and interpretation of international treaties, but has very little to say on the *content* of treaties.[18] That is left to contracting states to determine in accordance with their political influence on the world (or regional) stage. Nonetheless, in practice, the basic principle of contractual freedom is subject to some important qualifications. To highlight one example: under the doctrine of *jus cogens*, the validity of international agreements is considered conditional on states' compliance with an evolving set of specific preemptory legal norms.[19]

1.1.2 To What Extent Does International Law by Its Own Authority Provide for the Direct Penetration of Domestic Legal Systems?

International law does not by its own authority penetrate the domestic legal orders of states.[20] International law instead operates in its own sphere and leaves individual states free to determine the application and enforcement of international norms within national (or 'municipal') legal systems. As Cassese summarises:

> States consider that the translation of international commands into domestic legal standards is part and parcel of their sovereignty, and are unwilling to surrender it to international control ... As a consequence, each state decides, on its own, how to make international law binding on State agencies

[17] Cassese, *International Law*, n. 10, at pp. 5–6. For further examples, see Shaw, *International Law*, n. 8 at pp. 189.

[18] Vienna Convention on the Law of Treaties, 1155 U.N.T.S. 331, 8 I.L.M. 679. For discussion, see Aust, *Modern Treaty Law and Practice*, n. 8, and P. Reuter, *Introduction to the Law of Treaties* (London: Pinter, 1989).

[19] Cassese, *International Law*, n. 10 at pp. 218–219.

[20] See e.g., Cassese, *International Law*, n. 10 at p. 219; A. Nollkaemper, 'The Effects of Treaties in Domestic Law' in C. J. Tams, A. Tzanakopoulos and A. Zimmermann (eds.), *Research Handbook on the Law of Treaties* (Cheltenham: Elgar, 2014) at p. 124; E. Denza, 'The Relationship Between International Law and National Law' in Evans (ed.) *International Law*, n. 8 at p. 417 and Aust, *Modern Treaty Law and Practice*, n. 8 at p. 159.

and individuals and what status and rank to assign to it in the hierarchy of municipal sources of law.[21]

Similarly, as Denza observes:

> International law does not itself prescribe how it should be applied or enforced at the national level. It asserts its own primacy over national laws, but without invalidating those laws or intruding into national legal systems, requiring a result rather than a method of implementation. National constitutions are therefore free to choose how they give effect to treaties and to customary international law.[22]

1.1.3 *What Tools Are Available to States in Domestic Law to Manage the Internal Application of International Treaty Norms?*

At the national or 'municipal' level, states can exercise influence over the internal effect of international norms in a range of different ways. Most significantly, states are free to determine whether or not, and the conditions under which, international law has direct effect *domestically* (i.e., within their respective national legal systems). The attribution of direct effect to international norms as a matter of domestic law enables individuals to invoke them directly before national courts and tribunals. Furthermore, states are also able, through domestic law, to control the relationship between international law and municipal law in instances of conflict. Most importantly, this includes determining the rules that govern conflicts between international norms and provisions of domestic constitutions and/or national constitutional principles.

In practice, states have adopted a wide range of approaches to the integration of international legal norms into domestic legal systems.[23] At one end of the spectrum, states including Greece, France and the Netherlands provide generally for the automatic incorporation of treaty norms. The Netherlands is particularly open to international law. Article 93 of the Constitution provides that treaties and resolutions adopted by

21 Cassese, *International Law*, n. 10 at p. 220.

22 Denza, 'The Relationship between International Law and National Law', n. 20 at p. 412.

23 For a survey of approaches, see e.g., Aust, *Modern Treaty Law and Practice*, n. 8 at pp. 162–173; Nollkaemper, 'The Effects of Treaties in Domestic Law', n. 20 at pp. 138–142 and Shaw, *International Law*, n. 8 at pp. 98–129. See also earlier, F. G. Jacobs and S. Roberts (eds.), *The Effect of Treaties in Domestic Law* (London: Sweet and Maxwell, 1987). For a detailed critical cross-section of national approaches, see J. E. Nijman and A. Nollkaemper (eds.), *New Perspectives on the Divide between National and International Law* (Oxford: Oxford University Press, 2007).

international institutions shall, under specific instances, become binding after they are published.[24] Furthermore, Article 94 of the Constitution attributes primacy to such norms in instances of conflict with (ordinary) domestic law.[25] At the other end of the continuum, states such as Italy and the United Kingdom make the domestic application and enforcement of international norms subject to the prior enactment of national implementing measures.[26]

The preceding choices reflect national political preferences with respect to states' openness towards what is essentially 'foreign' law – the content of which states often do not exclusively control. As Nollkaemper notes:

> Blocking domestic effect may lead to an internationally wrongful act if the State does not perform its treaty obligations, but does preserve national policy space. A decision to grant a treaty full effect in national law may facilitate effective performance of international obligations, but comes at the price of national policy space, as it fixes the law at a level where it is beyond the control of individual States.[27]

The distribution of political power within individual states further conditions states' decisions over the domestic application and enforcement of international norms.[28] For instance, in a constitutional system structured around the supremacy of parliament (e.g., the United Kingdom), a decision to give immediate effect to international norms would radically adjust the balance of power between parliament and the courts – to the detriment of the former. The power of courts would be enhanced further still should parliament also elect to accord international norms primacy over conflicting domestic norms.[29] Federal states, such as Germany, face additional choices with respect to the vertical distribution of political authority. Decisions on whether and, more likely the conditions under

[24] Art. 93 provides that 'Provisions of treaties and of resolutions by international institutions which may be binding on all persons by virtue of their contents shall become binding after they have been published.'

[25] Art. 120 precludes national courts from reviewing the constitutionality of treaties.

[26] For the position under English law, see e.g., Lord Oliver in *JH Rayner* v. *Department of Trade and Industry* [1990] 2 AC 418.

[27] Nollkaemper, 'The Effects of Treaties in Domestic Law', n. 20 at pp. 124–125. See also, P. Reuter, *Introduction to the Law of Treaties* (London: Pinter, 1989) at pp. 20–23.

[28] Nollkaemper, 'The Effects of Treaties in Domestic Law', n. 20, at p. 125.

[29] See the United Kingdom, Arts. 2 and 3 of the European Communities Act 1972. See also Art. 3 of The Human Rights Act 1998, which directs national courts to interpret national law as a far as possible in line with (incorporated) Convention rights.

which, international norms should take effect within such states inevitably have a direct bearing on the distribution of power between state and federal authorities.

1.1.4 *What Tools Are Available to States in International Law to Manage the Internal Application of International Treaty Norms?*

States also enjoy considerable freedom to control the internal effect of international law when negotiating international treaties. In particular, they are free to agree, and consent to be bound by, specific rules on the domestic effect of international norms.[30] Article 46(1) of the European Convention of Human Rights (ECHR) provides one such example. Under that provision, contracting ECHR states have committed in international law to abide by (and, thus, give internal effect to) final judgments of the European Court of Human Rights (ECtHR) in cases to which they are party. Under the ECHR, the Committee of Ministers supervises contracting states' implementation of ECtHR judgments.[31] Should that Committee consider that an individual state has failed to comply with a final judgment of the ECtHR then it is empowered to refer the case back to the Court.[32] If the Court upholds the Committee's judgment on non-compliance, the case is returned to the Committee, which may then determine what, if any, measures to take against the defaulting State.[33]

States can also assert influence over the domestic effect of international norms at the international level by expressly consenting to attribute direct effect to specific treaty norms. More often, however, the direct effect of international norms arises *implicitly* where states consent to be bound by precisely worded treaty provisions that international courts and tribunals interpret as intending to confer specific rights on individuals that the latter may rely on before national courts.[34] In international law, the direct effect of treaty provisions was recognised by the Permanent Court of International Justice (PCIJ) in 1928.[35]

30 For an overview, see Nollkaemper, 'The Effects of Treaties in Domestic Law', n. 20 at pp. 130–149.

31 Art. 46(2) ECHR.

32 Art. 46(4) ECHR.

33 Art. 46(5) ECHR.

34 Nollkaemper, 'The Effects of Treaties in Domestic Law', n. 20 at p. 135. See also, T. Burgenthal, 'Self-Executing and Non-Self-Executing Treaties in National and International Law' (1992) IV *Recueil des Cors*, 303 at p. 319.

35 Shaw, *International Law*, n. 8 at p. 189; Cassese, *International Law*, n. 10 at pp. 218–219 and McCorquodale, 'The Individual and the International Legal System' in Evans (ed.),

In its Advisory Opinion in *Jurisdiction of the Courts of Danzig* the PCIJ concluded that,

> It may be readily admitted that, according to well-established principles of international law . . . an international agreement, cannot, as such, create direct rights and obligations for private individuals. But *it cannot be disputed that the very object of an international agreement, according to the intention of the Contracting Parties, may be the adoption by the Parties of some definitive rules creating individual rights and obligations enforceable by the national courts.*[36]

The PCIJ's Opinion in *Danzig Courts* highlights the significance of states' intentions in determining the direct effect of international agreements. It also reveals the important independent function that international courts and tribunals play in making such determinations in the exercise of their interpretative functions. This applies, *a fortiori*, where international agreements are silent on questions of direct effect.

Nonetheless, whatever rules states consent to be bound by at the international level, the effects of these rules within national legal systems remains – as previously discussed (see Section 1.1.2) – ultimately a matter for *domestic* law. As Nollkaemper reminds us, 'International law does not determine the domestic organization of states and cannot directly determine the powers of the organs of the state in the national legal order to give effect to treaties.'[37] In relation to domestic effect, it is perfectly possible, therefore, for states to agree to be bound by particular rules as matter of international law (i.e., in treaties), but thereafter to refuse (or simply fail) to give effect to those rules within their respective national legal systems. This possibility poses obvious challenges to the integrity and effectiveness of international law, but is legally within states' powers as sovereign actors in international law.

The UK, for instance, is presently refusing to implement the ECtHR's judgments on prisoner voting rights in contravention of Article 46(1) ECHR.[38] That provision commits contracting states to abide by the final judgments of the Strasbourg Court. Such behaviour is clearly regrettable

International Law, n. 8 at p. 307. For detailed analysis, see Parlett, *The Individual in the International Legal System*, n. 10 at pp. 16–26.

36 Advisory Opinion of 3 March 1928, *Jurisdiction of the Courts of Danzig*, PCIJ, Series B, No. 15 paras. 17–18 (emphasis added).

37 Nollkaemper, 'The Effects of Treaties in Domestic Law', n. 20 at pp. 13–131.

38 *Hirst* v. *the United Kingdom (No. 2)* [2005] ECHR 681. The deadline for the introduction of legislative proposals to amend s. 3 of the Representation of the People Act 1983 expired on 22 November 2012. For the UK Supreme Court's response, see *R. (on the application of Chester)* v. *Secretary of State for Justice* [2013] UKSC 63.

and gives rises to a breach of that State's obligations *in international law*. It does not, however, have any impact on the UK's continued right to determine the internal application of international norms. The domestic (and, in particular, direct) effect of treaties and other international obligations, ultimately remains the responsibility of individual states. International legal norms do not, as a matter of principle and state practice, take effect within national legal systems solely on the strength of their own authority.

1.2 The EU Treaties as Instruments of International Law

International law has provided, from inception to the present, the legal instruments to structure European integration.[39] This may surprise EU and international law scholars alike, but it remains fundamentally incontrovertible.

This section re-examines the EU Treaties' position on the formal status of Union law and the conditions under which it applies within Member States (Constitutional Issue No. 1) through the lens of international law. It begins with a brief look at the Treaty provisions governing the adoption, ratification and amendment of the EU Treaty framework (Section 1.2.1). Thereafter, it analyses the Treaties' statements on the domestic effect of EU norms – the principal issue with respect to Constitutional Issue No. 1 (Section 1.2.2). Finally, this section highlights the more innovative features of the EU Treaty framework as an instrument of international law (Section 1.2.3). These include, most notably, the preliminary reference procedure (Article 267 TFEU). That procedure constitutes a particularly novel mechanism to monitor *ex ante* Member State compliance with EU Treaty obligations.

Overall, as constitutional touchstones, the EU Treaties remain firmly embedded within the framework of international law. Under the EU Treaties, Union law retains its character as international law. Most strikingly in that regard, the EU Treaty framework makes no special provision for the application of Union law within Member States. On the contrary, the provisions governing the general application of EU law, the legal effects of judgments of the Court of Justice and the enforcement of EU legal norms all reinforce the conclusion that the relationship

[39] See de Witte, 'Using International Law for the European Union's Domestic Affairs', n. 9 at p. 134. See e.g., T. Hartley, 'The Constitutional Foundations of the European Union' (2001) 117 *Law Quarterly Review*, 225 at pp. 255–226.

between the Union and Member State legal orders remains ultimately grounded in the normative framework of public international law.

1.2.1 *Adoption, Amendment and Ratification*

The EU Treaties are (and have remained) strikingly conventional as instruments of international law.[40] The founding EEC Treaty and subsequent amending treaties were all concluded in accordance with the default rules set out in part two of the Vienna Convention on the Law of Treaties. On each occasion, Member States (Article 6 VCLT), represented by their designated plenipotentiaries (Article 7 VCLT), reached unanimous agreement on the adoption of the text of the treaty (treaties) (Article 9(1) VCLT). The entry into force of the agreed treaty (treaties) was conditional on signatory states subsequently expressing their consent to be bound in recognised form (Article 11 VCLT). In the context of European integration, states have consistently opted for the ratification option detailed in Articles 14 and 16 VCLT. Under Articles 54 TEU and 357 TFEU, the EU Treaties shall enter into force following: (1) ratification by each Member State in accordance with its respective constitutional requirements and (2) the deposit of all the instruments of national ratification with the Italian Government.[41]

Under Article 48 TEU, the entry into force of any amendments to the EU Treaties remains absolutely conditional upon the agreement of, and subsequent ratification by, all Member States. Important adjustments have been made to the legal framework structuring treaty amendment since the entry into force of the founding EEC Treaty. This includes, for instance, the introduction of a system of simplified treaty amendment in Articles 48(6)–(7) TEU. However, whilst significant in many other respects, the introduction of that procedure (and other changes) has not disturbed the fundamentals of EU Treaty adoption, amendment and ratification. That process remains entirely conditional on Member States reaching agreement on the adoption and entry into force of treaty revisions by common consent.[42] A transition to treaty amendment by

[40] De Witte, 'Using International Law for the European Union's Domestic Affairs', n. 9 at p. 135.

[41] See Art. 247 EEC and Art. 248 EEC respectively (now Art. 54 TEU and Art. 357 TFEU).

[42] Art. 50 TEU, inserted by the Lisbon Treaty and outlining the procedure for Member States to leave the European Union, is the exception. The conclusion of a withdrawal agreement pursuant to Art. 50(2) TEU requires the remaining Member States to approve that agreement by qualified majority.

majority decision-making would certainly make the process much more efficient. Such a move would also be entirely compatible with the Vienna Convention, but has not yet occurred.

1.2.2 *The Domestic Effect of EU Norms under the Treaty Framework*

In relation to the domestic effect of Union norms, the EU Treaties are also equally unremarkable as instruments of international law. A review of the provisions governing (1) the domestic application of EU law; (2) the legal effects of judgments of the Court of Justice; and (3) the enforcement of EU legal norms confirms that, under the Treaty framework, the formal status of EU law and the conditions under which it applies within Member States is governed by standard principles of international law.

Article 4(3) TEU sets out the Treaties' key statement on the domestic application of Union law.[43] According to that provision, 'Member States shall take any appropriate measure, general or particular to ensure fulfilment of the obligations arising out of the Treaties or resulting from the acts of the institutions of the Union.' Article 4(3) TEU does no more than bind Member States to the operation of orthodox principles of international law. In more specific terms, it attributes to Member States, as contracting parties, responsibility to perform EU Treaty obligations. It is also result-oriented as is characteristic of international legal obligations; its wording speaks to Member States' commitment to fulfil specific obligations arising under the Treaties, not the manner in which particular results are achieved. Most crucially, however, Article 4(3) TEU leaves individual Member States ultimately responsible for the application and enforcement of Union norms within national legal systems. Put bluntly, as the principal statement on the domestic effect of EU law, Article 4(3) TEU does nothing more than require Member States, in accordance with the standard approach in international law, to *give effect* to EU law internally as a source of binding legal norms.[44] No more is required.

An appraisal of the Treaties' statements on the domestic legal effects of EU Court judgments reinforces that conclusion. In parallel with Article 4(3) TEU, Article 260 TFEU provides that judgments of the

[43] See also, Art. 19(1) TEU: 'Member States shall provide remedies sufficient to ensure effective legal protection in the fields covered by Union law.'

[44] This applies also to Art. 101(2) TFEU, which states that anti-competitive agreements and decisions concluded between undertakings contrary to Art. 101(1) TFEU shall be 'automatically void'.

Court of Justice shall have only declaratory effect vis-à-vis Member States: 'If the Court of Justice of the European Union finds that a Member State has failed to fulfil an obligation under the Treaties, *the State shall be required* to take the necessary measures to comply with the judgment of the Court.'[45] Furthermore, Article 280 TFEU provides that judgments of the Court 'shall be enforceable under the conditions laid down in Article 299 TFEU'. The latter provision outlines the procedure for the enforcement of Commission and Council decisions within Member States, in particular those imposing pecuniary obligations on natural and legal persons. According to Article 299 TFEU, the execution of these decisions is expressly designated a matter for national law. Article 299 TFEU places a requirement on the relevant party to bring an action for enforcement before the designated competent authority of the Member States concerned to seek redress. On the strength of Article 280 TFEU, the same is to apply *mutatis mutandis* to decisions of the Court of Justice.

The Treaties' deference to Member States with respect to the internal application of EU legal norms does not, of course, preclude the direct penetration of Union law into national legal systems. It simply leaves that decision for determination by individual Member States, according to their respective constitutional preferences (see Section 1.2). Chapter 6 discusses the detail of Member State approaches to the domestic application of EU law.

A Member State's failure to give effect to EU law domestically constitutes – under the Treaty framework – a breach of its obligations in international law. That breach is not without consequences for the state concerned. On the contrary, the EU Treaties establish several procedures to address alleged infringements. Article 258 TFEU empowers the Commission to deliver 'reasoned opinions' to Member States in instances of alleged non-compliance with Treaty obligations.[46] Where the matter is not satisfactorily resolved within a specific timeframe, the Commission, acting as gatekeeper, may elect to bring the matter before the Court of Justice. Article 259 TFEU outlines a parallel (and rarely invoked) procedure for allegations of non-compliance instigated by

[45] Art. 260 TFEU (emphasis added). The Court of Justice recognised this point in its early case law. See Case 6/60, *Humblet* v. *Belgian State* EU:C:1960:48 at p. 569.

[46] See also, Art. 7 TEU, which establishes specific procedures to enforce the fundamental values enshrined in Art. 6 TEU against Member States.

other Member States.[47] Neither mechanism is atypical in the sphere of public international law. A successful action under either procedure may be considered to give rise to the declaration of a 'wrongful act' in international law on the part of the Member States concerned. It does not, however, take effect within domestic legal systems by its own authority.

1.2.3 *The EU Treaty Framework: Innovative Features*

Whilst entirely conventional in many respects, the EU Treaty framework has nonetheless always contained some more distinctive and innovative features. On domestic effect specifically, the EU Treaty framework has from the outset notably mandated that Member States ensure the 'direct application' of Regulations within national legal orders. According to (now) Article 288 TFEU, EU Regulations 'shall be binding in [their] entirety and directly applicable in all Member States'.

Conversely, Member States have also reached agreement through the EU Treaty framework to preclude the direct penetration of Union law into Member State legal systems in specific instances. For example, prior to the entry into force of the Lisbon Treaty, Article 34(2)(b)/(c) TEU provided that framework decisions and decisions adopted under Title VI of the (then) Treaty on European Union shall *not* entail direct effect. Similarly, post Lisbon, Article 1(2) of Protocol No. 30 on the Application of EU Charter of Fundamental Rights to Poland and the United Kingdom guarantees, for the avoidance of any doubt, that nothing in Title IV of that instrument establishes justiciable rights for individuals within the domestic legal orders of either Member State.[48]

The preliminary reference procedure is, however, without doubt, the EU Treaty framework's most innovative feature as an instrument of international law.[49] The establishment of that procedure, under which Member State courts may (and sometimes must) refer questions

[47] For rare exceptions see e.g., Case 141/78, *France* v. *United Kingdom (Marine Conservation)* EU:C:1979:225, Case C-388/95, *Belgium* v. *Spain (Designations of Origin)* EU:C:2000:244 and Case C-364/10, *Hungary* v. *Slovakia* EU:C:2012:630.

[48] Protocol (No. 30) on the Application of the Charter of Fundamental Rights of the European Union to Poland and to the United Kingdom [2008] OJ C 115/313.

[49] For analysis, see e.g., T. Tridimas, 'Knocking on Heaven's Door: Fragmentation, Efficiency and Defiance in the Preliminary Reference Procedure' (2003) 40(1) *Common Market Law Review*, 9 and M. Broberg and N. Ferger, *Preliminary References to the European Court of Justice* (Oxford: Oxford University Press, 2014).

of interpretation to the Court of Justice, modifies the standard approach to the monitoring and enforcement of state compliance with treaty obligations. In international law, states are generally held to account for infringements of their international obligations *ex post*; in other words, where it can be established that the contracting state – incorporating all its internal organs – has actually breached its international obligations. Under the EU Treaty framework, this approach is given expression through the existence of the infringement procedures in Articles 258 and 259 TFEU outlined earlier.

The preliminary reference procedure in Article 267 TFEU complements this framework by providing an additional mechanism to address potential compliance issues *within* domestic legal orders *ex ante* in collaboration with the Court of Justice.[50] Under Article 267 TFEU, national courts are empowered (and sometimes required) to request the Court's position on the interpretation or validity of EU law in connection with the application and enforcement of Union law within domestic legal systems. As Wyatt has argued:

> the Article [267 TFEU] procedure . . . allow[s] for "the clock to be stopped," and for questions which would have traditionally been framed as *ex post facto* in terms of responsibility, to be framed in terms of the duty of Member States, a duty in the case of treaty obligations apt for national judicial implementation, incumbent upon the courts of Member States.[51]

The preliminary reference is a rather innovative addition to the standard international law framework on domestic effect. In short, it gives Member States advance warning of potential breaches of EU law and invites one set of national actors (courts) to correct these through the framework of national law. Of course, as the next section argues, in the Court of Justice's hands, the preliminary reference procedure has taken on a very different procedural character.

[50] See here D. Wyatt, 'New Legal Order, or Old' (1982) 7 *European Law Review*, 147 at pp. 153–154 and M. Claes, *The National Courts' Mandate in the European Constitution* (Oxford: Hart Publishing, 2006) at pp. 247–248. On the origins of the Court's mandate, see M. Rasmussen, 'The Origins of a Legal Revolution: The Early History of the European Court of Justice' (2008) 81 *European Integration History*, 77 and A. Boerger-De Smedt, 'Negotiating the Foundations of European Law, 1950–57: The Legal History of the Treaties of Paris and Rome' (2012) 21(3) *Contemporary European History*, 339.

[51] D. Wyatt, 'New Legal Order, or Old', n. 50 at pp. 153–154.

2 Colliding Worlds: The Court of Justice *contra* the EU Treaty Framework

This section contrasts the Treaty framework's statements on Constitutional Issue No. 1 with the Court of Justice's institutional position. This enquiry unmasks the Court's position on the formal status of Union law and the conditions under which it applies within Member States as a striking act of constitutional contestation.

Section 2.1 summarises the substance of the Court's position on Constitutional Issue No. 1. Its approach comprises three interrelated claims – none of which align with the Treaty framework as constitutional touchstone. First, the Court asserts that the European Union constitutes a 'new legal order' distinct from ordinary international law.[52] Secondly, EU law is deemed 'autonomous' in character.[53] Thirdly, and most crucially, the Court has ruled that the application of Union law *within* Member States is exclusively a matter for Union law and governed by the principles of direct effect and primacy.[54]

Section 2.2 then reflects on the evolution of the Court's approach, which traces its origins back to its landmark judgments on direct effect and primacy: *Van Gend en Loos* and *Costa* v. *ENEL*.[55] The Court's conclusions in both decisions, to which it has since robustly adhered, capture that institution's particular normative view on the *finalité* of EU integration. As this chapter demonstrates through a fresh reinterpretation of the case law, that vision was projected onto the Treaty framework rather than deduced from it.

[52] Case 26/62, *van Gend & Loos*, n. 1 at p. 12. See also Case 6/64, *Costa*, n. 1 at p. 593; Opinion 1/09, *Draft Agreement on the Creation of a Unified Patent Litigation System*, n. 1 at para. 65 and Opinion 2/13, *Draft Agreement on Accession of the EU to the European Convention on Human Rights*, n. 1 at para. 157. See also, with respect to the Court's position on the autonomy of the EU legal order in the field of external relations, Opinion 1/91, *Draft agreement between the Community, on the one hand, and the countries of the European Free Trade Association, on the other, relating to the creation of the European Economic Area*, n. 1 at para. 1 and Opinion 1/00, *Proposed agreement between the European Community and non-Member States on the establishment of a European Common Aviation Area*, n. 1.

[53] Case 26/62, *van Gend & Loos*, n. 1 at p. 12. See also Case 6/64, *Costa*, n. 1 at p. 593, Opinion 1/91, Draft *agreement between the Community, on the one hand, and the countries of the European Free Trade Association, on the other, relating to the creation of the European Economic Area*, n. 1 at para. 2; Opinion 1/00, *Proposed agreement between the European Community and non-Member States on the establishment of a European Common Aviation Area*, n. 1 at paras. 5–46 and Opinion 2/13, *Draft Agreement on Accession of the EU to the European Convention on Human Rights*, n. 1 at paras. 158, 166 and 170.

[54] Case 26/62, *van Gend & Loos*, n. 1 at p. 12 and Case 6/64, *Costa*, n. 1 at p. 593.

[55] *Ibid.*

2.1 The Court of Justice and Constitutional Issue No. 1

The Court of Justice has shown very little regard for the Treaties' unambiguous statements on the formal status of Union law and the conditions under which it applies within Member States in the exercise of its attributed functions. In a most remarkable act of judicial creativity, the Court lost no time at all in exploiting its competence to issue *declaratory* judgments on the interpretation of EU law (Article 260 TFEU) that bind Member States *as a matter of international law* (Article 4(3) TEU) to formulate its own, very different position on Constitutional Issue No. 1. The result marks a clear break with the normative framework of international law that, as demonstrated above, continues to underpin European integration under the Treaty framework.

The Court of Justice has formulated and maintained a consistent and clear approach to determining the formal status of Union law and the conditions under which it applies within Member States. According to the Court, 'The founding treaties of the European Union, unlike ordinary international treaties, established a new legal order, possessing its own institutions, for the benefit of which the States have limited their sovereign rights, in ever wider fields, and the subjects of which comprise not only Member States but also their nationals.'[56]

The Court's approach to the formal status of EU law and its scope of application within Member State legal orders centres on three interrelated claims. First, as the preceding extract indicates, the Court of Justice asserts that the European Union constitutes a 'new legal order' distinct from ordinary international law. As Mayer observes, the Court has refined and experimented with different formulae over time to capture its view on the distinctive nature of EU integration.[57] More precisely, the Court has referenced the EU as a 'new legal order of international law';[58] its 'own legal system';[59] and a 'Community based

[56] Opinion 1/09, *Draft Agreement on the Creation of a Unified Patent Litigation System*, n. 1 at para. 65. See also earlier, Case 26/62, *van Gend & Loos*, n. 1 at p.12; Case 6/64, *Costa*, n. 1 at p. 593 and Opinion 1/91, *Draft agreement between the Community, on the one hand, and the countries of the European Free Trade Association, on the other, relating to the creation of the European Economic Area*, n. 1 at para. 1.

[57] F. C. Mayer, '*Van Gend en Loos*: The Foundation of a Community of Law' in M. Poiares Maduro and L. Azoulai (eds.), *The Past and Future of EU Law: The Classics of EU Law Revisited on the 50th Anniversary of the Rome Treaty* (Oxford, Hart Publishing: 2010) at p. 20.

[58] Case 26/62, *van Gend & Loos*, n. 1.

[59] Case 6/64, *Costa*, n. 1.

on the rule of law'.[60] The recent Opinion of the Full Court on EU accession to the ECHR revived the original conception of the EU as a 'new legal order' without any distinguishing references to international law.[61]

Secondly, alongside the 'new legal order' claim, the Court maintains and robustly defends the autonomy of EU law.[62] As an autonomous legal order, the normative authority of EU law is understood to flow directly from the Treaty framework itself as an 'independent source of law'.[63] Most importantly, the Court derives from its statements on the autonomy of the EU legal order an exclusive competence to determine the scope and validity of Union law to the exclusion of all of other actors.[64] That competence operates to exclude competing claims to (final) authority stemming from both national law and international law. Furthermore, the Court asserts an exclusive competence to adjudicate on the validity of secondary EU law. This seeks to preclude Member State courts from reviewing the validity of EU acts for compliance with national law, including domestic constitutions.[65] Finally, the Court is clear that international law cannot affect the autonomy of the EU legal order the observance of which it ensures by virtue of an exclusive jurisdiction.[66]

Thirdly, and most importantly, the Court's position on the formal status of EU law embodies a specific prescription with respect to the domestic application of Union law. The Court is uncompromising in its view that the

[60] Opinion 1/91, *Draft agreement between the Community, on the one hand, and the countries of the European Free Trade Association, on the other, relating to the creation of the European Economic Area*, n. 1 at para. 1.

[61] Opinion 2/13, *Draft Agreement on Accession of the EU to the European Convention on Human Rights*, n. 1, at para. 157.

[62] See e.g., Case 26/62, *van Gend & Loos*, n. 1 at p. 12; Case 6/64, *Costa*, n. 1 at p. 593 and Opinion 1/91, *Draft agreement between the Community, on the one hand, and the countries of the European Free Trade Association, on the other, relating to the creation of the European Economic Area*, n. 1 at para. 2; Opinion 1/00, *Proposed Agreement between the European Community and non-Member States on the establishment of a European Common Aviation Area*, n. 1 at paras. 5–46 and Opinion 2/13, *Draft Agreement on Accession of the EU to the European Convention on Human Rights*, n. 1 at paras, 158, 166 and 170.

[63] Case 6/64, *Costa*, n. 1 at p. 593.

[64] See e.g., Opinion 2/13, *Draft Agreement on Accession of the EU to the European Convention on Human Rights*, n. 1, esp. at paras. 174–176 and 198, 224, 234 and 246

[65] Case 6/64, *Costa*, n. 1; Case 11/70, *Internationale Handelsgesellschaft mbH* v. *Einfuhr- und Vorratsstelle für Getreide und Futtermittel* EU:C:1970:114; Case 106/77, *Amministrazione delle Finanze dello Stato* v. *Simmenthal SpA* EU:C:1978:49; Case 314/85, *Foto-Frost* v. *Hauptzollamt Lübeck-Ost* EU:C:1987:452 and Case C-399/11, *Melloni* EU:C:2013:107.

[66] Joined Cases C-402/05 P and C-415/05, *P Kadi and Al Barakaat International Foundation* v. *Council and Commission* EU:C:2008:461; Opinion 1/09, *Draft Agreement on the Creation of a Unified Patent Litigation System*, n. 1 and Opinion 2/13, *Draft Agreement on Accession of the EU to the European Convention on Human Rights*, n. 1.

internal effect of EU law is an exclusive matter for Union law (and the Court in particular) and not the responsibility of individual Member States.

In specific terms, the Court views the internal application of EU law as subject to the principles of direct effect and primacy. The concepts of direct effect and primacy are understood here as distinct from their international law context (see Section 1.2). According to the Court of Justice, EU legal norms do not merely have direct effect and take primacy over conflicting national law *as a matter of international law*. On the contrary, the Court asserts that Union law applies, *by its own authority*, within Member States legal orders; in other words, entirely independently of national constitutional law. That represents a radical break with the normative framework of international law that continues to structure EU integration under the Treaties.

References to the normative framework of international law are not, however, entirely absent from the Court's case law. For example, in *Brasserie du Pêcheur SA*, the Court of Justice expressly invoked established principles of public international law on collective responsibility in order to support its judgment on the application of its case law on state liability to national legislatures. In precise terms, the Court concluded that,

> [I]n international law a state whose liability for a breach of an international commitment is in issue will be viewed as a single entity, irrespective of whether the breach which gave rise to the damage is attributable to the legislature, the judiciary, or the executive. This must apply *a fortiori* in the Community legal order since all State authorities, including the legislature, are bound in performing their tasks to comply with the rules laid down by Community law directly governing the situation [at issue].[67]

The Court's reasoning demonstrates its openness to the normative framework of international law as a toolbox to develop principles of Union law – at least to the extent that that framework aligns with its own institutional preferences. Such alignment is, however, very much the exception, not the rule.

2.2 The Court's Position on Constitutional Issue No. 1: Origins and Evolution

The Court's position on the formal status of Union law and the conditions under which it applies within Member States traces its origins

[67] Joined Cases C-46/93 and C-48/93, *Brasserie du Pêcheur SA* v. *Bundesrepublik Deutschland and The Queen* v. *Secretary of State for Transport, ex parte: Factortame Ltd and others* EU:C:1996:79 at para. 34.

back to its landmark judgment in *Van Gend en Loos*.[68] In that decision, the Court of Justice was requested, by way of preliminary reference from the Dutch Tariefcommissie, to determine whether Article 12 EEC had direct effect. The Court of Justice was, of course, perfectly competent to answer such a question. It necessitated an interpretation of the Treaty, which fell within its responsibility under (now) Article 267 TFEU. Following the PCIJ's Opinion in *Danzig Courts* (see Section 1.1.4), it was also not unheard of for an international tribunal to be asked to rule on the direct effect of treaty norms as a matter of international law.

In its reply to the Dutch court, the Court of Justice concluded that Article 12 EEC was indeed directly effective. On its assessment,

> Article 12 contain[ed] a clear and unconditional prohibition which is not a positive but negative obligation. This obligation, moreover, is not qualified by any reservation on the part of states which would make its implementation conditional upon a positive legislative measure enacted under national law. The very nature of this prohibition makes it ideally adapted to produce direct effects in the legal relationship between Member States and their subjects.[69]

The Court's attribution of direct effect to Article 12 EEC is certainly open to question in light of the *Danzig* ruling. The wording of that provision, together with the arguments of the intervening Member State governments, leave real scope to doubt Member States' intention to confer rights on individuals directly in the area of customs policy. However, that is not the standout feature of the decision. The distinguishing feature in *Van Gend en Loos* is the Court's assertion of judicial control over the domestic application of EU legal norms as a matter of (then) *Community* law. That move marked the Court's first strike at the international law framework that, as argued earlier, still structures the internal application of Union law under the EU Treaties.

In *Van Gend en Loos*, the Court did not look to the Treaty's basic – and clear – statements on the rules governing the domestic effect of (then) Community legal norms. Had it done so, it would have found a clear answer: the internal effect of EU norms remained a matter for individual Member States. The Court's attribution of direct effect to Article 12 EEC required Member States to give effect to that ruling domestically, but did not prescribe how that result was to be achieved. Should a Member State

[68] For discussion, see B. de Witte, 'Direct Effect, Primacy, and the Nature of the Legal Order' in G. de Búrca and P. Craig (eds.), *The Evolution of EU Law* (2nd edn) (Oxford: Oxford University Press, 2011) at pp. 323–362.

[69] Case 26/62, *van Gend & Loos*, n. 1 at p. 13.

such as the Netherlands fail to do so, this would not be without legal consequences. Specifically, it would be open to the Commission and/or another Member State to instigate infringement proceedings against the defaulting State pursuant to (now) Articles 258 and 258 TFEU respectively.

The Court of Justice opted, however, for a subtle but radically different approach that contested the Treaty framework's unambiguous statements on Constitutional Issue No. 1. It ruled expressly that, as far as it was concerned, the principles of international law regarding the domestic effect of treaty norms embedded in the EU Treaty framework did *not* apply to the (then) EEC Treaty. The Court did so by adopting a broad teleological approach to treaty interpretation – a component part of the international law toolbox.[70] However, it is not *how* the Court ruled, but *what* the Court determined that is significant and, moreover, the source of contestation with the Treaty framework as constitutional touchstone. In its own words, the Court ruled in *Van Gend en Loos* that,

> Independently of the legislation of Member States, Community law . . . not only imposes obligations on individuals but is also intended to confer upon them rights which become part of their legal heritage. These rights arise not only where they are expressly granted by the Treaty, but also by reason of obligations which the Treaty imposes in a clearly defined way upon individuals as well as upon the Member States and upon the institutions of the Community.[71]

The key phrase in the Court's judgment was 'independently of the legislation of Member States'. Through that simple expression, the Court of Justice made a powerful and innovative claim to manage the internal application of EU treaty norms *as a matter of Union law*. This is qualitatively different from merely pronouncing that Article 12 EEC was capable of direct effect as an international treaty norm and, accordingly, obliging Member States to give effect to that decision domestically pursuant to (now) Articles 4(3) TEU and Articles 280 and 299 TFEU. It represented (and continues to represent) a remarkable act of judicial dynamism.

The Court's position on the domestic effect of EU law was subsequently further developed in the shadow of national constitution rules

[70] Case 26/62, *van Gend & Loos*, n. 1 at p. 12. See also Art. 31(1) VCLT.

[71] Case 26/62, *van Gend & Loos*, n. 1 at p. 12. See also Case 28/67, *Firma Molkerei-Zentrale Westfalen/Lippe GmbH* EU:C:1968:17 at p. 154: 'It is clear from the fundamental principles of the Treaty . . . that [Treaty] provisions, so far as by their nature they are capable of doing so, enter into national legal systems *without the assistance of any national measure*' (emphasis added).

governing the internal effect of international norms. In *Costa* v. *ENEL*, the Court took the next major step by asserting the primacy of Union law over conflicting provisions of national law. In *Van Gend en Loos* there had been no need for the Court of Justice to rule on the hierarchy of EU norms (and Article 12 EEC in particular) within domestic legal orders. Rather conveniently, the Netherlands Constitution already provided the desired response as a matter of national constitutional law. Article 94 thereof attributes primary to international norms in instances of conflict with provisions of (ordinary) Dutch law. The Court of Justice in *Van Gend en Loos* could therefore easily defer judgment on the primacy of EU law vis-à-vis national law within Member States.

Since *Costa* v. *ENEL*, the Court has repeatedly confirmed that, as a matter of Union law, EU norms take primacy over Member State law. Importantly, this applies without regard to the domestic constitutional status of the conflicting norm or whether it pre- or post-dates the entry into force of the EU law in question.[72] As the Grand Chamber summarised in *Melloni*, 'by virtue of the principle of primacy of EU law, which is an essential feature of the EU legal order, rules of national law, even of a constitutional order, cannot be allowed to undermine the effectiveness of EU law on the territory of that State'.[73]

Taken together, the Court's formative rulings on direct effect and primacy form part of a broader judicial vision of the European Union as a 'new legal order' that is autonomous and entirely distinct from the Treaty framework's clear statements on Constitutional Issue No. 1. As previously noted, the Court of Justice has reiterated in varying formulations its view that,

> The founding treaties of the European Union, unlike ordinary international treaties, established a new legal order, possessing its own institutions, for the benefit of which the States have limited their sovereign rights, in ever wider fields, and the subjects of which comprise not only Member States but also their nationals. The essential characteristics of the European Union legal order thus constituted are in particular its primacy over the laws of the Member States and the direct effect of a whole series of provisions which are applicable to their nationals and to the Member States themselves.[74]

[72] Case 11/70, *Internationale Handelsgesellschaft mbH*, n. 65 at para. 3.

[73] Case C-399/11, *Melloni*, n. 65 at para. 59.

[74] Opinion 1/09, *Draft Agreement on the Creation of a Unified Patent Litigation System*, n. 1 at para. 65.

Likewise, in its recent Opinion on the compatibility of the Draft Agreement for EU Accession to the ECHR with the Treaty framework, the Full Court ruled that:

> EU law is characterised by the fact that it stems from an independent source of law, the Treaties, by its primacy over the law of the Member States, and by the direct effect of a whole series of provisions which are applicable to their nationals and to the Member States themselves.[75]

These judgments leave no doubt as to the Court's view of the distinctive character of Union law and the EU legal order more generally. The question, of course, is what binds together its institutional statements on the formal status of Union law and the conditions under which it applies within Member States?

3 The Court of Justice, Constitutional Issue No. 1 and the 'Constitutionalisation' of the EU Legal Order

The Court's approach to determining the formal status of Union law and the conditions under which it applies within Member States is characteristic of an act of constitutional contestation with regard to the first key issue for EU constitutionalism. The EU Treaty framework remains firmly grounded in the normative paradigm of international law (Section 1.2). By contrast, the Court has sought to sever important links with that paradigm, accentuating the distinctiveness and autonomy of the EU as a 'new legal order' and by asserting full control over the domestic application of Union law (Section 2).

This section locates the Court's statements on Constitutional Issue No. 1 within a broader process of judicial 'constitutionalisation'.[76] It exposes its case law on the formal status of Union law and the conditions under which it applies within Member States as part of a wider judicial effort to recast the relationship between the Union and the Member States along domestic, rather than international lines (Section 3.1). As this section concludes, that effort has historically enjoyed strong support

[75] Opinion 2/13, *Draft Agreement on Accession of the EU to the European Convention on Human Rights*, n. 1 at para. 166.

[76] See Stein, 'Lawyers, Judges, and the Making of a Transnational Constitution', n. 5; Mancini, 'The Making of a Constitution for Europe', n. 5 and Weiler, 'The Transformation of Europe', n. 5. See also earlier, Green, *Political Integration by Jurisprudence*, n. 5.

among EU scholars, who were also instrumental in its construction as an act of constitutional contestation (Section 3.2).

3.1 The Court of Justice and the 'Constitutionalisation' of the EU Legal Order

In its best light, the Court's divergent position on Constitutional Issue No. 1 should be seen to form an integral component of its broader judicial vision of the European Union as a constitutional order in embryonic or quasi-federal form.[77] Its decisions on direct effect and primacy in *Van Gend en Loos* and *Costa* v. *ENEL*, respectively, are simply two steps on a judicial pathway that has sought progressively to recast the relationship between the Union and the Member States along domestic, rather than international lines.

The Court of Justice has taken further steps to detach the EU legal order from the international law framework embedded in the Treaties in many different ways. First, the Court has turned its back on the traditional international law paradigm through the simple *use of language*. Accordingly, the EU Treaties are no longer routinely referenced as international treaties, but as the basis of the European Union's 'constitutional charter'.[78] Similarly, when discussing EU competences, the Court emphasises the transfer of 'sovereign rights' by Member States to the Union institutions.[79] Implicit in that statement is the Court's belief that the Union itself is now the holder of sovereign rights – a status that, in international law, remains associated with states, not international organisations.

Secondly, the Court of Justice has skilfully inverted the orthodox relationship between the individual and the State as *subjects* of international law. In international law, states remain the primary subjects

[77] See in particular, Stein, 'Lawyers, Judges, and the Making of a Transnational Constitution', n. 5; Mancini, 'The Making of a Constitution for Europe', n. 5 and Weiler, 'The Transformation of Europe', n. 5 and K. Alter, *Establishing the Supremacy of European Law* (Oxford: Oxford University Press, 2001).

[78] Case 294/83, *Parti écologiste "Les Verts"* v. *European Parliament* EU:C:1985:166166 at para. 23. See also, Joined Cases C-402/05 P and C-415/0, *Kadi*, n. 66 at para. 281 and Opinion 2/13, *Draft Agreement on Accession of the EU to the European Convention on Human Rights*, n. 1 at para. 163.

[79] Case 26/62, *van Gend & Loos*, n. 1 at p. 12. See also, Case 6/64, *Costa*, n. 1 at p. 593 and Opinion 1/91, *Draft agreement between the Community, on the one hand, and the countries of the European Free Trade Association, on the other, relating to the creation of the European Economic Area*, n. 1 at para. 22 and Opinion 1/09, *Draft Agreement on the Creation of a Unified Patent Litigation System*, n. 1 at para. 65.

of legal obligations. Individuals generally feature only as the beneficiaries of specific rights, the enforcement of which typically remains entirely conditional on municipal law (see Section 1.1). In a radical departure from this model, the Court has repositioned individuals at the *centre* of European integration in a manner that is again more akin to the domestic legal context. That repositioning started in *Van Gend en Loos*, where the Court explicitly referenced its view that the subjects of the (then) Community as a 'new legal order' comprised 'not only Member States *but also their nationals*'.[80]

Subsequent cases have pushed the Court's statement in *Van Gend en Loos* much further to bring individuals to the very forefront of European integration. Most obviously, the Court has transformed ostensibly mundane Treaty provisions into 'fundamental freedoms' that individuals may rely on directly before national courts.[81] Thus, Article 34 TFEU, which commits Member States to abolish quantitative restrictions on imported goods and all measures having equivalent effect, has become an individual right to engage in cross-border trade.[82] In the same way, Articles 45, 49, 56 TFEU on the free movement of workers, freedom of establishment and free movement of services have all been reframed as fundamental rights that form part of the economic constitution of the EU legal order.[83]

Thirdly, as part of the process of judicial constitutionalisation, the Court has repositioned itself at the top of the 'new legal order' in the role of EU Supreme Court *de facto*. On the strength of its own jurisprudence, the Court now exercises functions and displays institutional behaviours that more closely reflect those of a constitutional court in the European continental tradition rather than those of an international tribunal.[84]

[80] Case 26/62, *van Gend & Loos*, n. 1 at p. 12 (emphasis added).

[81] Supporting that view, see e.g. M. Poiares Maduro, *We, The Court: The European Court of Justice and the European Economic Constitution* (Oxford: Hart Publishing, 1998) at pp. 166–175.

[82] See e.g., Case C-265/95, *Commission* v. *France (Strawberries)* EU:C:1997:595 at para. 32 and Case C-112/00, *Schmidberger, Internationale Transporte und Planzüge* v. *Republik Österreich* EU:C:2003:333 at paras. 54 and 59.

[83] See e.g., Case C-19/12, *Kraus* v. *Land Baden-Württemberg* EU:C:1993:125 at para. 16 and Case C-415/93, *Union royale belge des sociétés de football association ASBL* v. *Bosman* EU:C:1995:463 at para. 78.

[84] For discussion of the Court's role as an EU Constitutional Court, see e.g., A. Donner, 'The Constitutional Powers of the Court of Justice of the European Communities' (1974) 11 *Common Market Law Review*, 127; O. Due, 'A Constitutional Court for the European

Most clearly perhaps, the Court exploits the preliminary reference procedure as a means to extend the scope of its judicial review functions to scrutinise *de facto* the validity of Member State measures against the Treaty framework. That is a remarkable development, which further shifts the character of EU judicial adjudication firmly towards the domestic constitutional paradigm. It should be recalled that, under the EU Treaties, the Court of Justice enjoys only full powers of judicial review internally; in other words, with respect to acts of the *Union institutions*.[85] The Treaties grant the Court no comparable power to rule on the validity of provisions of Member State law. Yet, in effect, this is exactly what the Court now undertakes on a routine basis.

As Mancini argues, in responses to requests from national courts for interpretations of EU law,

> the Court does not confine itself to interpreting the Community rule; instead it enters into the heart of the conflict submitted to its attention, but takes the precaution of rendering it abstract, that is to say it presents it as a conflict between Community law and a hypothetical national provision having the nature of the provision in issue before the national court. The technique thus described … results in the Court of Justice acquiring a power of review which is analogous to – though of course narrower than – that routinely exercised by the Supreme Court of the United States and the constitutional courts of some Member States.[86]

Lenaerts' analysis of the Court's approach to the scope of its functions under the preliminary reference procedure is even stronger. In his view, using Article 267 TFEU, 'the Court of Justice … [goes] as far as it [can] to reach the same practical outcome as the one that would be obtained through a direct invalidation of Member State law'.[87]

Communities' in D. Curtin and D. O'Keeffe (eds.), *Constitutional Adjudication in European Community and National Law* (Butterworth: London, 1992); F. G. Jacobs, 'Is the Court of Justice of the European Communities a Constitutional Court?' in D. Curtin and D. O'Keeffe (eds.), *Constitutional Adjudication in European Community and National Law* (Butterworth: London, 1992); J. Rinze, 'The Role of the European Court of Justice as a Federal Constitutional Court' (1993) *Public Law*, 426 and more recently, B. Vesterdorf, 'A Constitutional Court for the EU?' (2006) 4(4) *International Journal of Constitutional Law*, 607 and J. Baquero Cruz, 'The Changing Constitutional Role of the European Court of Justice' (2006) 43(2) *International Journal of Legal Information*, 223.

85 See Art. 263 TFEU in combination with Art. 264 TFEU.

86 Mancini, 'The Making of a Constitution for Europe', n. 5 at p. 606. See also, H. Rasmussen, 'Why Is Article 173 Interpreted against Private Plaintiffs?' (1980) 5 *European Law Review*, 112 at p. 115.

87 K. Lenaerts, 'Constitutionalism and the Many Faces of Federalism' (1990) 38(2) *American Journal of Comparative Law*, 205 at p. 256.

The Court of Justice also displays more classically domestic institutional behaviours in other spheres of its activities. For example, its approach to the implementation of international law norms within the EU legal order is strikingly domestic in character. In parallel with the position adopted by many national constitutional courts when interpreting domestic constitutions, the Court of Justice has ruled that international norms do not take primacy over the EU Treaties. Its judgment in *Kadi*, on the relationship between Union law and the UN Charter, was explicit on that point. In that decision, the Grand Chamber ruled that, 'the obligations imposed by an international agreement cannot have the effect of prejudicing the constitutional principles of the EC Treaty'.[88] This is exactly the same reasoning that most Member State constitutional courts deploy in order to manage the reception of EU law within domestic legal systems (see further Chapter 6). It is the behaviour of a domestic constitutional court *par excellence*.

Finally, the Court's case law on implied powers provides a further example of the same phenomenon.[89] In *Commission* v. *Council (ERTA)*, the Court ruled that the existence (and subsequent exercise) of Community competence in the sphere of the common transport policy precluded Member States from concluding international agreements in the same substantive field. It ruled that, 'Each time the Community, with a view to implementing a common policy envisaged by the Treaty, adopts provisions laying down common rules, whatever form these may take, the Member States no longer have the right, acting individually or even collectively, to undertake obligations with third countries which affect those rules.'[90] As Weiler observes, the Court's approach on implied powers 'sidestepped' the presumptive rule of interpretation that applies to the determination of competences in international law. In its place, the Court again opted in favour of a solution that is taken straight from the toolbox of national constitutional interpretation.[91]

[88] Joined Cases C-402/05 P and C-415/0, *Kadi*, n. 66, at p. 285. International agreements may only be invoked to scrutinise *secondary* Union law. See *Kadi*, at paras. 304–309 and, earlier, Case C-61/94, *Commission* v. *Germany (International Dairy Agreement)* EU:C:1996:313 at para. 52 and Case C-311/04, *Algemene Scheeps Agentuur Dordrecht* EU:C:2006:23 at para. 25.

[89] See Case 22/70, *Commission* v. *Council (ERTA)* EU:C:1971:32. See also, e.g., Opinion 1/76, *Draft Agreement establishing a European laying-up fund for internal waterway vessels* EU:C:1977:63 and, in connection with the exercise of internal competences, Case C-176/03, *Commission* v. *Council (Environmental Sanctions)* EU:C:2005:542 at paras. 48–51.

[90] Case 22/70 *Commission* v. *Council (ERTA)*, n. 89 at para. 17.

[91] Weiler, 'The Transformation of Europe', n. 5 at p. 2407.

3.2 Support from the Sidelines: EU Legal Scholarship

There is nothing especially novel in arguing that the Court of Justice considers the EU legal order, and its own role therein, along more domestic than international lines. EU legal scholars were extremely quick to acknowledge the unifying federalising threads that underpin its case law on the formal status of EU law. The following three extracts authored in the 1960s by Valentine, Chavallier and Green, respectively, demonstrate this point clearly:[92]

> In interpreting the Treaties, the Court has adopted certain methods. It has also made certain assumptions, which are extremely important because these are not derived from the text of the Treaties but are a reflection of the Court's own views.[93]
>
> What is the thread binding these different judgments ... in which the Court asserts both its capacity of being the supreme interpreter of the Treaty and the needs of the Community? I think the key to all this is to be found in the simple fact that the Court is beginning to decide cases in the spirit of a national court and no longer of an international court.[94]
>
> The Court of Justice is building its own system of Community law, distinct and separate from the legal systems of the Member States, and from the legal system of traditional international law. If a label must be put on this legal system, the label "federal" would be appropriate, in the same sense that one speaks of a "federal" system of law in the United States.[95]

These initial accounts were subsequently refined by the work of scholars aligned to a new intellectual legal movement – 'integration through law'.[96] The basic and, to a large extent enduring, achievement of this influential movement was to reconstruct and defend the individual strands of the Court's case law on the formal status of EU law as an epic tale of judicial 'constitutionalisation'.[97] Thus, on Stein's classic account:

92 For an overview of initial scholarly reactions to the Court's early jurisprudence, see Green, *Political Integration by Jurisprudence*, n. 5 at pp. 463–490.

93 D. G Valentine, *The Court of Justice of the European Communities* (London: Stevens, 1965) at p. 370.

94 R. M. Chevallier, 'Methods and Reasoning of the European Court of Justice in Its Interpretation of Community Law' (1965) 2 *Common Market Law Review*, 21 at p. 25.

95 Green, *Political Integration by Jurisprudence*, n. 5 at p. 442.

96 M. Cappelletti, M. Seccombe and J. H. Weiler (eds.), *Integration through Law: Europe and the American Federal Experience* (Berlin: de Gruyter: 1986). For a retrospective, see D. Augenstein (ed.), *'Integration through law' Revisited: The Making of a European Polity'* (Farnham: Ashgate, 2012).

97 The constitutionalisation thesis emerged relatively early on in formative studies in comparative constitutionalism undertaken by scholars, see esp., Green, *Political Integration by Jurisprudence*, n. 5.

> The Court ... construed the European Community Treaties in a constitutional mode rather than employing the traditional international law methodology. Proceeding from a fragile jurisdictional base, the Court has arrogated to itself the ultimate authority to draw the line between Community law and national law. Moreover, it has established and obtained acceptance of the broad principle of direct integration of Community law into the national legal order of the member states and of the supremacy of Community law within its limited but expanded area of competence over any conflicting national law.[98]

Likewise, in what remains a landmark analysis of formative judicial developments with respect to the nature of EU law, Weiler argues that:

> The Treaties have been "constitutionalized" and the Community has become an entity whose closest structural model is no longer an international organization but a denser, yet non-unitary polity, principally the federal state. Put differently, the Community's "operating system" is no longer governed by general principles of public international law, but by a specific interstate governmental structure defined by a constitutional charter and constitutional principles.[99]

The 'constitutional' narrative of EU integration has proven incredibly resilient over time.[100] The Court, for its part, has not adjusted its basic understanding of the formal status of EU law and the rules governing its application within Member States. It remains fully committed to its formative conception of the Union as a 'new legal order' that is detached from the normative framework of international law and structured instead – at least implicitly – around domestic constitutional principles.[101] This is notwithstanding the emergence and subsequent proliferation of new approaches to European integration at variance with the traditional supranational or 'Community' model. In particular, and starting with the Single European Act, Member States have made increasing recourse to the institutional framework of intergovernmentalism as the basis for further integration.[102]

EU scholarship remains firmly attached to (and extremely defensive of) the Court's constitutionalisation narrative. As Davies and Rasmussen observe, 'Much of the legal and social science literature today unreflectively

[98] Stein, 'Lawyers, Judges, and the Making of a Transnational Constitution', n. 5 at p. 1.

[99] Weiler, 'The Transformation of Europe,' n. 5 at p. 2407.

[100] See M. Avbelj, 'Questioning EU Constitutionalisms' (2008) 9(1) *German Law Journal*, 1.

[101] See e.g., Opinion 2/13, *Draft Agreement on Accession of the EU to the European Convention on Human Rights*, n. 1.

[102] For analysis, see e.g., D. Curtin, 'The Constitutional Structure of the Union: A Europe of Bits and Pieces' (1993) 30(1) *Common Market Law Review*, 17.

analyses integration within some version of the Constitutionalisation paradigm.'[103] When necessary, EU scholars have adapted rather than abandoned the Court's institutional position on the formal status of EU law and the conditions under which it applies within Member States to fit the changing political context of European integration.[104] The most significant adjustment has been a shift towards the normative framework of (constitutional) pluralism.[105] Through the pluralist lens, the Court's proclamations concerning the formal status of EU law are placed *alongside* Member State conceptions of the EU legal order in a new, *heterarchical,* not hierarchical relationship.[106] This important evolution in EU legal scholarship is considered further in Chapter 6.

However, notwithstanding adjustments in the scholarship, the fact remains that the Court's position on Constitutional Issue No. 1 is based on a normative vision for EU integration that was (and still is) projected onto rather than deduced from the Treaty framework. In essence, the Court's 'new legal order' claim is premised on its basic assertion that the Treaty framework, as touchstone on the internal constitutionality of all EU institutional activity, has never actually meant what it so clearly states. EU law is not, as the Treaties prescribe, simply international law, but instead, in the Court's eyes, the basis of a 'new legal order' that is defined in opposition to the principles and practice of international law that remain firmly embedded in the Treaty framework as constitutional touchstone.

[103] B. Davies and M. Rasmussen, 'Towards a New History of European Law' (2012) 21(2) *Contemporary European History* 305 at p. 308. See also, Avbelj, 'Questioning EU Constitutionalisms', n. 100 at p. 1.

[104] For an overview of the principal responses, see Avbelj, 'Questioning EU Constitutionalisms', n. 100.

[105] See e.g., N. MacCormick, 'Beyond the Sovereign State' (1993) 56 *Modern Law Review*, 1; N. Walker, The Idea of Constitutional Pluralism' (2002) 65 *Modern Law Review*; J. Weiler, 'Federalism without Constitutionalism: Europe's Sonderweg' in K. Nicolaidis and R. Howse (eds.), *The Federal Vision* (Oxford: Oxford University Press, 2001); M. Poiares Maduro, 'Contrapunctual Law: Europe's Constitutional Pluralism in Action' in N. Walker (ed.), *Sovereignty in Transition* (Oxford: Hart Publishing, 2003) and M. Kumm, 'The Jurisprudence of Constitutional Conflict: Constitutional Supremacy in Europe before and after the Constitutional Treaty' (2005) 11 *European Law Review*, 262.

[106] For Jaklic, this constitutes the Ariadne's thread of pluralist discourse in EU integration. See K. Jaklic, *Constitutional Pluralism in the EU* (Oxford: Oxford University Press, 2015) at p. 5.

Concluding Remarks

Using the intellectual framework established in Chapters 1 and 2, Chapters 3, 4 and 5 of this book set out to assess how far EU judicial activity conforms to the Treaty framework and its statements on the three basic issues for EU constitutionalism. The overall argument developed across Chapters 3, 4 and 5 is that the Court's institutional positions on each of the three key issues for EU constitutionalism offer paradigmatic examples of what Chapter 2 defined as acts of constitutional contestation.

This chapter was specifically concerned with the Court's statements on the first issue for EU constitutionalism, addressing the formal status of Union law and the conditions under which it applies within Member States. In particular, it demonstrated that the Court of Justice has formulated and, thereafter, robustly defended its own position on that initial constitutional issue. In summary, its approach comprises three interrelated claims. First, the Court of Justice asserts that the European Union constitutes a 'new legal order' distinct from ordinary international law.[107] Secondly, EU law is deemed to be 'autonomous' in character.[108] Thirdly, and most crucially, the Court has ruled that the application of Union law within Member States is exclusively a matter for Union law and governed by the principles of direct effect and primacy.[109]

The Court's statements on the formal status of Union law and the conditions under which it applies within Member States remain external to, and in contestation with, the Treaty framework as constitutional

[107] See Case 26/62, *van Gend & Loos*, n. 1 at p. 12. See also Case 6/64, *Costa*, n. 1 at p. 593, Opinion 1/09, *Draft Agreement on the Creation of a Unified Patent Litigation System*, n. 1 at para. 65 and Opinion 2/13, *Draft Agreement on Accession of the EU to the European Convention on Human Rights*, n. 1 at para. 157. See also, with respect to the Court's position on the autonomy of the EU legal order in the field of external relations, Opinion 1/91, *Draft agreement between the Community, on the one hand, and the countries of the European Free Trade Association, on the other, relating to the creation of the European Economic Area*, n. 1 at para. 1 and Opinion 1/00, *Proposed agreement between the European Community and non-Member States on the establishment of a European Common Aviation Area*, n. 1.

[108] See e.g., Case 26/62, *van Gend & Loos*, n. 1 at p. 12; Case 6/64, *Costa*, n. 1 at p. 593 and Opinion 1/91, *Draft agreement between the Community, on the one hand, and the countries of the European Free Trade Association, on the other, relating to the creation of the European Economic Area*, n. 1, at para. 2; Opinion 1/00, *Proposed Agreement between the European Community and non-Member States on the establishment of a European Common Aviation Area*, n. 1 at paras. 5–46 and Opinion 2/13, *Draft Agreement on Accession of the EU to the European Convention on Human Rights*, n. 1 at paras. 158, 166 and 170.

[109] Case 26/62, *van Gend & Loos*, n. 1 at p. 12 and Case 6/64, *Costa*, n. 1 at p. 593.

touchstone. The EU Treaties (as amended) continue to accentuate the ordinary character of Union law as international law. Moreover, the EU Treaty framework also continues to make no special provision for the application of Union law within Member States. On the contrary, the provisions governing the general application of EU law, the legal effects of judgments of the Court of Justice and the enforcement of EU legal norms all reinforce the conclusion that the relationship between the Union and Member State legal orders remains ultimately grounded in the normative framework of international law.

The Court's approach to Constitutional Issue No. 1 traces its origins back to its landmark judgments on direct effect and primacy: *Van Gend en Loos* and *Costa* v. *ENEL*.[110] The Court's conclusions in both decisions, to which it has since robustly adhered, capture that institution's particular normative view on the *finalité* of EU integration. That vision, which appears impervious to changing (Member State) attitudes to EU integration over time,[111] was projected onto the Treaty framework rather than deduced from it. It forms the cornerstone of broader judicial efforts to recast the relationship between the Union and the Member States along domestic, rather than international lines – with the Court assuming for itself the role of EU Supreme Court *de facto* within that recast legal order.[112]

As an act of constitutional contestation, the survival of the Court's jurisprudence on Constitutional Issue No. 1 is ultimately conditional on the responses of the Court's principal interlocutors, namely: Member States and national courts. Without at least some degree of 'normalisation' by the Member States as Treaty signatories and, likewise, national courts as its institutional agents, the Court's assertion of control over, in particular, the internal effect of EU norms is entirely meaningless. It is simply the judicial equivalent of tilting at windmills. Chapter 6 explores the 'feedback loop' – the responses of the Court's key interlocutors to its position on, *inter alia*, the formal status of EU law as site of constitutional contestation.

110 *Ibid.*

111 See recently, e.g., Opinion 2/13, *Draft Agreement on Accession of the EU to the European Convention on Human Rights*, n. 1.

112 See Stein, 'Lawyers, Judges, and the Making of a Transnational Constitution', n. 5; Mancini, 'The Making of a Constitution for Europe', n. 5 and Weiler, 'The Transformation of Europe', n. 5. See also, earlier, Green, *Political Integration by Jurisprudence*, n. 5.

However, before closing the feedback loop in Chapter 6, this monograph continues its search for acts of constitutional contestation in relation to EU judicial activity. This begins in Chapter 4 with scrutiny of the Court of Justice's position on the locus of political authority within the EU legal order (Constitutional Issue No. 2) for compliance with the Treaty framework as constitutional touchstone.

4 The Court of Justice, the Treaty Framework and Constitutional Issue No. 2

> The Treaties set up a system for distributing power among the different Community institutions, assigning to each institution its own role in the institutional structure of the Community and the accomplishment of the tasks entrusted to the Community
>
> Case C-70/88, *Parliament and Council (Chernobyl)* EU:C:1990:217 at para. 21

Introduction

Chapters 3–5 of this book assess how far EU judicial activity conforms to the Treaty framework and its statements on the three basic issues for EU constitutionalism. This analysis is based on the normative framework established in Chapters 1 and 2, which defended the status, function and limits of the EU Treaties as principal touchstones on the internal constitutionality of all Union activity – including the work of the Court.

Chapter 3 assessed how far EU judicial activity conforms to the Treaty framework and its statements on the first issue for EU constitutionalism, namely the formal status of Union law and the conditions under which it applies within Member States. Using the intellectual framework developed in Chapters 1 and 2, that enquiry unmasked the Court's position on Constitutional Issue No. 1 as a clear example of what Chapter 2 characterised as an act of constitutional contestation.[1] This chapter embarks on the same enquiry in relation to the second issue for EU constitutionalism, concerning *the locus of political authority within the EU*

[1] Chapter 2 defined acts of *constitutional contestation* as measures developed by the EU institutions and/or Member States in tension with the Treaties' basic statements on the three fundamental issues for EU constitutionalism (Chapter 1). Along with acts of *constitutional supplementation*, acts of constitutional contestation condition the broader constitutional context that structures EU integration.

legal order. In summary, it argues that the Court's position on the locus of political authority within the EU legal order offers further paradigmatic examples of acts of constitutional contestation in the sphere of EU judicial activity.

In common with its position on Constitutional Issue No. 1 (Chapter 3), the EU Treaty framework sets out a clear position on the locus of political authority within the EU legal order. As argued in Chapter 1, that second key issue for EU constitutionalism has two dimensions: *constituent authority* and *EU policymaking authority*. With respect, first, to constituent authority, the EU Treaties leave no doubt whatsoever as to the position of Member States as the 'Masters of the Treaties'. Under the Treaty framework, Member States – acting collectively – retain full political control of the adoption, ratification and amendment of the Treaties. Secondly, with respect to EU policymaking, the Treaty framework entrusts primary responsibility to the Union's political institutions; principally, the Commission, European Parliament and Council of the European Union.[2] The EU Treaty framework brings together the competing political interests represented by these three key actors to produce policy outputs through a series of prescribed legislative procedures.

This chapter demonstrates that the Court has mounted a series of challenges to the locus of EU political authority under the Treaty framework. These challenges affect both dimensions of political authority sketched out earlier: (1) constituent authority (reserved to Member States as Treaty signatories) and also (2) EU policymaking authority (entrusted by Member States to the Union's political institutions).

Section 1 examines judicial challenges to constituent authority. It shows that the Court has repeatedly contested the fundamentals of constituent authority within the EU legal order. First, this can be seen in judicial efforts to undermine the exclusive competence of Member States to revise the Treaties pursuant to Article 48 TEU. Secondly, it is also clearly visible in the Court's disregard for additional expressions of constituent authority on discrete issues. These expressions include Member States' acts of constitutional supplementation (Chapter 2) addressing the rules governing the acquisition and loss of Member State nationality (*Rottmann*) and the terms of the EU's accession to the

[2] See also the role of the European Council in specific policy fields such as the Common Foreign and Security Policy (Title V, Chapter 2 TEU).

European Convention on Human Rights (ECHR) (*Opinion 2/13*).[3] With respect to both sets of examples, the Court employs the same underlying interpretative approach. Specifically, the Court asserts its own statements on the key issues for EU constitutionalism – developed independently of the Treaty framework – in order to overturn, qualify or simply interrogate these important statements of constituent authority.

Section 2 examines the Court's position on EU policymaking authority. In addition to contesting the Treaties' position on constituent authority, the Court of Justice is also responsible for a dramatic, unilateral restructuring of the institutional dynamics that govern EU policymaking under the Treaty framework. In summary, the Court has skilfully interposed itself alongside the Union's political institutions as *direct policymaker* in many key areas of EU policy. Section 2 examines the origins, nature and impact of the Court's direct policymaking platform as a further act of constitutional contestation with regard to the Treaty framework's statements on the locus of EU political authority.

1 Constituent Authority: The Court of Justice versus the EU Treaty Framework

This section assesses how far EU judicial activity complies with the Treaty framework's statements on constituent authority within the Union legal order. Section 1.1 begins with a brief restatement of the EU Treaties' position on that second key issue for EU constitutionalism. Thereafter, Section 1.2 exposes two sets of judicial challenges to the Treaty framework's clearly articulated statements on constituent authority within the EU. The first highlights examples of challenges to the Treaty framework's provisions on Treaty amendment (a competence reserved to Member States) (Section 1.2.1). The second unmasks judicial challenges to specific acts of constitutional supplementation. This includes the Court's review of supplementary Member State statements on the conditions governing the acquisition and loss of Member State nationality (*Rottmann*) and the terms of the EU's accession to the ECHR (*Opinion 2/13*) (Section 1.2.2).[4] Section 1.3 revaluates the Court's position within the Union legal order in light of its case law on constituent authority.

[3] Case C-135/08, *Rottman* v. *Freistaat Bayern* EU:C:2010:104 and Opinion 2/13, *Draft Agreement on Accession of the EU to the European Convention on Human Rights* EU:C:2014:2454.

[4] *Ibid.*

1.1 The EU Treaty Framework and Constituent Authority

The EU Treaties leave no doubt regarding the position of Member States – acting collectively – as the ultimate source of the EU's constituent political authority. As outlined in Chapters 1 and 3, the Union was (and remains) based on ordinary international treaties, negotiated and ratified by sovereign states on the strength of their continued collective political agreement to pursue European integration on the terms set out therein. The EU Treaty framework and its responses to the three issues for EU constitutionalism are the very embodiment of that collective political agreement.

The Treaty framework establishes the Court of Justice as an agent of the Member States.[5] As Treaty principals or 'Masters of the Treaties', the latter have collectively agreed, through the Treaties, to entrust to the Court of Justice responsibility to promote and, together with the Commission, monitor the performance of the EU Treaties. At times, that responsibility affords the Court considerable scope to influence the shape of EU norms and, more broadly, the development of European integration. This applies, in particular, with respect to the exercise of its interpretative competences.[6]

The EU Treaties are remarkably open-textured instruments, characterised by broad functional objectives and the inclusion of numerous provisions that demand additional clarification.[7] As is typical of international treaties, many of the EU Treaties' provisions conceal fundamental disagreement between Member States as treaty signatories on the specifics of key issues in European integration. For example, what exactly does Article 17(7) TEU mean when it obliges the European Council to 'take

[5] See also, A. Arnull, 'Me and My Shadow: The European Court of Justice and the Disintegration of European Union Law' (2007) 31 *Fordham International Law Journal*, 1174 at pp. 1175–1177. For analysis of the Court's agency role, see also, M. Pollack, *The Engines of Integration: Delegation, Agency, and Agency Setting in the European Union* (Oxford: Oxford University Press, 2003) and G. Garrett, 'International Cooperation and Institutional Choice: The European Community's Internal Market' (1992) 46 *International Organization*, 533.

[6] Pursuant to e.g., Art. 218(11) TFEU, Art. 258 TFEU, Art. 259 TFEU, Art. 263 TFEU and Art. 267 TFEU. For examples, see *Introduction*, n. 11–13 and the case law cited therein.

[7] On the functional character of EU competences, see recently, G. Davies, 'Democracy and Legitimacy in the Shadow of Purposive Competence' (2013) 21 *European Law Journal*, 2 at pp. 7–12. See also earlier, e.g., H. Farrell and A. Héritier, 'Contested Competences in Europe: Incomplete Contracts and Interstitial Institutional Change' (2007) 30 *West European Politics*, 227 and A. Stone Sweet, *The Judicial Construction of Europe* (Oxford: Oxford University Press, 2004) at pp. 24–31.

into account the elections to the European Parliament' when drawing up the list of candidates for the post of Commission President? Similarly, how far does the concept of 'official authority' in Article 51 TFEU stretch to limit the application of the Treaty provisions on intra-EU movement? The Court of Justice is established to resolve, when requested, such questions through the exercise of its interpretive functions.

Under the EU Treaty framework, judicial interpretation is not, however, without limits. Internally, judicial interpretation remains fundamentally constrained by the underlying character of the EU as a system of limited, attributed competences (Article 5 TEU).[8] The Court of Justice cannot, in the exercise of its attributed functions, break with the EU Treaties as constitutional touchstones (Chapter 1). Its inability to do so in specific instances may expose gaps or tensions within the Treaty framework. These gaps and tension may have potentially significant implications for European integration and, moreover, the institutional actors and individuals engaged and affected by that process. However, the Treaties do provide solutions for the resolution of such issues. Article 48 TEU establishes detailed procedures to revise the Treaties. Similarly, Article 352 TFEU makes provision, under specific circumstances, for Member States (subject to approval of, *inter alia*, national parliaments) to sanction extensions in Treaty competences where the present Treaties do not grant the Union institutions (sufficient) competence to act.

1.2 Judicial Challenges to Constituent Authority

The Court of Justice has repeatedly challenged the foundations of constituent authority under the Treaty framework in the exercise of its interpretative functions. This section identifies two sets of examples. First, the Court is shown repeatedly to have contested Member States' responsibility to revise the Treaties (Section 1.2.1). The EU Treaties continue (as before under the founding Treaty) to reserve that responsibility to the Member States acting collectively pursuant to, in particular,

[8] For analysis of *external* limits to EU judicial authority, see e.g., H. Rasmussen, *On Law and Policy in the European Court of Justice* (Dordrecht: Martinus Nijhoff, 1986); D. Keleman, 'The Political Foundations of Judicial Independence in the European Union' (2012) 19(1) *Journal of European Public Policy*, 43; D. S. Martinsen, *An Ever More Powerful Court? The Political Constraints of Legal Integration in the European Union* (Oxford: Oxford University Press, 2016) and M. Blauberger et al., 'ECJ Judges Read the Morning Papers. Explaining the Turnaround of European Citizenship Jurisprudence', *Journal of European Public Policy* (forthcoming, 2018).

Article 48 TEU. Secondly, the Court has also mounted additional challenges to the EU Treaties' position on constituent authority by disregarding specific acts of *constitutional supplementation* (Chapter 2) that Member States have adopted in order manage discrete issues in European integration (Section 1.2.2). These include, Declaration No. 2 on the rules governing the acquisition and loss of Member State nationality (*Rottmann*) and Protocol No. 8 on the terms of EU accession to the ECHR (*Opinion 2/13*).[9]

Constitutional Issues No. 1 and 3 are important background concerns in relation to both sets of examples. The Court's interventions to contest, first, Member States' responsibility to revise the Treaties (Section 1.2.1) and, secondly, specific acts of *constitutional supplementation* (Section 1.2.2) seek expressly to defend its institutional statements on *the formal status of Union law and the conditions under which it applies within Member States* (Constitutional Issue No. 1) and/or *the objectives, values and limits of EU integration* (Constitutional Issue No. 3). For the Court, these statements function as 'supra-constitutional' norms that it actively seeks to defend where challenged – including against clear statements of constituent authority. For example, in Section 1.2.1 the Court intervenes to defend its statements on *the formal status of Union law and the conditions under which it applies within Member States* (*Francovich*). Similarly, in Section 1.2.2 it asserts, *inter alia*, its institutional preferences with regard to *the objectives, values and limits of EU integration* in the specific area of EU citizenship rights (*Rottmann*).

1.2.1 *Judicial Challenges to Member States' Competence to Revise the Treaties*

Parliament v. *Council (Chernobyl)* and *Francovich*, on standing rights in annulment actions and reparation rights respectively, provide clear examples of judicial challenges to Member State competence to revise the EU Treaties pursuant to Article 48 TEU.[10] In *Parliament* v. *Council (Chernobyl)*, the European Parliament requested that the Court recognise its standing in annulment proceedings (now Article 263 TFEU). The Parliament had sought that recognition to enable it to contest the validity of a Council

[9] Declaration No. 2 on Nationality of a Member State [1992] OJ C 191/98 and Protocol No. 8 relating to Article 6(2) of the Treaty on European Union on the accession of the Union to the European Convention on the Protection of Human Rights and Fundamental Freedoms [2012] OJ C 326/273.

[10] Case C-70/88, *Parliament* v. *Council (Chernobyl)* EU:C:1990:217 and Joined Cases C-6/90 and C-9/90, *Francovich and Others* v. *Italy* EU:C:1991:428.

Regulation.[11] Specifically, it was seeking judicial review of the Commission's choice of legal basis for the draft Regulation. The Parliament had previously requested that the Commission prepare a new proposal based on an alternative provision: (then) Article 100a EEC. However, the Commission had opted not to do so, and the Council subsequently adopted the contested Regulation in its original form. Unfortunately for the European Parliament, the Treaty framework did not, at the material time, grant it standing to contest the Commission's decision on the appropriate legal basis for the adopted Regulation. The Court of Justice had previously confirmed that point expressly in its earlier judgment in *Parliament* v. *Council (Standing)*.[12] In no uncertain terms, it had ruled that, '[t]he applicable [Treaty] provisions, as they stand at present, do not enable the Court to recognize the capacity of the European Parliament to bring an action for annulment'.[13]

Revisiting the issue in *Parliament* v. *Council (Chernobyl)*, the Court of Justice adopted a very different approach, despite no changes to the Treaty framework in the intervening period. To begin with it appeared that nothing had changed; the Court acknowledged the European Parliament's continued exclusion as an applicant in annulment proceedings. It noted, as before, that,

> the Parliament does not have the right to bring an action for annulment under Article 173 of the EEC Treaty or under Article 146 of the Euratom Treaty . . . [it] is not included among the institutions which, like the Member States, can bring an action for annulment against any measure of another institutions. Furthermore, since the Parliament is not a legal person it [also] cannot bring an action before the Court under the second paragraph of the articles in question.[14]

However, for the Court, the Treaty's clear position on the European Parliament's standing rights – as a statement of Member State constituent authority – was no longer an obstacle to the recognition of such rights. Rather, that position simply formed the starting point of a broader judicial enquiry into the appropriate place for the European Parliament as an actor in annulment proceedings.

In substance, the Court ruled that the Parliament should enjoy standing before the Court to contest the validity of EU acts 'in defence of its prerogatives'.[15] That included, in the present case, instances where it

[11] For analysis, see e.g., G. Bebr, 'Case C-70/88, *European Parliament* v. *Council*, Judgment of the Court of Justice of 22 May 1990' (1991) 28(3) *Common Market Law Review*, 663.

[12] Case 302/87, *Parliament* v. *Council (Standing)* EU:C:1988:461.

[13] *Ibid.*, at para. 28.

[14] Case C-70/88, *Parliament* v. *Council (Chernobyl)* EU:C:1990:217 at paras. 12–14.

[15] *Ibid.*, at para. 31.

was open to the Parliament to contest the legal basis for EU instruments on the grounds that the Commission's choice was liable to affect its involvement in the adoption of the proposed measure.[16] As the Court summarised, 'Since the Parliament claims that its prerogatives were breached as a result of the choice of legal basis for the contested measure, it follows from all the foregoing that the present action is admissible.'[17]

The Court's challenge to constituent authority in *Parliament* v. *Council (Chernobyl)* did not explicitly reference its normative view of the Union as a 'new legal order' as the basis for recasting Member State preferences as Treaty principals. That move followed later (see *Francovich*). Instead, in *Parliament* v. *Council (Chernobyl)*, the Court justified its decision to recast the Treaty rules on the European Parliament's standing in annulment actions with reference to an (at the time) unwritten principle of 'institutional balance'. The EU Treaties, it ruled, were structured to disperse EU policymaking competence across the Union legislative institutions. That dispersal, the Court concluded, reflected a 'fundamental interest' in maintaining 'institutional balance', namely ensuring that each Union institution exercises its attributed powers with due regard for those of its counterparts.[18] On the strength of that unwritten principle alone, the Court concluded that, 'The absence in the Treaties of any provision giving the Parliament the right to bring an action for annulment ... cannot prevail over the fundamental interest in the maintenance and observance of the institutional balance laid down in the Treaties.'[19]

In *Francovich*, the Court of Justice went much further. In that case, the Court established, as a matter of Union law, an entirely new right to reparation.[20] It concluded that Member States were liable to compensate individuals for loss and damage that resulted from breaches of Union law for which they could be held responsible. This was a truly remarkable move for a Court that was (and remains) established to discharge agency functions within a system of limited attributed competences. The Court's reasoning in *Francovich* directly challenged the nature of the EU legal order as a system of limited attributed competences and, in

[16] At para. 30.
[17] At para. 31.
[18] See now Art. 13(2) TEU, which expressly mandates this requirement for inter-institutional co-operation between the EU institutions.
[19] At para. 26.
[20] Joined Cases C-6/90 and C-9/90, *Francovich and Others* v. *Italy*, n. 10.

particular, the position of Member States within that system as constituent authorities.

The EU Treaties make no provision for Member State liability towards individuals. This remains the case to date (i.e., under the present, post-Lisbon settlement). The scope of the Court's new *Francovich* remedy has been subsequently extended and refined, but never (as yet) integrated into the Treaty framework.[21] Instead, the Treaties have only ever provided (and continue to provide) for the contractual and non-contractual liability of the Union. With respect to the latter, Article 340 TFEU details, *inter alia*, that the Union shall make good any damage caused by its institutions or by its servants in the performance of their duties. The legal principles governing the terms of that obligation are to be determined in accordance with general principles that are common to the laws of the Member States.

The Court's reasoning in *Francovich*, directly challenging the position of Member States on reparation rights, is entirely self-referential.[22] The starting point of its analysis is its own institutional view on the position of individuals as the direct subjects of rights and obligations within the Union legal order as a 'new legal order' (Chapter 3). Specifically, the Court recalled its earlier normative assertion that,

> the EEC Treaty has created its own legal system, which is integrated into the legal systems of the Member States and which their courts are bound to apply. *The subjects of that legal system are not only the Member States but also their nationals. Just as it imposes burdens on individuals, Community law is also intended to give rise to rights which become part of their legal patrimony*. Those rights arise not only where they are expressly granted by the Treaty but also by virtue of obligations which the Treaty imposes in a clearly defined manner both on individuals and on the Member States and the Community institutions.[23]

[21] See e.g., Joined Cases C-46/93 and C-48/93, *Brasserie du Pêcheur SA* v. *Bundesrepublik Deutschland and The Queen* v. *Secretary of State for Transport, ex parte: Factortame Ltd and others* EU:C:1996:79; Case C-224/01, *Köbler* v. *Republik Österreich* EU:C:2003:513 and Case C-173/03, *Traghetti del Mediterraneo SpA* v. *Italy* EU:C:2006:391.

[22] See also, A. Bredimas, *Methods of Interpretation and Community Law* (Oxford: North Holland, 1978) at pp. 77–80, who identifies similar patterns of reasoning in the Court's (pre-*Francovich*) case law: 'the Court, instead of accounting mechanically the wishes of the authors, seems to consider [its view of] the Common Market as a fact, the existence of which it takes judicial notice and draws the consequences. Henceforth . . . the Court will seek less the effectiveness of the Treaty, i.e., the stages through which it is proper to pass in order to achieve an aim and which the Treaty authors foresaw, than the necessary consequences of this aim as settled'.

[23] Joined Cases C-6/90 and C-9/90, *Francovich and Others* v. *Italy*, n. 10 at para. 31 (emphasis added).

To that statement, the Court added references to its pre-existing case law on the duties of Member State courts vis-à-vis individuals: 'Furthermore, it has been consistently held that the national courts whose task it is to apply the provisions of Community law in areas within their jurisdiction must ensure that those rules take full effect and must protect the rights which they confer on individuals.'[24] Finally, reasoning backwards from its own assertions, the Court ruled that the effectiveness of *its* normative view of the EU legal order (Constitutional Issue No. 1) would be undermined if individuals were not entitled to claim reparation for losses for breaches of Union law that were attributable to Member States.[25] In this way, a powerful new legal right was born.

1.2.2 Judicial Challenges to Member States' Acts of Constitutional Supplementation

The second set of examples, discussing judicial challenges to more specific statements of constituent authority, exposes similar patterns of distinctly self-referential legal reasoning. In *Rottmann*, considered initially, the Grand Chamber invoked its normative view of Union citizenship as 'destined to be the fundamental status of nationals of the Member States' in order to recast clear statements of constituent authority on that issue.[26] In *Opinion 2/13*, examined subsequently, the Court of Justice referenced, as before in *Francovich*, its extra-Treaty position on the nature of the EU as a 'new legal order' in direct support of its decision to declare the Draft Agreement on ECHR accession incompatible with the Treaties.[27]

In *Rottmann*, the Court was requested to determine whether it was contrary to Union law for a Member State to withdraw nationality from one of its nationals where that status had been acquired by naturalisation but through deception.[28] The applicant, Dr Rottmann, was an Austrian national by birth who had subsequently applied for, and acquired, German

[24] *Ibid.*, at para. 32.
[25] At para. 33.
[26] Case C-135/08, *Rottman* v. *Freistaat Bayern*, n. 3.
[27] Opinion 2/13, *Draft Agreement on Accession of the EU to the European Convention on Human Rights*, n. 3. For discussion, see e.g., T. Lock, 'The Future of the European Union's Accession to the European Convention on Human Rights after Opinion 2/13: Is it Still Possible and is it Still Desirable?' (2015) 11(2) *European Constitutional Law Reviw*, 239 and B. de Witte and Š. Imamović 'Opinion 2/13 on Accession to the ECHR: Defending the EU Legal Order against a Foreign Human Rights Court' (2015) 40(5) *European Law Review*, 683.
[28] For analysis, see e.g., D. Kochenov, 'Case C-135/08, *Rottman* v. *Freistaat Bayern*' (Case Comment) (2010) 47(6) *Common Market Law Review*, 1831 and H. U. Jessurun D'Oliveira,

citizenship through nationalisation without declaring that he was the subject of criminal proceedings for alleged serious fraud in Austria. That failure constituted grounds for the revocation of his German citizenship as a matter of German administrative law. However, in the applicant's case, the withdrawal of his German nationality would risk rendering him stateless. Under Austrian law, Dr Rottmann had automatically lost his Austrian nationality upon nationalisation as a German citizen.

In the proceedings giving rise to the preliminary reference to the Court, the applicant argued that revoking his German nationality, and the potential statelessness that might follow, would, in turn, deprive him of his status as a Union citizen pursuant to Article 20 TFEU. That provision, introduced into the Treaty framework at Maastricht, establishes the status of Union citizenship. It provides that every person holding the nationality of a Member State shall be a citizen of the Union.

The EU Treaty framework was (and remains) absolutely clear on the derived character of Union citizenship: that status 'shall be additional to and not replace national citizenship'.[29] To reinforce that point, Member States had collectively and explicitly agreed as constituent authorities that the legal framework governing the acquisition and loss of Member State nationality – as the gateway to the benefits of Union citizenship – was an exclusive matter for domestic law. Specifically, Declaration No. 2 annexed to the Maastricht Treaty outlines in unambiguous terms that, 'The Conference declares that, wherever in the Treaty establishing the European Community reference is made to nationals of the Member States, *the question whether an individual possesses the nationality of a Member State shall be settled solely by reference to the national law of the Member State concerned*.'[30] Similarly, meeting in the European Council, the Heads of State and Government had agreed in the 'Edinburgh Decision' of 11 and 12 December 1992 that,

> The provisions of Part Two of the Treaty establishing the European Community relating to citizenship of the Union give nationals of the Member States additional rights and protection as specified in that Part. They do not in any way take the place of national citizenship. *The question whether an individual possesses the nationality of a Member State will be settled solely by reference to the national law of the Member State concerned.*[31]

'Case C-315/08 *Janko Rottman* v. *Freistaat Bayern*: Decoupling Nationality and Union Citizenship?' (Case Comment) (2011) 7(1) *European Constitutional Law Review*, 138.

29 See Art. 20 TFEU.

30 Declaration No. 2 on Nationality of a Member State, n. 9 (emphasis added).

31 Decision of the Heads of State and Government, meeting within the European Council at Edinburgh on 11 and 12 December 1992 concerning certain problems raised by

The Grand Chamber referenced both statements of constituent authority in its decision.[32] However, as before (see Section 1.2.1), it considered these acts of constitutional supplementation as simply the starting point of its own *de novo* enquiry into the relationship between EU law and domestic rules on the acquisition and loss of Member State nationality. In *Rottmann*, this enquiry centred on the Court's defence of its normative position on the status of Union citizenship as the 'fundamental status of nationals of the Member States'.[33] That position finds no basis within the EU Treaty framework. It has its origins in the Court's judgment in *Grzelczyk*, concerning the rights of Member State nationals to access certain non-contributory social benefits in another Member State of which he/she is not a national on the same terms as citizens of that State.[34]

In *Rottmann*, the Court's normative position on the fundamental nature of Union citizenship was used, in combination with its earlier case law, to leverage judicial space for it to engage directly in the scrutiny of domestic rules on the acquisition and loss of Member State nationality. This displayed a striking disregard for Member States' unambiguous position on that matter as 'Masters of the Treaties'. According to the Grand Chamber,

> As the Court has several times stated, citizenship of the Union is intended to be the fundamental status of nationals of the Member States . . . Thus, the Member States must, when exercising their powers in the sphere of nationality, have due regard to European Union law. *In those circumstances, it is for the Court to rule on the questions referred by the national court which concern the conditions in which a citizen of the Union may, because he loses his nationality, lose his status of citizen of the Union and thereby be deprived of the rights attaching to that status.*[35]

In the final analysis, the Court afforded Member States considerable discretion to determine the conditions under which, as a matter of EU law, nationality may be lawfully withdrawn where obtained through naturalisation by deception.[36] Most significantly, the Grand Chamber

Denmark on the Treaty of European Union (the 'Edinburgh Decision') [1992] OJ C 348/1 (emphasis added).

32 Case C-135/08, *Rottman* v. *Freistaat Bayern*, n. 3 at para. 40.

33 *Ibid.*, at para. 43.

34 Case C-184/99, *Grzelczyk* v. *Centre public d'aide sociale d'Ottignies-Louvain-la-Neuve* EU:C:2001:458.

35 Case C-135/08, *Rottman* v. *Freistaat Bayern*, n. 3 at paras. 43–46 (emphasis added).

36 At paras. 51–59.

ruled that Member States were not prevented from withdrawing nationality in such circumstances solely on the basis that the person in question had not (yet) recovered his or her previous nationality.[37]

Nonetheless, any degree of judicial deference conceded at the justification stage does not alter the character of the Court's direct challenge to constituent authority in *Rottmann*. Using its own jurisprudence – developed independently of both the Treaty framework and additional acts of constitutional supplementation – the Court opened up a protected sphere of Member State competence to full judicial scrutiny at Union level. As before in *Francovich*, the Court's own statements on the formal status of Union law and the conditions under which it applies within Member States (Constitutional Issue No. 1) and, here specifically, the nature of EU citizenship rights within that order (falling within Constitutional Issue No. 3) were elevated to the status of 'supra-constitutional values' in order to advance its institutional preferences on the scope of EU law.

The same underlying interpretative approach to specific statements of constituent authority is discernible in *Opinion 2/13* on the Draft Agreement on EU Accession to the ECHR.[38] In that Opinion, the Full Court was requested to assess the compatibility with the EU Treaties of the Draft EU/ECHR Accession Agreement. That Agreement was the product of considered negotiation between the EU and Council of Europe representatives led, from the Union's side, by the Commission acting on a mandate issued to it by Member States through the Council.[39] At its core, it sought to address the novel challenges posed by the Union's accession to the ECHR as a non-State actor.[40] In other words, under what conditions and with what necessary adjustments could the EU, as an international organisation with legal personality and established by international treaties, be integrated into the institutional framework of another international organisation?

The Member States, acting collectively as Treaty principals, have expressly mandated that the EU should accede to the Convention. The Lisbon Treaty inserted a new paragraph into Article 6 TEU, providing that

[37] At para. 57.

[38] Opinion 2/13, *Draft Agreement on Accession of the EU to the European Convention on Human Rights*, n. 3.

[39] See Council Decision authorising the Commission to negotiate the Accession Agreement of the European Union to the European Convention for the protection of Human Rights and Fundamental Freedoms (ECHR) [2010] 10817/10 for a heavily redacted version of the Council's mandate to the Commission.

[40] At para. 49. See also, paras. 155–156.

'the Union shall accede to the European Convention of Human Rights and Fundamental Freedoms'. The insertion of that provision, to establish a legal basis for ECHR accession, was agreed in direct response to the Court's earlier determination that the Union did not enjoy competence to accede to the Convention under the pre-existing EU Treaty framework.[41]

Protocol No. 8 outlines, in further detail, the Member States' collective position with regard to the precise terms of the Union's accession to the ECHR.[42] From the perspective of Member States as constituent authorities, that instrument states that the Accession Agreement drawn up to facilitate EU accession to the Convention must: (1) make provision for preserving the 'specific characteristics of the Union and Union law';[43] (2) not affect the competences of the Union or its institutions or, likewise, affect Member States' individual relationships with the ECHR;[44] and (3) not affect Article 344 TFEU on the settlement of disputes involving the interpretation or application of the Treaties.[45]

The concluded Draft Agreement negotiated with Convention representatives addressed in detail the unique challenges posed by the EU's accession to the ECHR as a non-State actor. For instance, agreement was reached on the Union's institutional participation in ECHR proceedings in instances where applications to the Strasbourg Court raised questions concerning the compatibility of Union law with Convention rights. Specifically, Article 3(2) of the Draft Agreement provides that, in such circumstances, the Union may become a 'co-respondent' to proceedings before the ECtHR and, moreover, that as co-respondent the Union is party to the case. In addition, Article 3(6) of the Draft Agreement outlines that, in proceedings to which the EU is co-respondent, the Court of Justice shall be afforded 'sufficient time' to make an assessment of the compatibility with Convention rights of the particular provisions of Union law at issue. Further provisions of the Draft Agreement make way for the Union's participation in the institutional architecture of the ECHR, including, among other things, its involvement (and voting rights) in the Assembly and Committee of Ministers and its contribution to expenditure.[46]

41 Opinion 2/94, *Accession by the Community to the European Convention for the Protection of Human Rights and Fundamental Freedoms* EU:C:1996:140.

42 Protocol No. 8 relating to Article 6(2) of the Treaty on European Union on the accession of the Union to the European Convention on the Protection of Human Rights and Fundamental Freedoms, n. 9.

43 Art. 1.

44 Art. 2.

45 Art. 3.

46 See e.g., Arts. 6, 7 and 8 of the Draft Agreement respectively.

Member States were in broad agreement that the Draft Agreement was compatible with the Treaties. The Commission also shared that view as designated EU negotiator.[47] In particular, Member States concurred with the Commission's assessment that the Draft Agreement preserved the 'specific characteristics of the Union and Union law' – the principal condition imposed on accession in Protocol No. 8.[48]

The Court of Justice, however, took a very different view. It declared the Draft Agreement incompatible with the EU Treaty framework. Indeed, the Full Court objected to the Draft Agreement on several grounds. These included: the Agreement's failure to ensure coordination between Article 53 ECHR and Article 53 EU on benchmark standards of fundamental rights protection; the absence of detailed arrangements in the Agreement to ensure that the specific characteristics of EU law were preserved in the operation of the co-respondent mechanism; and the Agreement's failure to have regard to those same characteristics in the specific field of EU Common Foreign and Security Policy.[49]

As before in *Francovich* and *Rottmann*, the Court's reasoning is strikingly self-referential. The Court again invoked its own case law on the formal status of Union law and the conditions under which it applies within Member States – developed in contestation with the Treaty framework as constitutional touchstone – to challenge the Member States' agreed position on ECHR accession. The Full Court was absolutely clear in its decision that, whatever Member States had agreed as constituent authorities, the terms of the EU's accession to the ECHR must fully respect the integrity of *its* particular normative view on Constitutional Issue No. 1. In its own words,

> The fact that the EU has a new kind of legal order, the nature of which is peculiar to the EU, its own constitutional framework and founding principles, a particularly sophisticated institutional structure and a full set of legal rules to ensure its operation, has consequences as regards the procedure for and conditions of accession to the ECHR.[50]

The Full Court attempted to link its extra-Treaty assertions regarding the nature and features of the EU legal order with the conditions for ECHR accession outlined by Member States. More precisely, the Court seized on the reference in Article 1 of Protocol No. 8 to the requirement to preserve

[47] Opinion 2/13, *Draft Agreement on Accession of the EU to the European Convention on Human Rights*, n. 3 at para. 73.
[48] At paras. 109, 117 and 118.
[49] See para. 258 for a summary of the Court's objections.
[50] At para. 158. See also, para. 66.

the 'specific characteristics' of the Union and Union law in the accession process. For the Court, the reference to 'specific characteristics' in the Protocol was read as synonymous with its jurisprudence on the nature of the EU as a 'new legal order' (Constitutional Issue No. 1).[51] However, reading the Protocol, together with Member States' submissions to the Court, it is far from clear that Member States had the Court's case law on the formal status of EU law (*Van Gend en Loos* et al.) in mind when drafting that condition.[52] On the contrary, their collective understanding of the specific characteristics of the Union and Union law was linked instead to the specific challenges arising in the accession process as a consequence of the EU's status as a non-State actor.

In particular, Article 1 of Protocol No. 8 links the notion of 'the specific characteristics of the Union and Union law' with two specific challenges that Member States sought to address in the accession process. The first of these concerns the need to ensure that detailed arrangements were made for the Union's possible participation in the Convention's control organs.[53] The second calls for the establishment of procedural mechanisms to ensure that proceedings that non-Member States and individuals raise before the European Court of Human Rights (ECtHR) are correctly addressed to (EU) Member States and/or the Union, as appropriate.[54] The Commission also shared this narrow reading of the 'specific characteristics' reference contained in the Protocol. In its submission to the Court, it noted expressly that,

> the *purpose* of the requirement in Article 1(a) of Protocol No. 8 EU to preserve the specific characteristics of the EU and EU law with regard to the specific arrangements for the EU's possible participation in the control bodies of the ECHR *is to ensure that the EU participates on the same footing as any other Contracting Party in the control bodies of the ECHR, that is to say, the ECtHR, the Assembly and the Committee of Ministers.*[55]

The Full Court's Opinion leaves no doubt that, irrespective of whether or not it complied with the conditions for accession agreed by Member States as constituent authorities, the Draft Agreement did not meet with its approval. That Agreement was incompatible with its own set

[51] See paras. 160–177.
[52] This conclusion is reinforced when considered alongside the reactions of the Court's interlocutors to its institutional position on the formal status of EU law and the rules governing its application within domestic legal systems. For full discussion, see Chapter 6.
[53] See also, para. 117.
[54] See also, para. 118.
[55] At para. 74 (emphasis added).

of preconditions governing the Union's future accession to the ECHR. These preconditions directly referenced its institutional position on the formal status of Union law and the conditions under which it applies within Member States (Constitutional Issue No. 1), regarding the nature of the Union as a 'new legal order' and the autonomy, primacy and direct effect of Union law.

Above all else, the Court appeared especially concerned with the threat posed to its role as the final arbiter on the interpretation of provisions of EU law. On the one hand, it accepted that, as a consequence of ECHR accession, the EU and its institutions, including the Court of Justice, would be subject to external control for compliance with Convention rights and obligations.[56] On the other hand, however, it was absolutely clear that accession to the ECHR must not affect, in any way, its institutional functions as the final arbiter on the interpretation of EU norms – including in the sphere of fundamental rights protection.[57] Furthermore, the Court of Justice was also not prepared to enable the Strasbourg Court (ECtHR) to scrutinise the Union's compliance with Convention rights in substantive fields of Union law over which its own jurisdiction is limited under the EU Treaties.[58]

1.3 The Court of Justice: From Agent to Trustee

The preceding examples (Section 1.2) clearly demonstrate that the Court has openly challenged the foundations of constituent authority in the exercise of its interpretative functions. First, in *Parliament* v. *Council (Chernobyl)* and *Francovich*, the Court was shown to contest the fundamental premise that the EU is a system of limited, attributed competences that, where necessary, leaves Member States responsible for any amendments to the Treaty framework. Secondly, the Court was also shown to have taken issue periodically with specific statements of Member State agreement on discrete matters, including the applicable rules governing the acquisition and loss of Member State nationality (*Rottmann*) and the terms of EU accession to the ECHR (*Opinion 2/13*).

With respect to both sets of examples, the Court employs the same underlying interpretative approach. More precisely, the Court asserts its own statements on the three main issues for EU constitutionalism – developed in contestation with the Treaty framework – in order to

[56] At para. 185.
[57] At para. 186.
[58] At para. 256.

overturn, qualify or simply interrogate statements of constituent authority. For instance, in *Francovich* and *Opinion 2/13*, the Court intervened to defend its statements *on the formal status of Union law and the conditions under which it applies within Member States* (Constitutional Issue No. 1). In *Rottmann*, however, it acted principally to assert its institutional preferences with regard to *the objectives, values and limits of EU integration* (Constitutional Issue No. 3) in the specific area of EU citizenship rights.

To the extent that it invokes its own normative statements on Constitutional Issues Nos. 1 and 3 in the above manner, the Court directly contests the Treaties' clear position on constituent authority (Constitutional Issue No. 2). In so doing, the Court effectively transforms its institutional role within the EU legal order. In *Parliament* v. *Council (Chernobyl)*, *Francovich, Rottmann* and *Opinion 2/13*, the Court of Justice did not see its institutional role as defined under the Treaty framework, namely as agent to the Member States as Treaty principals. Instead, the Court can be seen to have assumed the role of 'trustee' within the EU legal order. Exercising that role, the Court sees itself as tasked with responsibility to defend its own normative positions on the formal status of Union law (*Francovich* and *Opinion 2/13*) and the specific objectives, values and limits of EU integration (*Parliament* v. *Council (Chernobyl)* and *Rottmann*) – including against the Member States as Treaty signatories.[59]

Crucially, the Court does not exercise its self-asserted trusteeship functions in a neatly linear fashion. It is not entirely possible to predict exactly when it will invoke its own normative assertions on, for instance, the formal status of EU law (Constitutional Issue No. 1) or, likewise, the objectives, values and limits of EU integration (Constitutional Issue No. 3) in order to contest clear statements of constituent authority. On occasion, the Court has explicitly respected the EU Treaties' statements on the position of Member States as 'Masters of the Treaties'. This can be seen, for instance, in its review of Treaty rules on the standing rights of natural and legal persons in (now) Article 263 TFEU annulment proceedings – discussed further in Chapter 7.[60]

[59] On trusteeship, see e.g., S. Stone Sweet, 'The European Court of Justice and the Judicialization of EU Governance' (2011) *Faculty Scholarship Series*, Paper 70 and K. Alter, 'Agents or Trustees? International Courts in Their Political Context' (2008) 14(1) *European Journal of International Relations*, 33. The Court's engagement with the objectives, values and limits of EU integration under the Treaty framework as constitutional touchstone is explored in Chapter 5.

[60] See e.g., Case C-50/00 P, *Unión de Pequeños Agricultores* v. *Council* EU:C:2002:462. See also, e.g., Case 43/75, *Defrenne* v. *Société anonyme belge de navigation aérienne Sabena* EU:C:1976:56

2 Union Policymaking: The Court of Justice versus the EU Treaty Framework

In addition to contesting the Treaties' statements of constituent authority (Section 1), the Court of Justice is also responsible for a dramatic, unilateral restructuring of the institutional dynamics structuring EU policymaking under the Treaty framework. In summary, the Court has assumed for itself a direct role in key fields of EU policymaking that is qualitatively different to – and independent of – its attributed functions under the Treaties. More precisely, the Court has established and subsequently maintained a powerful independent role as *direct policymaker* in important fields of Union activity. The result is an effective 'decoupling' of EU policymaking from the carefully constructed model of *legislative* policymaking that remains firmly embedded in the Treaty framework as constitutional touchstone (Chapter 1).

Section 2.1 recalls the framework governing Union policymaking under the EU Treaties as constitutional touchstones. Section 2.2 begins by examining the origins of the Court's direct policymaking platform (Section 2.2.1). Following that, it highlights the growth and far-reaching scope of the Court's role as direct policymaker (Section 2.2.2). Thereafter, it considers the broader structural impact of the Court's challenge to the Treaty framework's statements on Union policymaking authority (Section 2.2.3). Finally, it concludes by discussing the resilience of the Court's assault on the Treaties' baseline position on Constitutional Issue No. 2 in the face of significant intervening changes (Section 2.2.4).

In short, the Court's assertion, and subsequence defence of, its direct policymaking platform has had a dramatic impact on the institutional dynamics of Union policymaking. The Treaty framework places Union policymaking competence squarely in the hands of the Union's political institutions. In so doing, it is conceived to foster a model of transnational regulatory co-operation that brings together a range of competing political interests in order to promote balanced policymaking. The transfer of regulatory competences to the Union legislature significantly decreases the scope for unilateral Member State action – and the influence of

at paras. 47–57 where the Court concluded that the EU Treaties could only be amended through the procedure prescribed therein. In that case, Member States had adopted a resolution on equal pay pursuant to Art. 119 EEC (now Art. 157 TFEU), which incorporated an agreement to extend the period for the implementation of that obligation beyond that outlined in the EEC Treaty.

national parliaments in particular. However, this loss is counterbalanced through efficiency gains and, at a more existential level, is also linked with the post-war 'rescue' of the European nation state.[61]

The Court's assumption of its role as direct policymaker – in contestation with the Treaty framework – has shattered the carefully balanced model for (Union) policymaking beyond the state. In place of the Treaty paradigm for *legislative* policymaking, the Court of Justice has established a *judicial* platform that, to a considerable extent, outsources to private actors responsibility for policy initiation. Once activated, that platform further undercuts the respective competences of the Union's political institutions in Union policymaking. In particular, the European Parliament and Member States forfeit their competences to influence, if not entirely control, EU policymaking. The Court's platform, with its adversarial dynamics, input restraints and private deliberations, displaces the Treaty legislative paradigm and its carefully structured model for open, deliberative policymaking.

The Court's subversion of the Treaty paradigm for legislative policymaking through its assumption of direct control over Union policymaking is historically rationalised (and justified) as a 'solution' to the crisis of decisional supranationalism that afflicted the (then) Community in its formative years.[62] That crisis has since been resolved through reforms to the Treaties' legislative processes. Notwithstanding these reforms, the Court has, however, never subsequently relinquished its role as direct Union policymaker. That role continues to exist *beyond* the Treaty framework as an important act of constitutional contestation, with a powerful and enduring impact on the institutional dynamics of EU integration.

2.1 EU Policymaking and the EU Treaties: Political Institutions, Attributed Powers and Institutional Balance

2.1.1 Political Institutions

The EU Treaties established and have subsequently maintained a consistent position on EU policymaking authority. As Treaty principals,

[61] See A. Milward, *The European Rescue of the Nation State* (2nd edn) (Abingdon: Routledge, 1999); G. Majone, *The Dilemmas of European Integration* (Oxford: Oxford University Press, 2005) and S. Weatherill, *Law and Values in the European Union* (Oxford: Oxford University Press, 2016).

[62] See J. H. H. Weiler, 'The Transformation of Europe' (1991) 100 *Yale Law Journal*, 2403.

Member States place that authority firmly in the hands of the Union's political institutions. Under the founding EEC Treaty, policymaking competence was vested in two main institutions: the Commission and the Council of Ministers. The European Parliament subsequently joined the aforementioned institutions to form what is now, in its default formation, a tripartite institutional framework.[63] In addition, and most recently, the Lisbon Treaty also established a new role for Member State parliaments in EU policymaking. Specifically, national parliaments are engaged to monitor the Union institutions' compliance with the principle of subsidiarity (Article 5(3) TEU) in areas of shared competence.

2.1.2 *Attributed Powers*

The Union's political institutions – the Commission, Council and Parliament – do not enjoy original (or even general) powers of action. On the contrary, the Treaty framework exhaustively circumscribes the specific powers of the Union's political institutions with regard to EU policymaking. This model reflects the nature of the European Union as a system of limited, attributed powers (Article 5 TEU). The EU Treaties enumerate a definitive list of provisions that expressly provide a legal basis for legislative policymaking across a broad spectrum of Union policy areas. These bases all display common features. More precisely, they detail the specific institutions empowered to act thereunder; the particular legislative procedure to be followed; the form of legal instrument that may be used; and the substantive parameters for Union policymaking.

By way of illustration, Article 46 TFEU, on the free movement of workers, provides that:

> The European Parliament and the Council shall, acting in accordance with the ordinary legislative procedure and after consulting the Economic and Social Committee, issue directives or make regulations setting out the measures required to bring about freedom of movement for workers, as defined in Article 45, in particular:
>
> (a) by ensuring close cooperation between national employment services;
> (b) by abolishing those administrative procedures and practices and those qualifying periods in respect of eligibility for available employment, whether resulting from national legislation or from agreements

[63] See also the increased role entrusted to European Council in specific policy fields such as the Common Foreign and Security Policy (Title V, Chapter 2 TEU).

previously concluded between Member States, the maintenance of which would form an obstacle to liberalisation of the movement of workers;

(c) by abolishing all such qualifying periods and other restrictions provided for either under national legislation or under agreements previously concluded between Member States as imposed on workers of other Member States conditions regarding the free choice of employment other than those imposed on workers of the State concerned;

(d) by setting up appropriate machinery to bring offers of employment into touch with applications for employment and to facilitate the achievement of a balance between supply and demand in the employment market in such a way as to avoid serious threats to the standard of living and level of employment in the various regions and industries

2.1.3 *Institutional Balance*

The division of political authority across the three Union institutions, together with the existence of distinctive legislative procedures in particular policy areas, is based on a guiding principle of institutional balance. In essence, that concept provides for the dispersal of EU political authority across different Union institutions, each of which represent competing political interests and must work together to produce legislative outputs. As Lenearts and Verhoeven summarise, 'Institutional balance is the prime device that brings together the various interests within the Union in a balanced manner and ties their discussions into an institutional frame in which, it is hoped, the narrow pursuit of self-interest can be overcome and replaced by a more emphatic, constructive debate on the "public good" within the European Union.'[64]

As a *political* principle, institutional balance functions primarily to describe (or account for) the prevailing distribution of political functions under the Treaties. The principle is itself entirely neutral about the precise apportioning of political authority within any polity. In other words, whilst that concept clearly describes the dispersal of political power across multiple institutions, it has little to say on exactly what form that should distribution must take. That choice remains with the relevant constituent actors. As Craig observes: 'Institutional balance is not . . . self-executing. It presumes by its very nature a normative and

[64] K. Lenearts and A. Verhoeven, 'Institutional Balance as a Guarantee for Democracy in EU Governance' in C. Joerges and R. Dehousse, *Good Governance in Europe's Integrated Market* (Oxford: Oxford University Press, 2002) at p. 43. See also, G. de Búrca, 'The Institutional Development of the EU: A Constitutional Analysis' in P. Craig and G. de Búrca (eds.), *The Evolution of EU Law* (Oxford: Oxford University Press, 1999) at p. 58.

political judgment as to which institutions should be able to partake of legislative and executive power, and it presumes also a view as to what constitutes the appropriate balance between them.'[65]

Within the EU legal order, the present model of institutional balance is the product of evolutionary change, managed by Member States as constituent authorities – with additional input from the Court of Justice (Section 2.2.). Member States have repeatedly amended the Treaty provisions governing the disposition of political authority for Union policymaking (Chapter 1). Notably, the evolution of European integration under the Treaty framework is characterised by the growth in the European Parliament's legislative competences.[66] The Single European Act began the process of transforming the European Parliament's institutional role within the EU legal order.[67] Following the entry into force of the Lisbon Treaty, the European Parliament is now, by default, co-legislature with the Council in most areas of Union policymaking.[68]

As a *legal* principle in EU integration, institutional balance has its origins in case law.[69] It now finds specific expression in Article 13(2) TEU, which provides that, 'Each institution [of the Union] shall act within the limits of the powers conferred on it in the Treaties and in conformity with the procedures and objectives set out in them.'

For the Court, institutional balance is, first and foremost, understood as a specific (horizontal) expression of the principle of conferral in Article 5(2) TEU. To borrow de Witte's terminology, it is now basically 'convenient shorthand' for the Treaty rules that govern the apportionment of policymaking competences between Union institutions in specific fields of activity – rules that the Union institutions are not open to reconfigure as they see fit.[70] In addition, and in its broadest formulation,

65 P. Craig, 'Institutions, Power, and Institutional Balance' in P. Craig and G. de Búrca (eds.), *The Evolution of EU Law*, n. 64. However, see Lenearts and Verhoeven, 'Institutional Balance as a Guarantee for Democracy in EU Governance', n. 64 at p. 47, who argue that 'institutional balance requires the makers of the European constitution to shape institutions and the interactions between them in such a manner that each interest and constituency present in the Union is duly represented and co-operates with others in the frame of an institutionalized debate geared towards the formulation of the common good'.

66 For analysis, see e.g., B Rittberger, *Building Europe's Parliament: Democratic Representation beyond the Nation State* (Oxford: Oxford University Press, 2005) and R. Corbett, F. Jacobs and M. Shackleton, *The European Parliament* (8th edn) (London: John Harper, 2011).

67 Single European Act [1987] OJ L 169/1.

68 Pursuant to Art. 289 TFEU and Art. 294 TFEU.

69 See e.g., *Parliament and Council (Chernobyl)*, n. 14, discussed in Section 1.2.1.

70 B. de Witte, 'The Role of Institutional Principles in the Judicial Development of the European Legal Order' in F. Synder (ed.), *The Europeanisation of Law: The Legal Effects of European Integration* (Oxford: Hart Publishing, 2000) at p. 92.

it also obliges Union institutions to co-operate with one another in the exercise of their respective attributed functions.[71]

Beyond that, there is little to support any claim that institutional balance functions as an independent and higher source of unwritten Union law; in other words, as a 'general principle' of EU law. The Court's decision on the standing rights of the European Parliament (*Parliament* v. *Council (Chernobyl)*) remains the exception (see Section 1.2.1).[72] In that case, the Court of Justice invoked the concept of 'institutional balance' as a (then) unwritten general principle of Union law in order to revise the Treaty rules governing European Parliament's standing rights in annulment actions – in a challenge to the Treaties' key statements on constituent authority.

2.2 Constitutional Contestation: The Court as Direct Policymaker

The EU Treaties have always attributed to the Court of Justice an important role in the management of the framework for Union *legislative* policymaking. The Court is engaged in that process in three principal respects. First, the Court contributes to substantive policymaking through its interpretation of the Treaties and provisions of secondary Union law.[73] Secondly, the Court achieves the same result through judicial review of EU legislative measures for compliance with the objectives, limits and values of EU integration set out in the Treaties (Constitutional Issue No. 3).[74] Finally, the Court plays a critical role in the management of the Treaty framework for legislative policymaking through the resolution of disputes between Union institutions regarding the limits of their respective roles under the EU Treaties.[75]

The Court of Justice's institutional influence on the substance and dynamics of EU policymaking now extends, however, far beyond its role in the management of the Treaty framework for legislative

71 See e.g., Case C-409/13, *Council* v. *Commission (Macro Financial Assistance)* EU:C:2015:217 and Case C-425/13, *Commission* v. *Council (Emissions Trading)* EU:C:2015:483.

72 *Parliament and Council (Chernobyl)*, n. 14.

73 Pursuant to Art. 267 TFEU.

74 Pursuant to Art. 218(11) TFEU, Art. 258 TFEU, Art. 259 TFEU and Art. 267 TFEU.

75 Disputes under this third heading typically arise in the context of annulment proceedings (Art. 263 TFEU). See e.g., *Council* v. *Commission (Macro Financial Assistance)*, n. 71 and *Commission* v. *Council (Emissions Trading)*, n. 71.

policymaking. In a remarkable and enduring challenge to that framework, the Court has interposed itself alongside the Union's political institutions as *direct policymaker* in many key areas of EU policy. Relying on its case law on the formal status of Union law and the conditions under which it applies within Member States (Constitutional Issue No. 1) (Chapter 3) in combination with the preliminary reference procedure, the Court has established a powerful, independent and hierarchically superior platform for judicial policymaking.[76] That platform was established in opposition to the EU Treaties and, importantly, continues to exist beyond that framework as a further act of constitutional contestation with regard to the locus of EU political authority (Constitutional Issue No. 2).

In output terms, the Court's direct policymaking platform is a remarkable story of success. Using EU norms that it has ruled directly effective, the Court of Justice has effectively *re-regulated* significant areas of economic and non-economic activity at Union level. Its contribution as direct policymaker spans the full spectrum of Union policymaking. The extensive list of examples includes the Court's establishment of the principle of mutual recognition in EU free movement law; its regulation of the conditions governing the award of public service compensation in the field of state aid; and the judicial construction of EU legal frameworks regulating the recognition of qualifications and Union citizen's access to cross-border healthcare services.[77] It is doubtful whether, absent its intervention, European integration would have reached such an advanced stage of development so quickly in these (and other) policy areas. Indeed, the impact of the Court's contribution in key areas of Union policymaking is so significant that, in several instances, the EU legislature has subsequently exercised its Treaty

[76] Chapter 5 discusses further the nature of the relationship between EU legislative and judicial policymaking through the lens of constitutional contestation developed in Chapter 2.

[77] See e.g., Case 120/78, *Rewe-Zentral AG* v. *Bundesmonopolverwaltung für Branntwein (Cassis de Dijon)* EU:C:1979:42 (mutual recognition); Case C-280/00, *Altmark Trans GmbH and Regierungspräsidium Magdeburg* v. *Nahverkehrsgesellschaft Altmark GmbH* EU:C:2003:415 (state aid); Case C-157/99, *Geraets-Smits* v. *Stichting Ziekenfonds VGZ and Peerbooms* v. *Stichting CZ Groep Zorgverzekeringen* EU:C:2001:404; Case C-372/04, *Watts* v. *Bedford Primary Care Trust and Secretary of State for Health* EU:C:2006:325 (cross-border healthcare services) and Case C-340/89, *Vlassopoulou* v. *Ministerium für Justiz, Bundes- und Europaangelegenheiten Baden-Württemberg* EU:C:1991:193 (recognition of qualifications).

competences simply to transpose the Court's substantive preferences into secondary Union.[78]

Nonetheless, regardless of its effectiveness, measured against the EU Treaty framework as constitutional touchstone, the Court's move to interpose itself as direct policymaker alongside the EU legislature is a striking act of constitutional contestation. It has radically restructured the locus of EU political authority within the EU legal order in relation to Union policymaking. Its effect is to 'decouple' EU policymaking from the paradigm for legislative policymaking embedded in the EU Treaties. In summary, Union policymaking is no longer driven, as the Treaties continue to prescribe, solely (or even primarily) by the Union's political institutions. Instead, advances in EU policy are frequently the result of judicial choices that take shape outside the carefully constructed Treaty framework for legislative policymaking.

2.2.1 *The Origins of the Court's Direct Policymaking Platform*

The Court's institutional position as independent policymaker traces its origins back to its formative case law on free movement. Its decision in *Reyners*, interpreting the Treaty provisions on the freedom of establishment, most clearly illustrates its move to decouple EU policymaking from the Treaty framework for legislative policymaking.[79] That case addressed the situation of a Dutch national, who had been refused entry to the Belgian Bar despite holding the prerequisite Belgian qualifications required for admittance. The applicant argued that the contested Belgian rules must be set-aside on the grounds that the Treaty conferred upon him a directly effective right not to be discriminated against on grounds of his nationality.

The prohibition of discrimination on nationality grounds in the field of establishment was set out in Article 52 EEC (now Article 49 TFEU). In line with the pattern embedded in the Treaty framework, that provision linked (and still links) Union policymaking directly with the legislative paradigm. Specifically, it outlined that,

> Within the framework of the provisions set out below, restrictions on the freedom of establishment of nationals of a Member State in the territory of another Member State shall be abolished by progressive stages in the course of

[78] See e.g., Directive 2011/24/EU of the European Parliament and of the Council of 9 March 2011 on the application of patients' rights in cross-border healthcare [2011] OJ L88/45.

[79] Case 2/74, *Reyners* v. *Belgian State* EU:C:1974:68.

> the transitional period. Such progressive abolition shall also apply to restrictions on the setting up of agencies, branches or subsidiaries by nationals of any Member State established in the territory of any Member State.
>
> Freedom of establishment shall include the right to take up and pursue activities as self-employed persons and to set up and manage undertakings, in particular companies or firms within the meaning of the second paragraph of Article 58, under the conditions laid down for its own nationals by the law of the country where such establishment is effected, subject to the provisions of the Chapter relating to capital.

The Treaty paradigm notwithstanding, the Court upheld the applicant's argument. It ruled that Article 52 EEC was directly effective and, further, directed the referring Belgian court to set aside the contested legislation in so far as it applied to non-Belgian (Member State) nationals such as Mr Reyners.

The Court did not conceal its move to decouple progress towards the elimination of obstacles to the freedom of establishment from the Treaty framework for legislative policymaking. On the contrary, it expressly ruled that the failure on the part of the (then) Community institutions (specifically: the Commission and Council) to enact a comprehensive programme of legislative measures to give effect to Article 52 EEC did not preclude the attribution of direct effect to that provision. According to the Court,

> Article 52 EEC . . . imposes an obligation to attain a precise result, *the fulfillment of which had to be made easier by, but not made dependent on, the implementation of a programme of progressive measures*. The fact that this progression has not been adhered to leaves the obligation itself intact beyond the end of the period provided for its fulfillment . . . It is not possible to invoke against such an effect the fact that the Council has failed to issue the Directives provided for by Articles 54 and 57 or the fact that certain of the Directives actually issued have not fully attained the objective of non-discrimination required by Article 52.[80]

The Court's parallel platform for judicial policymaking would not exist without its case law on *the formal status of Union law and the conditions under which it applies within Member States* (Constitutional Issue No. 1). Its substance draws on the central components of that case law; specifically, the judgments on the principles of direct effect and primacy. It will be recalled that, in combination, both principles demand – contrary to the

[80] *Reyners* v. *Belgian State*, n. 79 at paras. 26–29. (emphasis added). See also, thereafter, Case 11/77, *Patrick* v. *Ministre des Affaires Culturelles* EU:C:1977:113 at para. 10 and Case C-340/89, *Vlassopoulou*, n. 77 at para. 13.

position under the Treaty framework – the immediate application within national legal systems of Treaty provisions and provisions of secondary Union law that satisfy the Court's test for direct effect (Chapter 3). That test attributes direct effect to EU norms where these are judged (by the Court of Justice) to be sufficiently clear, precise and unconditional to be capable of immediate application with Member State legal systems.[81]

Of course, in *Reyners*, the Court was absolutely correct to point to the expiry of the transitional period – the date by which Member States had agreed to enact an ambitious programme of legislative measures in order to abolish restrictions on, *inter alia*, the freedom of establishment. In Article 7(2) EEC, Member States had committed to the progressive elimination of restrictions on intra-EU movement within twelve years of the entry into force of the founding Treaty. Nonetheless, it did not follow from that provision – or the terms of the EEC Treaty more generally – that the Community institutions' failure to realise that commitment empowered the Court of Justice to step in as substitute policymaker. It is certainly not atypical for international treaty norms to remain dormant as a result of inaction or incomplete action on the part of signatory states or the international institutions they establish to give effect to specific agreed commitments. The Court of Justice's decision to drive forward the Member States' partially realised programme of market integration by other means was its institutional choice.

Significantly, the Court's decision to advance economic integration through judicial lawmaking has been selective, not universal. For example, in *Casati*, the Court of Justice ruled that Article 67 EEC on intra-EU capital movements was not directly effective in its original form at the end of the transitional period.[82] The distinct approach taken in the

[81] See Case 26/62, *NV Algemene Transport- en Expeditie Onderneming van Gend & Loos* v. *Netherlands Inland Revenue Administration* EU:C:1963. See also, for Directives, e.g., Case 41/74, *van Duyn* v. *Home Office* EU:C:1974:133 and Case 148/78, *Criminal proceedings against Ratti* EU:C:1979:110.

[82] Case 203/80, *Criminal proceedings against Guerrino Casati* EU:C:1981:261 at para. 9. For analysis, see T. Horsley, 'Death, Taxes, and (Targeted) Judicial Dynamism: The Free Movement of Capital in EU Law' in A. Arnull and D. Chalmers (eds.), *The Oxford Handbook of European Union Law* (Oxford: Oxford University Press, 2015) and J. Usher, 'The Evolution of the Free Movement of Capital' (2008) 31 *Fordham International Law Journal*, 1533. See also, in the field of competition policy, the Court's approach to the interpretation of Art. 85(3) EEC (now Art. 101(3) TFEU). Prior to the enactment of Council Regulation 1/2003 EC on the implementation of the rules on competition laid down in Articles 81 and 82 of the Treaty [2003] OJ L1/1, attributing direct effect to Art. 101 TFEU in its entirety,

field of capital movements was prompted by judicial concerns regarding the economic and political consequences of decoupling – through the attribution of direct effect to Article 67 EEC – the process of abolishing restrictions on intra-Community capital movements from the Treaty framework for legislative policymaking. More precisely, the Court noted that liberalising restrictions would likely undermine Member States' economic policies and disrupt their respective balance of payments.[83] The effect of the Court's decision, however, was to preserve the integrity of the Treaty structure. More specifically, it functioned to ensure that the Council retained full control over the liberalisation of intra-Community capital movements in accordance with Article 69 EEC.

2.2.2 *The Evolution of the Court's Role as Direct Policymaker*

The Court's direct policymaking functions are no longer limited to managing intra-EU movement (see now: Articles 28, 30, 34, 35, 45, 49, 56 and 63 TFEU). The following provisions of the EU Treaties have also been declared directly effective, extending the Court of Justice's policymaking platform into other key spheres of Union activity:[84] Article 18 TFEU prohibiting discrimination on grounds of Member State nationality;[85] Article 21 TFEU establishing the rights of intra-EU movement for Union citizens;[86] Article 37 TFEU regulating state monopolies;[87] Articles 101 and 102 TFEU prohibiting, respectively, anti-competitive agreements and abuses of dominant positions within the internal market;[88] Article 106(2) TFEU regulating the provision of services of general economic interest;[89] Article 108(3) TFEU prohibiting the granting

the Court left the application of Art. 85(3) EEC to the Commission in accordance with the First Regulation implementing Articles 85 and 86 of the Treaty (Regulation No. 17) [1962] OJ 13/204.

83 Case 203/80, *Casati*, n. 82 at para. 9.

84 See A. Kaczorowska, *European Union Law* (London: Routledge, 2009) at pp. 305–306.

85 See e.g., Joined Cases C-92/92 and C-326/92, *Phil Collins* v. *Imtrat Handelsgesellschaft mbH* EU:C:1993:847 and Case C-281/98, *Angonese* v. *Cassa di Risparmio di Bolzano SpA* EU:C:2000:296.

86 See e.g., Case C-85/96, *Martínez Sala* v. *Freistaat Bayern* EU:C:1998:217 and Case C-493/99, *Baumbast and R* v. *Secretary of State for the Home Department* EU:C:2002:493

87 See e.g., Case 91/78, *Hansen GmbH & Co.* v. *Hauptzollamt Flensburg* EU:C:1979:65.

88 See e.g., Case 127/73, *BRT* v. *SABAM* EU:C:1974:25. For Art. 101(3) TFEU, see e.g., Case C-439/09 *Pierre Fabre Dermo-Cosmétique SAS* v. *Président de l'Autorité de la concurrence* ECLI:EU:C:2011:649.

89 See e.g., Case 127/73, *BRT* v. *SABAM*, n. 88.

of state aid without prior Commission notification;[90] and Article 157 TFEU on equal pay.[91]

The scope for the Court of Justice to function as direct policymaker is reinforced by its attribution of direct effect to provisions of secondary Union law[92] as well as provisions of international agreements.[93] It is extended further still by the Court's case law on the horizontal direct effect of specific EU norms.[94] The attribution of horizontal direct effect to certain EU norms enables individuals to engage the Court as direct policymaker in private disputes.

In addition to the aforementioned, the Court has recognised the existence of two further categories of directly effective primary EU norms. First, it has confirmed that provisions of the EU Charter of Fundamental Rights may have direct effect.[95] EU Charter provisions that meet the criteria for direct effect function as freestanding primary EU norms in the resolution of legal issues that are deemed to fall within the scope of Union law.[96] Secondly, the Court of Justice has recognised the direct effect of general (fundamental) principles of Union law. In *Mangold*, for example, the Grand Chamber ruled that the principle of non-discrimination on grounds of age constituted a 'general principle of Union law'.[97] That principle grants individuals a directly effective right to protection, the observance of which Member States courts are obliged to ensure in all circumstances falling within the scope of Union law. This

90 See e.g., Case 77/72, *Capolongo* v. *Azienda Agricole Maya* EU:C:1973:65.

91 Case 43/75, *Defrenne*, n. 60.

92 For Regulations, see e.g., Case 93/71, *Leonesio* v. *Ministero dell'agricoltura e foreste* EU:C:1972:39 and Case C-253/00, *Muñoz y Cia SA* v. *Frumar Ltd* EU:C:2002:497. For Decisions, see e.g., Case 9/70, *Grad* v. *Finanzamt Traunstein* EU:C:1970:78.

93 See e.g., Joined Cases 21–24/72, *International Fruit Company NV and others* v. *Produktschap voor Groenten en Fruit* EU:C:1972:115; Case 104/81, *Hauptzollamt Mainz* v. *C.A. Kupferberg & Cie KG* EU:C:1982:362 and Case T-115/94, *Opel Austria GmbH* v. *Council* EU:T:1997:3. However, contrast the position with respect to agreements concluded under the GATT/WTO framework, which the Court has ruled do not have direct effect. See e.g., Joined Cases 267/81, 268/81 and 269/81, *Amministrazione delle Finanze dello Stato* v. *SPI and SAMI* EU:C:1983:78 at para. 23

94 See e.g., Case 43/75, *Defrenne*, n. 60. (Art. 157 TFEU); Case C-281/98, *Angonese*, n. 85 (Art. 45 TFEU) and Case C-144/04, *Mangold* v. *Helm* EU:C:2005:709 (age discrimination).

95 See e.g., Case C-617/10, *Åklagaren* v. *Åkerberg Fransson* EU:C:2013:105 and Case C-650/13, *Delvigne* v. *Commune de Lesparre Médoc and Préfet de la* Gironde: EU:C:2015:648.

96 *Ibid.*

97 See e.g., Case C-144/04, *Mangold* v. *Helm*, n. 94; Case C-555/07, *Kücükdeveci* v. *Swedex GmbH & Co. KG* EU:C:2010:21 and Case C-441/14, *Dansk Industri (DI), acting on behalf of Ajos A/S* v. *Estate of Karsten Eigil Rasmussen* EU:C:2016:278.

includes the obligation to set aside any provisions of national law that conflict with that principle.[98]

2.2.3 *The Impact of the Court's Direct Policymaking Role on the Institutional Dynamics of EU Policymaking*

The Court's decoupling of EU policymaking from the Treaty's legislative processes through its attribution of direct effect to specific norms has radically altered the institutional dynamics of EU policymaking. This begins at the very start of the cycle with control over the initiation of EU policy. It continues thereafter to affect the approach to the formulation and enforcement of EU policy norms. The fact that the Court's decisions are not easy to overturn or adjust serves only further to entrench its institutional position within the Union legal order as direct policymaker.

In relation to policy initiation, the Court's assertion of direct policymaking functions shatters the Commission's monopoly to propose policy initiatives to promote the collective interests of the Union (Article 17(2) TEU). Responsibility is transferred instead outside the Treaties' institutional framework to individual party litigants, who engage the Court of Justice by requesting interpretations of directly effective provisions of EU law in proceedings before national courts.

Private actors were very quick to realise the new potential to advance their interests through the judicial process.[99] A review of the applications for preliminary rulings in any given year provides a snapshot of the range of natural and legal persons seeking to invoke EU norms that the Court of Justice has ruled directly effective in order to promote private interests.[100] Thus, looking back, it was a German importer seeking to contest German rules on the marketing of spirits that provided the Court of Justice with an opportunity to establish the principle of mutual

[98] Chapter 6 considers Member State reactions to this particular line of case law.

[99] For specific examples, see e.g., C. Barnard, 'A European Litigation Strategy: The Case of the Equal Opportunities Commission' in J. Shaw and G. More (eds.), *New Legal Dynamics of European Union* (Oxford: Oxford University Press, 1996). See also, R. Dehousse, *The European Court of Justice: The Politics of Judicial Integration* (London: MacMillan, 1998) at pp. 109–114. On 'adversarial legalism' as a mode of governance, see R. Kagan, *Adversarial Legalism* (Cambridge: Harvard University Press, 2001).

[100] See e.g., Annual Report 2016 of the Court of Justice, 'The Year in Review', available at: https://curia.europa.eu/jcms/upload/docs/application/pdf/2017-04/ragp-2016_final_en_web.pdf (accessed October 2017).

recognition in EU free movement law.[101] Similarly, it was a Belgian flight attendant who provided the Court with the opportunity to advance Union policymaking in the field of anti-discrimination law.[102] In addition, Member State nationals have also invoked the Court's direct policymaking platform to recast domestic rules on, *inter alia*, entry and residence, access to employment and entitlement to healthcare and social assistance.[103]

Ironically, the Commission has also activated the judicial process as a means to advance market integration, including, significantly, in instances where Treaty framework for legislative policymaking has stalled. Examples include its efforts to liberalise national insurance markets (e.g., *Commission* v. *Germany (Insurance Markets)*)[104] and, more recently, its litigation seeking to restructure the governance of newly privatised undertakings (e.g., *Commission* v. *Portugal (Golden Shares)*).[105] Member State efforts to block the Commission's effective circumvention of the EU legislative process in such instances have fallen on deaf ears. The Court has expressly ruled that the existence of the legislative platform for Union policymaking is not, in and of itself, an obstacle to the Commission's use of infringement proceedings to advance market integration by means of judicial interpretation. As the Court stated clearly in *Commission* v. *Germany (Insurance Markets)*,

> It is open to the Commission . . . to bring an action under Art [258 TFEU] if it considers that a Member State has failed to fulfil one of its obligations under the Treaty. *The mere fact that a proposal for a legislative measure, which if adopted and transposed into national law would terminate the infringements alleged by the Commission, has already been submitted to the Council does not prevent the Commission from bringing such an action.*[106]

Furthermore, the Court's direct policymaking platform has also radically altered the dynamics of policy *formation*. In judicial proceedings, the European Parliament, Commission and Council are engaged in shaping Union policy merely as party litigants or as interveners. In neither

[101] Case 120/78, *Cassis de Dijon*, n. 77.

[102] Case 43/75, *Defrenne*, n. 60. See also, e.g., Case 152/84, *Marshall* v. *Southampton and South-West Hampshire Area Health Authority* EU:C:1986:84.

[103] See e.g., Case C-85/96, *Martínez Sala*, n. 86; Case C-493/99, *Baumbast and R*, n. 86; Case C-138/02, *Collins* v. *Secretary of State for Work and Pensions* EU:C:2004:172; Case C-372/04, *Watts*, n. 77 and Case C-34/09, *Ruiz Zambrano* v. *Office national de l'emploi* EU:C:2011:124.

[104] Case 205/84, *Commission* v. *Germany (Insurance Markets)* EU:C:1986:463.

[105] Case C-367/98, *Commission* v. *Portugal (Golden Shares)* EU:C:2002:326.

[106] Case 205/84, *Commission* v. *Germany (Insurance Markets)*, n. 104 at paras. 6–7 (emphasis added).

capacity do any of these three political institutions enjoy powers of control and/or influence over the trajectory of Union policymaking comparable to those afforded to them under the Treaties' legislative procedures (most obviously: competence to veto unfavorable policy options). It is the Court of Justice that ultimately determines the scope and shape of EU policy through its interpretative choices. Its deliberations are conducted in secret, following a two-stage procedure before the Court: an exchange of written pleadings and a (usually) short public oral hearing.

The process of judicial policymaking thus contrasts markedly with the model for EU legislative policy making under the Treaty framework. Pursuant to Article 294 TFEU, the default legislative procedure, the formulation of policy choices undergoes a more rigorous, structured and transparent process of deliberative politics. That process begins with the Commission's submission to the European Parliament and Council of a draft legislative proposal. It then continues through a series of parliamentary readings until the European Parliament and Council reach agreement on a common position. Ultimately, unless the two institutions reach agreement on the draft act, that measure is not adopted. In accordance with the principle of inter-institutional balance (Section 2.1), the entire process is conceived to bring together and carefully balance the competing political interests represented by the Commission, Parliament and Council. By contrast, where the Court of Justice is engaged as direct policymaker, it falls principally to the Advocate General in her capacity as *amicus curiae* to furnish the Court with an impartial and reflective analysis of competing policy considerations.[107]

The Court's platform for direct Union policymaking also challenges the EU Treaties' position on the *enforcement* of EU policy norms. Specifically, it displaces the Commission's role under the Treaty framework as the principal enforcer of EU norms against recalcitrant Member States. Under the judicial model, individual litigants assume an important role alongside the Commission in the enforcement of Union law against Member States. This contribution is not, of course, what motivates individual litigants to raise proceedings before the Court (typically through Member State courts). They are concerned instead with the assertion of private interests. Nonetheless, it is a critical by-product of their efforts. As the Court stated in *Van Gend en Loos*, 'The vigilance of individuals concerned to protect their rights [using directly effective EU norms and the preliminary reference procedure] amounts to an effective

[107] For critique, see e.g., D. Bach-Golecka, 'Amicus Curiae or Primus Inter Pares? The Advocate General and the EU Institutional Framework' (2012) 54 *Studia Iuridica*, 7.

supervision in addition to the supervision entrusted by Articles 168 and 170 [now Articles 258 and 259 TFEU] to the diligence of the Commission and of the Member States.'[108]

Finally, it should be stressed that the strength of the Court's direct policymaking platform vis-à-vis the Treaty paradigm for legislative policymaking is reinforced by the fact that the Court's interpretative choices are not easily overturned. Member States can seek to undo or adjust the Court's case law by amending the Treaties (see further Chapter 6). However, this is not an easy task. Moreover, even where successful, it remains open to the Court subsequently to overturn, qualify or simply interrogate any renewed statements of constituent authority where these do not accord with its own institutional preferences (see Section 1 above). The same applies with respect to the Union legislature's efforts to correct the Court's interpretative choices through secondary EU law. Here the Court of Justice has also developed a range of techniques to manage any legislative responses to its choices as direct policymaker.[109]

2.2.4 The Resilience of the Court's Platform for Direct Policymaking

The Court's move to interpose itself alongside the Commission, Parliament and Council as direct policymaker has proven remarkably resilient. This is surprising given that its origins and normative justification are often linked to what Weiler characterised as the crisis of 'decisional supranationalism' that plagued the (then) Community in the early years of European integration.[110] According to that account, through its use of directly effective EU norms, the Court of Justice effectively stepped in to rescue the integration process at a time when the Treaty paradigm for legislative policymaking had all but stalled.

The intervening years have witnessed the 'unblocking' of this sclerosis. This started with the (re)introduction of qualified majority voting in the Council *de jure* and *de facto* through the Single European Act. It has continued with the introduction of further revisions to lubricate the Treaty legislative policymaking paradigm through, for example, the emergence of the (now default) ordinary legislative procedure (Article 294 TFEU).

[108] Case 26/62, *Van Gend en Loos*, n. 81.

[109] For analysis, see e.g., G. Davies, 'Legislative Control of the European Court of Justice' (2014) 51 *Common Market Law Review*, 1579 and, for a more optimistic appraisal, D. S. Martinsen, *An Ever More Powerful Court? The Political Constraints of Legal Integration in the European Union* (Oxford: Oxford University Press, 2015).

[110] See Weiler, 'The Transformation of Europe', n. 62.

Nevertheless, these key intervening changes have had no impact on the Court's assertion of direct policymaking functions in core areas of EU activity. On the contrary, the Court of Justice has continued, as before, to directly contest the EU Treaty framework's basic position on EU policymaking authority. Indeed, in the period since the adoption of the Single European Act, the Court has actually opted further to extend its reach as direct policymaker. It has, for instance, ruled even more Treaty provisions directly effective to enhance its potential sphere of influence significantly.[111] Likewise, the Court has expanded its case law on general principles as an additional set of directly effective norms.[112] Similarly, it has increasingly intervened as direct policymaker in private regulatory disputes through the development of its case law on horizontal direct effect.[113]

If the Court's move to interpose itself alongside the EU legislature as direct policymaker was motivated by a desire to 'rescue' the process of EU integration from decline, then the subsequent reinvigoration of that process has certainly not prompted the Court to relinquish that new function. As this chapter has argued, the Court has not only maintained, but also further reinforced, its institutional role as direct policymaker within the Union legal order. Crucially, that role continues to exist beyond the Treaty framework as an act of constitutional contestation with regard to Constitutional Issue No. 2.

Concluding Remarks

This chapter applied the intellectual framework developed in Chapters 1 and 2 to assess how far the Court's institutional position on the locus of political authority within the EU legal order (Constitutional Issue No. 2) conforms to the Treaty framework as constitutional touchstone. In summary, it demonstrated that the Court's position on the locus of political

[111] E.g., Arts. 20 and 21 TFEU on EU citizenship and Art. 63 TFEU on the free movement of capital. See respectively, e.g., Case C-85/96, *Martínez Sala*, n. 86; Case C-493/99, *Baumbast and R*, n. 86 and Joined Cases C-163/94, C-165/94 and C-250/94, *Criminal proceedings against Sanz de Lera and Others* EU:C:1995:451.

[112] See e.g., Case C-144/04, *Mangold* v. *Helm*, n. 94 and Case C-555/07, *Kücükdeveci* v. *Swedex GmbH & Co. KG*, n. 97.

[113] See e.g., Case C-415/93, *Union royale belge des sociétés de football association ASBL* v. *Bosman* EU:C:1995:463; Case C-281/98, *Angonese*, n. 85 and Case C-341/05, *Laval un Partneri Ltd* v. *Svenska Byggnadsarbetareförbundet* EU:C:2007:809.

authority within the EU legal order offers further paradigmatic examples of acts of constitutional contestation in the sphere of EU judicial activity. These acts affect both aspects of political authority identified in this chapter: (1) constituent authority (reserved to Member States as Treaty signatories) and also (2) EU policymaking authority (entrusted by Member States to the Union's political institutions).

Chapter 5 concludes the search for examples of judicial acts of constitutional contestation. It assesses how far the Court's interpretative choices *qua* Union institution comply with the EU Treaty framework's statements on the third issue for EU constitutionalism, concerning the objectives, values and limits of EU integration (Constitutional Issue No. 3).

5 The Court of Justice, the Treaty Framework and Constitutional Issue No. 3

[T]he Court act[s] as if it [is] in an empty jurisdictional space with no limitations on the reach of Community law.

J. H. H. Weiler, 'The Transformation of Europe' (1991) 100(8) *Yale Law Journal*, 2403 at 2440.

Introduction

This chapter completes the review of EU judicial activity for compliance with the EU Treaty framework as the principal touchstone on the internal constitutionality of all Union activity – including the work of the Court. Specifically, it identifies paradigmatic acts of constitutional contestation in EU judicial activity with regard to the Treaty framework and its statements on the *third* key issue for EU constitutionalism. That issue addresses *the objectives, values and limits of EU integration* (Constitutional Issue No. 3).

Scrutinising EU judicial activity for compliance with the Treaties' statements on the objectives, values and limits of EU integration is the most difficult of the three issues of EU constitutionalism to tackle. It is precisely here where the Treaties' function as touchstones on the internal constitutionality of EU institutional activity is at its least determinative. In particular, the EU Treaties now outline a broad spectrum of objectives (Chapter 1). These objectives are highly functional and pluralistic in character. Consequently, it can be difficult to adjudicate definitively on the internal constitutionality of the Court's (and other Union institutions') specific interpretative choices (or, similarly, to judge the relative constitutionality of one choice over another).[1]

[1] On the functional character of EU competences, see e.g., G. Davies, 'Democracy and Legitimacy in the Shadow of Purposive Competence' (2013) 21 *European Law Journal*, 2 at

The EU Treaties are not, however, so loosely drafted as to preclude any scrutiny of the Court's interpretative choices for compliance with their statements on Constitutional Issue No. 3.[2] This applies, *a fortiori*, with regard to the Treaty framework's statements on the *values and limits* that condition EU institutional activity. Indeed, the central claim in this chapter is that the Court's approach to the exercise of its interpretative functions may (and, moreover, should), as a matter of principle, be scrutinised for compliance with the full range of values and limits that now exist to structure EU institutional activity under the EU Treaty framework. The Court's adherence to these values and limits is especially pertinent where it is exercising its self-asserted functions as direct policymaker (Chapter 4).

The EU Treaties were shown to embody an increasingly broad set of normative values (Chapter 1). Under the founding Treaty, these values were principally linked to the realisation of economic objectives. In amended form, they now extend to include specific commitments to the fundamental values of respect for human dignity, freedom, democracy, equality, the rule of law and respect for human rights. In addition, the EU Treaty framework also now sets out a range of specific limits on EU policymaking – and EU institutional activity more broadly. These limits include overarching constitutional principles, such as the principles of conferral, subsidiarity and proportionality, as well as more specific exclusions or restraints on EU institutional activity.

Section 1 highlights the Court's use of directly effective EU norms as tools to override, sidestep or simply interrogate the Union legislature's clearly expressed preferences on matters of policy. The Court's use of directly effective EU norms in that manner provides further paradigmatic examples of constitutional contestation in EU judicial activity. Specifically, the Court's disregard for the integrity of EU legislative choices undermines the increased normative weight that the EU Treaty

pp. 7–12. For a critical perspective, see also, C. Kaupa, *The Pluralist Character of the European Economic Constitution* (Oxford: Hart Publishing, 2016).

[2] For earlier enquiries, see e.g., G. A. Bermann, 'Taking Subsidiarity Seriously: Federalism in the European Community and the United States' (1994) 94 *Columbia Law Review*, 331; T. Schilling, 'Subsidiarity as a Rule and a Principle' (1994) 14 *Yearbook of European Law*, 203; G. de Búrca, 'The Principle of Subsidiarity and the Court of Justice as an Institutional Actor' (1998) 36(2) *Journal of Common Market Studies*, 217; P. Craig, 'The ECJ and the *Ultra Vires* Action: A Conceptual Analysis' (2011) 48 *Common Market Law Review*, 395 and T. Horsley, 'Reflections on the Role of the Court of Justice as the "Motor" of European Integration: Legal Limits to Judicial Policymaking' (2013) 50 *Common Market Law Review*, 931.

framework now attaches to the *value of representative democracy* as the foundation of EU decision-making (falling within Constitutional Issue No. 3). Examples of the Court's use of its direct policymaking platform to undermine the EU legislature's political choices can be found across a broad spectrum of substantive policy areas. This section focuses on developments in two areas of Union policy in which the EU Treaties' position on the primacy of legislative policymaking is at its most explicit: (1) air transport services and (2) EU citizenship.

Section 2 exposes further acts of constitutional contestation in relation to the limits that the EU Treaties impose on EU legislative policymaking. In the exercise of its self-asserted direct policymaking functions, the Court is shown systematically to disregard key limits that the EU Treaties impose on EU *legislative* policymaking.[3] The Court's detachment of EU policymaking from the limits outlined in the Treaty framework defies functional expectations. As a consequence of its move to interpose itself alongside the Union legislature as direct policymaker, the Court of Justice should legitimately be expected to exercise its new role in accordance with the framework of limits structuring EU legislative policymaking. This applies, in particular, with respect to the application of the Treaties' most powerful normative restraints on EU policymaking: provisions that expressly exclude EU legislative competence.

The application *to the Court* of the framework of values and limits set out in the EU Treaties should not be considered limited to the examples highlighted in this chapter. As a matter of principle, the Court's institutional choices as direct policymaker should be considered subject to compliance with the full range of values and limits set out in the EU Treaty framework (Chapter 1).[4] Likewise, the search for sites of constitutional contestation in relation to Constitutional Issue No. 3

[3] See also, L. Azoulai, 'The "Retained Powers" Formula in the Case Law of the European Court of Justice: EU Law as Total Law?'(2011) 4(2) *European Journal of Legal Studies*, 192; L. Boucon, 'EU Law and Retained Powers of Member State' in L. Azoulai (ed.), *The Question of Competence in the European Union* (Oxford: Oxford University Press, 2014) and D. Damjanovic, '"Reserved Areas" of the Member States and the ECJ: The Case of Higher Education' in H-W. Micklitz and B. De Witte (eds.), *The European Court of Justice and the Autonomy of the Member States* (Antwerp: Insentia, 2012).

[4] See Horsley, 'Reflections on the Role of the Court of Justice as the "Motor" of European Integration', n. 2. For examples, see Bermann, 'Taking Subsidiarity Seriously', n. 2; Schilling, 'Subsidiarity as a Rule and a Principle', n. 2; de Búrca, 'The Principle of Subsidiarity and the Court of Justice as an Institutional Actor', n. 2; Craig, 'The ECJ and the *Ultra Vires* Action: A Conceptual Analysis', n. 2 and E. Cloots, *National Identity in EU Law* (Oxford: Oxford University Press, 2015).

can also be extended beyond a review of the Court's role as direct policymaker.[5] The case law on the General Court's non-contractual liability for damages as a consequence of its undue delay in hearing competition proceedings offers one specific example (see *Introduction*, Section I.3).

1 The *Values* of EU Policymaking: The Court of Justice versus the EU Treaty Framework

This section unmasks the Court's use of directly effective EU norms as tools to override, sidestep or simply interrogate the Union legislature's clearly expressed preferences on matters of policy. The Court's use of directly effective EU norms in that manner provides further paradigmatic examples of constitutional contestation in EU judicial activity. Specifically, the Court's disregard for the integrity of EU legislative choices undermines the increased normative weight that the EU Treaty framework now attaches to the value of representative democracy as the foundation of EU decision-making (falling within Constitutional Issue No. 3).

Sections 1.1 and 1.2 expose examples of judicial challenges to EU legislative choices in two specific substantive areas: air transportation (Section 1.1) and EU citizenship (Section 1.2). These two spheres of policymaking are especially well suited to analysis of the Court's relationship with the Union legislature as direct policymaker. In both areas, the EU Treaty framework is, as constitutional touchstone, at its most explicit with respect to the basic Treaty paradigm for Union legislative policymaking. In addition, the case law on air transportation and EU citizenship rights is ripe with illustrations of the Court's use of directly effective EU norms as tools to recast discrete legislative choices to match its own institutional preferences as direct policymaker. Section 1.3 then categorises judicial challenges to EU legislative choices (Sections 1.1 and 1.2) as acts of constitutional contestation with respect to the Treaty framework's position on Constitutional Issue No. 3. Specifically, it argues that the Court's use of directly effective EU norms to overturn EU legislative frameworks undermines the increased normative weight that the EU Treaties now attach to the value of representative democracy within the Union legal order.

[5] See Case T-577/14, *Gascogne Sack Deutschland GmbH* EU:T:2017:1. See also, Case T-673/15, *Guardian Europe* v. *European Union* EU:T:2017:377.

1.1 Air Transport

Air transport is an area of Union activity in which the Treaty framework is particularly explicit on the primary role for legislative policymaking.[6] Under Article 100(2) TFEU, EU policymaking in that field is *entirely* conditional on the Union legislature's decision to bring air (and sea) transportation within Title VI of Part 3 of the Treaty, which outlines its legislative competence in the area of transport policy.[7] Nonetheless, the Treaty framework notwithstanding, air transport is an area of EU policymaking in which the Court of Justice has repeatedly invoked EU norms that it has ruled directly effective as a means to contest the Union legislature's agreed regulatory preferences. Two sets of examples are highlighted here. The first example concerns the Court's approach as direct policymaker to the Union legislature's agreed policy position on air passenger compensation rights (*Sturgeon* and *Nelson and Others*)[8] (Section 1.1.1) The second example centres on the Court's use of directly effective EU norms to push the boundaries of EU integration on aircraft licensing beyond the limits established by the existing Union legislative framework in that area (*Neukirchinger* and *International Jet Management*)[9] (Section 1.1.2).

1.1.1 *Judicial Challenges to Regulation 261/2004 EU on Air Passenger Compensation Rights*

In *Sturgeon* and *Nelson and Others*, the Court invoked the principle of equal treatment to disregard the Union legislature's agreed position on the compensation rights of airline passengers.[10] Using Article 100(2) TFEU as a legal base, the EU legislature had enacted Regulation 261/2004 EU granting airline passengers travelling on flights within the EU and between the Member States and third countries specific rights to

[6] For an overview of the sector, see e.g., H. Kassim and H. Stevens (eds.) *Air Transport and the European Union: Europeanization and its Limits* (London: Palgrave, 2014).

[7] See also, Art. 58(1) TFEU, which provides that Title VI on transport shall govern services in the field of transport.

[8] Joined Cases C-402/07 and Case C-432/07, *Sturgeon* v. *Condor Flugdienst GmbH and Böck and Lepuschitz* v. *Air France SA* EU:C:2009:716 and Joined Cases C-581/10 and Case C-629/20, *Nelson and Others* v. *Deutsche Lufthansa AG and TUI Travel plc and Others* v *Civil Aviation Authority* EU:C:2012:657.

[9] Case C-382/08, *Neukirchinger* v. *Bezirkshauptmannschaft Grieskirchen* EU:C:2011:27 and Case C-628/11, *Criminal proceedings against International Jet Management GmbH* EU:C:2014:171.

[10] See S. Garben, 'Sky-High Controversy and High-Flying Claims? The *Sturgeon* Case Law in Light of Judicial Activism, Euroscepticism and Eurolegalism' (2013) 50(1) *Common Market Law Review*, 15

compensation with respect to cancelled and delayed flights.[11] Among other things, air passengers were entitled to claim compensation under Article 5 of the Regulation when airline operators had cancelled scheduled flights. The applicants in *Sturgeon* had suffered severe delays and sought compensation from their airline. They submitted that, for the purposes of compensation payments, the long delays they had suffered should be considered equivalent to situations in which flights are cancelled.

Regulation 261/2004 EU was absolutely clear on the distinct entitlements to compensation in connection with delayed versus cancelled flights. As the Court noted expressly, the Union legislature had opted *not* to grant airline passengers who had suffered flight delays equal rights to compensation as those enjoyed by passengers whose flights had been cancelled.[12] The Commission's Explanatory Note that accompanied the draft Regulation also reinforced that point. That Note outlined the Commission's clear intention, as author of the original legislative proposal, to differentiate between delayed and cancelled flights for the purposes of entitlements to compensation:

> Although passengers suffer similar inconvenience and frustration from delays as from denied boarding or cancellation, there is a difference in that an operator is responsible for denied boarding and cancellation (unless for reasons beyond its responsibility) but not always for delays. Other common causes are air traffic management systems and limits to airport capacity. As stated in its communication on the protection of air passengers, *the Commission considers that in present circumstances operators should not be obliged to compensate delayed passengers.*[13]

The Court of Justice acknowledged that, under Regulation 261/2004 EU, the categories of 'delayed' and 'cancelled' flights were distinctive and mutually exclusive. In specific terms, it ruled that flight cancellation involves the non-operation of a flight that was previously planned.[14] By contrast, a flight is deemed subject to delay for the purposes of the

[11] Regulation (EC) No 261/2004 of the European Parliament and of the Council establishing common rules on compensation and assistance to passengers in the event of denied boarding and of cancellation or long delay of flights [2004] OJ L 46/1.

[12] Joined Cases C-402/07 and Case C-432/07, *Sturgeon and Others*, n. 8 at paras. 40–41 and Joined Cases C-581/10 and Case C-629/20, *Nelson and Others*, n. 8 at para. 29.

[13] Proposal for a Regulation of the European Parliament and of the Council establishing common rules on compensation and assistance to air passengers in the event of denied boarding and of cancellation or long delay of flights COM(2001) 784 final (emphasis added).

[14] Joined Cases C-402/07 and Case C-432/07, *Sturgeon and Others*, n. 8 at para. 33.

Regulation where it is operated in accordance with the air carrier's original planning – irrespective of the severity of the delay.

On the facts, it was arguable that the applicants in *Sturgeon* had in fact suffered flight cancellations on the Court's interpretation, giving rise therefore to the compensation entitlements set out in Article 7 of the Regulation. That applied *a fortiori* with respect to the case that the applicants Bock and Lepuschitz had raised against Air France in the adjoining preliminary reference to the Court. In that case, the applicants had been offered (and accepted) tickets on an alternative flight operated by another airline, which was scheduled to depart the following day. Applying the Court's test for cancelled flights, it is not difficult to argue that the planning of that second flight was necessarily 'different from that of the flight for which the [original] booking was made'.[15]

The Court of Justice, however, opted for a radically different interpretation in its response to the referring court. In a direct challenge to the Union legislature's agreed position on the scope of air passengers' rights to compensation, the Court ruled that air passengers suffering delays should be entitled to compensation on broadly the same terms as those afforded to passengers whose flights had been cancelled. It openly acknowledged that this conclusion did not follow expressly from the Regulation, but proceeded regardless to restructure the EU legislative framework governing air passenger compensation rights.[16] In the final analysis, it concluded that:

> Regulation No. 261/2004 must be interpreted as meaning that passengers whose flights are delayed may be treated, for the purposes of the application of the right to compensation, as passengers whose flights are cancelled and they may thus rely on the right to compensation laid down in Article 7 of the regulation where they suffer, on account of a flight delay, a loss of time equal to or in excess of three hours, that is, where they reach their final destination three hours or more after the arrival time originally scheduled by the air carrier.[17]

The Court justified its decision to extend the scope of air operators' liabilities to cover losses incurred by passengers suffering flight delays with reference to the principle of equal treatment. On its interpretation, the principle of equal treatment required that the situation of passengers suffering long flight delays must be considered equivalent to that of passengers whose flights had been cancelled – notwithstanding

[15] *Ibid.*, at para. 35.
[16] *Ibid.*, at para. 41.
[17] *Ibid.*, at para. 69.

the absence of any reference to the existence of such a right in the Regulation.[18]

The Court was subsequently challenged on its use of the principle of equal treatment in order effectively to overturn the existing EU legislative framework governing the scope of air passenger compensation rights. In *Nelson and Others*, it was argued that the Court's interpretation of Regulation No. 261/2004 EU as imposing on airline operators an obligation to compensate passengers whose flights are delayed, 'disregard[ed] the intentions of the EU legislature and also the clear wording of that regulation, according to which compensation must be paid only in the event of denied boarding or flight cancellation'.[19] The Grand Chamber, however, rejected that challenge outright. Moreover, it restated in full its position on the existence in Union law of a right to compensation for long flight delays with express reference to the principle of equal treatment.[20]

1.1.2 Judicial Challenges to EU Regulations on Aircraft Licensing

The case law on air passenger compensation (Section 1.1.1) neatly illustrates the Court's application of directly effective EU norms as tools to contest the Union legislature's policy choices on discrete issues. Moving on to discuss aircraft licensing, *Neukirchinger* and *International Jet Management* provide examples of a related, but even bolder move.[21] In both decisions, the Grand Chamber openly challenged the Union legislature's competence under the Treaty framework – and Article 100(2) TFEU in particular – to determine the outer limits of EU integration in the air transport sector.

In *Neukirchinger*, the Court of Justice was requested to determine whether Union law precluded a Member State from requiring hot-air balloon operators to hold an air operator license to provide transport services within that State. The Treaty framework was clear that it did not. Article 58(1) TFEU provides for the exclusion of air transport services from the Treaty rules governing the free movement of services. As that provision stipulates, the freedom to provide services in the field of

[18] *Ibid.*, at para. 54. See thereafter, Joined Cases C-581/10 and Case C-629/20, *Nelson and Others*, n. 8 at para. 43.
[19] *Ibid.*, at para. 62.
[20] *Ibid.*, at para. 43.
[21] Case C-382/08, *Neukirchinger*, n. 9 and Case C-628/11 *International Jet Management*, n. 9. See T. Horsley, 'Case C-382/08, *Michael Neukirchinger* v. *Bezirkshauptmannschaft Grieskirchen*' (Case Annotation) (2012) 49(2) *Common Market Law Review*, 737.

transport is governed by the provisions on transport policy in Title VI of Part 3 of the TFEU.

That Title states clearly that EU integration in the sphere of air transport is conditional on the Union legislature's decision to enact legislative measures in that field pursuant to Article 100(2) TFEU. The EU legislature had made recourse to that provision to regulate key aspects of air transport. These measures included Regulation 2407/92 EEC on the licensing of air carriers within the European Union.[22] Crucially, however, the Union legislature had opted expressly *not* to regulate Member State rules on the licensing of non-power-driven aircraft such as hot-air balloons. Indeed, as Regulation 2407/92 EEC makes clear, the Union legislature had *explicitly excluded* such aircraft from the scope of the legislative framework on the licensing of air carriers enacted using Article 100(2) TFEU.[23]

The Grand Chamber acknowledged that, under the Treaty framework, the regulation of air transport services was subject to special rules. Moreover, it accepted that, exercising its competence under Article 100(2) TFEU, the Union legislature had excluded non-power-driven aircraft from the scope of Regulation 2407/92 EEC on the licensing of air carriers. Its position on that point was unambiguous:

> pursuant to Article 1(2) of Regulation No. 2407/92, the Council excluded the licensing of air carriers from the scope of that regulation where, for example, the carriage by air of passengers was performed by non-power-driven aircraft, thus including hot-air balloons. *In respect of modes of transport of that nature, the Council explicitly specified, in that provision, that national law governing operating licences was alone to apply.*[24]

'*Nevertheless*' (borrowing the Court's own language), the Grand Chamber concluded that the contested national rules requiring operators of hot-air balloon services to hold operating licenses was contrary to the (directly effective) principle of non-discrimination in Article 18 TFEU.[25]

Neither the Treaty framework nor, moreover, the Union legislature's exclusion of hot-air balloons from the scope of the EU legal framework on air transport altered that conclusion. For the Court, the express exclusion of non-power-driven aircraft from the scope of Regulation No. 2407/92 EEC did *not* mean that the Union legislature had intended

[22] Council Regulation (EEC) No. 2407/92 on licensing of air carriers [1992] OJ L 240/1.

[23] Art. 1(2).

[24] Case C-382/08, *Neukirchinger*, n. 9 at para. 25 (emphasis added).

[25] *Ibid.*, at para. 44.

to remove that mode of transport entirely from the scope of the Treaty. That line of judicial reasoning directly challenged the Union legislature's political preferences on the specific issue of air operator licenses. Even more strikingly, it undermined the Union legislature's competence to determine the extent to which the air transport sector is subject to Union law. In result, *Neukirchinger* leaves the Treaty paradigm for absolute legislative control in the air transport sector under Article 100(2) TFEU rather meaningless.

International Jet Management struck a further blow to the Treaty framework for legislative policymaking in the field of air transport. In that decision, the Grand Chamber was asked to determine whether Union law precluded German legislation that required operators of commercial flights between Member States and third countries to obtain prior authorisation before entering national airspace. Regulation 1008/2008 EU established a system of mutual recognition with respect to air operating licenses for commercial aircraft.[26] However, that Regulation only applied to govern the provision of *intra-EU* commercial flights.[27] The dispute at issue involved the provision of air transport services between the EU and third countries and did not fall within the scope of Regulation 1008/2008 EU.

As before in *Neukirchinger*, the Grand Chamber acknowledged that the Union legislature had not exercised its competence under Article 100(2) TFEU to establish common rules on air operating licenses with respect to non-EU commercial flights. '*Nevertheless*' (again, using the Court's language), it concluded that the contested German measure was subject to scrutiny against the prohibition of discrimination in Article 18 TFEU as a directly effective EU norm. According to the Grand Chamber,

> while it is true that the EU legislature has not, at this stage, under the shared competence conferred on it in the transport field by Article 4(2)(g) TFEU, adopted measures based on Article 100(2) TFEU on liberalisation of air transport services covering the routes between Member States and third countries, Article 18 TFEU may nevertheless be applied to such services, provided that they fall within the scope of application of the Treaties, within the meaning of that latter article.[28]

The Court's finding that the regulation of non-EU transport services fell within the scope of the Treaty for the purposes of Article 18 TFEU was

[26] Regulation (EC) No. 1008/2008 of the European Parliament and of the Council on common rules for the operation of air services in the Community [2008] OJ L 293/3.
[27] Art. 1.
[28] Case C-628/11, *International Jet Management*, n. 9 at para. 39.

based (again) on its assertion that the Union legislature had not expressly excluded non-EU commercial flights from the scope of Regulation 1008/2008 EU.[29] That is a remarkable line of argumentation when measured against the Treaty framework structuring EU policymaking in the area of air transport services. Article 100(2) TFEU leaves no doubt whatsoever that the EU Treaty framework vests primary responsibility for policy-making in that field to the Union legislature.

1.2 Union Citizenship

Union citizenship is a second sphere of EU policymaking that is rich with examples of the Court's use of directly effective EU norms as tools to challenge the Union legislature's substantive policy choices. In common with air transport (Section 1.1), it is also an area of Union activity in which the Treaty framework is especially explicit on the principal role for *legislative* policymaking as regards the scope and quality of EU legal rights. In particular, the Treaty framework – as constitutional touchstone – is absolutely clear that the rights of EU citizenship are subject to the conditions and limits outlined in the Treaties and, moreover, by the measures the EU legislature has adopted to give those rights effect (Article 20(2) TFEU).

Title II of Part 2 of the TFEU defines the status and rights of EU citizenship under the Treaties. Article 20 TFEU establishes the legal status of EU citizenship. That status is determined with reference to Member State nationality and is expressly defined as additional in character. That provision further outlines the range of rights that EU citizens enjoy. These rights include the right to move and reside freely within the territory of the Member States (Article 21 TFEU); the right to vote and to stand as candidates in elections to the European Parliament and in municipal elections in their Member States of residence under the same conditions as nationals of that State (Article 22 TFEU); the right to enjoy diplomatic and consular protection provided by other Member States in third countries in which they are not otherwise represented (Article 23 TFEU); and the right to petition the European Parliament, to apply to the European Ombudsman and to correspond with the EU institutions in any of the Treaty languages (Article 24 TFEU).

[29] *Ibid.*, at para. 42.

As in other areas, the Treaty framework accentuates the primary role for EU legislative policymaking to facilitate the exercise of the aforementioned rights of EU citizenship. Article 21(2) TFEU, for example, entrusts the EU legislature with competence to enact secondary legislation where 'action by the Union should prove necessary' to give effect to the right that Member State nationals enjoy as Union citizens to move and reside within the territory of the EU (Article 21 TFEU). Likewise, Article 22 TFEU requires the Council, after consulting the European Parliament, to adopt 'detailed arrangements' to give effect to EU citizens' electoral rights. More broadly, Article 25 TFEU empowers the Council to use the special legislative procedure to adopt legislative measures that seek to enhance the core rights of EU citizenship in Articles 21–24 TFEU.[30]

The Court of Justice's case law has repeatedly challenged the Treaty framework structuring EU legislative policymaking on Union citizenship rights.[31] This section highlights two particularly striking sets of examples concerning, first, its approach to EU citizens' entitlements to social security benefits (Section 1.2.1) and, secondly, its position on EU citizens' residence rights (Section 1.2.2). On both topics, the Court can be seen to invoke directly effective EU norms – and Articles 18, 20 and 21 TFEU in particular – as a means to recast the Union legislature's political choices on the scope and limits of EU citizenship rights.[32]

1.2.1 *Entitlements to Social Security Benefits*

Collins remains a standout instance of judicial recourse to directly effective norms to challenge the EU legislative framework governing social

[30] The entry into force of any enhancements is conditional on their ratification by Member States – offering Member States an additional degree of control as constituent authorities over the scope of EU citizenship rights.

[31] For analysis, see e.g., F. Wollenschläger, 'The Judiciary, the Legislature and the Evolution of Union Citizenship' in See P. Syrpis (ed.), *The Judiciary, the Legislature and the EU Internal Market* (Cambridge: Cambridge University Press, 2012); M. Dougan, 'The Constitutional Dimension to the Case Law on Union Citizenship' (2006) 31 *European Law Review*, 613 and E. Spaventa, 'Seeing the Wood despite the Trees? On the Scope of Union Citizenship and its Constitutional Effects' (2008) 45 *Common Market Law Review*, 13.

[32] Nic Shuibhne characterises this as a process of 'normative inversion'. See N. Nic Shuibhne, 'The Third Age of EU Citizenship: Directive 2004/38 in the Case Law of the Court of Justice' in Syrpis, *The Judiciary, the Legislature and the EU Internal Market*', n. 31 at p. 352. See also, S. O'Leary, 'Equal Treatment and EU Citizens: A New Chapter on Cross-Border Educational Mobility and Access to Student Financial Assistance' (2009) 34 *European Law Review*, 612.

security entitlements.[33] In that decision, the Court was requested to determine whether Member State nationals were entitled, as work seekers, to claim a non-contributory unemployment benefit (jobseeker's allowance) that required applicants to satisfy a habitual residence test. The EU Treaties and, moreover, Union legislative framework in force at the time were clear that such persons did not enjoy that right. Article 39 EC (now 45 TFEU) granted Member State nationals, *inter alia*, the right to accept offers of employment actually made and, further, to move freely within the territory of Member States for that purpose. Using Article 46 TFEU, the Union legislature had enacted several EU measures to facilitate the exercise of that provision. These included, in particular, Regulation 1612/68 EEC and Directive 68/360 EEC.[34] As the Full Court noted explicitly in its judgment, neither instrument afforded Member State nationals, as work seekers, a right to claim equal treatment with respect to non-contributory benefits such as the United Kingdom's jobseeker's allowance.[35]

The Full Court, however, was clearly dissatisfied with the legal landscape that prevailed at the time. It concluded that Member State nationals were necessarily entitled, as a matter of principle, to claim non-contributory social security payments designed to facilitate access to national employment markets. The Court's decision to do so relied on its invocation of Articles 18 and 21 TFEU – the Treaty provisions on equal treatment and Union citizenship – which the Court had ruled directly effective. These provisions were used effectively to (re)define the scope of EU policymaking in the sphere of work seekers' rights to match the Court's institutional preferences as direct policymaker. According to the Court,

In view of the establishment of citizenship of the Union and the interpretation in the case-law of the right to equal treatment enjoyed by citizens of the Union, it is no longer possible to exclude from the scope of Article 48(2) of the Treaty – which expresses

[33] Case C-138/02, *Collins* v. *Secretary of State for Work and Pensions* EU:C:2004:172. See also, Case C-258/04, *Office national de l'emploi* v. *Ioannis Ioannidis* EU:C:2005:559. See also, by analogy, the Court's case law on student maintenance and EU citizenship, e.g., Case C-209/03, *Bidar* v. *London Borough of Ealing and Secretary of State for Education and Skills* EU:C:2005:169.

[34] Regulation (EEC) No. 1612/68 of the Council on freedom of movement for workers within the Community [1968] OJ L 257/2 and Council Directive 68/360/EEC on the abolition of restrictions on movement and residence within the Community for workers of Member States and their families [1968] OJ L 257/13.

[35] Case C-138/02, *Collins*, n. 33 at paras. 33 and 44.

the fundamental principle of equal treatment, guaranteed by Article 6 of the Treaty – a benefit of a financial nature intended to facilitate access to employment in the labour market of a Member State.[36]

The Full Court's conclusions represent a direct challenge to the EU legislative framework established to structure access to non-contributory social security benefits.[37] Its judgment expresses the Court's apparent dissatisfaction with the appropriateness of the Union legislature's agreed position on social security entitlements that the latter had opted to make available to support Member State national's entry into national employment markets as work seekers. That dissatisfaction was, moreover, doubly contentious. At the time of the Court's decision, the Union legislature was in the final stages of legislating to provide enhanced protection for Member State social security systems in connection with the exercise of the Treaty's free movement rights. Specifically, Article 24(2) of the recently enacted Directive 2004/38 EC exempted Member States from any requirement to provide EU citizens with 'social assistance' to support their residency on the national territory as work seekers.[38]

1.2.2 Residence Rights

The case law on the delimitation of Union citizens' residence rights evidences the same disruptive judicial approach to Union policymaking – on an even greater scale. In this sphere, the Court has employed the Treaty provisions on Union citizenship as directly effective norms to sidestep entirely the EU legislative framework that was established to manage the scope of EU citizens' residence rights.

This move has its origins in *Baumbast*, in which the Court invoked Article 21 TFEU as a directly effective EU norm to review (and relax) the

[36] *Ibid.*, at para. 63 (emphasis added).

[37] It also represented a significant revision of its earlier case law. See esp., Case 316/85, *Centre public d'aide sociale de Courcelles* v. *Lebon* EU:C:1987:302 at para. 27.

[38] Directive 2004/38 EC of the Council and European Parliament on the right of citizens of the Union and their family members to move and reside freely within the territory of the Member States [2004] OJ L 158/77. In subsequent judgments, the Court has sought to defuse the tension that exists between its position in *Collins* and Art. 24(4) of Directive 2004/38 EC by stating that the provision of financial benefits that are intended to facilitate access to employment in the host Member State (at issue in *Collins*) do *not* fall within the meaning of 'social assistance' in Art. 24(2) of Directive 2004/38 EC. See e.g., Joined Cases C-22/08 and C-23/08, *Vatsouras and Koupatantze* EU:C:2009:344 at paras. 33–46.

detailed conditions that the Union legislature had opted to impose on the exercise of the right to reside within the territory of another Member State.[39] Specifically, the Court ruled that economically inactive[40] EU citizens could not be denied residence rights in Member States of which they are not nationals solely on the basis that they did not have comprehensive medical insurance – a requirement set out in Directive 90/364 EEC.[41] Likewise, in *Chen*, the Full Court held that a refusal to recognise the residence rights of a EU citizen on the basis that, as a minor, she did not *personally* satisfy the requirement in Directive 90/364 EEC to have 'sufficient resources' to support herself in the host Member State constituted a 'disproportionate interference' with the fundamental right to movement and residence conferred by Article 21 TFEU.[42]

However, the most profound challenge to the Treaty paradigm for legislative policymaking in the area of EU citizenship rights arose in *Ruiz Zambrano*.[43] In that case, the Court pushed its direct policymaking functions to the extreme in relation to the delineation of EU citizens' residence rights. The Grand Chamber employed Article 20 TFEU – which it had declared directly effective – to create an entirely new framework of residence (and also employment) rights for the third country national family members of a certain category of static Union citizen.

In *Ruiz Zambrano*, the Court was requested to determine whether EU law granted the third country national father of a (minor) EU citizen a right to reside in the territory of the Member State of which the latter was a national. The Union legislative framework was clear that it did not. Directive 2004/38 EC established residence rights for third country national family members only where Union citizens had exercised their Treaty rights to movement and residence. Likewise, Directive 2003/86 EC

[39] Case C-413/99, *Baumbast and R* v. *Secretary of State for the Home Department* EU:C:2002:493. See also earlier, Case C-85/96, *Martínez Sala* v. *Freistaat Bayern* EU:C:1998:217 and Case C-184/99, *Grzelczyk* v. *Centre public d'aide sociale d'Ottignies-Louvain-la-Neuve* EU:C:2001:458.

[40] Mr Baumbast had previously exercised his Treaty rights to intra-EU movement as a migrant worker, but at the material time had ceased to do so.

[41] Case C-413/99, *Baumbast and R*, n. 39 at para. 93.

[42] Case C-200/02, *Zhu and Chen* v. *Secretary of State for the Home Department* EU:C:2004:639.

[43] Case C-34/09, *Ruiz Zambrano* v. *Office national de l'emploi* EU:C:2011:124. For analysis, see e.g., H. Van Eijken and S. A. de Vries, 'A New Route into the Promised Land? Being a European Citizen after *Ruiz Zambrano*' (2011) 36 *European Law Review*, 704 and K. Hailbronner and D. Thym, 'Case C-34/09, *Gerardo Ruiz Zambrano* v. *Office national de l'emploi (ONEm)*, Judgment of the Court of Justice (Grand Chamber) of 8 March 2011' (Case Annotation) (2011) 48 *Common Market Law Review*, 1253.

on family reunification was inapplicable on the facts as that instrument does not apply to the family members of Union citizens.[44]

Accordingly, falling as it did outside the EU legislative framework enacted to give effect to Article 21 TFEU, the applicant's residence (and employment) rights might logically have been ruled an exclusive matter for national (Belgian) immigration law. The Member State governments intervening defended that conclusion. It was also the Commission's position. As the Court summarised,

> All governments which submitted observations to the Court and the European Commission argue that a situation such as that of Mr Ruiz Zambrano's second and third children, where those children reside in the Member State of which they are nationals and have never left the territory of that Member State, does not come within the situations envisaged by the freedoms of movement and residence guaranteed under European Union law. Therefore, the provisions of European Union law referred to by the national court are not applicable to the dispute in the main proceedings.[45]

That conclusion did not, of course, leave the applicant and his family without any potential redress, including, in particular, legal mechanisms to ensure compliance with fundamental rights standards. As a contracting party to the European Convention on Human Rights, the Belgian authorities' appraisal of Mr Ruiz Zambrano's legal position would be subject, ultimately, to external control for compliance with ECHR fundamental rights standards.[46]

The Grand Chamber in *Ruiz Zambrano* (and thereafter in the case of *Dereci*) did not conceal the finding that the existing EU legislative framework on citizenship rights did not cover the applicant's situation. The Court observed at the outset that, 'Directive 2004/38 ... applies to "all Union citizens who move to or reside in a Member State other than that of which they are a national, and to their family members ... " *Therefore, that directive does not apply to a situation such as that at issue in the main proceedings.*'[47] In *Dereci*, the Court also expressly acknowledged that the applicant's circumstances did not fall within the scope of Directive

[44] Art. 3(3) of Council Directive 2003/86/EC on the right to family reunification [2003] OJ L 251/12. See Case C-256/11, *Dereci and Others* v. *Bundesministerium für Inneres* EU: C:2011:734 at para. 47.

[45] Case C-34/09, *Ruiz Zambrano*, n. 43 at para. 37.

[46] See Case C-256/11, *Dereci and Others*, n. 44.

[47] Case C-34/09, *Ruiz Zambrano*, n. 43 at para. 39 (emphasis added). See also, Case C-256/11, *Dereci and Others*, n. 44 at para. 57.

2003/86 EC on family reunification.[48] It noted that, under Article 3(3) of that Directive, the provisions on family reunification did not apply to members of the family of Union citizens.[49]

Nevertheless, the Grand Chamber did not read the non-applicability of the existing EU legislative framework as exhaustive or, at the very least, as a statement of agreed political limits on the scope of EU citizens' rights. Rather, the Court took the non-applicability of Directives 2004/38 EC and Directive 2003/86 EC as simply a *starting point* in relation to judgments over the delineation of the rights of EU citizenship. Invoking Article 20 TFEU as a directly effective provision, the Grand Chamber asserted that, the Treaty framework notwithstanding, Union law granted a right of residence to the third country national father of two (minor) EU citizens in the Member State of which the Union citizens were nationals. That conclusion, the Court submitted, was necessary to safeguard the rights of the minor EU citizens to exercise their Treaty rights of EU citizenship. As the Court put it,

> Article 20 TFEU precludes national measures which have the effect of depriving citizens of the Union of *the genuine enjoyment of the substance of the rights conferred by virtue of their status as citizens of the Union*. A refusal to grant a right of residence to a third country national with dependent minor children in the Member State where those children are nationals and reside, and also a refusal to grant such a person a work permit, has such an effect.[50]

Considering the applicant's personal circumstances, the Court took the view that the refusal to secure Mr Ruiz Zambrano's residence rights as a matter of Union law would compel the EU citizens (his children) to leave the territory of the Union. Moreover, it concluded that the same result would likely necessarily follow should the Member State concerned refuse to grant a work permit to Mr Ruiz Zambrano.[51] Neither argument is persuasive. For one thing, the decision not to grant Mr Ruiz Zambrano a right of residence in the Member State of which his children are nationals would not legally compel the latter, as EU citizens, to leave the territory of the Union. On the contrary, the applicable Union

[48] Council Directive 2003/86/EC on the right to family reunification [2003] OJ L 251/12.

[49] Case C-256/11, *Dereci and Others*, n. 44 at para. 47. As the Court noted, the Commission had included reference to EU citizens who had not exercised their rights to movement and residence under Union law in its proposal for a Directive on Family Unification. However, this was deleted in the course of the legislative process. See *Dereci* at para. 49.

[50] Case C-34/09, *Ruiz Zambrano*, n. 43 at paras. 42 and 43 (emphasis added).

[51] *Ibid.*, at para. 43.

legislative framework guaranteed the entire Zambrano family the right to move to, and reside within, the territory of the other Member States in accordance with the conditions set out therein.

What the Grand Chamber was really saying in *Ruiz Zambrano* is that, in its view as direct policymaker, the existing legislative measures that the Union legislature had enacted to give effect to the Treaty rights on EU citizenship do not go far enough. More specifically, the Court challenged the Union legislature's express (and logical) decision to exclude the application of Union law to situations where Union citizens have not exercised their rights to intra-EU movement – so-called (wholly) internal situations. That exclusion, as *Ruiz Zambrano* makes strikingly clear, simply did not accord with the Court's own policy preferences as regards the scope of EU citizenship rights.[52] To justify its decision, the Grand Chamber recalled *its normative position* on the ultimate trajectory of Union citizenship as 'destined to be the fundamental status of nationals of the Member States'.[53] That position finds no support in the Treaty framework and exists solely on the strength of the Court's own earlier case law.[54]

1.3 The Court of Justice and the EU Legislature

Sections 1.1 and 1.2 exposed the Court's use of directly effective EU norms as tools to override or circumvent the EU legislature's agreed policy choices in air transport and Union citizenship rights, respectively. Further examples can be found in other policy areas. It is sufficient to recall here the Court's landmark judgments on the residence rights of

[52] See also, Davies, who references the Court's interpretation of secondary Union law 'in light of the castle of [directly effective] principles and idea[s] that it has built, and which it jealously guards against legislative corruption'. See G. Davies, 'Legislative Control of the European Court of Justice' (2014) 51 *Common Market Law Review*, 1579 at p. 1600.

[53] Case C-184/99, *Grzelczyk*, n. 39 at para. 31; Case C-413/99 *Baumbast and R*, n. 39 at para. 82; Case C-148/02 *Garcia Avello* v. *Belgian State* EU:C:2003:539 at para. 22; Case C-200/02, *Zhu and Chen*, n. 42 at para. 25 and Case C-135/08, *Rottman* v. *Freistaat Bayern* EU:C:2010:104 at para. 43.

[54] In its subsequent case law, the Court has taken steps to delimit the scope of EU citizenship rights in accordance with existing EU legislative frameworks. This is discussed further in Chapter 7. See e.g., Case C-333/13, *Dano and Dano* v. *Jobcenter Leipzig* EU:C:2014:2358 and Case C-67/14, *Jobcenter Berlin Neukölln* v. *Alimanovic and Others* EU:C:2015:597. The Court remains, however, an active policymaker in EU citizenship and other areas. See e.g., Case C-650/13, *Delvigne* EU:C:2015:648 (on electoral rights) and Case C-507/12, *Jessy Saint Prix* EU:C:2014:2007 (on free movement of workers).

third country national family members of Union citizens (*Metock*);[55] derogations to the right to equal treatment in the insurance market (*Test-Achats ASBL*)[56]; and the principle of non-discrimination on the grounds of age (*Mangold*).[57] The Court's exercise of its direct policymaking functions in this body of case law challenges the Treaty framework's status as constitutional touchstone in two ways. First, as Chapter 4 demonstrated, it directly contests the Treaties' basic statements on the locus of EU policymaking authority within the Union legal order (Constitutional Issue No. 2.). As argued in Chapter 4, the Treaty framework, as constitutional touchstone, vests primary responsibility for Union policymaking with the Union's political institutions, not the Court.

However, the Court's use of its direct policymaking functions to override or circumvent the EU legislature's agreed policy choices in areas such as air transport and Union citizenship is more than simply a challenge to the Treaties' statements on the locus of EU policymaking authority within the Union legal order. It also gives rise, secondly, to an example of constitutional contestation concerning the Treaty framework's statements on the core *values* that structure European integration thereunder. Specifically, it is argued that the Court's maintenance of its *primus inter pares* approach as Union policymaker (see Sections 1.1 and 1.2) has evolved to represent an increasingly powerful challenge to the Treaty framework's defence of a particular form of transnational representative democracy as a fundamental value in European integration.

Section 1.3.1 begins by tracing the emergence of representative democracy as a fundamental value in EU integration under the Treaty framework as constitutional touchstone. Section 1.3.2 then assesses how far the Court of Justice, acting as direct policymaker, has responded to the Treaties' progressive entrenchment of representative democracy as a normative value in European integration. It identifies the Court's failure to take account of the Treaty framework's evolving statements on representative democracy as a paradigmatic example of an act of *constitutional contestation* with regard to Constitutional Issue No. 3.

[55] See e.g., Case C-127/08, *Metock and Others* v. *Minister for Justice, Equality and Law Reform* EU:C:2008:449.

[56] See e.g., Case C-236/09, *Test-Achats ASBL and Others* v. *Conseil des ministres* EU:C:2011:100.

[57] Case C-144/04, *Mangold* v. *Helm* EU:C:2005:709 at para. 75. See thereafter, e.g., Case C-555/07, *Kücükdeveci* v. *Swedex GmbH & Co. KG*: EU:C:2010:21 and Case C-441/14, *Dansk Industri (DI), acting on behalf of Ajos A/S* v. *Estate of Karsten Eigil Rasmussen* EU:C:2016:278.

1.3.1 *The Emergence of European Representative Democracy as a Normative Value under the EU Treaty Framework*

When the Court first opted to interpose itself as direct policymaker – contrary to the Treaty framework (Chapter 4) – representative democracy was, at best, only an embryonic concern as a value in European integration. That concern was most visible through the collective agreement of Member States to include an Assembly composed of national parliamentarians within the institutional structure of the original Community. The powers of that unelected Assembly were, however, extremely limited.[58]

Beyond establishing the Assembly, the founding EEC Treaty was otherwise silent on representative democracy as a normative value structuring European integration. That omission was not unique. The founding Treaty included no references to any specific 'values' underpinning EU integration (Chapter 1). Of course, that did not mean that EU integration was not, from the outset, concerned with the promotion of a specific set of political and economic values. On the contrary, as argued in Chapter 1, through the EEC Treaty, the founding Member States expressed a qualified political commitment to the values of an open market economy based on the principles of non-discrimination and undistorted competition. In addition, the founding Treaty framework implicitly, but firmly, linked European integration to the rule of law as a normative value. As EU legal historians remind us, the Court of Justice was established principally to offer Member States and economic operators alike judicial protection against acts of the new Community institutions.[59] That task was embedded in the Court's overarching (and unchanged) mandate to ensure that, in the interpretation and application of the EEC Treaty, the 'law is observed'.

Representative democracy has since progressively emerged as a cornerstone value in EU integration under the Treaty framework. Initial efforts to embed democracy within the EU legal order linked EU integration to *national* democratic processes. The Treaty on European Union, for instance, introduced the first express reference to democracy as a founding principle of European integration with reference to the

[58] The Assembly's principal powers were consultative. It also enjoyed competence to pass motions of censure against the Commission (Art. 144 EEC).

[59] A. Boerger-De Smedt, 'Negotiating the Foundations of European Law, 1950–57: The Legal History of the Treaties of Paris and Rome' (2012) 21(3) *Contemporary European History*, 339 at p. 346.

democratic identities of the Member States. Pursuant to Article F of that Treaty, the newly established European Union committed to respect the 'national identities of its Member States, whose systems of government are founded on the principles of democracy'.[60] To the same end, the Maastricht Treaty introduced the principle of subsidiarity as a normative restraint on EU policymaking. That principle operates to protect the integrity of national democratic processes – specifically the regulatory decisions they make – by imposing important restrictions on the scope of EU policymaking in shared areas of competence.[61] Its introduction into the Treaty framework was linked to broader commitments to ensure that decisions are taken 'as closely as possible to the citizen[s] [they affect]'.

Following the entry into force of the Lisbon Treaty, the commitment to democracy has been recast as a fundamental value within the EU legal order. Moreover, it has also been further refined to reference, more expressly, a specific, networked model of transnational European representative democracy. Article 10 TEU, in particular, now outlines that,

> The functioning of the Union shall be founded on representative democracy. Citizens are directly represented at Union level in the European Parliament. Member States are represented in the European Council by their Heads of State or Government and in the Council by their governments, themselves democratically accountable either to their national Parliaments, or to their citizens. Every citizen shall have the right to participate in the democratic life of the Union. Decisions shall be taken as openly as possible and as closely as possible to the citizen. Political parties at European level contribute to forming European political awareness and to expressing the will of the citizens of the Union.[62]

The emergence of representative democracy as a foundational normative value has been accompanied by transformative changes to the framework for, and character of, EU policymaking under the EU Treaties. In more precise terms, repeated Treaty amendments have radically restructured the institutional balance governing EU policymaking in favour of increased democratic input and oversight. This process is most clearly exemplified by the growth of the European Parliament as both a directly

[60] The Treaty of Amsterdam amended Art. F TEU to read: 'The Union is founded on the principles of liberty, democracy, respect for human rights and fundamental freedoms, and the rule of law, principles which are common to the Member States.'

[61] See A. Estella, *The Principle of Subsidiarity and Its Critique* (Oxford: Oxford University Press, 2002).

[62] Art. 10 TEU. See also, the Opinion of Advocate General Poiares Maduro in C-411/06, *Commission* v. *Parliament and Council (Waste Shipments)* EU:C:2009:189.

elected institution of the Union and, moreover, an institution with increasing control over EU legislative processes. Following the entry into force of the Treaty of Lisbon, the European Parliament is now co-legislator with the Council by default.[63] Significantly, its sphere of influence as policymaker in that regard encompasses the full range of substantive policy areas over which the Court of Justice has interposed itself as direct policymaker.

A range of other intervening developments complements the European Parliament's emergence as a critical source of democratic input in connection with Union policymaking. The introduction of Article 10 TEU, with its reference to the dual basis of representative democracy within the EU legal order, has already been referenced. To this can be added, *inter alia*, the (earlier) establishment of new rights for EU citizens to vote and stand in elections to the European Parliament;[64] to petition the European Parliament;[65] to apply to the European Ombudsmen;[66] and to correspond with the EU institutions in any of the official languages of the Union.[67]

In addition, under the post-Lisbon Treaty settlement, Union citizens now have a direct stake in one of the most fundamental aspects of the policymaking process: policy initiation. Once the exclusive monopoly of the Commission, EU citizens now enjoy potential scope to shape the EU legislative agenda both indirectly through the European Parliament and now, post-Lisbon, directly through the European Citizens' Initiative (ECI).[68] The latter innovation requires the Commission to consider proposals for the adoption of EU legal acts in response to requests that enjoy the support of at least one million citizens from a minimum of a seven Member States.[69]

1.3.2 *The Court of Justice and Representative Democracy as a Normative Value under the Treaty Framework*

The Court of Justice is typically viewed as having played an active role in enhancing the value of representative democracy as a cornerstone of EU

63 Art. 289 TFEU and Art. 294 TFEU.
64 Art. 22 TFEU.
65 Art. 24 TFEU.
66 *Ibid.*
67 *Ibid.*
68 Art. 11(4) TEU.
69 Regulation (EU) No. 211/2011 of the European Parliament and of the Council on the citizens' initiative [2011] OJ L65/1.

policymaking.[70] It was the Court, for example, that shook the Community's political processes out of their sclerosis through its interventions as direct policymaker.[71] Similarly, it was the Court that challenged the collective position of Member States under the founding Treaty on the standing rights of the European Parliament in annulment actions. In *Parliament* v. *Council (Chernobyl)*, the Court of Justice ruled – contrary to the EU Treaties' statements on constituent power – that the European Parliament enjoyed competence to contest the validity of legal acts to defend its prerogatives (Chapter 4).[72]

This trend has continued. For example, the Court recently defended the integrity of the ECI with express reference to its function as a tool to enhance the democratic quality of Union policymaking. In *Anagnostakis* v. *Commission*, the Court ruled that Article 296 TFEU required the Commission to justify its refusal to register an application for an ECI. The introduction of the ECI at Lisbon was, the Court concluded, 'intended to reinforce citizenship of the Union and enhance the democratic functioning of the Union through the participation of citizens in the democratic life of the Union'.[73] However, the Court's contribution to the construction of the present model of European representative democracy is non-linear. What it has given in one context, it has more than taken back through the exercise of its direct policymaking functions in others. As Sections 1.1 and 1.2 clearly demonstrated, the Court of Justice asserts, where it sees appropriate, the primacy of its institutional preferences as direct policymaker to defeat (or step beyond) those of the Union legislature. Its case law on air transport and Union citizenship rights provided clear examples of the Court's use of directly effective EU norms to override or circumvent the EU legislature's agreed policy choices in both substantive areas.

Strikingly, the Court has not adjusted its approach as direct policymaker vis-à-vis the Union legislature to reflect the progressive qualitative changes to the democratic character of EU policymaking (outlined in Section 1.3.1). The fact that the Union legislature's preferences – as designated primary EU policymaker – are now formulated through increasingly enhanced democratic processes has not precipitated changes to the dynamics of

[70] See e.g., F. Mancini and D. Keeling, 'Democracy and the European Court of Justice' (1994) 57 *Modern Law Review*, 175 and K. Lenaerts, 'The Principle of Democracy in the Case Law of the European Court of Justice' (2013) 62 *International Comparative Law Quarterly*, 271

[71] See most clearly, its jurisprudence on mutual recognition, the substance of which precipitated key changes to legislative policymaking in the Common Market.

[72] Case C-70/88, *Parliament and Council (Chernobyl)* EU:C:1990:217.

[73] Case T-450/12, *Anagnostakis* v. *Commission* EU:T:2015:739 at para. 26.

judicial policymaking. To a great extent, the Court has retained its *primus inter pares* approach to the definition of the substance (and outer limits) of Union policymaking in areas over which it has opted – in contestation with the Treaty framework – to interpose itself alongside the EU legislature as direct policymaker.[74] For instance, as Sections 1.1 and 1.2 highlighted, the Court has not hesitated to recast the Union legislature's substantive preference on air passenger compensation rights (*Sturgeon and Others*) or, likewise, to step beyond the legislative frameworks governing the outer limits of Union citizenship (*Ruiz Zambrano*).[75]

There is a negative impact on the networked model of European representative democracy under Article 10 TEU whenever the Court uses EU norms that it has ruled directly effective in order to overturn or sidestep the Union legislature's policy preferences. Aside from the fact that the Treaty framework as constitutional touchstone does *not* attribute it any direct policymaking functions (Chapter 4), the Court fairs poorly in comparison to its political counterparts on the classic measures of comparative institutional analysis: democratic legitimacy and technical expertise.[76] Its judges are not elected, its deliberations are secret, and, as a court of general jurisdiction, it enjoys no specific expertise in the wide range of policy fields over which it intercedes to adjudicate.

The intensity of the Court's challenge to the value of representative democracy reaches its peak in areas of Union policymaking that are subject to the ordinary legislative procedure. In these areas, the EU legislature's substantive policy choices enjoy their strongest democratic credentials. Union legislation enacted under that (now, post-Lisbon, default) procedure engages the directly elected European Parliament as co-legislature with the Council. A number of the Court's decisions in which it opted, as direct policymaker, to recast the Union legislature's clearly articulated policy preferences considered in Sections 1.1 and 1.2 fall within this category. These include, the Court's judgments on the air passenger compensation (*Sturgeon* and *Nelson and Others*); the entitlements

74 Chapter 7 considers the exceptions, including aspects of its more recent case law on EU citizens' rights in e.g., Case C-333/13, *Dano*, n. 54; Case C-67/14, *Alimanovic and Others*, n. 54 and Case C-308/14, *Commission* v. *United Kingdom (Social Security)* EU:C:2016:436.

75 Joined Cases C-402/07 and Case C-432/07, *Sturgeon*, n. 8 and Case C-34/09, *Ruiz Zambrano*, n. 43.

76 See esp., Syrpis (ed.), *The Judiciary, the Legislature and the EU Internal Market*, n. 31 and P. Syrpis, 'The Relationship between Primary and Secondary Law in the EU' (2015) 52 *Common Market Law Review*, 461. See also, A. von Staden, 'The Democratic Legitimacy of Judicial Review Beyond the State: Normative Subsidiarity and Judicial Standards of Review' (2012) 10(4) *International Journal of Constitutional Law*, 1023.

of work seekers (*Collins* and *Vatsouras*); and the residence rights of static EU citizens (*Ruiz Zambrano*).

The tension with the value of representative democracy in the ordinary legislative procedure is further aggravated where the Treaty framework provides a role for Member State parliaments in Union policymaking.[77] The Lisbon Treaty integrated national parliaments into the Treaty paradigm for legislative policymaking. Member State parliaments are now expressly empowered to scrutinise EU legislative proposals in areas of shared competence for compliance with the subsidiarity principle. Their involvement in the *ex ante* scrutiny of EU legislative proposals for compliance with Article 5(3) TEU on subsidiarity enhances the democratic quality of the Treaties' legislative processes. National parliaments' interventions serve to protect the integrity of domestic democratic processes by policing the limits of the EU legislature's competences under the Treaty framework. In addition, their engagement as subsidiarity 'watchdogs' also provides an additional source of indirect democratic input into EU policymaking pursuant to Article 10 TEU.

Of course, the increased normative weight that the EU Treaty framework now places on the value of representative democracy within the Union legal order does not necessarily result in practical improvements. Indeed, the effectiveness of collective Member State efforts – through Treaty reform – to bolster the democratic credentials of Union policymaking is open to serious question. Turnout at European Parliamentary elections remains at historic lows and both the European Citizens' Initiative and Subsidiarity Early Warning System have recorded mixed operational success. Nonetheless, the existence of practical deficiencies in the political sphere does not undermine the argument that, under the Treaty framework, representative democracy now exists as an important normative value to guide the exercise of all EU institutional activity – including the work of the Court.

2 The *Limits* on EU Policymaking: The Court of Justice versus the EU Treaty Framework

In this section, the search for acts of judicial constitutional contestation with regard to Constitutional Issue No. 3 changes focus. The spotlight

[77] The same applies *mutatis mutandis* where directly effective EU norms are used to contest EU legislative acts that have their origins in ECI proposals. At the time of writing, no examples are forthcoming.

shifts from discussion of the Court's engagement with specific Treaty *values* along the *horizontal* axis to analysis of its compliance with specific Treaty *limits* on Union policymaking along the *vertical axis*.

This section assesses how far the Court's interpretative choices as direct policymaker conform to the Treaty framework's statements on the limits of Union policymaking. Section 2.1 provides an overview of the range of key limits that Member States have sought to impose on Union policymaking (Chapter 1). Section 2.2 constructs a functional argument to reinforce the central claim that underpins this section; namely, that, as direct policymaker, the Court of Justice is expected to adhere to the full range of limits that the Treaty framework imposes on Union policymaking. Thereafter, Section 2.3 scrutinises the Court's engagement as direct policymaker with a selection of the Treaties' most powerful restraints on Union policymaking: express exclusions on the adoption of EU harmonising measures (e.g., Article 168(5) TFEU and Article 153(5) TFEU).

In summary, the Court does not to consider itself subject to the framework of limits that the EU Treaties impose on Union *legislative* policymaking. In more precise terms, the Court can be seen routinely to determine the scope of its own policymaking functions – and thereby the reach of Union law into Member State legal systems – without reference to the increasing set of normative restraints that the EU Treaties impose, as constitutional touchstones, on EU policymaking activity. This defies functional expectations. As direct policymaker, the Court of Justice should legitimately be expected to engage with (and respect) the full range of limits that the Treaties impose – however imperfectly – on Union policymaking. The overall impact of the Court's approach is a loosening of the conception of the EU legal order as a system of limited attributed powers.[78]

Finally, Section 2.4 contextualises discussion of judicial engagement with Treaty limits on EU policymaking with reference to the existence of parallel sites of constitutional contestation in the *legislative* sphere. The Court of Justice is not alone in testing the limits that the EU Treaty

[78] See Azoulai, 'The "Retained Powers" Formula in the Case Law of the European Court of Justice: EU Law as Total Law?', n. 3 at p. 196 and S. Prechal, S. de Vries and H. van Eijken, 'The Principle of Attributed Powers and the "Scope of EU Law"' in L. F. M. Besselink, F. Pennings and S. Prechal (eds.), *The Eclipse of the Legality Principle in European Union* (Alphen aan den Rijn: Kluwer Law, 2011) at p. 246.

framework places on Union policymaking. The EU legislature also stands accused at specific points in time of attempting to circumvent the very same Treaty limits on EU policymaking. This includes, for instance, its use of broadly worded legal bases in the Treaties to sidestep the limits imposed on Union policymaking in specific substantive areas such as public health.[79] The existence of parallel sites of constitutional contestation in the political sphere does not, however, exonerate the Court and its interpretative choices as direct policymaker. It simply points to the existence of broader problems of competence control within the EU legal order.

2.1 Limits on Union Policymaking under the Treaty Framework

The EU Treaties place detailed limits on the scope of EU policymaking (Chapter 1). First, the Treaties include a range of provisions outlining the existence, and conditions of exercise of, all Union competences. First and foremost, Article 5(2) TEU frames the Union as a system of limited attributed competences, stating in explicit terms that competences not entrusted to EU institutions remain with the Member States. Articles 5(3) and Article 5(4) TEU prescribe that the exercise of Union competences must comply with the principles of subsidiarity and proportionality. Article 6 TEU in combination with Article 51(1) of the EU Charter makes all EU institutional activity conditional on compliance with EU fundamental rights standards.

Secondly, the EU Treaties contain a range of additional, more specific exclusions that supplement the aforementioned general competence norms. These include provisions such as Article 4(2) TEU which mandates, *inter alia*, that Union institutions must respect the national identities of the Member States in the exercise of their functions. That provision also makes explicit that national security remains the sole responsibility of Member States.[80] In addition, the Treaty framework also contains specific exclusions and/or restrictions on Union competence in discrete policy areas. For example, Article 168(5) TFEU precludes the harmonisation of national law and regulations in the field of public health. Likewise, Article 153(5) TFEU states that Union activity

[79] See e.g., Case C-376/98, *Germany* v. *European Parliament and Council (Tobacco Advertising)* EU:C:2000:544.

[80] See also, 346 TFEU.

in the sphere of social policy shall not extend to cover the regulation of pay, the right of association, the right to strike or the right to impose lockouts.

Finally, under the Treaties, the scope for Union policymaking is also conditioned by the substantive parameters outlined in specific Treaty provisions. For example, Article 57 TFEU specifies that the free movement of services entails the right of Member State nationals who are established in one Member State 'temporarily [to] pursue his activity in the Member State where the service is provided, under the same conditions imposed by that State on its own nationals'. Furthermore, that provision also defines 'services' to include activities of an industrial or commercial nature as well as the activities of craftsmen and the professions. Similarly, Article 50 TFEU on the freedom of establishment directs the EU legislature to enact Directives that seek, *inter alia*, to abolish national administrative practices that obstruct the freedom of establishment; enable nationals of one Member State to acquire property in other Member States; and ensure similar standards of corporate governance throughout the Union.

2.2 The Court as Direct Policymaker: Functional Expectations

Chapter 4 exposed the Court's move to interpose itself alongside the Union legislature as direct policymaker. That move was categorised as an act of constitutional contestation with regard to the Treaty framework's statements on the locus of EU political authority within the Union legal order (Constitutional Issue No. 2). Specifically, it directly contested the Treaties' continued attribution of primary responsibility for Union policymaking to the Union's political institutions, principally, the Commission, European Parliament and Council.

In making this move, the Court should legitimately have been expected to exercise its new role in accordance with the framework of limits summarised earlier (Section 1.1). The argument here is *functional*. Through its attribution of direct effect to a range of EU norms, the Court opted to assume additional, direct policymaking responsibilities in parallel to those formally attributed to the EU legislature under the Treaty framework. Accordingly, as direct policymaker, the Court should be expected to engage with (and respect) the full range of limits that the Treaties impose on Union policymaking. Put another way, the Court's decision to detach Union policymaking from the model of *legislative* policymaking prescribed by the Treaties (Chapter 4) does not in any sense provide a normative grounding for its disregard of the specific *limits* that the EU Treaties impose on Union policymaking.

The judgment in *Brown* on education rights offers a clear example of how the Court, as direct policymaker, should be expected to act to comply with the Treaties' statements on Constitutional Issue No. 3.[81] In *Brown*, the applicant, a dual British-French national, was refused access to a student maintenance allowance to support his university studies in Scotland on the basis that he did not meet the prescribed eligibility criteria. The contested national regulations required the applicant to satisfy a habitual residence test (to confirm his status as resident in Scotland) in order to qualify for an award – a classic manifestation of indirect discrimination. In the alternative, it was also open to the applicant to demonstrate that he had been employed in Scotland for at least nine of the preceding twelve months and, in addition, was enrolling in a vocational training programme in Scotland. The Court of Justice was requested to determine whether the contested national regulations were incompatible with Union law.

In its reply to the referring national court, the Court determined the scope of its own policymaking functions with close reference to the Treaty framework structuring EU *legislative* policymaking in the relevant area.[82] It did so by asserting the *potential* to activate its role as direct policymaker using Article 7 EEC (now Article 18 TFEU) on the prohibition of discriminatory treatment on grounds of nationality. In particular, it recalled its previous judgments on the application of that provision – which the Court had ruled directly effective[83] – to review Member State rules governing access to higher education.[84] However, thereafter and crucially, the Court also turned to consider the extent to which Member States had granted the Community institutions – meaning, of course, the Community *legislature* – competence in the particular area of application: education policy.

81 Case 197/86, *Brown* v. *The Secretary of State for Scotland* EU:C:1988:323. See also, earlier, Case 39/86, *Lair* v. *Universität Hannover* EU:C:1988:322 at paras. 11–16. The Court subsequently reconsidered its approach to student maintenance grants in Case C-209/03, *Bidar*, n. 33 at paras. 28–40.

82 See earlier, Case 293/83, *Gravier* v. *City of Liège* EU:C:1985:69 and Case 24/86, *Blaizot* v. *University of Liège* EU:C:1988:43.

83 See expressly, Case 24/86, *Blaizot*, n. 82 at para. 35.

84 At para. 15. To reach its conclusions on access to higher education, the Court had previous adopted a broad reading of the concept of 'vocational training' in the founding EEC Treaty. See e.g., Case 293/83, *Gravier*, n. 82 at paras. 19–25 and Case 24/86, *Blaizot*, n. 82 at paras. 15–24.

In the final analysis, the Court ruled that the applicant was not entitled to claim equal treatment with respect to the maintenance grant in question.[85] That determination – concerning the scope of application of Article 7 EEC as a directly effective EU norm – drew explicitly on its careful appraisal of the (then) Community's *legislative* competence in the field of education policy under the (then) EEC Treaty. At the material time, Community competence in that field was restricted to the enactment of specific measures in the area of social policy.[86] Most importantly, the EEC Treaty had granted the EU legislature no competence to regulate the provision of maintenance grants for university studies. In accordance with that position, the Court ruled that,

> at the present stage of development of Community law, assistance given to students for maintenance and for training falls in principle outside the scope of the EEC Treaty for the purposes of Article 7 thereof. It is, on the one hand, a matter of educational policy, *which is not as such included in the spheres entrusted to the Community institutions* and, on the other, a matter of social policy, which falls within the competence of the Member States *in so far as it is not covered by specific provisions of the EEC Treaty.*[87]

The Court's conclusions on the scope of EU competences under the Treaty and, thus, the reach of its own direct policymaking functions in *Brown*, offer a rare example of how the Court should be expected to act as parallel policymaker. *Contra Brown*, the Court does not, however, routinely take account of the Treaties' attribution (or, more problematically, express exclusion) of competence to the Union's *legislative* institutions in connection with decisions over the scope of its interpretative choices as direct policymaker.[88] For the Court, the reach of Union law into Member State legal systems is determined with exclusive reference to the scope of EU norms that it has ruled directly effective (e.g., Article 7 EEC, now Article 18 TFEU on non-discrimination).

Unlike in *Brown*, the Court typically resolves questions over the application of directly effective EU norms in substantive policy areas (such as education, criminal law or nationality law) that intersect with those norms without reference to the framework structuring EU legislative competences in those areas. This approach has facilitated a significant

[85] Case 197/86, *Brown*, n. 81 at para. 19.
[86] See in particular, Art. 118 EEC and Art. 128 EEC.
[87] Case 197/86, *Brown*, n. 81 at para. 18 (emphasis added).
[88] See Azoulai, 'The "Retained Powers" Formula in the Case Law of the European Court of Justice: EU Law as Total Law?', n. 3 at p. 196.

expansion in the reach of the Court's functions as EU policymaker. In effect, areas of Member State competence over which the Union's political institutions enjoy no (or restricted) *legislative* competence are simply subsumed within the scope of Union law – and the Court's policymaking platform, more specifically – in so far that they are judged to interfere with directly effective EU norms.

In one strand of its case law, the Court justifies its application of directly effective EU norms in intersecting policy fields by seeking to establish 'connecting factors' between the relevant field and the EU legal order broadly construed. References in the Treaty framework or provisions of secondary Union law – however oblique – to intersecting policy areas are used to establish a basis for judicial policymaking. In its early case law on education, for example, the Court relied on references to the (then) Treaty's embryonic statements on education and vocational training to conclude that the regulation of access to University education was 'not unconnected' with Community law.[89] That finding opened the door to the application of the principle of non-discrimination in that field as a directly effective EU norm.

Alternatively, and more frequently, the Court simply asserts the primacy of directly effective EU norms over all other intersecting areas with reference to its standard formula on retained powers.[90] This formula recognises, in accordance with the principle of conferral, that Member States retain competence in areas that have not been transferred to the EU institutions – exclusively or on a shared or complementary basis. At the same time, however, it establishes the Court's jurisdiction to scrutinise Member State measures for compliance with directly effective EU norms. Accordingly, the Court has consistently ruled that:

[89] Case 293/83, *Gravier*, n. 82 at paras. 19–25. See also, by analogy, the Court's approach to determining the scope of Union law for the purposes of defining when Member States are implementing or derogating from Union law. See M. Dougan, 'Judicial Review of Member State Action under the General Principles and the Charter: Defining the "Scope of Union Law"' (2015) 52 *Common Market Law Review*, 1246.

[90] See e.g., Case C-274/96, *Bickel and Franz* EU:C:1998:563 at para. 17 (as regards national provisions in the sphere of criminal legislation and the rules of criminal procedure); Case C-148/02, *Garcia Avello*, n. 53 at para. 25 (as regards national rules governing a person's name); Case C-403/03, *Schempp* v. *Finanzamt München V* EU:C:2005:446 at para. 19 (as regards national rules relating to direct taxation); Case C-145/04, *Spain* v. *United Kingdom (Electoral Rights)* EU:C:2006:543 at para. 78 (as regards national rules determining the persons entitled to vote and to stand as candidates in elections to the European Parliament) and Case C-135/08, *Rottman*, n. 53 at para. 45 (as regards the acquisition and loss of Member State nationality).

even if, in the areas which fall outside the scope of the Community's competence, the Member States are still free, in principle, to lay down conditions governing the existence and exercise of the rights in question, the fact remains that, when exercising that competence, the Member States must nevertheless comply with Community law.[91]

The Court's approach as direct policymaker is at its most contentious, however, where its application of directly effective EU norms intersects with express exclusions of EU legislative competence. These include, *inter alia*, Articles 147 TFEU and 149 TFEU on employment; Article 165 TFEU and Article 166 TFEU on education, vocational training, youth and sport; Article 167 TFEU on culture; Article 173 TFEU on industry; Article 195 TFEU on tourism; and Article 196 TFEU on civil protection. In each of these areas, the Court can be seen robustly to defend the view that directly effective EU norms displace these express exclusions on EU legislative competence. A similar approach can also be seen in its application of other key Treaty limits on EU policymaking such as Article 346 TFEU on national security.[92] At best, these provisions are recognised simply as potential derogations to specific EU norms that the Court has ruled directly effective – and subject to a strict proportionality assessment.[93]

2.3 The Court and Treaty Exclusions on EU Legislative Policymaking

This section explores the relationship between judicial policymaking (using EU norms ruled directly effective) and Treaty limits on EU legislative policymaking. It exposes the Court's systematic disregard, as direct policymaker, for the express exclusions that the EU Treaties impose on EU legislative policymaking. That approach places judicial policymaking in direct conflict with the Treaty framework's clearest normative

[91] Case C-438/05, *International Transport Workers' Federation and Finnish Seamen's Union* v. *Viking Line ABP* EU:C:2007:772 at para. 40 (and the case law cited therein).

[92] See e.g., Case 300/11, *ZZ* v. *Secretary of State for the Home Department* EU:C:2013:363; Case C-284/05, *Commission* v. *Finland (Military Equipment)* EU:C:2009:778; Case C-503/03, *Commission* v. *Spain (Schengen Information System)* EU:C:2006:74; Case C-490/04, *Commission* v. *Germany (Posted Workers)* EU:C:2007:430 and Case C-141/07, *Commission* v. *Germany (Pharmacies)* EU:C:2008:492.

[93] See esp., Case C-341/05, *Laval un Partneri Ltd* v. *Svenska Byggnadsarbetareförbundet* EU:C:2007:809 at paras. 103–11. See also, by analogy and with reference to Art. 4(2) TEU and Art. 346 TFEU on national security, Case 300/11, *ZZ* v. *Secretary of State for the Home Department*, n. 92 and Case C-284/05, *Commission* v. *Finland (Military Equipment)*, n. 92.

statements on the limits of EU integration (Constitutional Issue No. 3). It is a further paradigm example of an act of judicial constitutional contestation.

The case law on the reimbursement of the costs of medical treatments received abroad (Section 2.3.1), together with that governing the right to strike (Section 2.3.2), exemplifies the Court's use of directly effective EU norms to circumvent Member State efforts to impose express limits on Union legislative policymaking in specific policy areas. The choice of both these examples is illustrative. The Court's approach, as direct policymaker, to the EU Treaty framework's express exclusions on the adoption of harmonising measures in the field of public health (reimbursement for medical treatment received abroad) and social policy (the right to strike) applies *mutatis mutandis* to analysis of express exclusions in other substantive areas. Indeed, across all protected areas, the Court can be seen to invoke EU norms that it has ruled directly effective in order to circumvent the functioning of the Treaty framework as constitutional touchstone.[94] In contrast with *Brown*, the reach of the Court's direct policymaking functions using provisions that it had ruled directly effective is not circumscribed with reference to the restrictions that the EU Treaty framework imposes on EU legislative policymaking in specific intersecting areas. The overall effect is a dramatic weakening of the limits that the EU Treaties impose on Union institutional activity, with a detrimental impact on the vertical distribution of competences between the Union and Member States.[95]

2.3.1 *The Reimbursement of the Costs of Medical Treatments Received Abroad*

First, with respect to the framework of limits on public health, the Court of Justice has been repeatedly asked to rule on the compatibility with the EU Treaties – and Article 56 TFEU on services in particular – of Member State rules governing the reimbursement of medical treatments that EU

[94] See e.g., Case C-76/05, *Schwarz and Gootjes-Schwarz* v. *Finanzamt Bergisch Gladbach* EU:C:2007:492 at para. 70; Case C-372/04, *Watts* v. *Bedford Primary Care Trust* EU:C:2006:325 at para. 147; Case C-73/08, *Bressol and Others* v. *Gouvernement de la Communauté française* EU:C:2010:181 at para. 28; Case C-351/07, *Fachverband der Buch- und Medienwirtschaft* v. *LIBRO Handelsgesellschaft mbH* EU:C:2009:276 at para. 33 and Case C-268/06, *Impact* v. *Minister for Agriculture and Food and Others* EU:C:2008:223.

[95] See also, Prechal, de Vries, and van Eijken, 'The Principle of Attributed Powers and the "Scope of EU Law"', n. 78 at p. 246.

citizens receive elsewhere within the Union.[96] In each case, the Court has consistently ruled that, as a matter of principle, the imposition of prior authorisation requirements to sanction the reimbursement of patient expenditure constitutes a restriction on the free movement of intra-EU services, which Member States must justify as a matter of Union law.

Following a functional approach similar to that on display in *Brown*, the Court might have been expected to look expressly to the Treaty framework on Union legislative competences in both services and public health to determine the scope of its parallel policymaking functions. In *Brown*, the Court expressly recognised that the Treaties conferred on the Union legislature only very limited competences in education policy. Moreover, it acknowledged that these competences did *not* provide for the adoption of legally binding acts to regulate university maintenance grants. That conclusion was then directly transposed from the *legislative* to the *judicial* sphere to determine the scope of the Court's direct policy-making functions in parallel to those that the (then) Treaty granted to the Community legislature. In the final analysis, the Court considered that the absence of Community competence to enact legal (*legislative*) acts in the sphere of general education policy precluded its application of the principle of non-discrimination as a tool to regulate the conditions under which Member States may award student maintenance grants.

Much like education policy, Union competence in the sphere of public health was (and remains) extremely limited. Member States introduced specific exclusions on EU policymaking competence in that sphere at Maastricht.[97] In its post-Amsterdam revised form, applicable at the time of the Court's formative judgments on cross-border patient rights, Article 152 EC detailed the Union's extremely limited policymaking competences in the field of public health. Perhaps most crucially, Article 152(5) EC protected Member State competence to manage national healthcare systems. That provision outlined in express terms that, 'Community action in the field of public health shall fully respect the responsibilities of the Member States for the organisation and delivery of health services and medical care.'[98] The entry into force of the Lisbon Treaty has further

[96] See e.g., Case C-157/99, *Geraets-Smits* v. *Stichting Ziekenfonds VGZ and Peerbooms* v. *Stichting CZ Groep Zorgverzekeringen* EU:C:2001:404; Case C-385/99, *Müller-Fauré and van Riet* EU:C:2003:270 and Case C-372/04, *Watts*, n. 94.

[97] Art. 129 EEC.

[98] See now, in revised form, Art. 168(7) TFEU: 'Union action shall respect the responsibilities of the Member States for the definition of their health policy and for the organisation and delivery of health services and medical care. The responsibilities of the

reinforced Member State protection in the sphere of public health. In particular, Article 6(1) TFEU now expressly lists public health as a policy area in which the Union institutions enjoy only limited supporting, coordinating and supplementary competences. As such, the adoption of legally binding EU acts that entail the harmonisation of Member State public health measures is now explicitly excluded (Article 2(5) TFEU).

However, the Court's case law on the reimbursement of intra-EU medical treatments received abroad did not engage with that part of the Treaty framework and, specifically, the limits it defined on the scope of Union competences in the field of services and, more crucially, public health. Its approach as direct policymaker looked *neither* to the Treaty framework governing the adoption of EU legislative acts in the field of services, *nor* to the limits that the Treaties imposed on Union policymaking in the area of public health.

With respect to the framework on services, the Court demonstrated little interest in engaging with the substantive parameters that circumscribe EU legislative competence in the field of intra-EU services. Recalling its previous case law, the Court began by restating its earlier conclusions in *Luisi and Carbone*[99] that the personal scope of Article 56 TFEU necessarily extends to include Member State nationals in receipt of intra-EU services, including publicly funded healthcare treatments.[100] That decision, which subsequently opened the door to the exercise of its policymaking functions in the sphere of public healthcare and beyond, is fundamentally at odds with the substantive limits that the Treaties place on Union legislative policymaking in the fields of services.[101] Articles 56, 57 and 61 TFEU refer only to the right of Member State nationals established in one Member State temporarily to provide services to recipients established in another.[102] The Court's ruling that the Treaty provisions on services extended to include the receipt of services marked a significant expansion in Union policymaking competence.

Member States shall include the management of health services and medical care and the allocation of the resources assigned to them.'

99 Joined Cases 286/82 and 26/83, *Luisi and Carbone* v. *Ministero del Tesoro* EU:C:1984:35.

100 Case C-157/99, *Smits and Peerbooms*, n. 96 at para. 55; Case C-385/99 *Müller-Fauré and van Riet*, n. 96 at para. 39 and Case C-372/04, *Watts*, n. 94 at para. 87.

101 On this point, see the Opinion of Advocate General Trabucchi in Case 118/75, *Watson and Belmann* EU:C:1976:106.

102 See also, by analogy, the Court's inclusion of 'work seekers' within the scope of Art. 45 TFEU (free movement of workers) in light of substantive parameters outlined in Art. 45(3) TFEU.

Next, with regard to the framework of limits that the Treaties imposed on Union policymaking in public health and social policy, the Court ruled that these did *not* function to restrict the scope of its competence as direct policymaker. On the one hand, the Court recognised that Union law must respect Member State competence in the sphere of public health (and, by extension, social security).[103] On the other hand, though, it ruled that the exclusion of Union competence to enact legally binding EU measures in both areas had no impact on the scope of its competence as direct policymaker to achieve the same result using EU norms that it had declared directly effective. The Grand Chamber articulated this point clearly in *Watts* with express reference to the Treaty exclusions on Union (legislative) policymaking in the field of public health:

> according to Article 152(5) EC, Community action in the field of public health is to fully respect the responsibilities of the Member States for the organisation and delivery of health services and medical care. *That provision does not, however, exclude the possibility that the Member States may be required under other Treaty provisions, such as Article 49 EC . . . to make adjustments to their national systems of social security.*[104]

In line with its (by then) established approach, the Court concluded that Article 56 TFEU – as a directly effective EU norm – precluded Member State measures that are liable to prevent or deter the provision of intra-EU healthcare services from the position of both service provider and recipient.[105] The absence of EU policymaking competence in the field of public health, the special character of healthcare services or even the Treaties' explicit protection for national healthcare systems (Article 152(4) EC, now Article 168(7) TFEU) did not alter that conclusion. Far from being excluded, these areas were instead simply displaced by the Court's position on the scope of the Treaty provisions on intra-EU services – provisions that it had ruled directly effective to establish its platform as direct policymaker.

2.3.2 *The Right to Strike*

The case law on collective action (the right to strike) provides a further example of the Court's use of directly effective EU norms to circumvent the framework of Treaty limits governing EU legislative policymaking in

[103] Case C-157/99, *Smits and Peerbooms*, n. 96 at paras. 44–46; Case C-385/99, *Müller-Fauré and van Riet*, n. 96 at para. 100 and Case C-372/04, *Watts*, n. 94 at para. 92.
[104] Case C-372/04, *Watts*, n. 94 at paras. 146–147 (emphasis added).
[105] *Ibid.*, at paras. 94–98.

protected areas. In *Laval*, the Court of Justice was requested to rule on the relationship between (now) Article 56 TFEU on the freedom to provide services and the right, protected under Swedish law, to take collective action in employment disputes.[106] The applicant in the main proceedings, a Latvian undertaking providing services in Sweden, argued that a programme of collective action directed against it by Swedish trade unions infringed Article 56 TFEU. The collective action at the centre of the dispute was taken, in accordance with Swedish law, in an effort to compel Laval to adhere to national agreements on employment conditions in the building sector – conditions that were more generous than those applicable under Latvian law.

The EU Treaties grant the Union institutions only very limited policymaking competences in the sphere of social policy. Article 59 TFEU on services provides that the EU legislature may adopt directives to achieve the liberalisation of specific services – a broadly worded legal base. However, Article 153 TFEU provides that the Union institutions only enjoy supporting, coordinating and supplementary competences with respect to, *inter alia*, working conditions, social security and social protection of workers. In specific terms, Article 153(2) TFEU grants the Council and European Parliament competence to enact incentive measures designed to encourage co-operation between Member States. Such measures shall not, however, entail the harmonisation of national laws.

In addition, the EU legislature is expressly empowered to adopt minimum standards with respect to the objectives outlined in Article 153(1) TFEU, including working conditions, social security and social protection of workers. The adoption of such measures is, however, subject to the limits imposed by Articles 153(4)/(5) TFEU. Article 153(1) TFEU states explicitly that EU policymaking in the sphere of social policy shall not affect the right of Member States to define the fundamental principles of their social security systems and must not significantly affect the financial equilibrium thereof. Likewise, it shall not prevent any Member State from maintaining or introducing more stringent protective measures compatible with the Treaties. Finally, and crucially, Article 153(5) TFEU provides that Union action in the sphere of social policy shall not apply to pay, the right of association, the right to strike or the right to impose lockouts.

[106] Case C-341/05, *Laval un Partneri Ltd*, n. 93. See also, Case C-438/05, *Viking Line*, n. 91.

The EU legislature had made use of the Treaties' legal bases and, in particular, Article 57(2) EEC (now Article 59 TFEU) to enact a range of legislative measures in the field of services, including Directive 96/71 on the rights of posted workers.[107] In essence, the dispute in *Laval* required the Court to consider the specific relationship between, on the one hand, the EU legislative framework on posted workers and the Court's case law on Article 56 TFEU governing the free movement of services and, on the other hand, the right to take collective action regulated under national law and excluded from the scope of Union policymaking under Article 153 (5) TFEU. As before in its decisions on the reimbursement of intra-EU medical services (Section 2.3.1), the Grand Chamber attributed absolute priority to its case law on the free movement of services. It concluded that Article 56 TFEU precluded trades unions from attempting, by means of collective action, to compel a service provider established in another Member State to sign a collective agreement that regulated conditions of employment within the host State in the construction sector.[108]

Reaching that conclusion, the Court did not consider the Treaty limits on Union legislative policymaking in the sphere of social policy, and Article 153(5) TFEU (ex Article 137(5) EC) in particular, as relevant constraints on judicial policymaking. Both the Swedish and Danish governments had alerted the Court to the function of these important limits on Union legislative policymaking. In line with the functional approach adopted in *Brown* (Section 2.2), they submitted that the express exclusion of Union *legislative* competence in relation to the right to strike operated to restrict the scope for *judicial* policymaking in the same area using Article 56 TFEU on services.[109] The Court rejected that argument outright. According to the Grand Chamber, 'the fact that Article 137 EC [now Article 153(5) TFEU] does not apply to the right to strike or to the right to impose lockouts is not such as to exclude collective action such as that at issue in the main proceedings from the domain of freedom to provide services'.[110] More broadly, the Court in *Laval* reiterated that the absence (or the express exclusion) of Union competence in the Treaties in specific policy areas had no impact on the activation of its functions as direct policymaker. As the Grand Chamber put it, 'even though, *in the areas in which the Community does not have competence*, the Member States

107 Directive 96/71/EC of the European Parliament and of the Council of 16 December 1996 concerning the posting of workers in the framework of the provision of services [1997] OJ L 18/1.

108 Case C-341/05, *Laval un Partneri*, n. 93 at para. 120.

109 *Ibid.*, at para. 86.

110 *Ibid.*, at para. 88.

remain, in principle, free to lay down the conditions for the existence and exercise of the rights at issue, *they must nevertheless exercise that competence consistently with Community law*'.[111]

Ultimately, the requirement to comply with Union law, including where the Treaties grant the Union institutions no policymaking competence, translates into an obligation to adhere to the *Court's* interpretive choices. These choices are formulated, first and foremost, through its interpretation of EU norms that the Court has itself declared directly effective and, in some cases, also elevated to the status of 'fundamental' norms.[112] Any deference shown to Member States – and specific interests protected through the existence of limits in the Treaty framework – is relegated to the assessment of possible justifications for the restrictive national measure in question. The Court manages that assessment itself on a case-by-case basis. The proportionality test is a strict one, though not always applied with absolute consistency across (and within) different policy areas.

In relation to the right to strike, the Court ruled in *Laval* that the collective action taken was disproportionate to the public interest objective in protecting the rights of workers against the dangers of 'social dumping'.[113] By contrast, in *Viking Line*, the Grand Chamber concluded that collective action taken against a shipping line as part of a policy to combat the use of flags of convenience could, in principle, be justified as a matter of Union law.[114]

2.4 The Court of Justice as 'Detached' Policymaker

The Court's approach to the Treaty framework's *limits* on EU legislative competence defies expectations. As argued in Section 2.1, its move to interpose itself alongside the Union legislature as direct policymaker, gives rise to a strong functional argument that it should exercise its expanded institutional role in a manner that complies fully with the limits imposed on EU legislative policymaking. Put another way, the Court's decision to detach Union policymaking from the model of legislative policymaking

[111] *Ibid.*, at para. 87. See also, Case C-438/05, *Viking Line*, n. 91 at para. 40 (emphasis added).

[112] See with respect to Art. 56 TFEU on services, e.g., Case C-36/02, *Omega Spielhallen- und Automatenaufstellungs-GmbH* EU:C:2004:614 at para. 35.

[113] Case C-341/05, *Laval un Partneri*, n. 93 at para. 110.

[114] Case C-438/05, *Viking Line*, n. 91 at para. 90. With respect to the reimbursement of medical treatments received abroad (Section 2.3.1), the Court has recognised the ability of Member States to impose a requirement for prior authorisation as a proportionate restriction on the free movement of services. However, that requirement is subject to compliance with a set of specific conditions. See e.g., Case C-372/04, *Watts*, n. 94.

prescribed by the Treaties (Chapter 4) does not in any sense provide a normative basis for its subsequent disregard of the limits on EU policymaking outlined in the Treaties as constitutional touchstones.

In practice, however, this is precisely what has occurred. As the examples in Sections 2.3.1 and 2.3.2 illustrate, EU judicial policymaking routinely takes shape in an interpretative space that is, to a greater extent, detached from the limits that exist to govern EU legislative competence under the Treaty framework. In particular, the case law examined leaves no doubt that directly effective EU norms remain fully applicable where they intersect with areas of Member State policymaking on which the Treaties are *silent* as regards the existence of the Union *legislative* competences.[115] Moreover, and most contentiously, the Court's jurisprudence also confirms that directly effective EU norms function to displace any express *exclusions* on the adoption of EU harmonising measures (*Watts* and *Laval*).

The Court's use of EU norms that it has ruled directly effective in order to circumvent the exclusionary effect of such provisions has had a profound impact on the vertical distribution of competences between the EU and Member State legal orders.[116] It has facilitated what Weiler characterises as the 'absorption' of national law within the EU legal order.[117] Under that doctrine, all areas of Member State competence are potentially liable to scrutiny for compliance with the Court's case law on directly effective EU norms – irrespective of the existence of EU legislative competence in the relevant intersecting areas of application (e.g., education, public health and criminal law). That approach to the delineation of EU policymaking competences – and those of the Court of Justice in particular – contrasts markedly with that in *Brown* (Section 2.1).

The Court of Justice is not, of course, alone in testing the limits that the EU Treaty framework places on Union competences.[118] The EU legislature also stands accused at specific points in time of circumventing EU Treaty limits on Union policymaking. In particular, the EU legislature has invoked broadly worded legal bases in the EU Treaties in order

[115] See e.g., Case C-446/03, *Marks & Spencer plc* EU:C:2005:763 at para. 29; Case C-148/02, *Garcia Avello*, n. 53 at para. 25; Case C-224/02, *Pusa* v. *Osuuspankkien Keskinäinen Vakuutusyhtiö* EU:C:2004:273 at para. 22 and Case C-192/05, *Tas-Hagen* EU:C:2006:676 at paras. 21–22.

[116] Boucon, 'EU Law and Retained Powers of Member States', n. 3 at p. 187.

[117] J. H. H. Weiler, 'The Transformation of Europe' (1991) 100 *Yale Law Journal*, 2403 at p. 2438. See also, Azoulai, 'The "Retained Powers" Formula in the Case Law of the European Court of Justice: EU Law as Total Law?', n. 3.

[118] For discussion, see e.g., S. Weatherill, 'Competence Creep and Competence Control' (2004) 23(1) *Yearbook of European Law*, 1.

to circumvent such provisions. The EU legislature has, for instance, sought to use Article 114 TFEU – the Treaty legal basis for legislative policymaking in the internal market – as a foundation for the adoption of harmonising measures in protected areas of Member States competence.[119] For example, as Wyatt and Dashwood observe, in the area of public health,

> It was the Member States at the Maastricht IGC who drafted Article 168 TFEU (ex Art 152 EC) in a way specifically designed to place strict limits on Union competence in the field of public health; but a majority of the Member States [acting through the Council and together with the European Parliament] subsequently attempted to bypass exactly those same limits, through recourse to Article 114 TFEU, in order to achieve what they regarded as valuable social welfare objectives.[120]

The Court's expansive approach to Union policymaking (Section 2.3) has further aggravated problems of competence control in the *legislative* sphere. Its broad approach to the scope of directly effective EU norms, together with its disregard for the limits that the Treaty framework imposes on Union policymaking, functions to legitimise ambitious acts of EU legislative policymaking. The Patients Rights' Directive provides a good example of this dynamic at play.[121] The Court's prior application of the Treaty provisions on the free movement of services to establish a comprehensive legal framework governing EU citizens' right to access cross-border medical treatments (Section 2.3.1) provided cover for the Union legislature's subsequent use of Article 114 TFEU to enact that Directive. Had the Court adopted a stricter, functional approach to the scope of its competences as direct policymaker, the Union legislature may not have succeeded in using (or even attempted to use) the Treaties' internal market provision as a legal basis for legislative policymaking in the area of cross-border healthcare.

The EU legislature's efforts to sidestep specific Treaty limits on EU competences may often go unchallenged as acts of political constitutional contestation. This is particularly so where the Treaties mandate that

[119] See esp., Case C-376/98, *Germany* v. *European Parliament and Council (Tobacco Advertising)* EU:C:2000:544 and Case C-380/03, *Germany* v. *European Parliament and Council* (*Tobacco Advertising II*) EU:C:2006:772. See also, by analogy and more recently, the Eurozone States' establishment of the European Stability Mechanism outside the EU Treaty structure in contestation with the 'no-bailout clause' in Art. 125 TFEU (Chapter 2).

[120] *Wyatt and Dashwood's European Union Law* (Oxford: Hart, 2011) at p. 108.

[121] Directive 2011/24 EU on the application of patients' rights in cross-border healthcare [2011] OJ 88/45.

Member States – collectively through the Council – must exercise their legislative competences unanimously. In such cases, Member States (as constituent authorities) are effectively able to manage the scope of any encroachment into protected areas of national competence such as public health by consensus, subject, of course, to the consent of their institutional partners (e.g., European Parliament). By contrast, where the Treaties prescribe that, together with the Commission and European Parliament, Member States must act *by majority,* there is greater scope for challenges regarding the outer limits of EU legislative policymaking competence under the Treaties. Post-Lisbon, this is now the default approach to Union policymaking under the ordinary legislative procedure.

When contested, the Court of Justice has proved reluctant to challenge the Union legislature on its recourse to general legal bases in the Treaties as tools to circumvent more specific provisions that preclude the adoption of harmonising measures in areas such as public health; social policy; employment; and education, vocational training, youth and sport.[122] The Court has not, for example, adopted and enforced a robust doctrine of *lex specialis* to determine the relationship between such provisions. Instead, it has left the Union legislature broadly free to determine, through the political process, the restraining impact (if any) of Treaty provisions that purport expressly to exclude the adoption of binding EU harmonising measures in discrete policy areas. For example, the Court has consistently ruled that, 'provided that the conditions for recourse to [Article 114 TFEU] as a legal basis are fulfilled, the [Union] legislature cannot be prevented from relying on that legal basis on the ground that public health protection is a decisive factor in the choices to be made.'[123] Judicial interventions in disputes over the Union legislature's use of particular legal bases in the Treaty to support EU policymaking have focused primarily on other issues, notably questions of inter-institutional balance (Chapter 4).[124]

[122] For analysis of its judicial review of EU legislation enacted pursuant to Art. 114 TFEU, see e.g., S. Weatherill, 'The Limits of Legislative Harmonization Ten Years after Tobacco Advertising: How the Court's Case Law has Become a "Drafting Guide"' (2011) 12 *German Law Journal*, 827.

[123] Case C-491/01, *British American Tobacco (Investments) and Imperial Tobacco* EU:C:2002:741 at para. 62; C-434/02, *Arnold André* EU:C:2004:800 at para. 32; C-210/03, *Swedish Match* EU:C:2004:802 at para. 31 and C-380/03, *Germany* v. *Parliament and Council* EU:C:2006:772 at para. 39.

[124] See e.g., Case C-409/13, *Council* v. *Commission (Macro Financial Assistance)* EU:C:2015:217 and Case C-425/13, *Commission* v. *Council (Emissions Trading)* EU:C:2015:483.

The existence of parallel acts of constitutional contestation in the political sphere points to broader and more widely acknowledged issues of competence control within the EU legal order. It does not render the Court's interpretative choices as direct policymaker compliant with the Treaty framework as constitutional touchstone. It simply serves as a reminder that it is not only the Court's activities, but also those of the EU legislature (and also Member States) that may give rise to acts of constitutional contestation (see Chapter 2).

Concluding Remarks

This chapter completes the review of EU judicial activity for compliance with the EU Treaty framework as the principal touchstone on the internal constitutionality of all Union activity – including the work of the Court. Specifically, it identified paradigmatic acts of constitutional contestation with reference to the Treaty framework's statements on the third key issue for EU constitutionalism. That issue addresses the objectives, values and limits of EU integration (Constitutional Issue No. 3).

The Court of Justice, this chapter has argued, has shown little systematic regard for the ever-expanding range of limits that the EU Treaty framework prescribes to govern EU institutional activity. Likewise, it was argued that aspects of EU judicial activity also directly conflict with core values underpinning European integration under the EU Treaties as constitutional touchstones. This chapter highlighted two prominent examples of judicial challenges to the EU Treaties' prescriptions on the limits and values structuring EU integration.

Section 1 highlighted the Court's use of directly effective EU norms as tools to override, sidestep or simply interrogate the Union legislature's clearly expressed preferences on matters of policy. The Court's use of directly effective EU norms in that manner provided further paradigmatic examples of constitutional contestation in EU judicial activity. Specifically, the Court's disregard for the integrity of EU legislative choices undermines the increased normative weight that the EU Treaty framework now attaches to the *value of representative democracy* as the foundation of EU decision-making (falling within Constitutional Issue No. 3). Examples of the Court's use of its direct policymaking platform to undermine the EU legislature's political choices can be found across a broad spectrum of substantive policy areas. This chapter focused on developments in two areas of Union policy in which the EU Treaties' position on the primacy of legislative policymaking is at its most explicit: (1) air transport services and (2) EU citizenship.

Section 2 exposed further acts of constitutional contestation in relation to the *limits* that the EU Treaties impose on EU legislative policymaking. In the exercise of its self-asserted direct policymaking functions, the Court was shown systematically to disregard key limits that the EU Treaties impose on EU legislative policymaking.[125] The Court's detachment of EU policymaking from the limits outlined in the Treaty framework defies functional expectations. As a consequence of its move to interpose itself alongside the Union legislature as direct policymaker, the Court of Justice *should* legitimately be expected to exercise its new role in accordance with the framework of limits structuring EU legislative policymaking. This applies, in particular, with respect to the Treaties' most powerful normative restraints on EU policymaking: express exclusions on Union legislative competence.

The next chapter turns to examine the responses of the Court's key interlocutors to the acts of judicial constitutional contestation identified in Chapters 3–5. Put bluntly, the Court can say what it likes about the formal status of Union law and the conditions under which it applies within Member States (Constitutional Issue No. 1) (Chapter 3); the locus of political authority within the EU legal order (Constitutional Issue No. 2) (Chapter 4); and the objectives, values and limits of EU integration (Constitutional Issue No. 3) (Chapter 5). However, without the support of Member States, national courts and also most legal scholars, the Court's institutional preferences will, at best, simply not be implemented within Member States. Chapter 6 assesses how far the Court's acts of constitutional contestation have been 'normalised' *de jure* and/or *de facto* with the Treaty framework as constitutional touchstone.

[125] See also, Azoulai, 'The "Retained Powers" Formula in the Case Law of the European Court of Justice: EU Law as Total Law?', n. 3; Boucon, 'EU Law and Retained Powers of Member States', n. 3 and Damjanovic, '"Reserved Areas" of the Member States and the ECJ: The Case of Higher Education', n. 3.

6 The Feedback Loop

The Court of Justice and Its Interlocutors

The ECJ can say whatever it wants. The real question is why anyone should heed it.

K. Alter, 'The European Court's Political Power' (1996) 19 *West European Politics*, 458 at p. 459.[1]

Introduction

This chapter examines the responses of the Court's principal interlocutors (Member States, national courts and EU scholars) to the acts of judicial constitutional contestation identified in Chapters 3–5. Its principal aim is to assess the extent to which the Court's interlocutors – and, most crucially, Member States and national courts – have normalised the identified acts of judicial constitutional contestation *de jure* and/or *de facto*.

Section 1 assesses the responses of Member States – both collectively as Treaty signatories and also individually – to the Court's statements on the formal status of Union law and the conditions under which it applies within Member States (Constitutional Issue No. 1). As Treaty signatories, Member States have not taken steps to normalise *de jure* or *de facto* the Court's divergent position on Constitutional Issue No. 1. The Treaty framework, as the embodiment of the collective will of the Member States, continues as before to display all the hallmarks of ordinary treaties, the implementation of which is firmly rooted in the normative

[1] See also, B. de Witte, 'Direct Effect, Primacy, and the Nature of the Legal Order' in G. de Búrca and P. Craig (eds.), *The Evolution of EU Law* (2nd edn) (Oxford: Oxford University Press, 2011) at p. 346.

framework of international law. For individual Member States and their respective national courts, the domestic application of EU law also remains, in accordance with the EU Treaties, entirely contingent on *national* constitutional law. A review of the domestic constitutional landscape reveals the existence of twenty-eight different national approaches to the domestic implementation of EU law *as international law*. The process of domestic implementation is characteristically asymmetrical, predominantly court-led and largely stable as a matter of practical politics.

Section 2 considers Member State reactions to the Court's position on the locus of political authority within the EU legal order (Constitutional Issue No. 2) and the objectives, values and limits governing European integration (Constitutional Issue No. 3). Acting collectively as Treaty signatories, Member States have employed a range of distinct tools with varying degrees of intensity in response to the Court's statements on both issues.[2] These tools include attempts to reverse isolated decisions of the Court; to exclude its jurisdiction in sensitive policy areas; and to introduce discrete claw-back provisions into the Treaty framework. At national level, there is also (growing) evidence of Member State courts 'pushing back' against the Court of Justice. Specifically, a number of national courts have expressed clear concerns regarding the quality of the Court's engagement as direct policymaker with the objectives, values and limits governing European integration (Constitutional Issue No. 3).

Section 3 examines the response of EU legal scholars to the Court's jurisprudence on the three key issues for EU constitutionalism. EU scholars have taken a very different approach to Member States and national courts. This is most clear to see with regard to Constitutional Issue No. 1, addressing the formal status of Union law and the conditions under which it applies within Member States. In contrast to Member States, EU scholars have generally sought vigorously to defend the Court's vision of the Union as a 'new legal order' on its own terms, notwithstanding the continuing validity of the normative framework of international law as the basis of EU integration under the Treaties.[3] This position should not surprise. As noted in Chapter 3, legal scholars were very much in the vanguard when it came to supporting the Court in its formative efforts to break with the Treaty framework and its statements on the three issues for EU constitutionalism.

[2] See also, A. Arnull, 'Me and My Shadow: The European Court of Justice and the Disintegration of European Union Law' (2007) 31 *Fordham International Law Journal*, 1174.

[3] See esp., M. Avbelj, 'Questioning EU Constitutionalisms' (2008) 9(1) *German Law Journal*, 1.

EU legal scholars' robust defence of the Court's position on the three key issues for EU constitutionalism remains significant methodologically. It directly informs their approach to the scrutiny of EU judicial activity, including assessments of the Court's role as direct policymaker. Adhering to the Court's institutional statements, most EU legal scholars continue to see the Court of Justice in its own image as a *de facto* EU Constitutional Court that exercises near complete powers of judicial review both horizontally and vertically. That baseline, which remains wholly unsupported by the Treaties, has given rise to particular dynamics in assessments of judicial interpretation and its limits. Questions of legitimacy are construed not as matter of treaty interpretation, but as instances of *constitutional adjudication* in line with the view of the Court as a EU Supreme Court *de facto*. This entrenched perspective fundamentally obscures the Court's position within the EU legal order as an institution of the Union. It also entirely overlooks the application of the Treaty framework *to the Court* as constitutional touchstone – the focus of this monograph.

1 Member State Responses to Judicial Constitutional Contestation: Constitutional Issue No. 1

This section explores Member State responses to the Court's position on the formal status of Union law and the conditions under which it applies within Member States (Constitutional Issue No. 1). In Chapter 3, it was argued that the Court of Justice and the Treaty framework defend fundamentally different statements on that first issue for EU constitutionalism. The Treaties, as an expression of the collective will of the Member States, continue to anchor integration to the framework of international law. By contrast, the Court of Justice robustly defends a vision of the EU as a 'new legal order' that is defined in opposition to international law and characterised, most significantly, by the principles of direct effect and primacy of Union law.[4] The source of that judicial vision remains external to the Treaty framework. It represents the Court's projection onto the Treaty framework of a particular model of transnational political federalism.

[4] See e.g., Case 26/62, *Van Gend en Loos* EU:C:1963:1; Case 6/64, *Costa* v. *E.N.E.L* EU:C:1964:66; Opinion 1/91, *Draft agreement between the Community, on the one hand, and the countries of the European Free Trade Association, on the other, relating to the creation of the European Economic Area* EU:C:1991:490 and Opinion 2/13, *Draft Agreement on Accession of the EU to the European Convention on Human Rights* EU:C:2014:2454.

Section 1.1 reviews the responses of Member State governments *acting collectively as Treaty signatories* to the Court's position on the formal status of Union law and the conditions under which it applies within Member States. Thereafter, Section 2.2 considers the reactions of *individual* Member States – both founding and acceding. Analysis in both sections leads to the same overarching conclusion: there is little evidence to support the claim that Member States or their respective national constitutional courts have normalised the Court's case law on Constitutional Issue No. 1. It continues to exist *beyond* that framework as a paradigmatic act of judicial constitutional contestation.

1.1 The Collective Response: Member States as Treaty Signatories

As Treaty signatories, Member States have not taken steps to normalise *de jure* or *de facto* the Court's divergent position on the formal status of Union law and the conditions under which it applies within Member States. The Treaty framework, as the embodiment of the collective will of Member States as constituent authorities, continues as before to display all the hallmarks of ordinary treaties, the implementation of which is firmly rooted in the framework of international law (Chapter 3). Most significantly, the EU Treaties retain their original and unequivocal statements on the domestic effect of EU norms (now Article 4(3) TEU) and, likewise, on the declaratory nature of EU Court judgments (now Articles 280 and 299 TFEU).

Looking beyond these unequivocal statements, there is little to support the view that Member States have, the Treaty framework notwithstanding, normalised the EU Court's assertion of full control over the domestic application of Union law on the terms set out in its case law (*Van Gend en Loos* and *Costa* v. *ENEL*). This does *not* mean that Member States routinely refuse to give effect to the *substance* of the Court's statements on the formal status of Union law and the conditions under which it applies within Member States as a matter of *national* constitutional law. The argument here is simply that the Court of Justice's decisive move to break with the Treaties' statements on Constitutional Issue No. 1 continues to exist beyond the EU Treaty framework as an act of judicial constitutional contestation.

Nonetheless, it is possible to point to a range of intervening developments in an effort to defend the view that, as Treaty signatories, Member States have normalised the Court's position on Constitutional Issue No. 1. These developments include Member States' integration of *negative* references to the principle of direct effect into the Treaty framework (Section 1.1.1);[5] the adoption of Declaration No. 17 on the primacy of Union law (Section 1.1.2);[6] and, more strongly, express reference to the 'specific characteristics of the Union and Union law' in Protocol No. 8 on EU Accession to the European Convention on Human Rights and Fundamental Freedoms (Section 1.1.3).[7] Finally, it could also be argued that, for States that subsequently joined the (now) EU, the Court's position on Constitutional Issue No. 1 has been normalised as part of the EU accession *acquis* (Section 1.1.4).

On closer inspection, however, these developments – individually and jointly – do not support the assertion that, collectively, Member States have accepted *de facto*, if not *de jure*, the Court's divergent institutional position on the formal status of Union law and the conditions under which it applies within Member States. The status quo is instead one of political tolerance, with both sets of actors – Member States (acting collectively as Treaty signatories) and the Court of Justice – simply agreeing to disagree on Constitutional Issue No. 1.

1.1.1 *Negative References to Direct Effect in the Treaty Framework*

The principle of direct effect is a component part of the Court's divergent position on the *formal status of Union law and the conditions under which it applies within Member States*. According to the Court, under specific preconditions, EU norms enjoy direct effect within national legal systems *as a matter of Union law*; in other words, entirely independently of domestic law.

Member States have on several occasions amended the EU Treaties to insert references to that principle into the Treaty framework as constitutional touchstone – at least in the negative. For example, prior to the entry into force of the Lisbon Treaty, Article 34(2)(b)/(c) TEU provided that framework decisions and decisions adopted under Title VI of the then Treaty on European Union shall not entail direct effect. Similarly, post Lisbon, Article 1(2) of Protocol No. 30 on the Application of the EU Charter of Fundamental Rights to Poland and the United Kingdom guarantees, for the avoidance of any doubt, that nothing in Title IV of

[5] See e.g., historically, Art. 34(2)(b)(c) TEU.

[6] Declaration (No. 17) Concerning Primacy [2012] OJ C 326/346.

[7] Protocol (No. 8) relating to Article 6(2) of the Treaty on European Union on the accession of the Union to the European Convention on the Protection of Human Rights and Fundamental Freedoms [2012] OJ L326/273.

that instrument establishes justiciable rights for individuals within the domestic legal orders of either Member State.[8]

Member States' insertion of (negative) references to the direct effect of EU norms could be read as signalling their collective (implicit) acceptance of the Court's assertion of control over the domestic effect of EU law as a matter of Union law (*Van Gend en Loos*). However, this interpretation is problematic for two reasons. First, it sits awkwardly alongside the Treaty framework's unequivocal statements on the formal status of Union law and the conditions under which it applies within Member States.[9] These statements leave no doubt regarding the Treaties' continued adherence to the normative framework of international law as the basis for determining the relationship between Union and domestic law.

Secondly, as Treaty signatories, Member States are free to make determinations about the direct effect of particular Treaty norms as a matter of international law.[10] Indeed, as argued in Chapter 3, this is one of the principal ways through which States can seek to *influence* the domestic implementation of international norms – over which they ultimately retain full control – through the process of treaty-making. Accordingly, references to direct effect in the EU Treaty framework do not inherently challenge the integrity of the Treaties' adherence to the framework of international law as the basis for determining Constitutional Issue No. 1.

1.1.2 *Declaration No. 17 on the Primacy of Union Law*

Relatedly, it could also be argued that, acting collectively, Member States have normalised the Court's case law on the primacy of EU norms – *de facto* if not *de jure*. As argued in Chapter 3, as a key component of its institutional position on Constitutional Issue No. 1, the Court ruled that EU norms take priority over conflicting national law, regardless of the latter's status under domestic law.

At Lisbon, Member States took clear steps towards normalising the Court's primacy claim with the EU Treaty framework as constitutional

[8] Protocol (No. 30) on the application of the Charter of Fundamental Rights of the European Union to Poland and to the United Kingdom [2012] OJ C 202/312.

[9] See esp., Art. 4(3) TEU; Art. 19(1) TEU; Art. 260 TFEU; Art. 291(1) TFEU and Arts. 280 and 299 TFEU.

[10] See A. Nollkaemper, 'The Effects of Treaties in Domestic Law' in C. J. Tams, A. Tzanakopoulos and A. Zimmermann (eds.), *Research Handbook on the Law of Treaties* (Cheltenham: Elgar, 2014) at p. 135.

touchstone. In particular, Declaration No. 17, annexed to the EU Treaties now provides that,[11]

> The Conference recalls that, in accordance with well settled case law of the Court of Justice of the European Union, the Treaties and the law adopted by the Union on the basis of the Treaties have primacy over the law of Member States, under the conditions laid down by the said case law.[12]

The adoption of that Declaration at Lisbon introduced, for the time, express reference to the primacy of EU law within national legal orders. It also supersedes an earlier, and stronger, attempt to integrate primacy into the EU Treaty framework. Article I-6 of the now defunct Treaty establishing a Constitution for Europe[13] outlined that, 'The Constitution and law adopted by the institutions of the Union in exercising competences conferred on it shall have primacy over the laws of the Member States.'[14] It is easy to mistake the introduction of the first express reference to primacy in the Treaty framework, as anticipated by the failed Constitutional Treaty and now provided for in Declaration No. 17, for Member State acceptance of the Court of Justice's position on Constitutional Issue No. 1. However, scrutinised more closely, it is highly questionable whether even the legally binding provision in Article I-6 of the defunct Constitutional Treaty would have fully normalised the Court's conception of the European Union as a 'new legal order' in quasi-federal form.

As a Declaration annexed to the Treaties, the Member States' present commitment to primacy in Declaration No. 17 is non-binding – even as a matter of international law.[15] Moreover, even if it were legally binding, it would, at best, sit awkwardly alongside the Treaty framework. As restated earlier (Section 1.1), the EU Treaties continue unequivocally to link the EU legal order to the normative framework of international law through their clear (and unchanged) statements on the domestic effect of EU Treaty obligations and the legal effects of EU court judgments (see now, respectively, Article 4(3) TEU and Articles 280 and 299 TFEU). As argued in Chapter 3, the position would have been no different had the Constitutional Treaty entered into force.

[11] Declaration (No. 17) Concerning Primacy, n. 6.
[12] *Ibid.*
[13] Treaty establishing a Constitution for Europe [2004] OJ C 301/1.
[14] *Ibid.*
[15] See Case C-292/89, *Antonissen* EU:C:1991:80 at paras. 18–19; Case C-49/02, *Heidelberger Bauchemie GmbH* EU:C:2004:384 at para. 17 and Case C-345/04 P, *Gestoras Pro Amnistia and Others* v. *Council* EU:C:2007:115 at para. 60. For a summary, see A. Kaczorowska, *European Union Law* (3rd edn) (Abingdon: Routledge, 2013) at p. 112.

Moreover, and most crucially perhaps, any claim that Declaration No. 17 has effectively normalised the Court's case law on the formal status of Union law with the Treaty framework is open to serious question in light of Member State *practice*. A review of Member State responses to the Court's position on Constitutional Issue No. 1 makes it clear that Member States do *not* in fact accept the primacy of EU law 'under the conditions laid down by the said case law' as prescribed therein (Section 1.2). In reality, the Court of Justice's core claim that EU law takes effect within Member State legal orders *by virtue of its own authority* remains fundamentally contested.

1.1.3 *Protocol No. 8 on EU Accession to the European Convention on Human Rights*

A stronger normative basis for Member States' normalisation of the Court's case law on direct effect and primacy can arguably be found in the legally binding Protocol on EU accession to the European Convention on Human Rights and Fundamental Freedoms (Protocol No. 8).[16] That instrument commits the European Union to ensuring the preservation of the 'specific characteristics of the Union and Union law' in the process of negotiating the terms of the Union's accession to the ECHR.[17]

In *Opinion 2/13*, the Court of Justice lost no time in forging a link between Protocol No. 8 and its own statements on the formal status of Union law and the conditions under which it applies within Member States. However, as argued in Chapter 4, the wording of Protocol No. 8 does not actually support that move. On closer reading, the Court's case law on direct effect and primacy is not the focus of the Protocol. Rather, its reference to ensuring the preservation of the 'specific characteristics of the Union and Union law' in the accession process is focused, more specifically, on managing the status of the European Union as a non-State party within the ECHR legal order. In more precise terms, Article 1 of Protocol No. 8 obliges the Commission, under a mandate from the

[16] Protocol (No. 8) relating to Article 6(2) of the Treaty on European Union on the accession of the Union to the European Convention on the Protection of Human Rights and Fundamental Freedoms, n. 7. See also, Declaration No. 2 on Article 6(2) of the Treaty on European Union [2012] OJ C 202/337, which references the 'special features of Union law'.

[17] For analysis, see e.g., P. Gragl, *The Accession of the European Union to the European Convention on Human Rights* (Oxford: Hart Publishing, 2013).

Council, to address two key matters of concern in the Accession Agreement concluded with the ECHR. First, it requires agreement on the participation of the European Union institutions in the control bodies of the European Convention; secondly, it mandates the creation of special mechanisms to ensure that legal proceedings involving questions of Union law are correctly addressed to Member States and Union institutions.

1.1.4 *Normalisation as Part of the EU Accession* Acquis

Finally, it could be argued that, at least for States that have joined the (now) EU, the Court's statements on Constitutional Issue No. 1 have been effectively normalised as part of the EU accession *acquis*. The EU *acquis* references the accumulated legislation, legal acts and court decisions, which, together, constitute the entire body of European Union law. It forms the centerpiece of the arrangements for the accession of new Member States to the Union. Acceding states are required to adopt the entire EU *acquis* during a transitional period subject to strict monitoring.

The argument that, at least for acceding Member States, the Court's case law on the formal status of Union law and the conditions under which it applies within Member States has been normalised through the accession process is logical and appealing. However, it has a serious weakness: the Member States have never included the principles of direct effect or primacy as part of the accession *acquis*.[18] Beginning with the first wave of accession to the (then) Community in 1973, the Court's case law on direct effect and primacy has never formed part of any of the accession agreements concluded between the Member States and acceding states pursuant to (now) Article 49 TEU.

In fact, the Court's statements on Constitutional Issue No. 1 have only ever been referenced in the Commission's institutional Opinions on applications for EU accession.[19] In its institutional Opinions, it is the

[18] See also, B. de Witte, 'Direct Effect, Primacy, and the Nature of the Legal Order', n. 1 at p. 350.

[19] See e.g., Commission Opinion of 19 January 1972 on the application to the European Communities by the Kingdom of Denmark, Ireland, the Kingdom of Norway and the United Kingdom of Great Britain and Northern Ireland [1972] OJ L73/3; Commission Opinion of 19 April 1994 on the applications for accession to the European Union by the Republic of Austria, the Kingdom of Sweden, the Republic of Finland and the Kingdom of Norway [1994] OJ C 241/3; Commission Opinion of 19 February 2003 on the applications for accession to the European Union by the Czech Republic, the Republic of Estonia, the Republic of Cyprus, the Republic of Latvia, the Republic of Lithuania, the Republic of Hungary, the Republic of Malta, the Republic of Poland, the Republic of Slovenia and the

Commission, not Member States, that repeatedly restated the substance and importance of the Court of Justice's case law on the formal status of EU law. In its view,

> It is an essential feature of the legal order introduced by these Treaties that certain of their provisions and certain acts adopted by the institutions are directly applicable, that the law of the Union takes precedence over any national provisions which might conflict with it, and that procedures exist for ensuring the uniform interpretation of the law of the Union. Accession to the European Union implies recognition of the binding nature of these rules, observance of which is indispensable to guarantee the effectiveness and unity of the law of the Union.[20]

To summarise, for both existing and acceding Member States alike, the EU Treaty framework continues to provide clear statements on the formal status of Union law and the conditions under which it applies within Member States. Those statements remain fundamentally unaltered and firmly anchor the process of European integration to the normative framework of international law. The Court's institutional position on Constitutional Issue No. 1 continues to exist beyond the EU Treaty framework as an act of judicial constitutional contestation.

1.2 The National Response: Member States and National Courts

This section turns to consider *individual* Member States' responses to the Court's statements on formal status of Union law and the conditions under which it applies within Member States. Section 1.2.1 provides an overview of domestic reactions to the Court's position on Constitutional Issue No. 1 as an act of judicial constitutional contestation. Section 1.2.2 highlights the central role of national courts in managing the reception of EU law into domestic legal systems – in defence of the Treaty framework's position on Constitutional Issue No. 1. Finally, Section 1.2.3 explores the reasons why national courts have opted to give effect, as a matter of national law, to the *substance* of the Court's case law in *Van Gend en Loos* and *Costa.*

Slovak Republic [2003] OJ L235/3 and, most recently, Commission Opinion of 12 October 2011 on the application for accession to the European Union by the Republic of Croatia [2012] OJ L 112/3.

[20] See e.g., Commission Opinion on the application for accession to the European Union by the Republic of Croatia, n. 19, recital 10.

1.2.1 *Domestic Responses: Overview*

Member States, and their respective national courts, do not recognise the Court of Justice's institutional position on Constitutional Issue No. 1.[21] Instead, they adhere robustly to the Treaties' unambiguous statements on the formal status of Union law and the conditions under which it applies within Member States. As de Witte argues, for Member States and domestic courts alike, 'The idea that EU law can claim its primacy within the national legal order *on the basis of its own authority* seems as implausible as Baron von Munchhausen's claim that he had lifted himself up from the quicksand by pulling on his bootstraps.'[22] Rather, Member States and their respective national courts consider EU law to take effect domestically by virtue of provisions or instructions that are located *within* national constitutional systems.[23] That view on the internal application of EU norms is in absolute conformity with the normative framework of international law embedded in the Treaties. To repeat: that framework leaves individual states with full control over the internal application of treaty norms.[24]

For certain Member States, attributing domestic effect to the *substance* of the Court of Justice's case law on the direct effect and primacy of Union law was never problematic as a matter of national constitutional law.[25] This was particularly true, for example, for both Luxembourg and the Netherlands as founding Member States. In Luxembourg, national courts had already recognised the direct effect and primacy of international treaty norms as a matter of domestic constitutional law prior

[21] On national courts' reception of the Court's jurisprudence, see in particular, A. Oppenheimer (ed.), *The Relationship between European Community law and National Law: The Cases* (Vol. 1) (Cambridge: Cambridge University Press, 1994); A. Oppenheimer (ed.), *The Relationship between European Community Law and National Law: The Cases* (Vol. 2) (Cambridge: Cambridge University Press, 2004) and M. Claes, *The National Courts' Mandate in the European Constitution* (Oxford: Hart Publishing, 2006). See also, 'European Law and National Constitutions' in *Fide XX Congress: National Reports* (Vol. 1) (London: British Institute of International and Comparative Law, 2002).

[22] de Witte, 'Direct Effect, Primacy, and the Nature of the Legal Order', n. 1 at p. 351.

[23] See also, E. Denza, 'Placing the European Union in International Context: Legitimacy of the Case Law' in M. Adams, H. de Waele, J. Meeusen and G. Straetmans (eds.), *Judging Europe's Judges: The Legitimacy of the Case Law of the European Court of Justice* (Oxford: Hart Publishing, 2013) at p. 178.

[24] See Nollkaemper, 'The Effects of Treaties in Domestic Law', n. 10 at pp. 130–131 and E. Denza, 'The Relationship between International Law and National Law' in M. D. Evans (ed.) *International Law* (4th edn) (Oxford: Oxford University Press, 2014) at p. 412.

[25] Claes, *The National Courts' Mandate in the European Constitution*, n. 21, chapter 6.

to the EU Court's judgments in *Van Gend en Loos* and *Costa*.[26] The Constitution of the Netherlands was similarly well placed to give effect to the substance of the Court of Justice's position on Constitutional Issue No. 1. Article 93 of the Netherlands Constitution provides that treaties and resolutions adopted by international institutions shall, under specific instances, become binding after they are published.[27] Furthermore, Article 94 attributes primary to such norms in instances of conflict with (ordinary) domestic law.[28]

However, for most Member States (both founding and acceding) attributing domestic effect to the substance of the Court of Justice's case law on direct effect and primacy required differing degrees of national constitutional adjustment. For many Member States (again, both founding and acceding) the preferred solution has been to introduce changes to the domestic rules governing the internal effect of international norms.[29] Alternatively (or in addition), other Member States have opted to insert (or revise existing) 'enabling clauses' in national constitutions.[30] These clauses function to provide a domestic basis for the transfer of administrative, legislative and executive competences to the Union and its institutions pursuant to the EU Treaties.

Revisions to domestic rules on the internal effect of international and/or EU law do not generally expressly reference the Court's case law on direct effect and primacy. Explicit references feature only exceptionally. Most clearly, Article 2 of the Constitutional Act of the Republic of Lithuania on Membership of the Republic of Lithuania in the European Union provides that,

> The norms of the European Union law shall be a constituent part of the legal system of the Republic of Lithuania. Where it concerns the founding Treaties of

[26] See Cour de Cassation, Decision of 14 July 1954, Pas.lux, Vol. 16, 150. For discussion, see G. Wivines, 'Rapport Luxembourgeois' prepared for the XXth FIDE Congress (London: British Institute for International and Comparative Law, 2002) at pp. 24–25, cited in Claes, *The National Courts' Mandate in the European Constitution*, n. 21 at p. 151.

[27] Art. 94 provides that 'Provisions of treaties and of resolutions by international institutions which may be binding on all persons by virtue of their contents shall become binding after they have been published.'

[28] Art. 120 precludes national courts from reviewing the constitutionality of treaties. Despite the Netherlands Constitution's openness to the reception of the Court's case law, Claes notes that Dutch courts have not expressly referenced Art. 94 in connection with their attribution of internal effect to the jurisprudence on direct effect and supremacy. See Claes, n. 21 at pp. 150–151.

[29] See e.g., Art. 23 of the German Basic Law and Art. 8(3) of the Portuguese Constitution.

[30] See e.g., Art. 93 of the Spanish Constitution 1978.

the European Union, the norms of the European Union law shall be applied directly, while in the event of collision of legal norms, they shall have supremacy over the laws and other legal acts of the Republic of Lithuania.

Similarly, though in less equivocal language, the Third Amendment to the Irish Constitution provides that, 'No provision of this Constitution invalidates laws enacted, acts done or measures adopted by the State necessitated by the obligations of membership of the Communities or prevents law enacted, acts done or measures adopted by the Communities, or institutions thereof, from having the force of law in the State.'[31]

1.2.2 *Domestic Responses: The Role of National Courts*

Within both founding and acceding Member States, national courts have played a critical role in shaping the network of domestic rules that give internal effect to Union law in accordance with the demands of the EU Treaty framework as constitutional touchstone. Within most Member States it has fallen ultimately to national courts to supervise the process of domestic constitutional change. In particular, Member State courts have been tasked with reconciling the demands of the Court of Justice's case law on primacy – with its claim to precedence over *all* conflicting provisions of national law – with the defence of national constitutions and/or constitutional doctrines.

Broadly speaking, Member State courts have found a conceptual basis to facilitate the domestic application of EU norms with reference to one of two sets of national constitutional provisions (or a combined reading of both).[32] On the one hand, certain Member State courts have anchored the internal application of Union law principally to provisions of national constitutions that, like that of the Netherlands, provide for the domestic effect (and also priority) of international treaty norms.[33]

[31] See also, e.g., Art. 1A of the Constitution of Cyprus (introduced by amendment in 2006): 'No provision of the Constitution shall be deemed to annul laws enacted, acts done or measures taken by the Republic which become necessary by reason of its obligations as a member state of the European Union, nor does it prevent Regulations, Directives or other acts or binding measures of a legislative character, adopted by the European Union or the European Communities or by their institutions or competent bodies thereof on the basis of the Treaties establishing the European Communities or the Treaty of the European Union, from having legal effect in the Republic.'

[32] For analysis, see e.g., See Claes, n. 21, chapter 6.

[33] See e.g., Belgium (Cour de cassion (B), decision of 27 May 1971, *SA Fromagerie franco-Suisse Le* Ski, JT, 1971 460) and Luxembourg (Cour de Cassation, Decision of 14 July 1954, Pas. lux, Vol. 16, 150).

On the other hand, many national courts have found the primary basis to give effect to the substance of the Court's case law on Constitutional Issue No. 1 in constitutional enabling clauses or statutory provisions that provide the domestic basis for the transfer of Member State competences to the European institutions.[34]

In practical terms, the end result of this process of (ultimately) court-managed national constitutional adjustment may appear largely indistinguishable from domestic acceptance of the Court of Justice's case law *on its own authority*. However, the fundamental distinction that locks domestic constitutional responses to the normative framework of international law remains intact. As nearly all Member State courts continue to make clear when pushed, the decision to attribute internal effect to EU legal norms (and the conditions under which such effect shall be attributed) remains a matter for national (constitutional) law.

Indeed, the majority of Member State constitutional (or supreme) courts have made it clear that EU norms do *not* take primacy over (at least certain) provisions of national constitutions.[35] Parallel lines of interpretation can also be found in decisions of the United Kingdom courts – a Member State without a written constitution. The German Federal Constitutional Court's conditional view on the internal effect of Union law remains the most comprehensive.[36] That Court has repeatedly made it clear that the application of EU norms within Germany in accordance with the substance of the Court of Justice's case law on direct

[34] See e.g., Germany (Bundesverfassungsgericht, Decision of 30 June 2009, *Lisbon Decision*, 2 BvE 2/08); Italy (*Granital* Judgment No. 170/84 of 8 June 1984); United Kingdom (*R.* v. *Secretary of State for Transport, Ex p. Factortame and Others* (No. 2) [1991] 1 A.C. 603); Denmark (Danish Supreme Court, judgment of 6 April 1998, *Carlsen* v. *Rasmussen*, Case I 361/1997); Lithuania (Konstitucinis Teismas, ruling of 4 December 2008 on connecting the electricity network) and Latvia (Satversmes tiesa, judgment of 7 April 2009, *Lisbon*, Case No. 2008-35-01).

[35] Italy (Corte costituzionale, Decision n. 183/73 of 27 December 1973, *Frontini*, 18 Guir. Cost. I 2401) and Lithuania (Konstitucinis Teismas, ruling of 4 December 2008 on connecting the electricity network). See also Belgium (Arbitragehof/Cour d'Arbitrage, decision n. 26/92 of 16 October 1991, *Commune de Lanaken*). See also, analogously, for the UK (*R.* v. *Secretary of State for Transport, Ex p. Factortame and Others* (No. 2) [1991] 1 A.C. 603); Denmark (Danish Supreme Court, judgment of 6 April 1998, *Carlsen* v. *Rasmussen*, Case I 361/1997); Portugal (*Supremo Tribunal Administrativo*, 27 October 1999, Case 45389-A); Latvia (Satversmes tiesa, judgment of 7 April 2009, *Lisbon*, Case No. 2008-35-01); Czech Republic (*Ústanví soud*, judgment of 26 November 2008, *Treaty of Lisbon I*, PI. ÚS 19/08 and *Ústanví soud*, judgment of 3 November 2009, *Treaty of Lisbon II*, PI. ÚS 29/09)

[36] For analysis, see e.g., M. Payandeh, 'Constitutional Review of EU Law after *Honeywell*: Contextualizing the Relationship between the German Constitutional Court and the EU Court of Justice' (2011) 48 *Common Market Law Review*, 9.

effect and primacy is conditional, not absolute. The German Federal Constitutional Court's jurisprudence has evolved to assert competence to manage the domestic application of Union law on three key grounds. The first concerns the protection of fundamental rights;[37] the second addresses Union competences;[38] and, finally, the third relates to the defence of what the German Court considers the inalienable features of that State's constitutional identity.[39]

The imposition of limits on the domestic effect of Union law – as part of judicial processes of national constitutional adjustment – is a common feature across Member State legal systems. The imposition of such limits is also, in parallel with the assertion of domestic control over the internal effect of treaty norms more generally, entirely compatible with the principles and practice of international law firmly embedded in the EU Treaty framework. As Nollkaemper reminds us:

> On the whole, states have reserved the power under domestic law to limit the performance of treaty obligations where these may conflict with domestic law . . . Most states have declared their constitutions to be supreme. Such states do not accept the supremacy of treaties as a formal principle, but make the effect of international law contingent on substantive conformity with fundamental values enshrined in national law.[40]

1.2.3 *Explaining Domestic Constitutional Adjustment*

Separate to the discussion of *how* national courts adapted domestic rules on the implementation of international norms to give practical effect to the Court of Justice's statements on Constitutional Issue No. 1 is the question *why* they chose to do so.

It was always open to national courts to question the internal constitutionality of the Court's position on the formal status of EU law and ultimately take corrective action. As Weatherill notes, national courts should not be understood as simply 'unthinking agents of the Court of Justice.'[41] Individual Member State courts could, for example,

[37] Bundesverfassungsgericht, Decision of 29 May 1974, *Solange I*, BVerfGE 37, 271.
[38] Bundesverfassungsgericht, Decision of 12 October 1993, *Treaty of Maastricht*, BVerfGE 89, 155.
[39] Decision of 30 June 2009, BVerfGE 123, 267.
[40] Nollkaemper, 'The Effects of Treaties in Domestic Law', n. 10 at pp. 143–144.
[41] S. Weatherill, 'The Court's Case Law on the Internal Market: "A Circumloquacious Statement of the Result, Rather than a Reason for Arriving at It?"' in Adams, de Waele, Meeusen and Straetmans, *Judging Europe's Judges*, n. 23 at p. 90.

have simply declared that, in their view, the Court of Justice's institutional position on Constitutional Issue No. 1 was *ultra vires* under the EU Treaties. Similarly, national courts could have ruled that the existing domestic framework on the implementation of international norms precluded the attribution of internal effect to the substance of the Court of Justice's judgments on direct effect and primacy. Of course, such determinations would have consequences for the state concerned. That Member State would likely quickly find itself the addressee of Article 258 TFEU infringement proceedings for its alleged non-compliance with its obligations under the Treaty.

EU Scholars have offered a range of possible explanations for national courts' decisions to attribute internal effect to the substance of the Court's case law on direct effect and primacy.[42] As Claes notes, it is difficult to determine the precise reasons why individual national courts chose to adapt national legal frameworks in order to implement the Court's rulings in *Van Gend en Loos* and *Costa*.[43] However, the following have been offered as key factors that likely shaped domestic judicial responses. The traditional legalist approach accentuates the normative pull of law. As Alter argues, 'legalist approaches see national judiciaries as having been convinced by legal arguments of the validity of the supremacy [primacy] of EC law over national law, and of the importance of national courts applying the supreme EC law in their own jurisprudence'.[44] Relatedly, the empowerment thesis emphasises the relationship between the domestic implementation of the principles of direct effect and primacy and the position of Member State courts within national constitutional orders. Put simply, national courts were motivated to adjust domestic rules governing the internal effect of international norms to match the Court of Justice's jurisprudence as a means to enhance their own institutional competences. As Weiler points out, accepting the substance of direct effect and primacy, 'Lower courts

[42] For discussion, see J. H. H. Weiler, 'The Least Dangerous Branch: A Retrospective and Prospective of the European Court of Justice in the Arena of Political Integration' in J. H. H. Weiler, *The Constitution of Europe: 'Do the New Clothes Have an Emperor?' And Other Essays on European Integration* (Cambridge: Cambridge University Press, 1999); K. Alter, *Establishing the Supremacy of European Law* (Oxford: Oxford University Press, 2001), chapter 5 and Claes, *The National Courts' Mandate in the European Constitution*, n. 21, chapter 9.

[43] Claes, *The National Courts' Mandate in the European Constitution*, n. 21 at p. 265.

[44] K. Alter, 'Explaining National Court Acceptance of European Court Jurisprudence: A Critical Evaluation of Theories of Legal Integration,' in A. M. Slaughter, A. Stone Sweet and J. H. H Weiler (eds.), *The European Court and National Courts – Doctrine and Jurisprudence: Legal Change in its Social Context* (Oxford: Hart Publishing, 1998) at p. 222.

and judges were [in many instances] given the facility to engage with the highest jurisdiction in the Community and, even more remarkable, to gain the power of judicial review over the executive and legislative branches, even in those jurisdictions were such power was weak and non-existent.'[45] Equally, national judges may have been influenced by the responses of their counterparts in other Member States in a process of judicial cross-fertilisation.[46] Most strikingly perhaps, the French *Conseil d'Etat's* attention was notably drawn to the fact that its approach to implementing the Court of Justice's case law on primacy was out of step with that of other Member States courts. As the *commissiarie de government* noted in his opinion to that Court:

> So far as foreign courts are concerned ... all I would say is that your Court [*Conseil d'Etat*] is now the last which formally refuses to apply the Community measures which are contradicted by later [national] laws. By way of example, it is sufficient to mention that the Constitutional Court of the Federal Republic of Germany for its part finally accepted the opposite principle no less than eighteen years ago, by decision of 9 June 1971. And even more significant is the case of the Italian Constitutional Court which, although hindered by a dualist legal tradition ... finally went so far as to authorise the ordinary courts of their own motion not to apply law contrary to Community regulations by an important judgment of 8 June 1984, *Granital*.[47]

Finally, national judicial responses to the Court's statements on Constitutional Issue No. 1 may also have been influence by other broader contextual factors. These include, for instance, changing Member State attitudes to the implementation of international norms within domestic legal systems, coupled with the steady growth and political acceptance of judicial review powers within European democracies.[48] Equally, another explanatory factor could be the role and influence of an emergent transnational EU legal community that has remained strongly supportive of

[45] J. H. H Weiler, 'Journey to an Unknown Destination: A Retrospective and Prospective Analysis of the European Court of Justice in the Arena of Political Integration' (1993) 31 *Journal of Common Market Studies*, 417 at p. 425. See also, Claes, *The National Courts' Mandate in the European Constitution*, n. 21 at pp. 255–257.

[46] Claes, *The National Courts' Mandate in the European Constitution*, n. 21 at pp. 258–260.

[47] Opinion of Patrick Frydman, *Commissaire du government* in Conseil d'Etat, Decision of 20 October 1989, *Nicolo*, RTDeur., 136. The *Commissaire du government* is a member of the Conseil d'Etat whose role it is to provide that Court with an advisory opinion for its consideration prior to delivery of judgment. See Alter, *Establishing the Supremacy of European Law*, n. 42 at p. 139.

[48] On the rise of constitutional politics within Europe, see S. Stone Sweet, *Governing with Judges* (Oxford: Oxford University Press, 2001).

the Court of Justice's approach to the nature and objectives of European integration (see further Section 3).[49]

2 Member State Responses to Judicial Constitutional Contestation: Constitutional Issues No. 2 and No. 3

This section considers Member State reactions to the Court's position on the locus of political authority within the EU legal order (Constitutional Issue No. 2) (Chapter 4) and, relatedly, on the objectives, values and limits governing European integration (Constitutional Issue No. 3) (Chapter 5). Following the structure in Section 1, Section 2.1 reviews the responses of Member State governments *acting collectively as Treaty signatories*. Thereafter, Section 2.2 considers the reaction within *individual* Member States.

At *Union* level, Member States have used a range of distinct tools with varying degrees of intensity in response to the Court's statements on Constitutional Issues No. 2 and No. 3.[50] These include isolated attempts to reverse specific decisions of the Court; to exclude its jurisdiction in sensitive policy areas; and to introduce discrete claw-back provisions into the Treaty framework. At *national* level, there is also (growing) evidence of Member State courts 'pushing back' against the Court of Justice. Specifically, a number of national courts have expressed (increasing) concern with regard to the quality of the Court's engagement as direct policymaker with the Treaty framework's statements on the objectives, values and limits governing European integration (Constitutional Issue No. 3).

2.1 The Collective Response: Member States as Treaty Signatories

Acting collectively as Treaty signatories, Member States have not normalised the Court's challenge to the Treaty framework's statements on the locus of political authority within the EU legal order (Constitutional Issue No. 2). In particular, the Court's move to interpose itself as direct policymaker in key areas continues to exist beyond the Treaty framework as an act of constitutional contestation. As outlined in Chapter 4, the EU Treaties continue to vest principal responsibility for Union policy-making with the EU's political institutions, not the Court.

[49] Alter, *Establishing the Supremacy of European Law*, n. 42 at p. 58.

[50] See also, Arnull, 'Me and My Shadow: The European Court of Justice and the Disintegration of European Union Law', n. 2.

As an act of constitutional contestation, the Court's assertion of direct policymaking functions has, however, not gone unchallenged.[51] At *Union level*, Member States have introduced various measures in response to the Court's challenge to the Treaty framework's statements on the locus of EU policymaking authority within the Union legal order (Constitutional Issue No. 2). Relatedly, Member States have also challenged the Court's conclusions, as direct policymaker on the objectives, values and limits governing European integration (Constitutional Issue No. 3). The solutions adopted fall into two broad categories. The first set of measures has sought to revise, or at least adjust, the Court's substantive policy choices on discrete issues such as the scope of the principle of equal treatment. The second set of tools attempts to shape the parameters for *future* judicial policymaking or, through the imposition of limits on the Court's jurisdiction, to exclude it completely.

2.1.1 Member State Interventions to Recast Judicial Policy Choices

The Barber Protocol annexed to the Treaty of Maastricht is characteristic of the first category of response.[52] In *Barber*, the Court of Justice ruled that Article 119 EC (now Article 157 TFEU) – a directly effective EU norm prohibiting discriminatory treatment on grounds of sex – was applicable to private employee pensions. Alarmed by the potentially disruptive impact of the Court's judgment on the pensions sector, Member States sought by means of a new Protocol to embed within the Treaty framework the narrowest permissible reading of the Court's judgment. In more precise terms, the Protocol outlined that,

> For the purposes of Article 119 of this Treaty, benefits under occupational social security schemes shall not be considered as remuneration if and in so far as they are attributable to periods of employment prior to 17 May 1990, except in the case of workers or those claiming under them who have before that date initiated legal proceedings or introduced an equivalent claim under the applicable national law.

[51] See esp., the United Kingdom's (unsuccessful) proposals to curb the Court's functions in the run-up to the Amsterdam ICG. For analysis, see A. Arnull, 'The ECJ, the UK and the IGC' (1996) 21 *European Law Review*, 349. See also, Alter, *Establishing the Supremacy of European Law*, n. 42 at pp. 197–198.

[52] See also, e.g., Protocol 17 (now 35) on Art. 40.3.3 of the Constitution of Ireland – in response to Case C-159/90, *Grogan* EU:C:1991:378 and Protocol (now 32) concerning Denmark – reacting to Case C-305/87, *Commission* v. *Greece* EU:C:1989:218.

Article 119 EC was itself also revised following another ruling of the Court of Justice that did not accord with the Member State's consensus view on matters of sex discrimination. In *Kalanke*, the EU Court had ruled that the prohibition on sex discrimination prohibited affirmative action measures that guaranteed women absolute and unconditional priority with respect to appointment and promotion.[53] In its view, such measures could not be justified under the terms of the derogation in Article 2(4) of Directive 76/207 EEC, which provided that the general principle of equality in the employment sphere was 'without prejudice to measures to promote equal opportunity for men and women, in particular by removing existing inequalities which affect women's opportunities'.[54] The Court's conclusion on that point did not find favour with Member State governments, prompting revisions to the text of Article 119 EC at Amsterdam. A new paragraph was inserted into that provision, which now outlines contra *Kalanke* that,

> With a view to ensuring full equality in practice between men and women in working life, the principle of equal treatment shall not prevent any Member State from maintaining or adopting measures providing for specific advantages in order to make it easier for the underrepresented sex to pursue a vocational activity or to prevent or compensate for disadvantages in professional careers.

Subsequently, Member States have revised the EU Treaties to establish an exceptional basis for the legislative override of the Court's decisions in the area of capital movements. Article 65(4) TFEU, introduced at Lisbon, empowers Member States – through the Council – to reverse the Court of Justice's decisions on the existence of national restrictions imposed on extra-EU capital movements. It provides that, 'the Council, acting in accordance with a special legislative procedure, may unanimously, and after consulting the European Parliament, adopt measures which constitute a step backwards in Union law as regards the liberalisation of the movement of capital to or from third countries'. Article 65(4) TFEU stands alone in the Treaty framework as an example of a legislative 'claw back' provision that enables Member States to recast politically unfavourable judicial choices in the specific area of external capital movements. Its closest equivalent in the Treaties is Article 108(2) TFEU,

53 Case C-450/93, *Kalanke* v. *Freie Hansestadt Bremen* EU:C:1995:322.

54 *Ibid.*, at paras. 16–24. Council Directive 76/207/EEC of 9 February 1976 on the implementation of the principle of equal treatment for men and women as regards access to employment, vocational training and promotion, and working conditions [1976] OJ L39/40.

which permits Member States, acting unanimously through the Council in exceptional circumstances, to declare the provision of State Aid 'compatible' with the internal market.[55]

2.1.2 *Member State Interventions to Manage the Scope for Future Judicial Policymaking*

In the run-up to the Intergovernmental Conference at Amsterdam, the United Kingdom tabled a particularly far-reaching set of proposals to curb the Court's jurisdiction and, thus, its functions as direct policymaker.[56] Among other things, the United Kingdom advocated the introduction of a new Protocol to restrict the Court's interpretative choices. Under that Protocol, 'when faced with more than one possible interpretation of provisions of Community law, the Court shall, unless there is a clear contrary intention, prefer the interpretation which least constrains the freedom of the Member States'. The United Kingdom's specific proposals failed to gain broad support in the negotiations leading up to the adoption of the Treaty of Amsterdam. However, through repeated amendments to the EU Treaties, Member States have nonetheless collectively agreed on a range of other initiatives that have sought to manage the scope of the Court's functions as direct policymaker.

First, Member States have annexed a number of non-binding Declarations to the EU Treaty framework in an effort to circumscribe the parameters for Union policymaking in discrete substantive areas. For example, Declaration No. 2 on Nationality of a Member State, annexed to the final act of the Treaty on European Union, sets out the view of Member States as Treaty signatories that the acquisition and loss of nationality remains a matter for national law alone.[57] It outlines that, 'The Conference declares that, wherever in the Treaty establishing the European Community reference is made to nationals of the Member States, the question whether an individual possesses the nationality of

[55] The Court has adopted a strict approach to the Council's exceptional competence to intervene in the control of state aid under that provision. See e.g., Case C-110/02, *Commission* v. *Council (State Aid)* EU:C:2004:395 at paras. 28–51 and Case C-117/10, *Commission* v. *Council (State Aid)* EU:C:2013:786 at paras. 50–60.

[56] For analysis, see Arnull, 'The ECJ, the UK and the IGC', n. 51. See also, Alter, *Establishing the Supremacy of European Law*, n. 42 at pp. 197–198.

[57] Declaration No. 2 on Nationality of a Member State [1992] OJ C 191/98. See also, e.g., Declaration on Article 8a of the EEC Treaty [1987] OJ C 169/24 on the deadline for the completion of the internal market.

a Member State shall be settled solely by reference to the national law of the Member State concerned.' More recently, the Lisbon Treaty introduced Declaration No. 1 concerning the Charter of Fundamental Rights of the European Union.[58] That Declaration restates, albeit without express reference to the Court of Justice, that the EU Charter does not extend the competences of the Union beyond those in the Treaties.

Secondly, Member States have inserted a number of Protocols into the Treaty framework. These legally binding instruments are typically conceived to grant specific legal guarantees to individual Member States. For example, Protocol No. 21 enshrines into primary law a guarantee that the Court's decision interpreting (now) Title V of Part 3 of the TFEU will not be binding upon or applicable within the United Kingdom or Irish legal systems.[59] Similarly, Protocol No. 30 offers the United Kingdom and Poland additional reassurance that the attribution of legal effect to the EU Charter of Fundamental Rights does not extend the competence of, *inter alia*, the Court of Justice to declare the laws, regulations or administrative provisions, practices or action of either Member State incompatible with the fundamental rights reaffirmed therein.[60]

Similarly, the (now-defunct) Decision of the European Council on a new settlement for the United Kingdom within the European Union included legal guarantees – concluded outside the EU Treaty framework (see Chapter 2) – against expansive judicial interpretation in specific areas.[61] In particular, Member States collectively agreed that the reference in the Treaty framework to the achievement of an 'ever closer Union among the peoples of Europe' does not apply to the United Kingdom. In wording that directly targets the Court of Justice, the Decision states unambiguously that,

> The references in the Treaties and their preambles to the process of creating an ever closer union among the peoples of Europe do not offer a legal basis for extending the scope of any provision of the Treaties or of EU secondary legislation. They should not be used either to support an extensive interpretation of the

[58] Declaration concerning the Charter of Fundamental Rights of the European Union [2012] OJ C 202/337.

[59] Protocol No. 21 on the Position of the United Kingdom and Ireland in Respect of the Area of Freedom, Security and Justice [2012] OJ C 202/295.

[60] Protocol No. 30 on the Application of the Charter of Fundamental Rights of the European Union to Poland and to the United Kingdom [2012] OJ C 202/312.

[61] Decision of the Heads of State or Government, meeting within the European Council, concerning a New Settlement for the United Kingdom within the European Union [2016] EUCO 4/16.

competences of the Union or of the powers of its institutions as set out in the Treaties.[62]

Thirdly, and most powerfully, Member States have attempted to limit the scope for judicial policymaking prospectively by introducing limits on the Court's jurisdiction. Beginning at Maastricht, Member State governments have agreed (and thereafter revised) exclusions to the Court's jurisdiction in discrete and politically sensitive fields of Union policymaking. Article L of Title VII of the Treaty on European Union (Maastricht) excluded the Court of Justice from exercising its functions in areas governed within (what were then) the Second and Third Pillars (Common Foreign and Security Policy and Justice and Home Affairs respectively). The Court's jurisdiction in both areas has subsequently increased over time through further Treaty amendment, not least as aspects of the Third Pillar were transferred into the (then) EC Treaty. Existing exclusions were, however, maintained for the benefit of those Member States that chose to opt out of the policy areas in question (see Protocol 21).

Relatedly, restricting access to the preliminary reference procedure has further restrained the Court's influence in certain policy areas. Pre-Lisbon, Court's jurisdiction in the Third Pillar (Title VI on Police and Judicial Co-operation in Criminal Matters) was conditional on Member States accepting its jurisdiction by way of declaration. Likewise, Article 68(1) EC limited the availability of preliminary references to the Court of Justice in specific areas to national courts of last instance.

Post-Lisbon, the EU Treaty framework continues largely to exclude the Court's jurisdiction in the field of Common Foreign and Security Policy. Its competence in that sphere is limited to monitoring compliance with Article 40 TEU, which mandates that activities within the CFSP shall not impact on Union competences in other areas. The Court also enjoys jurisdiction to review the legality of measures adopted against individuals. As far as the preliminary reference procedure is concerned, the Lisbon Treaty provides for the abolition of restrictions subject to the transitional arrangements outlined in Protocol No. 36.[63]

[62] *Ibid.*, at p. 16. See also, similarly, the guarantee on national security (applicable to all Member States) at p. 18: 'Article 4(2) of the Treaty on European Union confirms that national security remains the sole responsibility of each Member State. This does not constitute a derogation from Union law and should therefore not be interpreted restrictively. In exercising their powers, the Union institutions will fully respect the national security responsibility of the Member States.'

[63] Protocol No. 36 and Transitional Provisions [2012] OJ C 202/321.

2.2 The National Response: Member States and National Courts

This section considers *national* responses to the Court's statements on the locus of political authority within the EU legal order (Constitutional Issue No. 2) (Chapter 4) and, relatedly, on the objectives, values and limits governing European integration (Constitutional Issue No. 3) (Chapter 5).

At national level, there is (growing) evidence of Member State courts 'pushing back' against the Court of Justice. Several Member State courts have indicated that they consider the attribution of domestic effect to the Court's decisions as direct policymaker ultimately conditional on its respect for the Treaties' statements on *the objectives, values and limits governing European integration*. This includes, first and foremost, the principle of conferral in Article 5(2) TEU. The application of that Treaty provision *to the Court* as direct policymaker is most developed in the jurisprudence of the German Federal Constitutional Court. That Court has maintained, at least in theory if not entirely in practice, a robust position that Article 5(2) TEU operates as a source of normative restraint on EU institutional activity – including the activities of the Court of Justice.

Section 2.2.1 reviews the German Federal Constitutional Court's judgment in *Honeywell* as the trailblazing example of national courts 'pushing back' against the Court of Justice's interpretative choices as direct policymaker. Section 2.2.2 then considers further manifestations of 'push back' across the broader body of national case law.

2.2.1 The German Federal Constitutional Court in Honeywell

The German Federal Constitutional Court's judgment in *Honeywell* provides a clear illustration of its approach to the external scrutiny of EU institutional activity for compliance with Article 5(2) TEU.[64] In that decision, the German Court was invited to activate its 'ultra vires' review to challenge the internal constitutionality of the Court of Justice's ruling in *Mangold*.[65] In that case, the Grand Chamber had proclaimed the existence of the principle of non-discrimination of age as a directly

[64] Bundesverfassungsgericht, Decision of 6 July 2010, *Honeywell*, 2 BvR 2661/06. For analysis, see Payandeh, 'Constitutional review of EU law after *Honeywell* ', n. 36

[65] Case C-144/04, *Mangold* v. *Helm* EU:C:2005:709. For criticism, see J. Mazak and M. Moser, 'Adjudication by Reference to General Principles of EU Law: A Second Look at the Mangold Case Law' in Adams et al., *Judging Europe's Judges*, n. 23.

effective 'general principle' of EU law, the full effectiveness of which national courts were obliged to ensure.[66]

The Court of Justice's decision in *Mangold* is in basic tension with the Union legislature's decision on the scope of application of the non-discrimination principle in the employment sector. It is a paradigm example of an act of judicial constitutional contestation. Crucially, the Court's assertion of non-discrimination on grounds of age as a directly effective general principle of Union law extended its scope of application beyond the terms of Directive 2000/78 EC establishing a general framework for equal treatment in employment and occupation.[67] The Court's approach effectively sidestepped the legal framework established to give effect to the principle of non-discrimination in that Directive, not least by making that principle immediately applicable in employment disputes between private individuals and in advance of the deadline for the Directive's transposition.

Ruling the complaint admissible, the German Federal Constitutional Court restated its competence as a matter of domestic constitutional law to scrutinise EU institutional activity for compliance with the Treaties. Moreover, it also confirmed the consequences of any transgression with respect to the application of EU norms within the German legal order. In its own words it outlined that,

> The Federal Constitutional Court is ... empowered and obliged to review acts on the part of the European bodies and institutions with regard to whether they take place on the basis of manifest transgressions of competence ... and where appropriate to declare the inapplicability of acts for the German legal system which exceed competences.[68]

With direct reference to EU judicial activity, the German Court linked its review of Article 5(2) TEU compliance to changes to 'clearly recognisable statutory decisions which may even be explicitly documented in the wording (of the Treaties)' or likewise the Court of Justice's creation of 'new provisions without sufficient connection to legislative statements'.[69] Further development of the law through judicial interpretation

[66] Case C-144/04, *Mangold* v. *Helm*, n. 65 at para. 75. See thereafter, e.g., Case C-555/07, *Kücükdeveci* v. *Swedex GmbH & Co. KG* EU:C:2010:21 and Case C-441/14, *Dansk Industri (DI), acting on behalf of Ajos A/S* v. *Estate of Karsten Eigil Rasmussen* EU:C:2016 278.

[67] Council Directive 2000/78/EC establishing a general framework for equal treatment in employment and occupation [2000] OJ L 303/16.

[68] Bundesverfassungsgericht, Decision of 6 July 2010, *Honeywell*, 2 BvR 2661/06 at para. 55.

[69] *Ibid.*, at para. 64.

is considered especially problematic where the Court of Justice makes 'fundamental policy decisions over and above individual cases' or takes decisions that precipitate 'structural shifts ... in the system of the sharing of constitutional power and influence'.[70]

The legal framework established by the German Federal Constitutional Court to monitor the internal constitutionality of EU judicial activity is only loosely based on the Treaty framework. The concept of an '*ultra vires*' act developed by that Court and employed in *Honeywell* essentially superimposes a particular (German) understanding of the limits imposed on the Court of Justice under the principle of conferral in Article 5(2) TEU. That understanding links the notion of transgression to four key concerns without further express reference to the detailed framework of limits and values on Union institutional activities that are set out in EU Treaties as constitutional touchstones.

In summary, the German Court's *ultra vires* review is concerned, first, with the strength of the relationship between, on the one hand, the Court of Justice's interpretative choices and, on the other hand, the text of the Treaties, EU legislation and principles established within its previous case law. Secondly, the German Court highlights the Court of Justice's development of legal principles without sufficient regard to the policy choices of the Union legislature as a potential trigger for its *ultra vires* review. Thirdly, the German Court takes issue with attempts by the Luxembourg Court to use individual disputes as vehicles to formulate fundamental statements of policy of broader application. Its final concern addresses the consequences of the Court of Justice's interpretative choices. More precisely, the German Court indicates that it may step in to correct judicial development of EU norms that lead to the reconfiguration of the institutional balance governing Union policymaking established by the Treaties.

In his dissenting Opinion, Judge Landau had forcefully argued that the *Mangold* judgment unequivocally transgressed the limits of a constitutionally legitimate EU institutional act. On his analysis,

> With its judgment in the case of *Mangold*, the Court of Justice [had] manifestly transgressed the competences granted to it to interpret Community law with the *Mangold* judgment and acted ultra vires. The question left open by the Senate majority, namely whether the Court of Justice of the European Union departed from the area of justifiable interpretation – including further developing the law – with its judgment, is manifestly to be answered in the affirmative.[71]

[70] *Ibid.*

[71] *Ibid.*, at paras. 94–116

However, the majority Opinion disagreed. The conclusion that the Court of Justice's decision in *Mangold* did not constitute a manifest transgression of EU competences under the Treaties was highly deferential to the Luxembourg Court – a matter on which Judge Landau was most critical.[72] On each of the points raised, the majority Opinion ruled that the Court of Justice had not acted contrary to (its interpretation of) the principle of conferral in Article 5(2) TEU. Absolving the Court of Justice, it concluded that,

> A sufficiently qualified breach by the Court of Justice of the principle of conferral cannot be ascertained. Neither the opening of the field of application of Directive 2000/78/EC to cover cases which were to particularly attain the objective of the vocational integration of long-term unemployed older workers (aa), nor the advance effect of Directive 2000/78/EC, which was yet to be transposed in Germany, presumed by the Court of Justice (bb), nor the derivation of a general principle of the prohibition of discrimination based on age (cc), led to a structurally significant shift to the detriment of Member State competences.[73]

2.2.2 *'Push Back' as a Broader Constitutional Phenomenon*

The review of EU judicial activity for compliance with the EU Treaties, and Article 5(2) TEU in particular, is most developed in the German legal system. However, the German Federal Constitutional Court is not alone in voicing concerns over the compatibility of certain of the Court of Justice's interpretative choices with the principle of conferral. Several Member State constitutional courts have integrated parallel mechanisms for *ultra vires* review, following the lead set by the German Court.[74] Significantly, there is also evidence of 'push back' on the part of individual Member State courts with respect to the internal constitutionality of the Court of Justice's policy choices in practice, not just theory. This

[72] He criticises his colleagues for 'shying away from effectively implementing [the Court's previous case law on the conditionality of EU law within Germany] in practice'. See Bundesverfassungsgericht, Decision of 6 July 2010, *Honeywell*, 2 BvR 2661/06 at para. 106.

[73] See also, at para. 68: 'it is irrelevant whether the outcome found in the *Mangold* ruling can still be gained by recognised legal interpretation methods and whether any existing shortcomings would be evident'.

[74] See e.g., Tribunal Constitucional, Declaration 1/2004 of 13 December 2004 (Spain); Trybunal Konstytucyjny, Decision of 11 May 2004, *Accession Treaty*, K 18/04 and Trybunal Konstytucyjny, Decision of 24 November 2010, *Lisbon Treaty*, K 32/09 (Poland); Ústanví soud, judgment of 26 November 2008, *Treaty of Lisbon I*, PI. ÚS 19/08 (Czech Republic) and *R (HS2 Action Alliance Ltd)* v. *Secretary of State for Transport* [2014] UKSC 3 (United Kingdom).

includes further domestic challenges to the Court's judgment in *Mangold* as well as criticism of other key decisions of the Luxembourg Court.

In *Ajos*, the Supreme Court of Denmark went a step further than the *Bundesverfassungsgericht* in its reaction to the Court of Justice's ruling in *Mangold*.[75] Most strikingly, the Supreme Court refused to apply the prohibition of discrimination on grounds of age, as a general principle of Union law, in a private dispute concerning entitlement to severance pay under Danish law. The Danish Court justified its decision not to attribute domestic effect to the Court's *Mangold* case law with reference to the Danish Act of Accession. According to the Danish Court, that Act did not foresee the application – within Denmark – of directly effective legal norms that did not have a legal basis in specific provisions of the EU Treaties. Specifically, it ruled that,

> there is no basis for holding that the EU law principle prohibiting discrimination on grounds of age which, according to the EU Court of Justice, is to be found in various international instruments and in the constitutional traditions common to the Member States – that is to say, legal sources corresponding to those referred to in Article 6(3) TEU – have been made directly applicable in Denmark by the Law on accession.[76]

Judicial challenges at Member State level to the Court of Justice's interpretative choices as direct policymaker are not exclusively concerned with the internal constitutionality of the *Mangold* judgment. For example, in *G1 (Sudan)* v. *Secretary of State for the Home Department*, Lord Justice Laws of the Court of Appeal for England and Wales mounted a strong critique of the Grand Chamber's ruling on EU citizenship in *Rottmann*.[77] In that decision, the Court of Justice had ruled that Member States were required to have 'due regard' to Union law when applying national rules on the acquisition and loss of nationality (see Chapter 4).[78] Rejecting the appeal, Lord Justice Laws took specific issue with the

[75] Danish Supreme Court, judgment of 6 December 2016, *Dansk Industri (DI) acting for Ajos A/S* v. *The estate left by A*, Case I 15/2014. Unofficial translation available at www.supremecourt.dk/supremecourt/nyheder/pressemeddelelser/Documents/Judgment%2015-2014.pdf (accessed October 2017). For analysis, see e.g., M. R. Madsen, H. P. Olsen and U. Šadl, 'Competing Supremacies and Clashing Institutional Rationalities: The Danish Supreme Court's Decision in the *Ajos* Case and the National Limits of Judicial Cooperation' (2017) 23(1) *European Law Journal*, 140.

[76] Case No. 15/2014, *Dansk Industri (DI) acting for Ajos A/S*, n. 75 at p. 47.

[77] *R. (on the application of G1 (Sudan))* v. *Secretary of State for the Home Department* [2012] EWCA Civ 867 and Case C-135/08, *Rottman* v. *Freistaat Bayern* EU:C:2010:104.

[78] Case C-135/08, *Rottman*, n. 77 at para. 45.

Court's competence to impose any such obligation on Member States as a matter of Union law:

> I have with great respect found some difficulties with the reasoning in *Rottmann* (para 37) … *Upon what principled basis, therefore, should the grant or withdrawal of State citizenship be qualified by an obligation to "have due regard" to the law of the European Union?* It must somehow depend upon the fact that since the entry into force of the Maastricht Treaty in 1993 EU citizenship has been an incident of national citizenship, and "citizenship of the Union is intended to be the fundamental status of nationals of the Member States". But this is surely problematic. EU citizenship has been attached by Treaty to citizenship of the Member State. It is wholly parasitic upon the latter … *I am none the wiser as to the juridical basis of an obligation to "have due regard" to the law of the European Union in matters of national citizenship.*[79]

Furthermore, Lord Justice Laws was very clear that, however reasoned, the Grand Chamber's ruling could not be taken to establish a general obligation on Member States to have regard to the Treaty provisions on Union citizenship when applying domestic rules on the acquisition and loss of nationality. To do so, Lord Justice Laws contended, would raise questions over the existence of the Court of Justice's competence under the EU Treaties to regulate national citizenship. On his analysis,

> The conditions on which national citizenship is conferred, withheld or revoked are integral to the identity of the nation State. They touch the constitution; for they identify the constitution's participants. *If it appeared that the Court of Justice had sought to be the judge of any procedural conditions governing such matters, so that its ruling was to apply in a case with no cross-border element, then in my judgment a question would arise whether the European Communities Act 1972 or any successor statute had conferred any authority on the Court of Justice to exercise such a jurisdiction.*[80]

Lord Justice Laws' remarks on the limits of the Court of Justice's policy-making competence in the field of EU citizenship provide a further, albeit implicit awareness the function of Article 5(2) TEU (conferral) as a limit its competence as direct policymaker. His Opinion strongly

[79] *R. (on the application of G1 (Sudan))*, n. 77 at para. 38 (emphasis added). See also *R (HS2 Action Alliance Ltd)* v. *Secretary of State for Transport* [2014] UKSC 3 and Ústanví soud, judgment of 31 January 2012, *Slovak Pensions*, Pl. ÚS 5/12. The Court's judgment on air passenger rights in Joined Cases C-402/07 and Case C-432/07, *Sturgeon* v. *Condor Flugdienst GmbH and Böck and Lepuschitz* v. *Air France SA* EU:C:2009:716 (see Chapter 5) has attracted particular criticism from a number of national courts. For analysis, see S. Garben, 'Sky-High Controversy and High-Flying Claims? The *Sturgeon* Case Law in Light of Judicial Activism, Euroscepticism and Eurolegalism' (2013) 50(1) *Common Market Law Review*, 15.

[80] *R. (on the application of G1 (Sudan))*, n. 77 at para. 43 (emphasis added).

implies that any transgression on the part of the Court of Justice with regard to Article 5(2) TEU would attract the same sanction developed by the German Federal Constitutional Court (as mentioned earlier): the denial of domestic effect to the Luxembourg Court's decision as a matter of *national* constitutional law.[81]

3 Reponses in the EU Scholarship

This section examines EU legal scholars' responses to the Court's jurisprudence on the three key issues for EU constitutionalism. Overall, most EU scholars have taken a very different approach to Member States and national courts. This is most clear to see with respect to Constitutional Issue No. 1, addressing the formal status of Union law and the conditions under which it applies within Member States. Unlike Member States and national courts (Sections 1 and 2), EU scholars have generally sought vigorously to defend the Court's vision of the Union as a 'new legal order' *on its own terms*, notwithstanding the continuing validity of the normative framework of international law as the basis for EU integration under the Treaties.[82]

EU legal scholars' defence of the Court's statements on the formal status of Union law and the conditions under which it applies within Member States is significant. It directly informs their approach to the scrutiny of EU judicial activity, including assessments of the Court's role as direct policymaker. Adhering to the Court's institutional statements, EU legal scholars continue to see the Court of Justice in its own image as a *de facto* EU Constitutional Court that exercises near-complete powers of judicial review both horizontally and vertically. That baseline, which remains wholly unsupported by the Treaties, has given rise to particular dynamics in assessments of judicial interpretation and its limits. Questions of legitimacy are construed not primarily as matters of treaty interpretation, but, in line with the Court's case law, as instances of *constitutional adjudication*. This entrenched perspective fundamentally obscures the Court's position within the EU legal order *as an institution of the Union*. It also entirely overlooks the application of the Treaty framework *to the Court* as constitutional touchstone – the focus of this monograph.

[81] The Opinion of Laws LJ met with Supreme Court approval in *Pham* v. *Secretary of State for the Home Department* [2015] UKSC 19.

[82] See esp., Avbelj, 'Questioning EU Constitutionalisms', n. 3.

Section 3.1 examines legal scholars' robust defence of the Court's statements on the formal status of Union law and the conditions under which it applies within Member States (Constitutional Issue No. 1). Thereafter, Section 3.2 highlights the enduring impact of that defence on legal writing on the Court. It constructs a fivefold typology of current legal scholarship on the Court.

3.1 EU Scholars and the Formal Status of EU Law: Defending the Judicial Vision

EU scholars have fought very hard to defend the Court of Justice's institutional statements on the formal status of Union law and the conditions under which it applies within Member States.[83] This is despite the continued validity of the normative framework of international law under the EU Treaties. Specifically, a number of legal writers have turned to the theoretical framework of (constitutional) pluralism in an effort to 'rescue' the Court's institutional position on Constitutional Issue No. 1 as an act of judicial constitutional contestation.[84]

Pluralist discourse (re)conceptualises the relationship between Union and Member State legal orders as one of heterarchy not hierarchy. In summary, pluralist scholars consider the Treaty framework's and the Court's divergent statements on Constitutional Issue No. 1 as independent and *equally valid* sovereign claims that co-exist within a shared legal framework. As Klemen summarises, for pluralists,

> the European constitution is not ultimately derived from, and so hierarchically inferior to, national constitutional authority. Nor are the national constitutions ultimately grounded in, and thus hierarchically subordinated to, the European constitutional authority. Instead, both of these are and should be self-standing, and thus co-equal, sources of constitutional authority that overlap *heterarchically*

[83] See esp., D. Curtin, 'The Constitutional Structure of the Union: A Europe of Bits and Pieces' (1993) 30(1) *Common Market Law Review*, 17.

[84] N. MacCormick, 'Beyond the Sovereign State' (1993) 56 *Modern Law Review*, 1; N. Walker, The Idea of Constitutional Pluralism' (2002) 65 *Modern Law Review*, 317; J .H. H. Weiler, 'Federalism without Constitutionalism: Europe's Sonderweg' in K. Nicolaidis and R. Howse (eds.), *The Federal Vision* (Oxford: Oxford University Press, 2001); M. Poiares Maduro, 'Contrapunctual Law: Europe's Constitutional Pluralism in Action' in N. Walker (ed.), *Sovereignty in Transition* (Oxford: Hart Publishing, 2003) and M. Kumm, 'The Jurisprudence of Constitutional Conflict: Constitutional Supremacy in Europe before and after the Constitutional Treaty' (2005) 11 *European Law Review*, 262.

over a shared piece of territory so that neither of them is really the ultimate authority.[85]

The emergence of pluralist discourse in EU legal scholarship in the 1990s can be seen as a direct response to Member States' refusal to normalise – *de jure* or *de facto* – the Court of Justice's position on Constitutional Issue No. 1. That refusal posed a significant intellectual challenge for legal scholars. As argued in Chapter 3, EU legal scholars had previously rationalised the Court's statements on Constitutional Issue No. 1 as part of an ongoing exercise to 'transform' the (then) Community into a transnational quasi-federal legal order.[86]

Member States' refusal to normalise the Court's statements on Constitutional Issue No. 1 *de jure* or *de facto* required EU legal scholars to refresh the foundations of the Court's normative view of the EU as a quasi-federal transnational legal order. The original constitutionalisation narrative no longer matched the legal and political reality of European integration. Pluralism provided EU legal scholars with the necessary intellectual platform to square the circle. As Avbelj summarises,

> The new wave of [pluralist] constitutionalism has strived to distinguish itself from the classical constitutionalism due to its too strong reliance on the framework of a federal state, and due to its excessive and unrealistic insistence on unity, uniformity and overall hierarchical top-down constitutional structure of the Union. As these kind of, more or less, unilaterally imposed constitutional characteristics have never been truly internalized by [the] national constitutional pole of integration ... the revised constitutionalisms recognized the need for more imaginative solutions.[87]

In contrast to Member State responses (Section 1), pluralist accounts of EU integration continue to accept the ultimate validity of the Court of Justice's position on Constitutional Issue No. 1. The Court's jurisprudence on direct effect and primacy – as before under the original 'constitutionalisation' thesis – underpins pluralist theories of European integration. Indeed, despite the apparent shift away from the language

[85] J. Klemen, *Constitutional Pluralism in the EU* (Oxford: Oxford University Press, 2014) at pp. 4–5.

[86] See E. Stein, 'Lawyers, Judges, and the Making of a Transnational Constitution' (1981) 75 *American Journal of International Law*, 1; F. Mancini, 'The Making of a Constitution for Europe' (1989) 26 *Common Market Law Review*, 595 and J. H. H. Weiler, 'The Transformation of Europe' (1991) 100 *Yale Law Journal*, 2403. See also, earlier, A. W. Green, *Political Integration by Jurisprudence* (Leiden: Sijthoff, 1969).

[87] Avbelj, 'Questioning EU Constitutionalisms', n. 3 at p. 22.

of hierarchy and competing sovereign claims, pluralist accounts remain premised on an acceptance of the Court of Justice's case law on direct effect and primacy. As Avbelj argues, 'the revised constitutionalisms have inherited the formal constitution from the classical constitutional narrative. The doctrines of supremacy, direct effect, pre-emption and human rights protection, establishing a hierarchical structural framework of the integration have, despite the widespread commitments to constitutional pluralism, largely remained the unquestioned Articles of Faith.'[88]

EU scholars working within the recast pluralist paradigm simply accept – as before – the basic validity of the Court's position on Constitutional Issue No. 1 on its own terms. The only difference is that, through the pluralist lens, the Luxembourg Court's claims are placed in a new relationship with those of the Member States. In that relationship, the Court of Justice's institutional position is attributed *equal status* with the contrary views maintained by Member States. As outlined earlier, the latter position, which remains embedded in the EU Treaties as constitutional touchstones, continues to conceptualise European integration with explicit reference to the principles and practice of international treaty law.

3.2 Legal Scholarship on the Court: A Fivefold Typology

Legal scholars' adherence to, and (through pluralism) defence of, the Court's statements on Constitutional Issue No. 1 matters. It directly conditions their responses to critiquing the Court of Justice. In line with their acceptance of the Court's response on that first issue for EU constitutionalism, most legal scholars continue – both explicitly and implicitly – to view the Luxembourg Court in its own image; that is, as a *de facto* EU Constitutional Court that, the Treaties notwithstanding, exercises near-complete judicial review powers both horizontally and vertically.

From that perspective, it is possible to sketch out a broad typology of five principal measures of legitimacy in the main English language legal studies of the Court and judicial interpretation. That typology is indicative of general trends in the literature and is not exhaustive. Legitimacy is, of course, a hotly contested and multifaceted concept, and this section

[88] See also, Avbelj, 'Questioning EU Constitutionalisms', n. 3 at pp. 23–24.

does not offer or superimpose a fixed definition.[89] Rather, it uses the existing literature to construct an understanding of how EU legal scholars understand legitimacy in connection with the scrutiny of EU judicial activity. In other words, this chapter does *not* ask what legitimacy *can be*, but rather *how it is presently constructed* in the EU scholarship on the Court.

As our typology reveals, aspects of the existing scholarship critiquing EU judicial interpretation overlap with the specific acts of judicial constitutional contestation identified in Chapters 3–5. For example, the Court's position on the formal status of EU law and the conditions under which its applies within Member State (Constitutional Issue No. 1) (Chapter 3) shares much in common with criticism of the Court's broad functional approach to Treaty interpretation (the third approach in our typology). Likewise, the Court's use of directly effective EU norms to challenge the Union legislature's policy choices (Constitutional Issue No. 3) (Chapter 5) may be linked with analysis of the Court of Justice's compliance with generally accepted standards of good constitutional adjudication (the fifth approach). The important point to stress, however, is that the overlapping concerns raised in the existing scholarship on these and other matters do not expressly link criticism of the Court's interpretative choices with the function of the EU Treaty framework as constitutional touchstone. It is that omission that this monograph addresses.

The *first* approach in our typology scrutinises EU judicial activity for compliance with the Court's own standards of judicial interpretation – standards that, as is generally accepted, typically privilege a highly functional approach to interpretation that is predisposed to advancing European integration. On that approach, which underpins much of the scholarship on EU law, the assessment of the Court's performance as a judicial institution is largely self-referential.

Bengoetxea's study of the Court's interpretative methods is the primary example of this broad self-referential approach to the scrutiny of

[89] For analysis of conceptions of legitimacy in EU judicial interpretation, see e.g., G. A. Caldeira and J. L. Gibson, 'The Legitimacy of the Court of Justice in the European Union: Models of Institutional Support' (1995) 89 *American Political Science Review*, 356 and N. Huls, M. Adams and J. Bomhoff (eds.), *The Legitimacy of Highest Courts' Rulings: Judicial Deliberations and Beyond* (The Hague: Asser Press, 2009). See also, V. A. Schmidt, 'Democracy and Legitimacy in the European Union' in E. Jones, A. Menon and S. Weatherill (eds.), *The Oxford Handbook of the European Union* (Oxford: Oxford University Press, 2012).

EU judicial activity.[90] Building on the work of MacCormick and Weinberger on the Institutional Theory of Law, Bengoetxea offers a rational reconstruction of the Court's interpretative framework, coupled with a normative argument that the validity of its judgments should be assessed against that framework.[91] For Bengoetxea, what gives individual judgments their legitimacy is the extent to which they may be said to fit the institutional form of its previous decisions – a form which is itself generated by the Court through its practice. More recently, Beck has revived interest in the study of the Court's own interpretative techniques in connection with the justification of judicial decisions.[92] His particular focus is on the identification and systematisation of the range of 'steadying factors' that exist to manage judicial decision-making as an exercise in legal reasoning.[93]

The self-referential approach to legitimacy conditions much of the scholarship on EU law. It also underpins key works on the Court in political science literature.[94] Broadly speaking, the Court s confirmed preference for a broad and highly functional approach to interpretation is viewed uncritically as the accepted paradigm structuring EU judicial lawmaking and its limits. Its normative support is drawn, on the one hand, from an acceptance among scholars of the Court's view of the European Union as a 'new legal order' detached from the normative framework of international law. It is reinforced, on the other hand, by a belief that the new legal order justifies the Court's assertion of distinctive interpretative tools – and its preference for a teleological interpretation in particular. As Conway notes,

> The attributed novelty or *sui generis* character [of the EU legal order] was a potent tool for establishing a new frame of reference freed from pre-existing ideas of the normative limits on institutional powers of government, and seems to have been consciously deployed with this in mind. The effect was to make criticism of the

90 J. Bengoetxea, *The Legal Reasoning of the European Court of Justice: Towards a European Jurisprudence* (Oxford: Oxford University Press, 1993).

91 N. MacCormick and O. Weinberger, *An Institutional Theory of Law: New Approaches to Legal Positivism* (Dortrecht: Springer, 1986).

92 G. Beck, *The Legal Reasoning of the Court of Justice of the EU* (Oxford: Hart Publishing, 2013). See also, S. Sankari, *European Court of Justice Legal Reasoning in Context* (Groningen: Europa Law Publishing, 2013).

93 Beck, *The Legal Reasoning of the Court of Justice of the EU*, n. 92, chapter 11.

94 A. Stone Sweet, *Governing with Judges*, n. 48; A. Stone Sweet, *The Judicial Construction of Europe* (Oxford: Oxford University Press, 2004) and K. Alter, *The European Court's Political Power* (Oxford: Oxford University Press, 2009).

EU institutions, and of the ECJ in particular, based on a traditional separation of powers seem misdirected or outmoded.[95]

The strength of the Court's dynamism in key areas has often left scholars to play catch-up in their efforts to rationalise (and legitimise) its approach to interpretation in line with its institutional preferences. Poiares Maduro, for example, retrospectively fashioned a new normative model to justify the Court's dynamic approach to the interpretation of Article 34 TFEU on the free movement of goods.[96] On his analysis, that body of jurisprudence finds justification in its corrective impact on national political processes. The Court's intervention, it is argued, functions in proxy for the political interests of 'out of state' actors that are not represented at Member State level. Needless to say, such justification is entirely absent from the Court's own reasoning.[97] Similarly, from a political science perspective, Stone Sweet has (re)modeled the Court of Justice to align more closely with its repeated challenges to Member States as constituent authorities. On his analysis, the Court of Justice may be understood as a 'trustee' of European integration (and thus, unilateral defender of its values as it sees them) as opposed to simply an agent of the Member States.[98]

The self-referential character of much of the scholarship on EU law – and judicial interpretation more specifically – is linked in part to the unquestionable effectiveness of the Court's work to advance integration. On a measure of output legitimacy that accepts its preferred approach to judicial interpretation, the Court has historically scored highly. It may claim considerable institutional responsibility for the successful completion of a functioning internal market; the advancement of economic and social objectives; and the enhancement of fundamental rights within the Union. However, as a proxy for legitimacy, effectiveness is, of course, no longer beyond challenge. In particular, as integration has broadened and

95 G. Conway, *The Limits of Legal Reasoning and the European Court of Justice* (Cambridge: Cambridge University Press, 2012) at p. 39.

96 M. Poiares Maduro, *We the Court: The European Court of Justice and the European Economic Constitution* (Oxford: Hart Publishing, 1998). See also, with respect more generally to the constitutional foundations of the EU legal order, R. Barents, *The Autonomy of Community Law* (The Hague: Kluwer, 2004) and R. Schutze, *From Dual to Cooperative Federalism: The Changing Structure of European Law* (Oxford: Oxford University Press, 2009).

97 Poiares Maduro, *We the Court*, n. 96, chapter 5.

98 S. Stone Sweet, 'The European Court of Justice and the Judicialization of EU Governance' (2011) *Faculty Scholarship Series*, Paper 70. For broader discussion, see also, K. Alter, 'Agents or Trustees? International Courts in Their Political Context' (2008) 14(1) *European Journal of International Relations*, 33.

deepened, scholars have expressed increased concern about the Court's role in the development of Union policymaking.[99] There is, *inter alia*, open disagreement with respect to the Court's interpretative choices in specific fields of policymaking, its encroachment into national welfare systems and its privileged treatment of individual rights over collective interests.[100]

The *second* of our key measures of legitimacy is not content to view the world of judicial interpretation as the Court of Justice sees it. Instead, the aim in this second strand of scholarship is to formulate and defend alternative normative models of judicial reasoning to manage the exercise of the Court's interpretative functions. This remains very much a minority position in the legal scholarship, with Conway's study occupying a central position among the body of critical outliers.[101] In summary, Conway constructs a normative scheme of judicial reasoning that is rooted in a fixed hierarchy of interpretive norms. That hierarchy privileges ordinary linguistic interpretation, coupled, where necessary, with a model of 'objective originalist interpretation' over the Court's current highly functional approach, which he characterises as 'meta-teleological' in character.[102] In the final analysis, under this normative framework, 'A judge should decide on the basis of the most specific legal or constitutional provision, as supplemented by originalist interpretation if ordinary meaning is not decisive, and should explain and justify the extent of choice within that framework.'[103] Conway defends his alternative normative model with reference to the separation of powers, which, he maintains, is linked to the 'twin pillars of modern constitutionalism: democracy and the rule of law'.[104] He is critical of efforts by the Court,

[99] See e.g., D. Grimm, 'The Democratic Costs of Constitutionalisation: The European Case' (2015) 21(4) *ELJ* 460 and F. Scharpf, 'Perpetual Momentum: Directed and Unconstrained?' (2012) 19(1) *Journal of European Public Policy*, 127.

[100] See e.g., C. Newdick, 'Citizenship, Free Movement and Health Care: Cementing Individual Rights by Corroding Social Solidarity' (2006) 43(6) *Common Market Law Review*, 1645; S. Gerards, 'Pluralism, Deference and the Margin of Appreciation Doctrine' (2011) 17(1) *European Law Review*, 80 and F. de Witte, 'Sex, Drugs & EU law: The Recognition of Moral and Ethical Diversity in EU Law' (2013) 50(6) *Common Market Law Review*, 1545.

[101] See J. Bengoetxea, 'Text and Telos in the European Court of Justice: Four Recent Takes on the Legal Reasoning of the ECJ' (2015) *European Constitutional Law Review*, 184 at p. 196

[102] Defined, in full, as: 'meta-teleological interpretation, where broad systemic considerations [are] used to justify an interpretation that [is] contrary to both text and to legal tradition'. See Conway, *The Limits of Legal Reasoning and the European Court of Justice*, n. 95 at p. 205.

[103] Conway, *The Limits of Legal Reasoning and the European Court of Justice*, n. 95 at p. 163.

[104] *Ibid.*, at p. 279.

but also in the scholarship, to detach the EU legal order from traditional (Western) accounts of the separation of powers through, in particular, appeals to the distinctive substitute concept of 'institutional balance'. Conway's normative scheme of judicial reasoning targets the Court of Justice but is presented as scalable to other non-EU judicial institutions.

A *third* and equally critical perspective maintains that the legitimacy of EU judicial interpretation is conditional on adherence to the text of the Treaties as a specific canon of interpretation.[105] This perhaps now rather unfashionable approach reached its peak in the mid-1990s but remains detectable in more recent studies. Both Beck and Conway, for instance, attributed particular importance to textual analysis within their respective analyses of EU legal reasoning.[106] In particular, Beck is highly critical of the Court of Justice's departure from textual interpretation in its approach to Article 125 TFEU – the so-called 'no bail-out' clause – in *Pringle*. In rather unvarnished terms, he concludes his study with an assertion that,

> In *Pringle*, the Court turned the natural meaning of Article 125 TFEU on its head and ignored specific monetary and economic policy Treaty objectives . . . It appears that in the current emergency situation, written EU law no longer imposes any effective constrains on the judiciary and that in critical cases which may fundamentally affect the integration process within the EU and the Eurozone as a whole, the law is becoming what the judges say it is whatever the natural meaning of the written law and whatever the written law actually says.[107]

The essence of the third critique is that, through its institutional preference for a broad functional approach to judicial interpretation, the Court of Justice is departing from accepted canons of interpretation recognised in both international and national law. Hartley concluded that its preference to depart from the natural meaning of Treaty provisions could only be explained with reference to its 'pursuance of a settled and consistent policy of promoting European federalism', which also facilitated the extension of the Court's own powers.[108] His critical study

[105] See e.g., the academic exchange between T. Hartley, 'The European Court, Judicial Objectivity and the Constitution of the European Union' (1996) 112 *Law Quarterly Review*, 95 and A. Arnull, 'The European Court, Judicial Objectivity: A Reply to Professor Hartley' (1996) 112 *Law Quarterly Review*, 411.

[106] See also, H. Rasmussen, *On Law and Policy in the European Court of Justice* (Dordrecht: Martinus Nijhoff Publishing, 1986) at p. 12 and, more recently, J. Snell, 'The Legitimacy of Free Movement Case Law: Process and Substance' in Adams et al., *Judging Europe's Judges*, n. 23.

[107] Beck, *The Legal Reasoning of the Court of Justice of the EU*, n. 92 at p. 449.

[108] Hartley, 'The European Court, Judicial Objectivity and the Constitution of the European Union', n. 105 at p. 95.

identified a range of decisions in which the Court of Justice had, in his view most egregiously, ruled contrary to the clear text of the Treaty. These included its judgments in *Van Duyn* (on the direct effect of Directives); *SPI* (on the Court's jurisdiction to hear preliminary references to interpret the GATT); and *Les Verts* (on the European Parliament's standing rights in direct actions for annulment).[109]

Rasmussen's landmark and highly critical work on the Court defines the *fourth* strand of the legitimacy matrix.[110] In a nod to political science, his work accentuates the importance of *external reactions* to the Court's jurisprudence as a measure of legitimacy. As a matter of principle, Rasmussen has no objections to judicial lawmaking *per se* – an activity that he actually defends as a public good under certain preconditions. In particular, he maintains that the EU Court should use its interpretative discretion as a tool to correct (temporary) 'legislative inertia' in Union legislative processes.[111] His concern is, more broadly, with the Court's promotion of integration in the absence of legislative impasses and, most crucially, without due regard for the external responses to its judgments. On his analysis,

> a careful monitoring of the responses of the countervailing powers to activist judgments, and activist series of judgments, offers an adequate tool for establishing when judicial activism is no longer socially acceptable … Only the responses from the body politic offer a satisfactory guideline for assessing when an acceptable judicial activism has become unacceptable … [J]udicial research of activism phenomena must move on to a registration and weighing of both positive and negative policy inputs.[112]

Ultimately, Rasmussen's critique is much less radical than legend now has it. As his conclusions demonstrate, his basic aim is simply to reduce what might be termed the 'non-acceptability' of EU Court decisions through improvements to its decision-making and docket control processes.[113] On the first issue, he calls for the Court to have access to, and engage fully with, detailed social, economic and technical information in

109 Case 41/74, *Van Duyn* v. *Home Office* EU:C:1974:133; Joined Cases 267/81, 268/81 and 269/81, *Amministrazione delle Finanze dello Stato* v. *SPI and SAMI* EU:C:1983:78 and Case 294/83, *Parti écologiste "Les Verts"* v. *European Parliament* EU:C:1986:166.

110 Rasmussen, *On Law and Policy in the European Court of Justice*, n. 106.

111 *Ibid.*, at pp. 8–9.

112 *Ibid.*, at p. 188.

113 See Rasmussen, *On Law and Policy in the European Court of Justice*, n. 106, chapters 13 and 14, respectively.

order to support its interpretive choices – labelled 'socio-economic fact briefings'.[114] The concern here is essentially to enhance the quality of the Court's interpretative functions, largely by bringing judicial adjudication closer in line with the Union's deliberative policymaking processes. On the second point, Rasmussen argues for the introduction of a stricter system of docket control at the Court, drawing comparisons with the US Supreme Court. A stricter mechanism, he maintains, would furnish the Luxembourg Court with an effective tool to enable it to manage its exposure to potentially contentious acts of judicial policymaking.[115]

Once again, there are traces of the third approach to legitimacy, pioneered by Rasmussen, across the body of legal scholarship critiquing EU judicial interpretation. Bobek, for example, has argued that, within the context of the preliminary ruling procedure, the legitimacy of the Court's approach should be measured, in part, with reference to the needs and reasonable expectations of Member State courts. More specifically, he concludes that:

> The yardstick for assessing the legitimacy of the Court's case law is . . . functional legitimacy with respect to national courts. Feasible, understandable guidance, which is at least somewhat compatible with the work and function of a normal, mortal judge, can be considered legitimate. Conversely, case law setting impossible requirements, uselessly upsetting or completing atomising national procedures, disregarding Member States' courts interest in the name of full effectiveness of EU law will be, in the eyes of national judges, devoid of such functional legitimacy.[116]

Finally, EU legal scholars scrutinise EU judicial activity for compliance with generally accepted standards of good constitutional adjudication. This *fifth* approach is by far the most dominant, with concerns over the *quality* of the Court's reasoning entirely eclipsing all others as the most serious deficiency. As Adams et al. summarise, scholarly critiques of the legitimacy of the EU Court's interpretative choices for adherence to (Western) norms of good constitutional adjudication are essentially reducible to probing, 'Whether the [Court's] judgments display sufficient consistency, whether the outcomes are well-founded, whether the

[114] *Ibid.*, chapter 13.

[115] *Ibid.*, chapter 14.

[116] R. Bobek, 'Of Feasibility and Silent Elephants: The Legitimacy of the Court of Justice through the Eyes of National Courts' in Adams et al., *Judging Europe's Judges*, n. 23 at p. 214.

results were reasonably predictable and whether the ECJ defers to the EU legislature and the Member States whenever appropriate.'[117] On the separation of powers, scholars periodically express concerns with specific decisions of the Court that are considered to trespass the proper limits of its judicial role. In recent years, its judgments in, for instance, *Mangold*, *Test Achats*, *Sturgeon and Others*, *Rottmann*, and *Ruiz Zambrano* have attracted particular criticism in that regard.[118] In summary, under this fifth model, there is broad agreement that the Court of Justice's legitimacy is threatened to the extent that it encroaches on the functions of both Member State and EU legislatures. However, as Mazak and Moser rightly note, there is no consensus on the precise 'Archimedean point' at which (legitimate) judicial interpretation becomes (illegitimate) judicial policy-making under the notorious *gouvernement des juges*.[119] Most scholars recognise the existence of limits to proper judicial adjudication as a matter of principle, but are rather quick to exonerate the Court of Justice from any serious wrongdoing in individual instances.[120] Critique, where it exists, is still rather muted – a point to which this chapter will return shortly.

Consistency is another key theme in the scholarship assessing the Court of Justice's performance as a *de facto* EU Constitutional Court. Nic Shuibhne's work in the area of EU free movement law presently offers the most comprehensive study on this point. Her work scrutinises the judicial development of the scope of the EU Treaty provisions on intra-EU movement from the perspective that sustaining case law coherence is a vital 'constitutional responsibility' of the Court of Justice.[121] On her analysis,

> Judges [at the Court of Justice] can properly be expected – and obliged – to be aware of the existing corpus of law and to add judgments to that framework in full consciousness of the public legal resource being unpacked, expanded, and

[117] M. Adams et al., 'Introduction: Judging Europe's Judges', in Adams et al., *Judging Europe's Judges*, n. 23 at p. 8.

[118] Case C-144/04, *Mangold*, n. 65; Case C-236/09, *Test-Achats ASBL and Others* v. *Conseil des ministres* EU:C:2011:100; Joined Cases C-402/07 and Case C-432/07, *Sturgeon*, n. 79; Case C-135/08, *Rottman*, n. 77 and Case C-34/09, *Ruiz Zambrano* v. *Office national de l'emploi* EU:C:2011:124.

[119] J. Mazak and M. Moser, 'Adjudication by Reference to General Principles of EU Law: A Second Look at the Mangold Case Law', in Adams et al., *Judging Europe's Judges*, n. 23 at pp. 64–67.

[120] See recently and forcefully, J. H. H. Weiler, 'Epilogue: Judging the Judges – Apology and Critique' in Adams et al., *Judging Europe's Judges*, n. 23.

[121] N. Nic Shuibhne, *The Coherence of EU Free Movement Law: Constitutional Responsibility and the Court of Justice* (Oxford: Oxford University Press, 2013).

sometimes profoundly changed in consequence. Added to that, the application of appropriate practices of engaging with existing authority is how the judges then show us their work'[122]

Nic Shuibhne identifies a number of sites of fragmentation in the Court's jurisprudence on intra-EU movement, together with their drivers. Her conception of constitutional responsibility is constructed with reference to standards of good constitutional adjudication outlined by the International Law Commission.[123] Although she does not conclude that there is any 'major breakdown or crisis' in the EU Court's case law, she exposes the existence of 'distinct pockets of damaging case law fragmentation', which generate a 'systemic problem' for legitimacy that is greater than the sum of its parts.[124]

The final component of the constitutional adjudication critique – concerning the quality of the Court's reasoning – is a topic on which there is the strongest, and most critical consensus in the legal scholarship. Whereas most scholars operating within the fifth paradigm ultimately defend the Court's approach to the exercise of its interpretative functions, nearly all accept deficiencies in the quality of its reasoning. The Court of Justice's reasoning has been characterised as 'cryptic and Cartesian'[125] and 'circumloquacious'[126] or, more often, just simply poor.[127] Decisions of immense constitutional, political and socio-economic significance are routinely delivered as short, sparsely reasoned proclamations. The Grand Chamber's 2009 decision in *Ruiz Zambrano*, conferring upon third country national parents the right to reside (and work) in the Member State of which their children are nationals, is a standout example (Chapter 5).[128] That seismic legal development in the scope of protection afforded to EU citizens and their third country national family members – beyond the scope of the applicable EU legislative framework – was delivered in just seven short substantive paragraphs.

122 *Ibid.*, at p. 7.
123 *Ibid.*, chapter 1.
124 *Ibid.*, at pp. 257–259.
125 J. H. H. Weiler, 'Epilogue: The Judiciary Après Nice' in G. de Búrca and J. H. H. Weiler (eds.), *The European Court of Justice* (Oxford: Oxford University Press, 2001) at p. 225.
126 S. Weatherill, 'The Court's Case Law on the Internal Market: A Circumloquacious Statement of the Result, Rather than a Reason for Arriving at It?' in Adams et al, *Judging Europe's Judges*, n. 23.
127 See e.g., K. Heilbronner and D. Thym, Case C-34/09, *Gerardo Ruiz Zambrano* v. *Office national de l'emploi (ONEm)*, Judgment of the Court of Justice (Grand Chamber) of 8 March 2011 (Case Comment) (2011) 49 *Common Market Law Review*, 1253 and N. Nic Shuibhne, 'Seven Questions for Seven Paragraphs' (Editorial) (2011) 36 *European Law Review*, 161.
128 Case C-34/09, *Ruiz Zambrano*, n. 118.

3.3 Legal Scholarship on the Court: Summary

Overall, the five broad strands of critique in the legal scholarship all display a strong degree of deference to the Court of Justice. This is most clear to see, of course, with respect to the first approach, which conceives legitimacy as a self-referential exercise in monitoring the Court against its own standards. Historically, EU scholars have proved extremely reluctant to find fault with the Luxembourg Court. Alter describes the early literature on the Court as the product of a 'legal lobby in support of ECJ jurisprudence and ECJ authority'.[129] Similarly, writing in 1996, Shaw pointed to the general acceptance of the Court's 'constitutionalisation' narrative among legal scholars.[130] As Conway notes, this reluctance to criticise the Court of Justice may, in part, be explained with reference to the uniquely proximate relationship between officials at the Court (and those working within the Union institutions more generally) and the academic community.[131] The strength of that institutional incestuousness has undoubtedly diminished over time, but its footprint remains nonetheless.

Isolated challenges to the Court of Justice – and the legitimacy of EU judicial interpretation – have historically been met with robust responses. Most famously perhaps, Rasmussen's (in places)[132] admittedly rather provocative study on the Court was the object of fierce derision in the commentary.[133] Similarly, EU writers close to the Court were quick to come to its defence when its departure from the ordinary meaning of Treaty provisions was put under the spotlight in subsequent analyses.[134]

129 Alter, *Establishing the Supremacy of European Law*, n. 42 at p. 58.

130 J. Shaw, European Legal Studies in Crisis? Towards a New Dynamic' (1996) 16(2) *Oxford Journal of Legal Studies*, 231 at p. 233.

131 Conway, *The Limits of Legal Reasoning and the European Court of Justice*, n. 95 at pp. 55–56.

132 See in particular, his characterisation of the Court of Justice's case law on the direct effect of Directives as 'revolting judicial behaviour'. Rasmussen, *On Law and Policy in the European Court of Justice*, n. 106 at p. 12.

133 See esp., J. H. H. Weiler, 'The Court of Justice on Trial: A Review of Hjalte Rasmussen, *On Law and Policy in the European Court of Justice*' (1987) 24 *Common Market Law Review*, 555. See also, M. Cappelletti, 'Is the European Court of Justice "Running Wild?"' (1987) 12 *European Law Review*, 4 and A. G. Toth, 'On Law and Policy in the European Court of Justice' (1987) *Yearbook of European Law*, 411.

134 See e.g., Arnull, 'The European Court, Judicial Objectivity', n. 105 and D. Edward, 'Judicial Activism – Myth or Reality' in A. Campbell and M. Voyatzi (eds.), *Legal Reasoning and Judicial Interpretation in European Law: Essays in Honour of Lord Mackenzie Stuart* (London: Trenton Publishing, 1996). See also, K. Lenaerts, 'The Court's Outer and Inner Selves: Exploring the External and Internal Legitimacy of the European Court of Justice', in Adams et al., *Judging Europe's Judges*, n. 23, chapter 1.

The passage of time has witnessed an increased openness towards and interest in less deferential approaches to the Court of Justice, as exemplified by Conway's and Nic Shuibhne's critical studies. This no doubt reflects the inherently cyclical nature of legal research as a discipline, where the forgotten is readily resurrected and re-examined as a means to shatter ossified intellectual paradigms. At the same time, it also likely reflects an increasingly shared awareness of the strengths and weakness of the Court's approach. Nonetheless, and whilst a welcome trend, critical analysis of the EU Court and the exercise of its interpretative functions remains tied to the legitimacy typology sketched out earlier.

Most legal scholars, however critical, continue to see the Court as that the institution wishes to be seen, namely as a *de facto* EU Constitutional Court. Analysis of the application of the EU Treaty framework *to the Court* as an institution of the Union – the focus of this monograph – is virtually absent from the current legitimacy matrix. As the preceding typology has shown, the concerns that several commentators have raised with respect to the Court's interpretative choices do overlap, to a certain extent, with the acts of judicial constitution contestation identified in Chapters 3–5. However, these parallels notwithstanding, a fundamental distinction remains: the existing scholarship does not expressly link scrutiny of the Court's interpretative choices with the function of the EU Treaty framework as constitutional touchstone.

Concluding Remarks

This chapter examined the responses of the Court's principal interlocutors (Member States, national courts and EU scholars) to the acts of judicial constitutional contestation identified in Chapters 3–5. Its principal aim was to assess the extent to which the Court's interlocutors – and, most crucially, Member State and national courts – have normalised the identified acts of judicial constitutional contestation through acceptance *de jure* or *de facto*.

Section 1 assessed the responses of Member States – both collectively as Treaty signatories and also individually – to the Court's statements on the formal status of Union law and the conditions under which it applies within Member States (Constitutional Issue No. 1) (Chapter 3). As Treaty signatories, Member States were shown not to have normalised *de jure* or *de facto* the Court's divergent position on Constitutional Issue No. 1. The Treaty framework, as the embodiment of the collective will of Member States as constituent authorities, continues as before to display all the hallmarks of ordinary treaties, the implementation of which is firmly rooted in the framework of international law. For individual Member States and their respective national courts, the domestic application of EU law also remains, in accordance with the EU Treaties, entirely contingent on national constitutional law. A review of the domestic constitutional landscape revealed the existence of twenty-eight different national approaches to the domestic implementation of EU law as international law. The process of domestic implementation is characteristically asymmetrical, predominantly court-led and largely stable as a matter of practical politics.

Section 2 considered Member State reactions to the Court's position on the locus of political authority within the EU legal order (Constitutional Issue No. 2) (Chapter 4) and the objectives, values and limits governing European integration (Constitutional Issue No. 3) (Chapter 5). Acting collectively as Treaty signatories, Member States were shown to have employed a range of distinct tools with varying degrees of intensity in response to the Court's statements on both issues.[135] These tools are comprised of isolated attempts to reverse specific decisions of the Court; to exclude its jurisdiction in sensitive policy areas; and to introduce discrete clawback provisions into the Treaty framework. At *national* level, there is also (growing) evidence of Member State courts 'pushing back' against the Court of Justice. National courts have expressed clear concerns regarding the quality of the Court's engagement as direct policy-maker with the objectives, values and limits governing European integration (Constitutional Issue No. 3) (Chapter 5).

Importantly, Member State responses to the Court's statements on all three Constitutional Issues do not close the 'feedback loop'. On the contrary, the responses at both Union and national levels remain in a dynamic relationship with the Court of Justice, which may yet have another opportunity to (re)assert its institutional preferences against those of the Member States. Indeed, where Member States have secured collective agreement at Union level to reverse specific decisions of the Court, exclude its jurisdiction or introduce specific clawback provisions, the Court of Justice has often subsequently succeeded, at least in part, in curtailing the scope of these measures.[136] Equally, it is also open to the

[135] See also, Arnull, 'Me and My Shadow: The European Court of Justice and the Disintegration of European Union Law', n. 1.

[136] See e.g., Case C-57/93, *Vroege* EU:C:1994:352 (interpreting the Barber Protocol) and Case C-105/03 *Pupino* EU:C:2005:386 (interpreting Art. 34(2)(b) TEU).

Court of Justice to respond to instances of 'push back' on the part of national courts. Here the Court has proven decidedly less responsive as its adherence to its jurisprudence on non-discrimination on grounds of age (*Mangold*) and air passenger rights (*Sturgeon and Others*) demonstrates. In these and other areas, the Court of Justice has robustly defended its institutional preferences despite strong criticism from numerous Member State courts.[137]

Section 3 examined EU legal scholars' responses to the Court's jurisprudence on the three key issues for EU constitutionalism. EU scholars have taken a very different approach to Member States and national courts. This is most clear to see with respect to Constitutional Issue No. 1, addressing the formal status of Union law and the conditions under which it applies within Member States (Chapter 3). In contrast to Member States, EU scholars have sought vigorously to defend the Court's vision of the Union as a 'new legal order' *on its own terms*, notwithstanding the continuing validity of the international law framework as the basis of EU integration under the Treaties.[138] This position should not surprise. The Court's transformation of the EU legal order through its responses on the three issues for EU constitutionalism – and Constitutional Issue No. 1, in particular – was, to a considerable extent, 'co-produced' with EU legal scholars.

EU legal scholars' general adherence to, and robust defence of, the Court's responses on the key issues for EU constitutionalism is significant. It directly informs approaches to the scrutiny of EU judicial activity, including assessments of the Court's role as direct policymaker. Adhering to the Court's institutional statements, most EU legal scholars continue to see the Court of Justice in its own image as a *de facto* EU Constitutional Court that exercises near-complete judicial review powers both horizontally and vertically. That baseline, which remains wholly unsupported by the Treaties, was shown to have given rise to particular dynamics in assessments of judicial interpretation and its limits. Questions of legitimacy are construed not with reference to the Treaty framework as constitutional touchstone, but instead as instances of constitutional adjudication, in line with the Court's institutional position on the three key issues for EU constitutionalism. The main

[137] See e.g., Case C-555/07, *Kücükdeveci*, n66; Joined Cases C-581/10 and Case C-629/20, *Nelson and Others* v. *Deutsche Lufthansa AG and TUI Travel plc and Others* v. *Civil Aviation Authority* EU:C:2012:657 and Case C-441/14, *Ajos A/S* v. *Estate of Karsten Eigil Rasmussen*, n. 66.

[138] See esp., Avbelj, 'Questioning EU Constitutionalisms', n. 3.

criticism in the legal scholarship at present is with the economy and quality of the Court's reasoning.

Chapter 7 concludes the assessment of EU judicial activity for compliance with the EU Treaty framework as constitutional touchstone. It brings together the conclusions in Chapters 3–5 (isolating acts of judicial constitutional contestation) with analysis, in this chapter, of the responses of the Court's interlocutors. The result is the identification of three contemporary problems with EU judicial lawmaking. Thereafter, it offers four specific reform proposals in outline form in an effort to enhance the legitimacy of EU judicial activity.

7 Conclusion

Three Contemporary Problems, Four Reform Proposals

Whilst the Court's contribution to European integration is widely considered beneficial in politically correct discourses, its impact on the constitutional balance of the multilevel European polity does raise serious problems . . . The question is whether there are, or could be, countervailing mechanisms that would defend or restore the constitutional balance.

F. Scharpf, 'Perpetual Momentum: Directed and Unconstrained?' (2012) 19(1) *Journal of European Public Policy*, 127 at p. 134.

Introduction

This book has assessed how far the Court of Justice complies with the EU Treaty framework in the exercise of its attributed functions. The use of the EU Treaty framework to scrutinise the Court's interpretative choices is an innovative approach to the study of EU judicial lawmaking and its limits. Legal scholars (and the Court itself) presently overlook the application *to the Court* of the EU Treaty framework as a tool to determine the internal constitutionality of its institutional activities. The core claim of this book is that such an entrenched perspective fundamentally obscures the Court's position within the EU legal order as an institution of the Union. The implications of that claim are potentially transformative when coupled with the Court's historically dynamic approach to the exercise of its interpretative functions.

Chapter 1 explored the status and function of the EU Treaty framework as principal touchstone on the internal constitutionality of EU judicial activity. It argued that the EU Treaties indeed remain the key baselines when assessing the internal constitutionality, and hence legitimacy, of all Union institutional activity – including the work of the Court. Furthermore, the EU Treaty framework was also shown to provide clear statements on what this book defined as the three basic issues for

EU constitutionalism: *the formal status of Union law and the conditions under which it applies within Member States* (Constitutional Issue No. 1); *the locus of political authority within the EU legal order* (Constitutional Issue No. 2); and *the objectives, values and limits governing European integration* (Constitutional Issue No. 3).

Chapter 2 placed analysis of the EU Treaty framework's status and function as constitutional touchstone within the broader legal and political context that structures EU integration. In summary, it argued that the Treaties' function as touchstones is conditioned by acts of *constitutional supplementation* and *constitutional contestation*. The former, constitutional supplementation, references acts of the EU institutions (and also Member States) that elaborate – but do not fundamentally contest – the EU Treaties' basic statements on the three key issues for EU constitutionalism. By contrast, the latter refers to acts of the EU institutions (and Member States) that expressly contest the Treaties' clear position on the three basic issues for EU constitutionalism.

Chapters 3–5 employed the framework developed in Chapters 1–2 to identify specific acts of *judicial* constitutional contestation across all three key issues for EU constitutionalism. Chapter 6 then considered the *responses* of the Court's interlocutors (Member States, national courts and EU scholars) to the acts of judicial constitutional contestation identified in Chapters 3–5. Its principal aim was to assess the extent to which the Court's interlocutors – and, most crucially, Member States and national courts – have normalised the acts of judicial constitutional contestation with the Treaty framework *de jure* or *de facto*.

This chapter considers the implications that follow the assessment of EU judicial activity for compliance with the EU Treaty framework as constitutional touchstone. Section 1 begins by identifying three contemporary problems with EU judicial lawmaking. These problems emerge by reading the conclusions in Chapters 3–5 (isolating acts of judicial constitutional contestation) alongside the responses of the Court's interlocutors explored in Chapter 6. Thereafter, Section 2 argues that the existence of these problems places the Court of Justice at the very centre of crucial debates over EU integration, its limits and, most acutely, the democratic credentials of Union policymaking.

The application of the Treaty framework *to the Court* as a means to problematise that institution's role within the EU legal order represents this monograph's primary contribution to the scholarship on European integration. Nonetheless, by way of conclusion, this book also asks how the Court and its interlocutors can (and should) respond to the existence of the three contemporary problems for EU judicial activity identified in this chapter. Section 3 offers some initial reflections in response to that important second-order concern. Specifically, it sets out four reform proposals to manage the Court's institutional role within the Treaty framework as a Union institution. The four proposals are presented in outline form only as part of a constructive effort to enhance the legitimacy of the Court's contribution to EU integration.

1 Three Contemporary Problems for EU Judicial Lawmaking

1.1 Problem No. 1: Judicial Challenges to Constituent Authority

The first contemporary problem centres on the Court's approach to *constituent authority*. As a review of its case law has exposed, the Court of Justice has repeatedly challenged clear statements of constituent authority. In particular, the Court routinely invokes its own institutional responses on the three issues for EU constitutionalism – developed without regard to the Treaty framework as constitutional touchstone – as 'supra-constitutional norms' to overturn, adjust or simply interrogate clear statements of constituent authority (Chapter 4). Examples include its use of its institutional position on the formal status of Union law and the conditions under which EU law applies within national legal systems (Constitutional Issue No. 1) to challenge the competence of Member States to revise the Treaties pursuant to (now) Article 48 TEU (e.g., *Parliament* v. *Council (Chernobyl)* and *Francovich*).[1] Similarly, in *Opinion 2/13*, the Court explicitly referenced its institutional statements on Constitutional Issue No. 1 to support its conclusion that the Draft EU/ECHR Accession Agreement was incompatible with Union law.[2]

The Court's institutional approach to constituent authority within the Union legal order persists as a paradigm example of judicial constitutional contestation. As Chapter 6 demonstrated, the Court's position on the locus of political authority within the EU legal order (Constitutional Issue No. 2) – and constituent authority specifically – has not been

[1] Case C-70/88, *Parliament and Council (Chernobyl)* EU:C:1990:217 and Joined Cases C-6/90 and C-9/90, *Francovich and Others* v. *Italy* EU:C:1991:428.

[2] Opinion 2/13, *Draft Agreement on Accession of the EU to the European Convention on Human Rights* EU:C:2014:2454. See also, with specific reference to the Court's position on the autonomy of Union law, Opinion 1/91, *Draft agreement between the Community, on the one hand, and the countries of the European Free Trade Association, on the other, relating to the creation of the European Economic Area* EU:C:1991:490 at para. 2 and Opinion 1/09, *Draft Agreement on the Creation of a Unified Patent Litigation System* EU:C:2011:123 at para. 67.

normalised with the Treaty framework *de jure* or *de facto* Crucially, *neither* the Treaty framework *nor* Member States and their national courts recognise the Court's powerful claim to act as the 'Trustee' of what *it* sees as the guiding principles of European integration. EU legal scholars are alone in defending the Court's divergent approach to constituent authority within the Union legal order. In contrast to the position of Member States and national courts, most writers accept (and rigorously defend) the validity of the Court's institutional statements on the three key issues for EU constitutionalism on the Court's own terms.

As constitutional touchstone, the Treaty framework continues as before under the founding EEC Treaty to establish the Court of Justice within the Union's institutional structure as an agent of the Member States.[3] As Treaty principals or 'Masters of the Treaties', the latter have maintained their collective agreement, through the treaties, to entrust to the Court of Justice responsibility to promote and, together with the Commission, monitor the performance of the EU Treaties. At times, that responsibility affords the Court considerable scope to influence the shape of EU norms and, more broadly, the development of European integration. Judicial interpretation is not, however, without limits. As this book has argued throughout, judicial interpretation remains fundamentally constrained by the Treaty framework as constitutional touchstone – including its unambiguous statements on the locus of constituent authority within the Union legal order.

1.2 Problem No. 2: Judicial Challenges to Treaty Limits on EU Policymaking

The second contemporary problem focuses on *the quality of the Court's engagement, as direct policymaker, with the range of limits that the EU Treaties impose on Union policymaking*. The problem here is most acute where the Court invokes EU norms that it has declared directly effective to neutralise the protective effects of Treaty exclusions on Union *legislative*

[3] See also, A. Arnull, 'Me and My Shadow: The European Court of Justice and the Disintegration of European Union Law' (2007) 31 *Fordham International Law Journal*, 1174 at pp. 1175–177. For analysis of the Court's agency role, see also, M. Pollack, *The Engines of Integration: Delegation, Agency, and Agency Setting in the European Union* (Oxford: Oxford University Press, 2003) and G. Garrett, 'International Cooperation and Institutional Choice: The European Community's Internal Market' (1992) 46 *International Organization*, 533.

competences.[4] Chapter 5 highlighted a range of examples. These focused on the Court's application of the Treaty provisions on intra-EU movement to circumvent express limits on EU legislative competence in discrete areas such as employment (Articles 147 TFEU and 149 TFEU); social policy (153(5) TFEU); education, vocational training, youth and sport (Article 165 TFEU and Article 166 TFEU); culture (Article 167 TFEU); public health (Article 168(7) TFEU); industry (Article 173 TFEU); tourism (Article 195 TFEU) and civil protection (Article 196 TFEU). In each of these areas, the Court was shown robustly to defend the view that directly effective EU norms *displace* express exclusions on EU legislative competence.[5]

The Court's disregard, as direct policymaker, for the limits that the EU Treaty framework imposes on Union legislative policymaking persists as an act of judicial constitutional contestation. First, as Chapters 4 and 6 demonstrated, the Court's move to interpose itself alongside the EU legislature as direct policymaker remains at odds with the Treaty framework's clear position on *the locus of political authority within the EU legal order* (Constitutional Issue No. 2). In line with the founding Treaty, the EU Treaties continue to vest primary responsibility for EU policymaking with the Union's political institutions, namely the Commission, European Parliament and Council. It is these three institutions that the Treaty framework principally empowers to work together in differing formations to produce specific policy outputs.[6]

Secondly, the Court's approach to the restraints that the EU Treaty framework imposes on Union legislative policymaking remains in basic tension with the Treaties' key statements on the *limits* on EU policymaking (Constitutional Issue No. 3). As direct policymaker, the Court should be expected to engage with (and respect) the full range of limits that the Treaties impose on Union policymaking. The argument here is

[4] See e.g., Case C-157/99, *Smits and Peerbooms* EU:C:2001:404; Case C-385/99, *Müller-Fauré and van Riet* EU:C:2003:270; Case C-372/04, *Watts* v. *Bedford Primary Care Trust* EU:C:2006:325 and Case C-438/05, *International Transport Workers' Federation and Finnish Seamen's Union* v. *Viking Line ABP* EU:C:2007:772.

[5] A similar approach can also be seen in its approach to other key Treaty limits on EU policymaking such as Arts. 346 TFEU on national security interests. See e.g., Case 300/11, *ZZ* v. *Secretary of State for the Home Department* EU:C:2013:363; Case C-284/05, *Commission* v. *Finland (Military Equipment)* EU:C:2009:778; Case C-503/03, *Commission* v. *Spain (Schengen Information System)* EU:C:2006:74; Case C-490/04, *Commission* v. *Germany (Posted Workers)* EU:C:2007:430 and Case C-141/07, *Commission* v. *Germany (Pharmacies)* EU:C:2008:492.

[6] See also the role of the European Council in specific policy fields such as the Common Foreign and Security Policy (Title V, chapter 2 TEU).

functional. Through its attribution of direct effect to a range of EU norms, the Court opted to assume additional, direct policymaking responsibilities in parallel to those formally attributed to the EU legislature under the Treaty framework. Its decision to detach Union policymaking from the model of *legislative* policymaking prescribed by the Treaties does not in any sense provide a normative grounding for its disregard of the specific limits that the EU Treaties impose on Union policymaking.

1.3 Problem No. 3: Judicial Challenges to EU Legislative Frameworks

The third contemporary problem is also concerned with the Court's exercise of its (self-asserted) direct policymaking functions – this time along the horizontal axis. Specifically, it is argued that the Court is on normatively contentious ground whenever it opts to *invoke directly effective norms as tools to override, adjust or step beyond the EU legislature's clearly articulated policy choices*. Examples include the Court's application of the principle of equal treatment to circumvent the Union legislature's unambiguous policy choices in the fields of air transport[7] and non-discrimination law.[8] To the same effect, the Court has also repeatedly invoked the Treaty provisions on EU citizenship to recast the boundaries of the EU legislative framework governing the scope of EU citizens' rights of residence and equal treatment.[9]

The Court's use of its direct policymaking platform in order to override, adjust or step beyond the EU legislature's clearly articulated policy choices also remains at odds with the EU Treaty framework. Again, in common with Problem No. 2 (Section 1.2), it contests the EU Treaties' unambiguous statements on the locus of political authority within the EU legal order (Constitutional Issue No. 2). However, along the horizontal axis, the normative tensions run much deeper. Specifically, the

[7] Joined Cases C-402/07 and Case C-432/07, *Sturgeon* v. *Condor Flugdienst GmbH and Böck and Lepuschitz* v. *Air France SA* EU:C:2009:716; Case C-382/08, *Neukirchinger* v *Bezirkshauptmannschaft Grieskirchen* EU:C:2011:27.

[8] Case C-236/09, *Test-Achats ASBL and Others* v. *Conseil des ministres* EU:C:2011:100 and Case C-144/04, *Mangold* v. *Helm* EU:C:2005:709 at para. 75. See e.g., Case C-555/07, *Kücükdeveci* v. *Swedex GmbH & Co. KG* EU:C:2010:21 and Case C-441/14, *Dansk Industri (DI), acting on behalf of Ajos A/S* v. *Estate of Karsten Eigil Rasmussen* EU:C:2016:278.

[9] See e.g., Case C-138/02, *Collins* v. *Secretary of State for Work and Pensions* EU:C:2004:172; Case C-127/08, *Metock and Others* v. *Minister for Justice, Equality and Law Reform* EU:C:2008:449 and Case C-34/09, *Ruiz Zambrano* v. *Office national de l'emploi* EU:C:2011:124.

Court's application of directly effective norms as tools to contest and/or reshape the EU legislature's clearly articulated policy choices is fundamentally at odds with the EU Treaty framework's increasingly strong normative commitment to the value of representative democracy.[10] That commitment finds its clearest expression in Article 10 TEU, which defines representative democracy as the fundamental basis for all EU decision-making.

The Court's recourse to EU norms that it has ruled directly effective to override, adjust or step beyond the EU legislature's clearly articulated policy choices often yields positive outcomes for individual litigants. Nonetheless, measured against the Treaty framework as constitutional touchstone, it has a remarkably distortive effect on Union policymaking. The Court's use of directly effective EU norms to challenge the EU legislature's clearly articulated policy choices disrupts the carefully balanced (and democratically superior) Treaty paradigm for legislative policymaking (Chapter 4).

2 The Three Contemporary Problems: Challenges to the Legitimacy of European Integration

The Court of Justice's challenges to constituent authority (Problem No. 1); to Treaty limits on EU Policymaking (Problem No. 2); and to EU legislative frameworks (Problem No. 3) position that institution at the very centre of crucial debates over EU integration, its limits and, most acutely, the democratic credentials of Union policymaking.[11]

Successive Treaty amendments have sought to place clearer limits on the existence and exercise of EU competences, as well as to introduce new safeguards to protect Member State autonomy in sensitive policy areas.[12] In parallel, far-reaching reforms have also been introduced into

[10] See also, D. Grimm, 'The Democratic Costs of Constitutionalisation: The European Case' (2015) 21(4) *European Law Journal*, 460.

[11] See also, F. Scharpf, 'Perpetual Momentum: Directed and Unconstrained?' (2012) 19(1) *Journal of European Public Policy*, 127 and Grimm, 'The Democratic Costs of Constitutionalisation: The European Case', n. 10.

[12] See the introduction, at Maastricht, of e.g., Art. 3b EEC (now Art. 5 TEU) (on conferral, subsidiarity and proportionality); at Amsterdam, of e.g., Art. F(3) TEU (on national identity), Art. K(5) TEU (on national security), Art. 129(5) EEC (now Art. 168(7) TFEU) (on protection of national healthcare systems); and, at Lisbon, of e.g., Art. 4 TEU and Arts. 2–6 TFEU (on categories of competence), Art. 6 TEU (on the legal status of the EU Charter of Fundamental Rights), Art. 50 TEU (on Member State withdrawal) and Art. 65(4) TFEU (on Member State control over the liberalisation of external capital movements).

the Treaty framework in an effort to bolster the democratic qualities of Union policymaking.[13] Under the post-Lisbon settlement, EU citizens are now positioned at the centre of EU policymaking processes. Citizens contribute to EU policymaking through a multidimensional network of direct engagement (European Citizens' Initiative), direct representation (European Parliament) and also indirect representation (Council and Member State parliaments).[14]

These (and other related) reform initiatives amount to very little if the Court of Justice – one of the most powerful and influential institutions of the Union – remains free to act independently of the Treaty framework as constitutional touchstone. Specifically, judicial challenges to constituent authority (Problem No. 1) and EU legislative frameworks (Problem No. 3) directly undermine progressive efforts to enhance the democratic qualities of EU decision-making. The Court's use of its direct policymaking functions without regard for the ever-increasing range of limits that the EU Treaties now impose on EU legislative policymaking (Problem No. 2) is equally problematic. More precisely, it functions to undermine the effectiveness of ongoing efforts to clarify and, importantly, delimit the scope of Union competence.

The Court of Justice is not, of course, the only institution in history that stands accused of having acted to empower itself against, or at least over and above, the terms of its founding constitutional charter. Similar patterns of institutional self-aggrandisement can be seen in the evolution of various domestic and international legal orders. The US Supreme Court, for example, asserts competence to review the constitutionality of statutes and treaties for compliance with the US Constitution – a competence it claims to derive, in part, from a founding document that makes no reference to the existence of any such power of judicial

[13] See the introduction, in the Single European Act, of e.g., Art. 6 (establishing the co-operative legislative procedure); at Maastricht, of e.g., Art. 8d EEC (now Art. 24 TFEU) (establishing EU citizens' right to petition the European Parliament and engage the EU Ombudsman); at Amsterdam, of e.g., Art. 189b (see now Arts. 289 and 294 TFEU) (extending the co-decision procedure) and, at Lisbon, of e.g., Art. 10 TEU (on the dual democratic basis of the Union), Art. 11(4) TEU and Regulation (EU) No 211/2011 of the European Parliament and of the Council on the citizens' initiative [2011] OJ L65/1 (establishing the European Citizens' Initiative) and Art. 12 TEU (on the role of national parliaments).

[14] See Art. 10 TEU. For judicial confirmation see e.g., Case C-589/15 P, *Anagnostakis* v. *Commission* ECLI:EU:C:2017:663 (on the ECI).

review.[15] As even one of that Court's most ardent textualists,[16] Justice Scalia, conceded,

> The Constitution of the United States says nowhere that the Supreme Court shall be the last word on what the Constitution means. Or that the Supreme Court shall have the authority to disregard statutes enacted by the Congress of the United States on the ground that in its view they do not comport with the Constitution. It doesn't say that anywhere. We [the Supreme Court Justices] made that up.[17]

Comparable trends of judicial empowerment can also be seen in the international context. The Appellate Body of the World Trade Organization, for example, has also transformed its institutional role through judicial interpretation in a manner that challenges contracting parties' clear intentions with respect to the scope and nature of its functions within the WTO legal order.[18]

Likewise, within the EU legal order, the Court of Justice is also not alone in contesting the Treaty framework's responses on the three key issues for EU constitutionalism. As Chapter 2 demonstrated, Member States have mounted periodic challenges to the Treaties' functioning as constitutional touchstones. These include, for instance, making adjustments to the prevailing institutional balance governing Union policy-making under the Treaties and the use of external international treaties to circumvent the Treaty framework's prescribed procedures for Treaty reform.[19] Similarly, as Chapter 5 highlighted, the EU's political and

[15] See also, in the international context and with reference to the activities of the Appellate Body of the World Trade Organization, e.g., R. H. Steinberg, '*Judicial Lawmaking at the WTO: Discursive, Constitutional, and Political Constraints*' (2004) 98 *American Journal of International Law*, 247.

[16] On textualism (or original intent) as a theory of judicial interpretation, see e.g., A. Scalia and B. A. Garner, *Reading the Law: The Interpretation of Legal Texts* (St Paul: Thomson West, 2012).

[17] See A. Scalia, 'Judicial Adherence to the Text of Our Most Basic Law: A Theory of Constitutional Interpretation', public lecture delivered at The Catholic University of America, Washington, DC on 18 October 1996, cited in L. Goldstone, *The Activist: John Marshall, Marbury v. Madison, and the Myth of Judicial Review* (New York: Walker, 2008) at p. 1.

[18] For discussion, see e.g., Steinberg, 'Judicial Lawmaking at the WTO: Discursive, Constitutional, and Political Constraints', n. 15.

[19] See e.g., *Bulletin of the European Communities*, March 1966, 3–66, pp. 5–11 (The so-called 'Luxembourg Compromise'); Treaty establishing the European Stability Mechanism [2012] T/ESM LT/EN 1, and the (now-defunct) Draft Decision of the Heads of State or Government, meeting within the European Council, concerning a New Settlement for the United Kingdom within the European Union [2016] EUCO 4/16.

administrative institutions have tested the limits of the EU Treaties as a source of normative restraint on the exercise of their attributed functions. The EU legislature's effort to circumvent express limits on EU competence through recourse to broadly worded legal bases in the Treaties provides one set of examples.[20]

The identification of acts of judicial self-empowerment in other contexts, as well as evidence of acts of political constitutional contestation within the Union legal order, does not exonerate the Court of Justice. It simply points to the existence of broader issues of internal constitutionality not only within the EU, but also in other legal systems. Moreover, it also highlights the wider significance of the innovative intellectual framework developed in this monograph to scrutinise EU judicial activity. The concepts of constitutional supplementation and constitutional contestation developed in Chapter 2 can be used (or adapted) to provide a normative framework to scrutinise the internal constitutionality of institutional activity within any legal order based on the rule of law. The challenge, of course, is to identify clear statements on the three key issues for constitutionalism within individual legal systems – a relatively straightforward task with reference to the European Union as a system of attributed powers based on international treaties.

3 The Court of Justice and the EU Treaty Framework as Constitutional Touchstone: Four Proposals for Reform

How can (and should) the Court and its interlocutors respond to the existence of our three contemporary problems for EU judicial interpretation? By way of conclusion, this section offers four reform proposals in response to this critical second-order question. The first and second proposals are the most significant. They do not require Treaty amendment and can be actioned immediately. The third and fourth proposals are presented as supplementary. They outline possible options for reform to enhance further the legitimacy of EU judicial activity by aligning this more closely with the Treaty framework as constitutional touchstone.

[20] See most clearly, the EU legislature's use of Art. 114 TFEU (ex Art. 95 EC) and esp. Case C-376/98, *Germany* v. *European Parliament and Council (Tobacco Advertising)* EU:C:2000:544. See also, pre-Lisbon, its use of Art. 235 EC – the so-called 'flexibility clause' (now, in revised form, Art. 352 TFEU).

3.1 Proposal No. 1: Closer Judicial Engagement with the Treaty Framework

The first proposal mandates that the Court of Justice engages more closely with the EU Treaties in the exercise of its interpretative functions as a Union institution. The application *to the Court* of the Treaty framework as constitutional touchstone places important demands on that institution. In abstract terms, it requires the Court to transition to a conceptual understanding of its position within the EU legal order that more fully reflects its status as a Union institution under the Treaty framework. That requirement can be broken down into three specific normative prescriptions.

First, as constitutional touchstone, the Treaty framework demands that the Court should demonstrate greater sensitivity towards clear statements of constituent authority in the exercise of its interpretative functions. In particular, the Court should refrain from invoking its own responses on the first issue for EU constitutionalism – developed in contestation with the EU Treaty framework – in order to recast the preferences of Member States as constituent authorities. The application of its case law on, for example, the autonomy, direct effect and primacy of EU law as 'supra constitutional norms' to that effect is irreconcilable with the Treaties' unambiguous position on the status of Member States as 'Masters of the Treaties'.[21]

Secondly, when acting as direct policymaker, the Treaty framework demands that the Court of Justice engage much more closely and critically with the limits that this framework imposes on *legislative* policymaking (and EU institutional activity more broadly).[22] The Court's continued exercise of its *de facto* policymaking functions beyond the Treaties must be viewed as contingent on its adherence to the framework of limits that the Treaty framework places on EU legislative policymaking. The argument here is *functional*. The Court has opted to interpose itself alongside the EU legislature as direct policymaker. Accordingly, the

[21] See e.g., Case C-70/88, *Parliament and Council (Chernobyl)*, n. 1; Joined Cases C-6/90 and C-9/90, *Francovich and Others*, n. 1 and Opinion 2/13, *Draft Agreement on Accession of the EU to the European Convention on Human Rights*, n. 2. See also, with specific reference to the Court's position on the autonomy of Union law, Opinion 1/91, *Draft agreement between the Community, on the one hand, and the countries of the European Free Trade Association, on the other, relating to the creation of the European Economic Area*, n. 2 at para. 2 and Opinion 1/09, *Draft Agreement on the Creation of a Unified Patent Litigation System*, n. 2 at para. 67.

[22] See Chapter 1 (Section 2.3.3) and Chapter 5 (Section 2.1) for an overview of the applicable Treaty limits on Union policymaking.

exercise of its functions in that capacity should be considered subject, as a matter of principle, to the same normative restraints that bind the EU legislature.

The application of Treaty limits *to the Court* as direct policymaker is also not without its difficulties given, in particular, the open-textured nature of many of the applicable limits. Nevertheless, the Court of Justice is not excused from its responsibilities as an institutional actor simply on the grounds that compliance may prove challenging. On the contrary, as a consequence of the Court's move to interpose itself alongside the Union legislature as direct policymaker, that institution is obliged to overcome difficulties and engage fully with the limits structuring EU legislative policymaking. At the very least, the Court should not openly circumvent the clearest set of normative restraints that the EU Treaty framework imposes on EU policymaking: express exclusions on EU legislative competence.[23]

Thirdly, the application *to the Court* of the Treaty framework as constitutional touchstone also demands that the Court reshape its relationship with the EU legislature. Specifically, it mandates that the Court of Justice refrain from using provisions of EU law that it has ruled directly effective as tools to override, adjust or step beyond the EU legislature's clearly articulated policy choices.[24] The use of its direct policymaking platform to that effect is open to challenge with reference to existing abstract theories of comparative institutional analysis (Chapter 5). Measured against the Treaty framework, however, it must be also considered to exist in fundamental tension with the Treaties' explicit commitment to the value of representative democracy as the basis for all EU decision-making.

A closer look at the Court's jurisprudence confirms that adjustment is possible. Significantly, the Court of Justice has, at various points in time, opted to exercise its adjudicative functions in a manner closely aligned with the Treaties' key statements on EU constitutionalism. This can be seen, for instance, in its initial approach to the Treaty provisions on intra-EU capital movements (Section 3.1.1);[25] its review of Treaty rules

[23] See e.g., Art. 153(5) TFEU (social policy), Art. 168(7) TFEU (on public health) and Art. 346 TFEU (on national security).

[24] See e.g., Case C-138/02, *Collins*, n. 9; Case C-144/04, *Mangold*, n. 8; Case C-555/07, *Kücükdeveci*, n. 8; Case C-127/08, *Metock and Others*, n. 9; Joined Cases C-402/07 and Case C-432/07, *Sturgeon*, n. 7; Case C-382/08, *Neukirchinger*, n. 7; Case C-34/09, *Ruiz Zambrano*, n. 9 and Case C-236/09, *Test-Achats ASBL and Others* v. *Conseil des ministres*, n. 8.

[25] Case 203/80, *Criminal proceedings against Guerrino Casati* EU:C:1981:261.

on the standing rights of natural and legal persons in (now) Article 263 TFEU annulment proceedings (Section 3.1.2);[26] and, finally, aspects of its post-*Ruiz Zambrano* case law on EU citizenship (Section 3.1.3).[27] The challenge for the Court is to benchmark this approach to EU judicial interpretation in the exercise of all its institutional functions.

3.1.1 *Article 67 EEC on Capital Movements*

The Court's formative approach to Article 67 EEC (now Article 63 TFEU) on capital movements offers a clear example of enhanced judicial respect for the restraining impact of the EU Treaty framework as constitutional touchstone.[28] More precisely, its decision in *Casati* demonstrates the Court's sensitivity towards the (then) Treaty's statements on the locus of EU political authority within the Union legal order (Constitutional Issue No. 2). In that case, the Court was invited to rule whether Article 67 EEC had direct effect – the gateway to establishing a role for direct judicial policymaking in the free movement of capital. In contrast to its decisions on the related Treaty provisions on goods, services and persons, the Court ruled that Article 67 EEC was not directly effective as a matter of Union law (in other words, in accordance with its judgment in *Van Gend en Loos*).

The effect of that decision was to preserve the integrity of the Treaty paradigm for *legislative* policymaking in one specific aspect of the (then) common market. The Court's refusal to extend the benefits of its *Van Gend en Loos* judgment to the area of capital movements had the effect of leaving it to the EU legislature (here: Commission and Council) to determine the scope, depth and pace of progress with regard to the abolition of Member State restrictions on intra-EU capital movements. This process took shape incrementally through the Union legislature's use of the legal basis for the adoption of harmonising measures (Article 69 EEC) to

26 Case C-50/00 P, *Unión de Pequeños Agricultores* v. *Council* EU:C:2002:462.

27 Case C-333/13, *Dano and Dano* v. *Jobcenter Leipzig* EU:C:2014:2358 and Case C-67/14, *Jobcenter Berlin Neukölln* v. *Alimanovic and Others* EU:C:2015:597.

28 See also, in the field of competition policy, the Court's approach to the interpretation of Art. 85(3) EEC (now Art. 101(3) TFEU). Prior to the enactment of Council Regulation 1/2003 EC on the implementation of the rules on competition laid down in Arts. 81 and 82 of the Treaty [2003] OJ L1/1, attributing direct effect to Art. 101 TFEU in its entirety, the Court left the application of Art. 85(3) EEC to the Commission in accordance with the First Regulation implementing Arts. 85 and 86 of the Treaty (Regulation No. 17) [1962] OJ 013 p. 204.

enact a series of Council Directives.[29] It culminated in the entry into force of Directive 88/361 EEC, which effected the liberalisation of all capital movements listed in Annex I of that Directive.[30]

Following revisions to the Treaty at Maastricht, the Court of Justice ruled the revised Article 67 EEC (now Article 63 TFEU) directly effective.[31] This had the consequence of bringing that provision into line with the related Treaty rules on the free movement of goods, persons and services. In so doing, the Court completed its interposition as direct policymaker in the field of EU internal market law – having previously ruled the Treaty provisions on goods, persons and services directly effective many years before. Nonetheless, prior to the Court's attribution of direct effect to Article 63 TFEU, the Treaty paradigm for legislative policymaking in the sphere of intra-EU capital movements remained intact. Thus, until that point, the free movement of capital was uniquely distinguished among the provisions on intra-EU movement.[32] It was the only area of the internal market that was liberalised as the Treaty prescribes: primarily through EU legislative initiatives.

3.1.2 *Standing Rights in Annulment Proceedings*

The jurisprudence on the standing rights of natural and legal persons under Article 263 TFEU offers a second example of an approach to EU judicial interpretation that is sensitive to the restraining impact of the EU Treaty framework as constitutional touchstone. Here the Court's interpretative choices as a Union institution demonstrate awareness of the Treaties' statements on constituent authority (Constitutional Issue No. 2).

In *Unión de Pequeños Agricultores* v. *Council*, the Court of Justice was faced with powerful calls to enhance the standing rights of natural and legal

[29] For analysis, see T. Horsley, 'Death, Taxes, and (Targeted) Judicial Dynamism: The Free Movement of Capital in EU Law' in A. Arnull and D. Chalmers (eds.), *The Oxford Handbook of European Union Law* (Oxford: Oxford University Press, 2015) and J. Usher, 'The Evolution of the Free Movement of Capital' (2008) 31 *Fordham International Law Journal*, 1533.

[30] Directive 88/361/EEC of 24 June 1988 for the implementation of Article 67 of the Treaty [1988] OJ L 178/5.

[31] The Court conformed the direct effect of (now) Art. 63(1) TFEU in Joined Cases C-163/94, C-165/94 and C-250/94, *Criminal proceedings against Sanz de Lera and Others* EU:C:1995:451 at paras. 40–48.

[32] Art. 63(1) TFEU remains distinguished with reference to its scope. Uniquely among the EU Treaty provisions on free movement, Art. 63(1) TFEU applies externally to restrictions on capital movements between Member States and third countries. See e.g., Case C-101/05, *Skatteverket* v. *A* EU:C:2007:804.

persons to contest third party EU legal acts (principally: Regulations and Directives).[33] Under what is now Article 263(4) TFEU, the standing rights of particular categories of applicant is conditional on individuals satisfying the cumulative tests of direct and individual concern.[34] The Court had interpreted both tests restrictively – particularly the latter. In *Plaumann*, it ruled that,

> Persons other than those to whom a decision is addressed may only claim to be individually concerned if that decision affects them by reason of certain attributes which are peculiar to them or by reason of circumstances in which they are differentiated from all other persons and by virtue of these factors distinguishes them individually just as in the case of the person addressed.[35]

Admittedly, the Court could have improved the standing rights of natural and legal persons – at least in part – through adjustments to its own jurisprudence. However, as the Court noted, both criteria (and that of individual concern in particular) could not simply be set aside through judicial (re)interpretation without undermining the integrity of the Treaty framework.[36] Accordingly, the Court of Justice concluded, with express reference to the Treaty amendment procedure in (now) Article 48 TEU, that it was for the Member States as constituent authorities to revise the wording of Article 263 TFEU should they consider this appropriate. In its view,

> While it is, admittedly, possible to envisage a system of judicial review of the legality of Community measures of general application different from that established by the founding Treaty and never amended as to its principles, it is for the Member States, if necessary, in accordance with Article 48 [TEU], to reform the system currently in force.[37]

Member States duly responded to the Court's direction, integrating an additional standing test into the existing annulment action through the Lisbon Treaty. The revised Article 263 TFEU now enables natural and legal persons to challenge 'regulatory act[s] which [are] of direct

[33] Case C-50/00 P, *Unión de Pequeños Agricultores*, n. 26.

[34] See Case 25/62, *Plaumann* v. *Commission* EU:C:1963:17.

[35] *Ibid.*, at p. 107.

[36] Case C-50/00 P, *Unión de Pequeños Agricultores*, n. 26 at para. 44.

[37] *Ibid.*, at para. 45. Contrast this approach to Constitutional Issue No. 2 with e.g., the Court's earlier ruling on the European Parliament's standing rights in annulment actions in Case C-70/88, *Parliament and Council (Chernobyl)*, n. 1 at para. 26 (discussed in Chapter 4).

concern to them and [do] not entail implementing measure[s]' before the General Court.[38]

3.1.3 *EU Citizenship*

Finally, in its post-*Ruiz Zambrano* citizenship case law, the Court of Justice has taken clear steps to reorientate its jurisprudence on EU citizens' residence rights more closely around the limits set by the Union legislature. This is most visible in its judgments on entitlements to social assistance benefits.[39] Beginning with *Dano*, the Grand Chamber has repeatedly ruled that the establishment of a right of residence under the terms of EU secondary legislation was a precondition for the application of the right to equal treatment with respect to access to social assistance in the host Member State.

The applicant in *Dano* was a Romanian national resident in Germany and not economically active. The German authorities had refused her application for payment of a non-contributory benefit (jobseeker's allowance). The applicant challenged this refusal, arguing, *inter alia*, that it was contrary to Union law and the principle of non-discrimination in Articles 18 and 45 TFEU. The Grand Chamber rejected that claim. Moreover, and crucially for present purposes, it forged an express link between the application of the principle of non-discrimination and the provisions of Directive 2004/38 EC. Specifically, the Court ruled that the applicant was unable to invoke the protection of that principle on the basis that she was not resident in Germany in accordance with the terms of the Directive. According to the Court,

[38] The addition of that new admissibility test has, however, had little practical impact on the standing rights of natural and legal persons in annulment actions. The Court of Justice has since ruled that *legislative* measures did *not* fall within the scope of the revised wording of Art. 263 TFEU. See e.g., Case C-583/11P, *Inuit Tapiriit Kanatami and Others* v. *Parliament and Council* EU:C:2013:625 at paras. 69–77.

[39] Case C-333/13, *Dano*, n. 27; Case C-67/14, *Alimanovic and Others*, n. 27 and Case C-299/14, *Garcia-Nieto and Others* EU:C:2016:114

For analysis and criticism, see e.g., T. Thym, 'The Elusive Limits of Solidarity: Residence Rights and Social Benefits for Economically Inactive Union Citizens' (2015) (52) *Common Market Law Review*, 17; N. Nic Shuibhne, 'Limits Rising, Duties Ascending: The Changing Legal Shape of Union Citizenship' (2015) 52 *Common Market Law Review*, 889 and H. Verschueren, 'Preventing "Benefit Tourism" in the EU: A Narrow or Broad Interpretation of the Possibilities offered by the ECJ in *Dano*' (2015) 52 *Common Market Law Review*, 363.

> Article 20(2) TFEU expressly states that the rights conferred on Union citizens by that article are to be exercised *'in accordance with the conditions and limits defined by the Treaties and by the measures adopted thereunder'*. Furthermore, under Article 21(1) TFEU too the right of Union citizens to move and reside freely within the territory of the Member States is *subject to compliance with 'the limitations and conditions laid down in the Treaties and by the measures adopted to give them effect'*.
>
> It follows that, so far as concerns access to social benefits, such as those at issue in the main proceedings, *a Union citizen can claim equal treatment with nationals of the host Member State only if his residence in the territory of the host Member State complies with the conditions of Directive 2004/38*.[40]

Subsequent decisions have confirmed the Court's revised approach in *Dano* to the determination of the scope of EU citizens' rights to access certain social assistance benefits. In *Alimanovic*, for example, the Grand Chamber upheld the German authorities' refusal to award the applicants the same jobseeker's allowance on the basis that they also did not satisfy the residence conditions in Directive 2004/38 EC.[41]

Overall, the result of the above judgments on social welfare entitlements is a return to a position that more fully accords with the Treaties' statements – as constitutional touchstones – on Constitutional Issue No. 2, concerning the locus of EU political authority within the Union legal order.[42] As argued in Chapter 5, the EU Treaties continue to vest primary responsibility for Union policymaking with the Union legislature. More precisely, Article 21(2) TFEU entrusts the EU legislature with competence to enact secondary legislation where 'action by the Union should prove necessary' to give effect to the right that Member State nationals enjoy as Union citizens to move and reside within the territory of the EU (Article 21 TFEU). Likewise, Article 25 TFEU empowers the Council to use the special legislative procedure in order to adopt legislative measures that seek to enhance the core rights of EU citizenship in Articles 21–24 TFEU.[43]

[40] Case C-333/13, *Dano*, n. 27 at paras. 60 and 69 (emphasis added). See also, Case C-67/14, *Alimanovic and Others*, n. 27 at para. 49 and Case C-299/14, *Garcia-Nieto and Others*, n. 39 at para. 38. See also, with reference to the judgment in *Dano*, Case C-308/14, *Commission* v. *United Kingdom (Social Security)* EU:C:2016:436 at para. 68.

[41] Case C-67/14, *Alimanovic and Others*, n. 27.

[42] The Court remains, however, an active policymaker in EU citizenship and other areas. See e.g., Case C-650/13, *Delvigne* EU:C:2015:648 (on electoral rights) and Case C-507/12, *Jessy Saint Prix* EU:C:2014:2007 (on free movement of workers).

[43] The entry into force of any enhancements is conditional on their ratification by Member States – offering Member States an additional degree of control as constituent authorities over the scope of EU citizenship rights.

In addition, the Court's reorientation of its interpretative choices as direct policymaker aligns more closely with the Treaties' statements on *the objectives, values and limits of EU integration* (Constitutional Issue No. 3). First, with respect to *limits*, the Court's judgment in *Dano* explicitly recognises that the Treaty provisions on EU citizenship – which the Court has declared directly effective to establish its role as direct policymaker – are subject to express limits. In particular, the Treaty framework is clear that the rights of EU citizenship are subject to the conditions and limits outlined in the Treaties and, moreover, by the measures the EU legislature has adopted in order to give those rights effect (Article 20(2) TFEU).[44] Secondly, the Grand Chamber's approach as direct policymaker with regard to the rights of EU citizenship in *Dano* supports the Treaty framework's increased commitment to the *value* of representative democracy as the basis for Union policymaking (Article 10 TEU). Its decision to restrict the application of Union law – and, more specifically, the scope of the non-discrimination principle – to the conditions set out in Directive 2004/38 EC demonstrates respect for the Union legislature's agreed position on the appropriate scope of EU citizenship rights.

The consequences of the Court's alignment of its choices as direct policymaker around those of the Union legislature are, without question, deeply problematic for individual applicants that do not meet the criteria outlined in Directive 2004/28 EC. However, this finding alone does not justify breaking with the Treaty framework as constitutional touchstone. Criticism of the prevailing legal conditions is justified, but should be directed principally towards the Union legislature for its failure to ensure sufficient protection for some of the most vulnerable mobile Union citizens and their dependents.

3.2 Proposal No. 2: A Revised Approach to Scrutiny of the Court

The second reform proposal targets EU legal scholarship. The application *to the Court* of the Treaty framework as constitutional touchstone requires legal commentators to revise the intellectual paradigm that presently structures both explanatory and normative critiques of that institution and its case law (Chapter 6). EU legal scholars lost sight long

[44] Supporting this view, see esp., K. Hailbronner, 'Union Citizenship and Access to Social Benefits' (2005) 42(5) *Common Market Law Review*, 1245 at pp. 1266–1267.

ago of the Treaties' function as the principal touchstones against which the internal constitutionality of all EU institutional activity must ultimately be measured.[45]

Most academic writers still tend to see the Court as that institution itself wishes to be seen, namely as a *de facto* EU Constitutional Court. This normative perspective has had a significant impact on the evolution of legal scholarship on the Court. In more specific terms, scholars' strict adherence to (and robust defence of) the Court's statements on the three key issues for EU constitutionalism has steered their attention away from analysis of EU judicial activity for compliance with the Treaty framework as constitutional touchstone. Instead, EU legal writers focus on scrutinising the Court's activities against universal (Western) conceptions of the separation of powers and/or key procedural benchmarks of good constitutional adjudication; principally, coherence, consistency and the quality of legal reasoning.[46]

The application of the Treaty framework *to the Court* as an institution of the Union requires EU scholars to break with the existing paradigm and adopt a new, enhanced 'way of seeing' the Court.[47] That recast approach should take full account of the Court of Justice's position within the EU legal order as not simply a judicial institution, but also

45 For exceptions, see G. A. Bermann, 'Taking Subsidiarity Seriously: Federalism in the European Community and the United States' (1994) 94 *Columbia Law Review*, 331; T. Schilling, 'Subsidiarity as a Rule and a Principle' (1994) 14 *Yearbook of European Law*, 203; G. de Búrca, 'The Principle of Subsidiarity and the Court of Justice as an Institutional Actor' (1998) 36(2) *Journal of Common Market Studies*, 217; P. Craig, 'The ECJ and the *Ultra Vires* Action: A Conceptual Analysis' (2011) 48 *Common Market Law Review*, 395; T. Horsley, 'Reflections on the Role of the Court of Justice as the "Motor" of European Integration: Legal Limits to Judicial Policymaking' (2013) 50 *Common Market Law Review*, 931 and Cloots, *National Identity in EU Law* (Oxford: Oxford University Press, 2015).

46 See e.g., J. Bengoetxea, *The Legal Reasoning of the European Court of Justice: Towards a European Jurisprudence* (Oxford: Oxford University Press, 1993); M. Poiares Maduro, *We the Court: The European Court of Justice and the European Economic Constitution* (Oxford: Hart Publishing, 1998); G. Conway, *The Limits of Legal Reasoning and the European Court of Justice* (Cambridge: Cambridge University Press, 2012); G. Beck, *The Legal Reasoning of the Court of Justice of the EU* (Oxford: Hart Publishing, 2013); S. Sankari, *European Court of Justice Legal Reasoning in Context* (Groningen: Europa Law Publishing, 2013); M. Adams, H. de Waele, J. Meeusen and G. Straetmans (eds.), *Judging Europe's Judges: The Legitimacy of the Case Law of the European Court of Justice* (Oxford: Hart Publishing, 2013) and N. Nic Shuibhne, *The Coherence of EU Free Movement Law: Constitutional Responsibility and the Court of Justice* (Oxford: Oxford University Press, 2013).

47 Borrowing from J. Berger, *Ways of Seeing* (London: Penguin Classics, 2008).

as an institution of the Union pursuant to Article 13 TEU.[48] The prevailing paradigm is by no means redundant as a normative framework to scrutinise the legitimacy of EU judicial activity. It is simply *incomplete* to the extent that it fails to take sufficient account of the duality of the Court's institutional position within the Treaty framework.

Along with the Court, legal writers have a responsibility to engage with the duality of the Court of Justice's role under the EU Treaties. In more specific terms, they should acknowledge and actively interrogate the consequences that attach to the application of the EU Treaties *to the Court* as the principal touchstones on the internal constitutionality of all Union institutional activity – including the work of the Court. This will serve directly to assist the Court to meet its obligations to comply with the Treaty framework in the exercise of its institutional functions (see Proposal No. 1).

3.3 Proposal No. 3: Improving the Quality of the EU Treaty Framework

Member States also have a critical role to play in connection with the application of the Treaty framework to the Court of Justice *qua* Union institution. In the first instance, Member States, acting collectively, are responsible as Treaty signatories for enhancing the clarity of the EU Treaties. Thus, it falls to Member States to ensure that in so far as possible, the EU Treaties set out relatively clear statements on, for instance, the limits and values structuring EU policymaking (Constitutional Issue No. 3).

Treaty drafting is a complex art, and the provisions of international treaties are often worded to conceal fundamental disagreement between contracting parties over key issues. Yet, as Chapters 4 and 6 demonstrated, Member States have in fact previously been rather successful in securing agreement on unambiguous and tightly drafted statements on, for example, the limits imposed on EU policymaking in specific areas. Further efforts to reach similar agreement on such matters can only support the Court in its efforts to internalise the demands of the Treaty framework as normative touchstone (summarised in Section 3.1).

[48] See also, Horsley, 'Reflections on the Role of the Court of Justice as the "Motor" of European Integration: Legal Limits to Judicial Policymaking', n. 46 and J. Snell, 'The Legitimacy of Free Movement Case Law: Process and Substance' in Adams et al., *Judging Europe's Judges*, n. 47.

Examples of tightly worded statements of constituent authority include Article 21 TFEU on EU citizenship, together with Declaration No. 2 on the rules governing the acquisition and loss of Member State nationality (Chapter 5). The first of these statements defines the status and core rights of EU citizenship in fairly clear terms. Together with the provisions that follow, Article 21 TFEU also reinforces the primary role for legislative policymaking in the development of these important substantive rights – noting, expressly, the restraining impact of EU legislative measures such as Directive 2004/38 EC on the scope of EU citizenship rights. With particular regard to the acquisition and loss of EU citizenship, Declaration No. 2 annexed to the Maastricht Treaty offers additional statements of constituent authority, albeit non-binding. That Declaration outlines in clear terms that, 'The Conference declares that, wherever in the Treaty establishing the European Community reference is made to nationals of the Member States, the question whether an individual possesses the nationality of a Member State shall be settled solely by reference to the national law of the Member State concerned.'[49] Further examples of unambiguous statements of constituent authority can be found throughout the Treaty. For example, in the sphere of air transport, Article 100(2) TFEU is absolutely clear that EU policymaking in that field is conditional on the Union legislature's decision to bring air (and sea) transportation within Title VI of the Treaty on Transport (Chapter 5). Likewise, Article 125 TFEU leaves little scope for doubt on Member States' collective intention to prohibit the provision of direct financial assistance to struggling Eurozone states (Chapter 2).

3.4 Proposal No. 4: Establishing a New EU Framework for Compliance Monitoring

The final proposal calls upon the Member States (and legal scholars) to consider the added value of establishing a stronger institutional framework to facilitate more effective scrutiny of EU judicial activity for compliance with the EU Treaties as constitutional touchstones. The Lisbon Treaty introduced, to positive effect, a similar mechanism to provide for enhanced scrutiny of the EU legislature's choices in areas of shared responsibility.[50] As Chapter 1 highlighted, national parliaments

[49] Declaration No. 2 on Nationality of a Member State [1992] OJ C 191/98 (emphasis added).
[50] See Art. 12 TEU and Protocol (No. 2) On the Application of the Principles of Subsidiarity and Proportionality [2016] OJ 201/206, establishing the subsidiarity early warning

are now empowered to submit reasoned opinions to the Commission objecting to draft EU legislative proposals on subsidiarity grounds. Where prescribed thresholds are met, these reasoned opinions trigger the review of the contested legislative draft. The introduction of this new mechanism has not comprehensively resolved competence control problems in EU legislative activity. Nonetheless, it has recorded some success in enhancing the Union legislature's compliance with the Treaty framework as constitutional touchstone (at least with regard to Article 5(3) TFEU on subsidiarity).[51]

Member States, acting collectively as Treaty signatories, should be encouraged to apply similarly fresh and ambitious thinking with respect to EU judicial activity. This applies, *a fortiori*, with respect to monitoring the Court's exercise of its direct policymaking functions. As Chapters 4 and 5 exposed, there are strong *functional parallels* between the Union legislature's exercise of its attributed policymaking functions and the Court's assumption of direct policymaking functions using EU norms that it has ruled directly effective. Moreover, a review of the Court's activities as direct policymaker exposed significant problems. In more precise terms, the Court of Justice was shown, as direct policymaker, routinely to disregard the limits that the EU Treaty framework imposes on Union legislative policymaking (Problem No. 2). Equally, the Court was also shown to invoke directly effective EU norms to override, adjust or step beyond the EU legislature's clearly articulated policy choices in tension with the Treaties' statements on the value of representative democracy as the basis for EU decision making (Problem No. 3).

Certain Member State courts have already asserted claims to act as 'watchdogs' of EU judicial activity for compliance with the Treaty framework as constitutional touchstone.[52] The German Federal Constitutional Court has championed this supervisory function, but similar judicial sentiments now reverberate widely in the jurisprudence of most Member

procedure. For analysis, see e.g., P. Kiiver, *The Early Warning System for the Principle of Subsidiarity* (London: Routledge, 2012) and A. Cygan, 'The Parliamentarisation of EU Decision-Making: The Impact of the Treaty of Lisbon on National Parliaments' (2011) 36 *European Law Review*, 480.

51 For analysis, see e.g., F. Fabbrini and K. Garnat, 'Yellow Card, but no Foul: The Role of National Parliaments under the Subsidiarity Protocol and the Commission Proposal for an EU Regulation on the Right to Strike' (2013) 50 *Common Market Law Review*, 115. See also, Kiiver, *The Early Warning System for the Principle of Subsidiarity*, n. 50 and A. Cygan, *Accountability, Parliamentarism and Transparency in the EU* (Cheltenham: Elgar, 2013).

52 Borrowing from I. Cooper, 'The Watchdogs of Subsidiarity: National Parliaments and the Logic of Arguing in the EU' (2006) 44 *Journal of Common Market Studies*, 281.

State constitutional and/or supreme courts.[53] However, at present, national judicial interjections remain fragmented and linked, first and foremost, to domestic conceptions of the legitimacy of EU judicial activity. In place of the EU Treaties as constitutional touchstones, national courts increasingly assert the defence of domestic constitutional values and/or national conceptions of 'constitutional identity' as the operative limits on EU institutional activity.[54] Acting collectively as Treaty signatories, Member States could usefully consider how these embryonic *national* assertions of judicial competence could be transformed into a more effective and co-ordinated system of EU-level competence control.

This could be achieved in a variety of different ways. One option would be to resurrect earlier proposals, including arguments in favour of establishing a 'European High Court' with competence to hear appeals from national courts of last instance against the Court of Justice's judgments in preliminary rulings.[55] However, there is clear scope to move beyond existing templates. In particular, Member States could consider the extent to which granting new powers to (certain) domestic courts might function effectively to enhance the monitoring of the Court of Justice's compliance with the Treaties as constitutional touchstones. National courts could, for example, be granted new powers to submit reasoned opinions to the Luxembourg on the interpretation of EU norms *ex ante*. In its current form, the Statute of the Court of Justice does not guarantee domestic courts (other than the referring court *in casu*) the right to

[53] On the German Court's response see, Bundesverfassungsgericht, Decision of 29 May 1974, *Solange I*, BVerfGE 37, 271; Bundesverfassungsgericht, Decision of 12 October 1993, *Treaty of Maastricht*, BVerfGE 89, 155 and Decision of 30 June 2009, BVerfGE 123, 267. On the relationship between the Court of Justice and National Courts, see e.g., B. de Witte, J. A. Mayoral, U. Jaremba, M. Wind and K. Podstawa (eds.), *National Courts and EU Law: New Issues, Theories and Methods* (Cheltenham: Elgar, 2016) and M. Claes, M. de Visser, P. Popelier and C. Van de Heyning (eds.), *Constitutional Conversations in Europe: Actors, Topics and Procedure* (Antwerp: Insentia, 2012).

[54] See e.g., Decision of 30 June 2009, BVerfGE 123, 267 (Germany); *Ústanví soud*, judgment of 26 November 2008, *Treaty of Lisbon I*, PI. ÚS 19/08 and *Ústanví soud*, judgment of 3 November 2009, *Treaty of Lisbon II*, PI. ÚS 29/09 (Czech Republic), Conseil Constitutionnel, Décision No. 2006–540 DC, 27 July 2006 and Conseil Constitutionnel, Décision No. 2006–543 DC, 30 November 2006 (France) and Trybunal Konstytucyjny, Decision of 24 November 2010, *Lisbon Treaty*, K 32/09 (Poland). On national identity in EU law, see E. Cloots, *National Identity in EU Law* n. 45.

[55] See J. H. H. Weiler, 'Epilogue: The Judicial Après Nice' in G. de Búrca and J. H.H. Weiler (eds.), *The European Court of Justice* (Oxford: Oxford University Press, 2001). See also, Lindseth's proposal for a 'Conflicts Tribunal' in P. L. Lindseth, *Power and Legitimacy: Reconciling Europe and the Nation-State* (Oxford: Oxford University Press, 2010) at pp. 266–277.

submit observations to the Court of Justice.[56] Alternatively, Member States could look to national and/or Union political institutions to monitor the Court's compliance with the Treaty framework as constitutional touchstone. Such an approach would also have the added advantage of further increasing the degree of democratic input and control over Union policymaking.

Concluding Remarks

The Court of Justice is a powerful institution that has driven forward the process of European integration. It has done so largely without regard to the function of the EU Treaty framework as the principal touchstone on the internal constitutionality of all Union institutional activity. This is despite the fact that, under the EU Treaties, the Court of Justice is established as an institution of the Union and, moreover, in its own case law has repeatedly reiterated that the validity of all Union institutional activity is conditional on compliance with the EU Treaties.[57]

In a case of 'do as I say, not as I do', the Court has adopted and robustly defended its own positions on the three key issues for EU constitutionalism. On *the formal status of Union law and the conditions under which it applies within Member States* (Constitutional Issue No. 1), the Court has recast the fundamental character of the Union as a transnational legal order anchored to the framework of international law (Chapter 3). Likewise, it has formulated independent institutional statements on Constitutional Issue No. 2), concerning *the locus of political authority within the EU legal order* (Chapter 4). Finally, exercising its direct policymaking functions, the Court has mounted systematic challenges to the Treaty framework's clear statements on *the objectives, values and limits governing European integration* (Constitutional Issue No. 3) (Chapter 5).

The Court's divergent institutional approach across all three issues for EU constitutionalism has radically restructured European integration. Under the terms of the Court's case law, the EU legal order is not an international organisation established by ordinary international treaties and operationalised in accordance with the principles and practice of

[56] See Protocol No. 3 on the Statute of the Court of Justice of the European Union [2016] OJ C 202/210, Arts. 23 and 40.

[57] Joined Cases C-402/05 P and C-415/05, *P Kadi and Al Barakaat International Foundation* v. *Council and Commission* EU:C:2008:461 at para. 281; Case 294/83, *Parti écologiste "Les Verts"* v. *European Parliament* EU:C:1986:166 at para. 23 and Opinion 2/13, *Draft Agreement on Accession of the EU to the European Convention on Human Rights* EU:C:2014:2454 at para. 163.

international treaty law. It is a 'new legal order' that is defined *in opposition to* international law and structured around principles that form the cornerstones of federal legal orders.[58] Within that recast legal order, Union policymaking across a wide spectrum of substantive areas is now driven ultimately, not by the Union legislature, but rather by judicial policymaking. The Court of Justice's attribution of direct effect and primacy to a range of EU norms has effectively decoupled the process of Union policymaking from the Treaty paradigm for *legislative* policymaking. Finally, and most contentiously, the Court has repeatedly challenged the Treaties' statements on the most fundamental baseline in EU integration: the position of Member States (acting collectively) as 'Masters of the Treaties'.

The Court's transformation of the EU legal order through its adoption and defence of independent positions on the three key issues for EU constitutionalism has considerably advanced European integration. This has benefitted not only the European Union and its institutions (including the Court itself), but also Member States and their citizens. For example, as Chapter 4 highlighted, the Court's move to interpose itself as direct policymaker alongside the EU legislature in the 1970s – at odds with the (then) Treaty's statements on Constitutional Issue No. 2 – broke the legislative sclerosis that threatened to derail European integration. Without the Court's attribution of direct effect and primacy to them, many of the Treaty provisions would arguably have amounted to very little through the Treaty paradigm for legislative policymaking.

In addition, as direct policymaker, the Court's institutional approach to treaty interpretation has significantly advanced the rights of EU citizens in key fields of Union policymaking. Engaging the Court of Justice as direct policymaker using the preliminary reference procedure, EU citizens have succeeded in directly shaping Europe's legislative agenda. In substantive terms, this has facilitated a remarkable expansion in individual rights within the EU legal order. Chapter 5 exposed specific examples in the fields of medical services, air transportation and most strikingly, EU citizenship. In these and other areas, Europe's citizens have worked together with the Court of Justice to advance the protection of both economic and non-economic rights within the EU legal order. The impact of the dynamics of adversarial legalism within the EU legal order is so great that, in many instances, the Union legislature has

[58] See e.g., Case 26/62, *Van Gend en Loos* EU:C:1963:1 at p. 12 and Opinion 1/09, *Draft Agreement on the Creation of a Unified Patent Litigation System*, n. 2 at para. 65.

subsequently done little more than simply transpose the Court's policy choices into secondary legislation.

However, as this monograph has unmasked, the Court's institutional break with the Treaty framework as constitutional touchstone to promote (its conception of) European integration is also associated with significant costs. Specifically, the Court's lack of engagement with the Treaty framework in the exercise of its own functions as a Union institution was shown to aggravate problems of *competence control* within the EU legal order and, relatedly, ever-increasing concerns over the *democratic quality of Union policymaking*. This aggravation is the result of three contemporary phenomena in EU judicial activity: the Court's challenges to constituent authority (Problem No. 1); its disregard, as direct policymaker, for the range of *limits* that the EU Treaties impose on Union policymaking (Problem No. 2); and, finally, its use of directly effective EU norms as tools to override, adjust or step beyond the Union legislature's clearly articulated policy choices (Problem No. 3). The negative effects of these three problems far outweigh concerns over the quality of the Court's approach to the scrutiny of acts of *other* EU institutions for compliance with the Treaty framework as constitutional touchstone – the familiar line of critique.

It is no secret that the European Union has struggled for decades to manage questions of competence control and concerns regarding the democratic quality of Union policymaking (as well as its proximity to Union citizens). These concerns have only grown as the objectives of European integration have multiplied through successive Treaty amendments and EU institutional activity has assumed direct control over areas of policymaking that involve deeply contested political judgments and redistributive policymaking.

Member States have duly responded with a range of new initiatives spanning the introduction of express exclusions of Union competence; increases in the European Parliament's powers; the integration of national parliaments into the institutional architecture; and the establishment of the European Citizen's Initiative. These initiatives have recorded mixed success as devices to reinforce EU competence control and enhance the democratic credentials of Union policymaking. However, regardless of their success (or lack thereof), existing reforms remain an *incomplete prescription* to the Union's persisting legitimacy concerns. They leave the exercise of the functions of the Union's most powerful institution, the Court of Justice, unchecked against the Treaty framework as constitutional touchstone.

To date, EU legal scholars have generally avoided pressing the Court on this critical blind spot. In part, this is likely the product of their long-standing support for (and forceful defence of) the Court's divergent statements on the three key issues for EU constitutionalism. In other words, most EU legal scholars simply do not acknowledge the existence of the underlying normative problem. Relatedly, there is still a general reluctance among EU legal writers to criticise the Court.[59] This is perhaps understandable considering the response that any criticism of the Court tends to attract from that institution's strong supporters – justifiably in some cases, less so in others.

Nevertheless, despite continued broad support for the Court, most EU legal scholars are clearly uncomfortable with (at least) some aspects of the Court's institutional role. This discomfort is detectable even where the Court's substantive judgments align with liberal outcomes (which legal scholars tend to favour instinctively), notably: the advancement of individual rights (e.g., *Collins, Metock* and *Ruiz Zambrano*).[60] It is also verified empirically by the resurgence in the number of publications interrogating the legitimacy and constitutional impact of EU judicial lawmaking following yet another wave of highly significant EU Court decisions.[61] At a minimum level, legal commentators appear to agree that the Court's decisions as direct policymaker are often insufficiently reasoned (Chapter 6).[62] Scharpf's analysis of the dynamics of judicial policymaking captures the prevailing sentiment in EU legal scholarship neatly:

59 See also, Conway, *The Limits of Legal Reasoning and the European Court of Justice*, n. 46 at pp. 55–56.

60 Case C-138/02, *Collins*, n. 9; Case C-127/08, *Metock and Others* v. *Minister for Justice, Equality and Law Reform* EU:C:2008:449 and Case C-34/09, *Ruiz Zambrano* v. *Office national de l'emploi* EU:C:2011:124.

61 See e.g., Conway, *The Limits of Legal Reasoning and the European Court of Justice*, n. 46; H. W. Micklitz and B. de Witte (eds.), The European Court of Justice and the Autonomy of the Member States (Antwerp: Insentia, 2012); Adams et al., *Judging Europe's Judges*, n. 46; Beck, *The Legal Reasoning of the Court of Justice of the EU*, n. 46; M. Dawson, B. de Witte and E. Muir (eds.), *Judicial Activism at the European Court of Justice* (Cheltenham: Elgar, 2013) and N. Nic Shuibhne, *The Coherence of EU Free Movement Law: Constitutional Responsibility and the Court of Justice*, n. 46.

62 See e.g., J. H. H. Weiler, 'Epilogue: The Judiciary *Après* Nice' in G. de Búrca and J. H. H. Weiler (eds.), *The European Court of Justice* (Oxford: Oxford University Press, 2001) at p. 22; K. Heilbronner and D. Thym, 'Case C-34/09, *Gerardo Ruiz Zambrano* v. *Office national de l'emploi (ONEm)*, Judgment of the Court of Justice (Grand Chamber) of 8 March 2011 (Case Comment)' (2011) 49 *Common Market Law Review*, 1253 and N. Nic Shuibhne, 'Seven Questions for Seven Paragraphs' (Editorial) (2011) 36 *European Law Review*, 161.

> Whilst the Court's contribution to European integration is widely considered beneficial in politically correct discourses, its impact on the constitutional balance of the multilevel European polity does raise serious problems ... The question is whether there are, or could be, countervailing mechanisms that would defend or restore the constitutional balance'[63]

In response to such concerns, this monograph has turned to the Treaty framework in the search for countervailing mechanisms that are capable of restoring 'constitutional balance' within the EU legal order. It has done so at an extremely difficult juncture in European integration. The prevailing political climate is characterised by a succession of crises. The instinctive pull to defend the European Union and its institutions under such circumstances is strong – all the more so in view of the resurgence of political movements within many Member States that consciously *mis*inform Europe's citizens about the purpose, structure and costs of European integration.

Yet, even at times of political crisis, it is the responsibility of legal scholars to ask difficult questions and offer critical perspectives. In that spirit, the core thesis developed in this monograph has challenged head-on many of the things that EU legal writers defend (or at least have come to accept) as incontrovertible 'truths' in European integration. This is done not to undermine the Court or, more broadly, to support further denigration of the European Union and its institutions. Rather, this book's central argument and four concluding reform proposals are united in service of a common aim: enhancing the legitimacy of EU judicial lawmaking. This can only be achieved by engaging fully with the Treaty framework as principal touchstone on the internal constitutionality of all EU institutional activity – including the work of the Court.

[63] Scharpf, 'Perpetual Momentum: Directed and Unconstrained?', n. 11 at p. 134.

Index

For EU product safety concerns, contact us at Calle de José Abascal, 56–1°, 28003 Madrid, Spain or eugpsr@cambridge.org.

www.ingramcontent.com/pod-product-compliance
Lightning Source LLC
LaVergne TN
LVHW010055220926
848484LV00005BA/1079

9781107124035